Postcolonial Ecologi

Postcolonial Ecologies

Literatures of the Environment

Edited by
Elizabeth DeLoughrey and
George B. Handley

OXFORD
UNIVERSITY PRESS

Oxford University Press, Inc., publishes works that further
Oxford University's objective of excellence
in research, scholarship, and education.

Oxford   New York
Auckland   Cape Town   Dar es Salaam   Hong Kong   Karachi
Kuala Lumpur   Madrid   Melbourne   Mexico City   Nairobi
New Delhi   Shanghai   Taipei   Toronto

With offices in
Argentina   Austria   Brazil   Chile   Czech Republic   France   Greece
Guatemala   Hungary   Italy   Japan   Poland   Portugal   Singapore
South Korea   Switzerland   Thailand   Turkey   Ukraine   Vietnam

Copyright © 2011 by Oxford University Press, Inc.

Published by Oxford University Press, Inc.
198 Madison Avenue, New York, New York 10016

www.oup.com

Oxford is a registered trademark of Oxford University Press

All rights reserved. No part of this publication may be reproduced,
stored in a retrieval system, or transmitted, in any form or by any means,
electronic, mechanical, photocopying, recording, or otherwise,
without the prior permission of Oxford University Press.

Library of Congress Cataloging-in-Publication Data
Postcolonial ecologies : literatures of the environment / edited by Elizabeth DeLoughrey and
George B. Handley.
   p. cm.
ISBN 978-0-19-539442-9 (cloth : alk. paper)—ISBN 978-0-19-539443-6 (pbk. : alk. paper)
1. Commonwealth literature (English)—History and criticism. 2. Ecology in literature.
3. Human ecology in literature. 4. Postcolonialism in literature. 5. Ecocriticism. I. DeLoughrey,
Elizabeth M., 1967- II. Handley, George B., 1964-
PR9080.5.P68   2010
820'.936—dc22   2010013325

Printed in the United States of America

Contents

Contributors vii

Introduction: Toward an Aesthetics of the Earth 3
Elizabeth DeLoughrey and George B. Handley

PART I. CULTIVATING PLACE

1. Cultivating Community: Counterlandscaping in Kiran Desai's *The Inheritance of Loss* 43
   Jill Didur

2. Haiti's Elusive Paradise 62
   LeGrace Benson

3. Toward a Caribbean Ecopoetics: Derek Walcott's Language of Plants 80
   Elaine Savory

PART II. FOREST FICTIONS

4. Deforestation and the Yearning for Lost Landscapes in Caribbean Literatures 99
   Lizabeth Paravisini-Gebert

5. The Postcolonial Ecology of the New World Baroque: Alejo Carpentier's *The Lost Steps* 117
George B. Handley

6. Forest Fictions and Ecological Crises: Reading the Politics of Survival in Mahasweta Devi's "Dhowli" 136
Jennifer Wenzel

PART III. THE LIVES OF (NONHUMAN) ANIMALS

7. Stranger in the Eco-Village: Environmental Time, Race, and Ecologies of Looking 159
Rob Nixon

8. What the Whales Would Tell Us: Cetacean Communication in Novels by Witi Ihimaera, Linda Hogan, Zakes Mda, and Amitav Ghosh 182
Jonathan Steinwand

9. Compassion, Commodification, and *The Lives of Animals*: J. M. Coetzee's Recent Fiction 200
Allison Carruth

10. "Tomorrow There Will Be More of Us": Toxic Postcoloniality in *Animal's People* 216
Pablo Mukherjee

PART IV. MILITOURISM

11. Heliotropes: Solar Ecologies and Pacific Radiations 235
Elizabeth DeLoughrey

12. Activating Voice, Body, and Place: Kanaka Maoli and Ma'ohi Writings for Kaho'olawe and Moruroa 254
Dina El Dessouky

13. "Out of This Great Tragedy Will Come a World Class Tourism Destination": Disaster, Ecology, and Post-Tsunami Tourism Development in Sri Lanka 273
Anthony Carrigan

14. In Place: Tourism, Cosmopolitan Bioregionalism, and Zakes Mda's *The Heart of Redness* 291
Byron Caminero-Santangelo

Works Cited 309
Index 337

Contributors

LeGrace Benson holds a Ph.D. from Cornell University and an M.F.A. from the University of Georgia. Currently she is director of the Arts of Haiti Research Project, associate editor of the *Journal of Haitian Studies*, and a member of the board of the Haitian Studies Association. Author of a number of articles in scholarly journals, she has also contributed chapters to books concerning educational, environmental, and arts issues in Haiti and the wider Caribbean. She held a Cornell University Civic Fellowship in 2003–04 and was a visiting researcher in the Center for Black Studies Research at the University of California, Santa Barbara, in 2005–06. Benson has taught the history of art at Cornell and Wells College and has served as associate dean at Wells and Empire State College of the State University of New York, where she directed the program in arts, humanities and communications. Her current book, *How the Sun Illuminates Under Cover of Darkness*, examines the works of Haitian artists in light of the unique environment, history, and religions of Haiti from the Taíno-Columbian encounter through the present era (Ian Randle Publishers, forthcoming).

Byron Caminero-Santangelo is an associate professor at the University of Kansas. He is coeditor, with Garth Myers, of *Environment at the Margins: Literary and Environmental Studies in Africa* (forthcoming, University of Ohio Press) and author of *African Fiction and Joseph Conrad: Reading Postcolonial Intertextuality* (SUNY Press, 2005). Some of his recent articles include "Different Shades of Green: Ecocriticism and African Literature," *African*

Literature: An Anthology of Criticism and Theory (Blackwell, 2007); "Of Freedom and Oil: Nation, Globalization, and Civil Liberties in the Writing of Ken Saro-Wiwa," *Research in English and American Literature* (2006).

Anthony Carrigan is a lecturer in English at Keele University, United Kingdom. He is the author of *Postcolonial Tourism: Literature, Culture, and Environment* (Routledge, 2011) and has published on a range of postcolonial topics including tourism, environment, and indigeneity. He has contributed to special issues of the *Journal of Commonwealth and Postcolonial Studies* and *ISLE: Interdisciplinary Studies in Literature and Environment* on postcolonial ecocriticism, and his next research project explores postcolonial literature and disaster from an ecocritical perspective.

Allison Carruth is an assistant professor of English and core faculty member in Environmental Studies at the University of Oregon. She has published essays in *Modern Fiction Studies, Modern Drama*, and *Modernism/Modernity* and has completed a book manuscript entitled *Global Appetites: Imagining the Power of Food*. She is currently developing a second book project that investigates how developments in the molecular and material sciences are shaping visions of sustainability, environmental justice, and the green city in contemporary culture.

Elizabeth DeLoughrey is an associate professor of English at the University of California, Los Angeles. She is the author of *Routes and Roots: Navigating Caribbean and Pacific Island Literatures* (University of Hawai'i Press, 2007) and coeditor, with Renée Gosson and George Handley, of *Caribbean Literature and the Environment: Between Nature and Culture* (University of Virginia Press, 2005). With Cara Cilano she edited a special issue of *ISLE: Interdisciplinary Studies of Literature and the Environment* on postcolonial ecocriticism (2007) and is currently completing a manuscript about environmental globalization in the postcolonial tropics.

Jill Didur is an associate professor in the Department of English at Concordia University in Montreal. She is the author of *Unsettling Partition: Literature, Gender, Memory* (University of Toronto Press, 2006) and coeditor of special issues of *Cultural Studies: Revisiting the Subaltern in the New Empire* and *Cultural Critique: Critical Posthumanism*. Her current book project, *Gardenworthy: Plant-hunting in South Asian Literature and Travel Writing*, examines the discursive and material links among the memoirs and plant-collecting practices of colonial botanists, contemporary postcolonial writing about the Himalayas, and alpine and rock gardening culture globally.

Dina El Dessouky holds a master's degree in literature at the University of California, Santa Cruz, and is currently working on her doctoral dissertation, tentatively titled, "Indigenous Articulations of Identity and Island Space in Kanaka Maoli and Ma'ohi Literature of the Nuclear Free and Independent Pacific Era." Her dissertation focuses on how indigenous Hawaiians and French Polynesians shape new identities in relation to recent colonial uses of their land and sea territories as zones for nuclear and military weapons testing and tourism. She serves as event coordinator of the Pacific Islands Research Cluster through the Center for Cultural Studies at UCSC.

George Handley is professor of humanities at Brigham Young University. Author of *Postslavery Literatures in the Americas* (University of Virginia Press, 2000) and most recently, *New World Poetics: Nature and the Adamic Imagination of Whitman, Neruda, and Walcott* (University of Georgia Press, 2007), he is also the coeditor of *Caribbean Literature and the Environment* (University of Virginia Press, 2006) with Elizabeth DeLoughrey and Renée Gosson. He is an inaugural member of the executive board and program chair for the International American Studies Association, and his articles have appeared in *Callaloo, American Literature, Mississippi Quarterly, ISLE,* and others.

Pablo Mukherjee grew up and was educated in Calcutta, Oxford, and Cambridge. He is currently an associate professor in the Department of English and Comparative Literary Studies at Warwick University. He is the author of *Crime and Empire* (Oxford University Press, 2003) and *Postcolonial Environments* (Palgrave, 2010), as well as articles on colonial and postcolonial literatures and cultures and Victorian studies. He is currently researching and publishing on two new areas—Victorian natural disasters and Victorian world literary systems. He has also reviewed films, theater, and visual arts for national media in the United Kingdom.

Rob Nixon is the Rachel Carson Professor of English and Creative Writing at the University of Wisconsin, Madison. He is the author of *London Calling: V. S. Naipaul, Postcolonial Mandarin* (Oxford University Press); *Homelands, Harlem and Hollywood: South African Culture and the World Beyond* (Routledge); and *Dreambirds: The Natural History of a Fantasy* (Picador). *Dreambirds* was selected as a Notable Book of 2000 by the *New York Times Book Review* and as one of the ten best books of the year by *Esquire*. It was also serialized as the Book of the Week on BBC radio. His book *Slow Violence and the Environmentalism of the Poor* is forthcoming from Harvard University Press, and he is a frequent contributor to the *New York Times*. His writing has also appeared in the *New Yorker, Atlantic Monthly, London Review of Books, Times Literary Supplement, Village Voice,* the *Nation,* the *Guardian, Outside, Chronicle of Higher Education,* the *Independent, Critical Inquiry, Social Text, Journal of Commonwealth and Postcolonial Studies, Ariel, Black Renaissance/Renaissance Noire,* and elsewhere.

Lizabeth Paravisini-Gebert is a professor of Caribbean culture and literature in the Department of Hispanic Studies and the Program in Africana Studies at Vassar College, where she holds the Randolph Distinguished Professor Chair. She is also a participating faculty member in the programs in American Culture, Latin American Studies, and Environmental Studies. She received a B.A. in comparative literature from the University of Puerto Rico and an M.A., an M.Phil., and a Ph.D. in comparative literature from New York University. She is the author of a number of books, among them *Phyllis Shand Allfrey: A Caribbean Life* (1996), *Jamaica Kincaid: A Critical Companion* (1999), *Creole Religions of the Caribbean* (2003, with Margarite Fernández Olmos), and most recently, *Literatures of the Caribbean* (2008). Her biography of Cuban patriot José Martí (*José Martí: A Life*) is forthcoming. Her most recently completed book project, *Endangered Species: Ecology and the Discourse of the Caribbean Nation*, has just been submitted for publication. She is at work on *Glimpses of Hell*, a study of the aftermath of the 1902 eruption of the Mont Pelée volcano of Martinique, and on *Painting the Caribbean (1865–1898): Frederic Church, Camille Pissarro, Paul Gauguin, and Winslow Homer*.

Elaine Savory is an associate professor of literary studies at the New School University, New York City. She coedited *Out of the Kumbla: Caribbean Women and Literature* and has written *flame tree time* (poems), *Jean Rhys*, and *The Cambridge Introduction to Jean Rhys*. She has also published widely on Caribbean and African literature, especially on poetry, drama and theater, women's writing, and literary history. She is presently completing *The Quarrel with Death: Elegiac Poetry in the Shadow of Empire*, and editing the MLA *Approaches to Teaching the Work of Kamau Brathwaite*.

Jonathan Steinwand is a professor of English at Concordia College in Moorhead, Minnesota. His courses include global literature, Pacific Islands literatures, literary criticism, and British literature from *Paradise Lost* to *Frankenstein*. His publications include "How a Local Work Can Make Core Questions Hit Home: Winona LaDuke's *Last Standing Woman*" in *The Wider World of Core Texts and Courses* and "The Future of Nostalgia in Friedrich Schlegel's Gender Theory: Casting Aesthetics beyond Ancient Greece and Modern Europe toward a Future Germany" in *Narratives of Nostalgia, Gender, and Nationalism*. He is currently working on *The Survivance of Enchantment in the Secularizing Encounter: From the Gothic to the Postcolonial*, a study tracing the enchanted countermemory that persists from the Gothic to the postcolonial in spite of the hegemonic forces of disenchantment that drive secular modernity.

Jennifer Wenzel is an associate professor in the Department of English Language and Literature at the University of Michigan. Previous publications include "Petro-Magic-Realism: A Political Ecology of Nigerian Literature" (*Postcolonial Studies*), "The Pastoral Promise and the Political

Imperative: The *Plaasroman* Tradition in an Era of Land Reform" (*Modern Fiction Studies*), and "Epic Struggles over India's Forests in Mahasweta Devi's Short Fiction" (*Alif*). The author of *Bulletproof: Afterlives of Anticolonial Prophecy in South Africa and Beyond* (University of Chicago Press and University of KwaZulu-Natal Press, 2009), she is currently at work on a book project entitled "Reading for the Planet: World Literature and Environmental Crisis."

Postcolonial Ecologies

For Edouard Glissant, in memoriam

Introduction

Toward an Aesthetics of the Earth

Elizabeth DeLoughrey and George B. Handley

> For a colonized people the most essential value, because the most concrete, is first and foremost the land: the land which will bring them bread and, above all, dignity.
>
> Franz Fanon, *The Wretched of the Earth*, 9

> If there is anything that radically distinguishes the imagination of anti-imperialism, it is the primacy of the geographical in it. Imperialism after all is an act of geographical violence through which virtually every space in the world is explored, charted, and finally brought under control. For the native, the history of colonial servitude is inaugurated by the loss of locality to the outsider; its geographical identity must thereafter be searched for and somehow restored. . . . Because of the presence of the colonizing outsider, the land is recoverable at first only through imagination.
>
> Edward Said, *Culture and Imperialism*, 77

Writing in 1961 at the tail end of the Algerian War of Independence, Martinican author Franz Fanon identified the land as a primary site of postcolonial recuperation, sustainability, and dignity.[1] A generation later, the Palestinian scholar Edward Said argued that the imagination was vital to liberating land from the restrictions of colonialism and, we might add, from neocolonial forms of globalization. Here Said framed postcolonial writing ecologically, positioning it as a process of recovery, identification, and historical mythmaking "enabled by the land" (78). While he foregrounds the vital role of the literary imagination in the process of decolonization, Said doesn't elaborate on the challenges such imaginative recovery inevitably confronts: How can an author recover land that is already ravaged by the violence of history? How can nature be historicized without obscuring its ontological difference from human time? Moreover, what becomes of this need for a renewed sense of place when colonialism and globalization deny local land sovereignty, and when pollution, desertification, deforestation, climate change, and other forms of global environmental degradation remind us so forcefully of the ecological interdependencies of any given space?

Said's work helps us to see that to speak of postcolonial ecology is to foreground a spatial imagination made possible by the experience of place. Place has infinite meanings and morphologies: it might be defined geographically, in terms of the expansion of empire; environmentally, in terms of wilderness or urban settings; genealogically, in linking communal ancestry to land; as well as phenomenologically, connecting body to place. In emphasizing the production of history in the making of the global south, postcolonial studies has utilized the concept of place to question temporal narratives of progress imposed by colonial powers. As Guyanese author Wilson Harris has observed, "a civilization which is geared towards progressive realism cannot solve the hazards and dangers and the pollution which it has inflicted upon the globe" within the same epistemological framework ("Fabric" 73). Place encodes time, suggesting that histories embedded in the land and sea have always provided vital and dynamic methodologies for understanding the transformative impact of empire and the anticolonial epistemologies it tries to suppress.

Historicization has been a primary tool of postcolonial studies and, as Said and Fanon imply, it is central to our understanding of land and, by extension, the earth. In order to engage a historical model of ecology and an epistemology of space and time, Harris suggests that we must enter a "profound dialogue with the landscape" (75). This historical dialogue is necessary because the decoupling of nature and history has helped to mystify colonialism's histories of forced migration, suffering, and human violence. Following Harris's model, we foreground the landscape (and seascape) as a participant in this historical process rather than a bystander to human experience. Engaging nonhuman agency creates an additional challenge because nature's own processes of regeneration and change often contribute to the burial of postcolonial histories.[2] A postcolonial ecocriticism, then, must be more than a simple extension of postcolonial methodologies into the realm of the human material world; it must reckon with the ways in which ecology does not always work within the frames of human time and political interest. As such, our definition of postcolonial ecology reflects a complex epistemology that recuperates the alterity of both history *and* nature, without reducing either to the other.[3]

I. COLONIALISM AND THE "OFFENCE AGAINST THE EARTH"

Although it has been suggested that some postcolonial writers have not been attentive to nature, there are many examples from the mid-twentieth century of authors who were grappling with the relationship between landscape and colonization. Nearly a half a century before Said's observations about the geographical imperative of postcolonial literature, the Guyanese author and decolonization activist Martin Carter published in 1951 a poem about "Listening to the Land," which stressed the importance of paying heed to the histories of colonial violence embedded in the earth. The narrator repeatedly describes how he "bent" and "kneeled" down, in anticipation of listening, but confesses that "all (he) heard was tongueless whispering/as if some buried slave wanted to speak again" (89). Written in an era of decolonization and postcolonial nationalism, Carter's poem suggests both the *recuperative* role of place, defining land via relations of property rather than as "earth" or "landscape," while also demonstrating the impossibility of fully *translating* place because of the historical violence that produces "tongueless whispering." He foregrounds the discursive paradox of recovering a "tongueless" land and history, highlighting the poetic tensions of postcolonial ecology. We might say, then, that the imagination Said describes as necessary must be a poetic, world-making one, in which the human relationship to the more-than-human world and to a buried past must be reached for and conceived even if this nationalist recovery risks being romantic (Said *Culture and Imperialism* 78). Carter's postcolonial ecology, however, is hardly a bucolic pastoral, which would pose a landscape outside of the relations of property, or would idealize the relations of human labor and land.[4] Harris has observed that the Caribbean is "a landscape saturated by traumas of conquest" (*Whole Armour* 8). Instead of a pastoral or wilderness narrative, we see in Carter's poem that the land is a witness to the ongoing legacy of the plantocracy, a history that is vital to understanding modernity and yet seems without voice. Has the slave lost his or her tongue due to the alienation of the Middle Passage or by the violence of a master? Is the whispering "tongueless" because the relationship between human and land, or poet and place, lacks a common language? The poem's final line, that the "buried slave wanted to speak again," stimulates the reader's desire to connect the past and present through a natural (but not ahistorical) representation of land even while acknowledging the discursive limitations of that desire.

In his 1950 New World epic of a postcolonial imaginary in *Canto General*, Pablo Neruda writes of a tree of life that is "nutrido por muertos desnudos, / muertos azotados y heridos [nourished by naked corpses, / corpses scourged and wounded]" (478/71). Unlike Genesis, the tree's life stands in dialectical relation to the colonial destruction that has preceded it:

> sus raíces comieron sangre
> y extrajo lágrimas del suelo:
> las elevó por sus ramajes,
> las repartió en su arquitectura. (478)
>
> its roots consumed blood,
> and it extracted tears from the soil:
> raised them through its branches,
> dispersed them in its architecture. (72)

Neruda's poem, like Carter's and many other postcolonial works, foregrounds an ancestral relationship to place and the challenges posed by its discursive recuperation. This representation of place is symbolized by a nature nurtured by the violated bodies of colonial history, a literal engagement with what Harris refers to as "the living fossil of buried cultures" (*Explorations* 90). This is a genealogical claim, however, that has no illusions that ancestry provides an unambiguous and exclusive claim to land as territory. Instead, it admits that what is buried can never be recovered, thereby humanizing the landscape through death while also sacralizing it for the secular historical project of decolonization.

In the same era, Nigerian author Chinua Achebe emphasized the radical ontological shift in understanding place that occured through the process of European colonialism and Christian missionization in his well-known 1958 novel *Things Fall Apart*. Although this is rarely if ever cited as an ecocritical text, Achebe's inscription of the transition from Igbo to British colonial rule in West Africa anticipates Said's description of the need for the imagination in responding to "the loss of locality to the outsider." In describing the community's burial ground, Achebe's narrator comments, "the land of the living was not far removed from the domain of the ancestors. There was coming and going between them. . . . A man's life from birth to death was a series of transition rites which brought him nearer and nearer to his ancestors" (122). This dynamic model of land extends genealogically from the past to the future; women hoping to become pregnant visit an "ancient silk-cotton tree which was sacred" that holds the "spirits of good children . . . waiting to be born" (46). Achebe's representation of the ontology of land is not an idealization of tradition; the novel repeatedly demonstrates how patriarchal privilege and forms of exclusion are also locally embedded and naturalized. Thus attachment to the land or localism itself is not an inherently ethical or ecological position.[5] Nevertheless, we might describe his novel as one that evidences how deeply the community's language and being are constituted by the land and how that dynamic relationship shifts radically according to the social, cultural, and linguistic force of empire. What Edouard Glissant has called the "language of landscape" (*Caribbean Discourse* 146) is manifested by the paradox of Achebe writing in English to describe the way indigenous language is produced through the lived experience of ancestral land.

When one character asks, "does the white man understand our custom about land?" the other retorts, "How can he when he does not even speak our tongue?" (176). In the Caribbean context of transplantation and diaspora, Glissant has argued that "the individual, the community, the land are inextricable in the process of creating history. Landscape is a character in this process. Its deepest meanings need to be understood" (*Caribbean Discourse* 105–6). The postcolonial ecology of *Things Fall Apart* is evident in the way that language develops in a long historical relationship to a particular environment and culture and becomes integral to the process of recuperation, even if this recuperation is necessarily limited.

Over the course of Achebe's novel, the villagers move from an ancestral conception of belonging to the land embedded in language and cosmology toward an abstract and delocalized Christian god imported by colonialism. This is reminiscent of what environmental historian Donald Worster describes as a Christian imperialism that "stripped from nature all spiritual qualities and rigidly distanced it from human feelings—promoting a view of creation as a mechanical contrivance" ("Nature's Economy" 29). Achebe's villagers are forced into a new ontological relation in which "the justice of the earth goddess" (125) and other deities of the natural world are dismissed by Christian missionaries as "gods of deceit" to be replaced by "only one true God" who controls "the earth, the sky, you and me and all of us" (146). Certainly there are signals in the novel that suggest that the protagonist Okonkwo has betrayed the community's ethic of natural justice before the arrival of the missionaries. But the final violent break from a natural justice embedded in ancestral landscape to the imposition of a foreign colonial court is symbolized in the novel's final devastating scene, in which Okonkwo hangs himself, an act understood by Igbo to be "an offense against the Earth" (207). In response, the colonial commissioner orders all of the witnesses to be brought to colonial court (208) and imagines documenting Okonkwo's death as "new material . . . not a whole chapter but a reasonable paragraph" for his book, chillingly titled *The Pacification of the Primitive Tribes of the Lower Niger* (209). Achebe's bleak vision of the possibilities of recuperation is evident in the novel's narrative shift in the final paragraph to a colonial perspective. This self-reflexive commentary about the limitations of an English-language recuperation of the precolonial past likens the distanced colonial view of Igbo ecology in *The Pacification* to the novel *Things Fall Apart*. Like Carter, Achebe foregrounds the difficulties in recovering subaltern oral histories in the realist mode of written English, additionally highlighting how language embeds the legal structures of colonial dispossession. By extension, Achebe's novel calls attention to the failures of mimesis—the direct apprehension and imitation of the physical world. Instead mimesis becomes a postcolonial poetics, an activity of self-reflexive and self-conscious world making.[6]

The impossibility of recuperating nature and the precolonial past—two forms of alterity that in these examples are analogous—reminds us of

Gayatri Chakravorty Spivak's gloss on deconstruction as critiquing that which we cannot not want ("Woman" 45). Building upon Spivak, Donna Haraway has described the concept of "nature" as "that which we cannot not desire. Excruciatingly conscious of nature's discursive constitution as 'other' in the histories of colonialism, racism, sexism and class domination of many kinds, we nonetheless find ... something we cannot do without, but can never 'have'" ("Promises of Monsters" 296). Haraway insists that we "find another relationship to nature besides reification and possession" (296), which is a way of saying that we need to establish another relationship to alterity itself. Demanding an imagination of a totality and an otherness that nevertheless cannot be possessed marks the central common ground between ecocritical and postcolonial critique.[7]

In beginning with these literary examples, written in a mid-century era of intense global decolonization, we hope to foreground the ways in which material, discursive, and ontological relations with the land are mutually constitutive. These texts also suggest that since the environment stands as a nonhuman witness to the violent process of colonialism, an engagement with alterity is a constitutive aspect of postcoloniality. Addressing historical and racial violence is integral to understanding literary representations of geography, particularly because the land is "saturated by traumas of conquest" (Harris ibid). Glissant argues that this is why a postcolonial ecology cannot be interpolated as a pastoral but rather an untranslatable historical record of a "fight without witnesses" (*Discours antillais* 177). Since it is the nature, so to speak, of colonial powers to suppress the history of their own violence, the land and even the ocean become all the more crucial as recuperative sites of postcolonial historiography. Nature, in Beverly Ormerod's analysis, is the past's "only true guardian ... history waits, latent, in Caribbean nature, which is filled with sorrowful reminders of slavery and repression" (*French West Indian* 170), a point invoked by poets like Derek Walcott who turn to the sea to recover the suppressed bodies of colonial violence. This makes the process of conservation and sustainability all the more ontologically powerful, because a gesture of destruction against land and sea, then, simultaneously becomes an act of violence against collective memory.[8]

In the opening of this collection, we've drawn from earlier works in postcolonial literature to suggest that the global south has contributed to an ecological imaginary and discourse of activism and sovereignty that is not derivative of the Euro-American environmentalism of the 1960s and '70s. Most of the recent scholarship theorizing the development of ecocriticism and environmentalism has positioned Europe and the United States as the epistemological centers, while the rest of the world has, for material or ideological reasons, been thought to have arrived belatedly, or with less focused commitment, to an ecologically sustainable future. Certainly there are important distinctions, for example, between what Lawrence Buell has famously called the "environmental imagination" as it has been produced by privileged subjects in the northern hemisphere, and the

Introduction

"environmentalism of the poor" (Guha and Martinez-Alier *Varieties of Environmentalism*) associated with the global south.[9] These distinctions have been articulated in recent years during a remarkable turn in which ecocritical methodologies have been adapted for rethinking postcolonial literature as well as a recognition on the part of mainstream American ecocritics of the need to engage in more globally nuanced terms. Our interest here is to briefly outline how these epistemological differences may have been produced and to advance the conversation by highlighting where these disparate fields have shared concerns and goals.

While we recognize the differences between the varied forms of ecocriticism and postcolonialism, we are concerned that the production of a discourse of irreconcilable differences between these fields serves to relegate postcolonial literatures and methodologies to the footnotes of mainstream ecocritical study and tends to homogenize the complexity of ecocritical work. In fact, adopting one genealogy of ecocriticism as the normative one that is blind to race, class, gender, and colonial inequities tends to marginalize the long history of precisely this critique articulated by indigenous, ecofeminist, ecosocialist, and environmental justice scholars and activists, who have theorized the relations of power, subjectivity, and place for many decades. As Graham Huggan and Helen Tiffin point out in their recent book *Postcolonial Ecocriticism: Literature, Animals, Environment*, "[t]he easy assertion, for instance, that the postcolonial field is inherently anthropocentric (human-centred) overlooks a long history of ecological concern in postcolonial criticism; while any number of examples could be mustered to fend off the counter-charge that eco/environmental studies privileges a white male western subject, or that it fails to factor cultural difference into supposedly universal environmental and bioethical debates" (3). Our hope in *Postcolonial Ecologies* is to outline a broader, more complex genealogy for thinking through our ecocritical futures and a turn to a more nuanced discourse about the representation of alterity, a theorization of difference that postcolonialists, ecofeminists, and environmental activists have long considered in terms of our normative representations of nature, human and otherwise.[10]

II. ENVIRONMENT AND EMPIRE: UNCOVERING ROOTS

It has been over a decade since the *New York Times* declared the "Greening of the Humanities," a remarkable shift that highlights the role of literature in mediating environmental knowledge and in articulating a poetics of place in the alienating wake of globalization. This change has revitalized the humanities, offering a methodology for thinking through the complexity of environmental histories and imagining new directions for our ecological futures. While this ecocritical turn in literary studies has produced an innovative body of scholarship, including an international conference association and multiple journals,[11] scholars have lamented that the dominant discourse of the field continues to be marked by an

Anglo-American and a national framework rather than engaging broader contexts. In fact, in commenting on this celebratory *New York Times* article, Rob Nixon points out that all of the two dozen or so "green" authors cited are American. He finds this to be a peculiar emphasis since it was written precisely at the moment when the international community was mobilizing to prevent Ken Saro-Wiwa and his Nigerian colleagues from being sentenced to death for their resistance to what the Ogoni leader called "ecological genocide" perpetuated by oil companies in the Niger Delta.[12]

Paradoxically, as American ecocriticism expands and gains increasing relevance in the context of our global environmental crisis, its major narrative threads are producing a more narrow and nationalist genealogy of origin. This general lack of engagement with postcolonial methodologies and contexts is peculiar because an ecological approach to literature by definition is not restricted by geopolitical borders, language, and nationality. By insisting on the vitality and even necessity of a postcolonial ecocritical frame, our collection foregrounds literature's engagement with the globalization of the environment, a process that has been formulated by a long and complex history of empire. Colonialism must not be understood as a history relegated to the periphery of Europe and the United States, but rather a process that also occurred within and that radically changed the metropolitan center. The ongoing refusal to see the interdependent histories of metropole and colony implicitly relegates postcolonial ecocriticism to the margins of Euro-American discourse.[13] Similarly, to deny colonial and environmental histories as mutually constitutive misses the central role the exploitation of natural resources plays in any imperial project. We see Worster's basic argument, for example, that rivers tell us much about "the flow of power in history" as one model of postcolonial ecology that brings these relationships back into focus (*Rivers of Empire* 17). In sum, our collection begins with the premise that postcoloniality has not come belatedly to the discourse of ecology because of the intextricability of environmental history and empire building.

There is ample scholarship demonstrating that Western discourses of nature and the environment have been shaped by the history of empire. Generally speaking, historians are more conversant with these global connections than literary scholars. The eighteenth-century European mania for plant collecting, particularly New World flora, enabled the production of Carolus Linnaeus's binomial plant taxonomies and developed into a hierarchy of species backed by an emergent Enlightenment science. Mary Louise Pratt observes that "Linnaeus' system alone launched a European knowledge-building enterprise of unprecedented scale and appeal" (25). This represented a radical new mapping of global space through one common language (Latin), bringing into being a new European "planetary consciousness" (9). This eighteenth-century homogenization of the natural world has been addressed in Jamaica Kincaid's wry gloss:

> These countries in Europe shared the same botany, more or less, but
> each place called the same thing by a different name; and these people
> who make up Europe were (are) so contentious anyway, they would
> not have agreed to one system for all the plants they had in common,
> but these new plants from far away, like the people far away, had no
> history, no names, and so they could be given names. And who was
> there to dispute Linnaeus, even if there was someone who would listen? (*My Garden (Book)*: 122)

Our entire planet has been biotically reconfigured due to this long history of what Richard Grove calls "green imperialism," a process that foregrounds the etymological definition of diaspora as the spreading of seeds, and destabilizes our association of flora and fauna with a natural (read: autochthonous) landscape. The binonomial taxonomy of all the flora and fauna of the globe, an empirical and imperial project, has been likened by Vandana Shiva to the current practice of patenting life forms and appropriating indigenous knowledge for transnational corporations, something that produces a "monoculture of knowledge" (*Biopiracy* 9). Having created a taxonomy for that which is visible, science in the service of transnational capitalism now charts and patents a microscopic map of life. Shiva observes, "capital now has to look for new colonies to invade and exploit for its further accumulation. These new colonies are, in my view, the interior spaces of the bodies of women, plants, and animals" (*Biopiracy* 5).

Of course, biopiracy is a material as much as a discursive practice; Michel Foucault reminds us that "the theory of natural history cannot be disassociated from that of language" (*Order of Things* 157). Although Foucault overlooked the structures of colonialism, Kincaid does not. She observes, "this naming of things is so crucial to possession—a spiritual padlock with the key thrown irretrievably away—that it is a murder, an erasing" (*My Garden (Book)*: 122). This legacy of capturing and renaming nature leaves the postcolonial writer in the position of having to renegotiate the terms of taxonomy, struggling to articulate new relationships and new meanings in the tired language of empire. This process tends to render language more ironic, self-reflexive, and unstable, as we've seen in our previous literary examples. This self-conscious process of renaming and revisioning is a subversion of the colonial language of taxonomy, discipline and control, and a key element in postcolonial literary production.[14]

Just as the British Museum and Kew Gardens were constituted by the flora, fauna, and human knowledges extracted from the colonies, the discourse of natural history was articulated in terms of biotic nations, kingdoms, and colonists, reflecting the "language of expansionist power" (Browne "Science" 468).[15] Paradoxically, the construction of a taxonomy produces homogenization and difference. As Foucault observes, "for taxonomy to be possible . . . nature must be truly continuous, and in all its plenitude. Where language required the similarity of impressions, classification requires the principle of the smallest possible difference between things" (*Order* 159). Thus these new taxonomies of flora and fauna instituted a hierarchy of human species through this episteme of difference, contributing to biologically determinist discourses of race, gender, and nature. Although European Enlightenment thought was diverse and often contradictory, to different extents philosophers such as Georges-Louis Leclerc, Comte de Buffon, Charles-Louis de Secondat, Baron de Montesquieu, David Hulme, Georg Wilhelm Friedric Hegel, and Immanuel Kant all articulated some form of climatic determinism, asserting that the peoples of the tropics were unable to attain the moral and cultural heights of northern Europe and to produce history.[16] As such, the determinist discourse of colonial (tropical) place was often used to justify the practice of slavery and the denial of citizenship and subjectivity to non-Europeans. This also led to the colonial classification of indigenous peoples as fauna rather than as human beings, notably in Australia until as late as 1967.[17]

Since the material resources of the colonies were vital to the metropolitan centers of empire, some of the earliest conservation practices were established outside of Europe. As Grove has shown, tropical island colonies were crucial laboratories of empire, as garden incubators for the transplantation of peoples and plants and for generating the European revival of Edenic discourse. Eighteenth-century environmentalism derived from colonial island contexts in which limited space and an ideological model of utopia contributed to new models of conservation (*Green Imperialism* 229–30). By the mid-eighteenth century, tropical island colonies were at the vanguard of establishing forest reserves and environmental legislation (266).[18] These forest reserves, like those established in New England and South Africa, did not necessarily represent "an atavistic interest in preserving the 'natural' or the ancient and primeval" but rather a "more manipulative and power-conscious interest in constructing a new landscape by planting trees or, conceivably, marking out reservations" (280).

In sum, European Enlightenment knowledge, natural history, conservation policy, and the language of nature—the very systems of logic that we draw from today to speak of conservation and sustainability—are derived from a long history of the colonial exploitation of nature, as well as the assimilation of natural epistemologies from all over the globe. As such, this in turn diversifies our understandings of the genealogy of European knowledge as it expanded, adapted, borrowed, and outright stole from distant cultural and material contexts. This complex history plays an integral part in our current models of ecological sustainability. As Grove's history of ecological thought demonstrates, the environmental sciences that tell us that we can no longer afford to ignore our human impact on the globe are an ironic by-product of a global consciousness derived from a history of imperial exploitation of nature. In fact, if we turn to this deeper history, we see how colonial violence was mystified by invoking a model of conserving an untouched (and often feminized) Edenic landscape. Thus the nostalgia for a lost Eden, an idealized space outside of human time, is closely connected to displacing the ways that colonial violence disrupted human ecologies.[19]

To speak of postcolonial ecology is to foreground the historical process of nature's mobility, transplantation, and consumption. The new material resources of the colonies literally changed human bodies and national cultures as New World foods such as tomatoes, potatoes, maize, chili peppers, peanuts, cassava, and pineapple were transplanted, naturalized, and creolized all over the globe, while Asian and African crops such as sugarcane and coffee became integral to the plantocracies of the Americas. The early colonial transplantation of American food crops, what Alfred Crosby terms the "Columbian exchange," doubled the populations of parts of Africa, Asia, and Europe, directly contributing to their industrialization and expansion. In some colonial contexts, these food introductions also catalyzed the rise of monocrop agriculture, susceptibility to drought, and pestilence; dependence upon singular staples triggered severe famines in the British colonies of Ireland and India.[20] This rapid global agricultural change was an important antecedent to the twentieth-century "green revolution" in which the introduction of genetically modified seeds, agrichemicals, and a fossil-fuel based monoculture was expected to eliminate starvation in developing nations, but in many cases contributed to malnutrition, famine, social instability, and large-scale ecological problems.[21] Tracing out these histories of nature is vital to understanding our current era in which a "new green revolution" is radically changing postcolonial ecologies, particularly evident in the recent "African land grab" by countries seeking to fuel the expanding ethanol industry and to replace territory that may be lost through global climate change.[22]

We are all products of this long process of "ecological imperialism," a term Crosby uses to describe the "portmanteau biota" of plants, animals, and pathogens that enabled the expansion of Europe and radically transformed the globe. Although Crosby tends to emphasize European male agency over other subjects of history and almost reiterates the biological determinism of the colonial past, his scholarship is also a useful reminder of the ways in which biotic agents were participants in human history and the radical ecological changes wrought by empire.[23] His work and that of many other environmental historians has helped to underscore the biological dimensions of human history that both shape and are shaped by human agency, thus helping us to come to understand human choices in broader and more ecological contexts. Edward Said has drawn from Crosby's discussion of ecological imperialism to consider how this history might be adopted by the anticolonial poet. He concludes that "a changed ecology also introduced a changed political system that, in the eyes of the nationalist poet or visionary, seemed retrospectively to have alienated the people from their authentic traditions" (Said 77). As such, we see that biotic and political ecologies are materially and imaginatively intertwined, and that one vital aspect of postcolonial ecology is to reimagine this displacement between people and place through poetics.

III. GENEALOGIES OF ECOCRITICISM: RHIZOMATIC ROOTS

Given the ample body of scholarship on nature and empire, we must ask, why are environmental concerns often understood as separate from postcolonial ones? Why are they perceived to have emerged as parallel rather than as interrelated disciplines? Part of the answer lies in the recent intellectual genealogies of ecocriticism, which configure postcolonial concerns and methodologies to be secondary developments, a "second wave" to an unmarked American origin.[24] Yet as we have demonstrated, there is an ample body of work in both the history of empire as well as postcolonial ecocriticism to suggest that there is no lack of available literature and scholarship.[25] So why doesn't the history of empire or postcolonial studies appear in dominant discourses of ecocriticism? While ecocritical genealogies have different forms and may be written along the lines of chronology, thematics, epistemologies, and pedagogies, we find that most are organized around American (and to a lesser extent English) texts.[26] The *Johns Hopkins Guide to Literary Theory and Criticism's* 2005 entry on "Ecocriticism," for instance, focuses almost entirely on American authors, drawing upon the important work of Aldo Leopold, Cheryll Glotlfelty, and Lawrence Buell. Although the entry is written as a chronology, scholars who question the normative ecological subject and his/her relation to place (including nation) appear in the tail end of the essay, despite the fact that these publications predate the other critics. Thus the work of ecofeminists who have theorized the naturalizing discourse of gender and empire such as Annette Kolodny, Carolyn Merchant, and Val Plumwood appear in the conclusion, while the scholarship of Donna Haraway, which has consistently engaged postcolonial studies, does not appear at all.[27] The author acknowledges that "ecocritical practice appears to be dominated by American critics and an ever-solidifying American ecocritical canon," yet postcolonial studies is mentioned only once in the final paragraph as a "new area" without any references (Milne n.p.). Ursula Heise's important essay, "The Hitchhiker's Guide to Ecocriticism," published a year later, reiterates a similar genealogy and while providing an engaging and nuanced intellectual profile of the field and calling attention to the process by which these genealogies are written, generally sidesteps ecofeminist and postcolonial approaches in theorizing the human relationship to place.[28] At American ecocritical conferences and in recent publications, we see an increasing tendency to naturalize a dominant American origin for ecological thought, and by extension a displacement of postcolonial, feminist, ecosocialist, and environmental justice concerns as outside the primary body of ecocritical work, even in the cases where they predate later, more mainstream forms. As we know, the discourse of nature is a universalizing one, and thus ecocriticism is particularly vulnerable to naturalizing dominant forms of environmental discourse, particularly those that do not fundamentally engage with questions of difference, power, and privilege.[29]

Part of this intellectual streamlining derives from the conflation of environmental texts, such as Rachel Carson's 1962 *Silent Spring*, with ecocriticism, the literary methodology that developed in the 1990s. Most introductions to the field, like Greg Garrard's important volume *Ecocriticism*, attribute modern environmentalism to Carson's influential book (1). While Garrard's work is helpfully organized around environmental tropes, a methodology that presses the linearity of strict chronologies, American ecocriticism in general is backdated and often streamlined by many scholars in ways that obfuscate its complex, multidisciplinary, and even contradictory strands. Moreover, the single genealogical emphasis on Carson overlooks other foundational sources, such as the ecosocialist Murray Bookchin's previously published book about pesticides entitled *Our Synthetic Environment*, as well as the environmental activism coordinated by Puerto Rican poet Juan Antonio Corretjer against pesticide use by American agribusiness, discussed by Lizabeth Paravisini-Gebert later in this volume. We recognize the need for field synopses and do not advocate drawing a hard line between environmental and ecocritical methodologies because they have developed in conversation and reflect intrinsically hybrid discourses.[30] Nor do we question the important legacy of Rachel Carson. However, we do want to call attention to an implicit production of a singular American ecocritical genealogy that, like all histories, might be reconfigured in broader, more rhizomatic, terms. A founding narrative of modern environmental ethics could just as well include Mahatma Gandhi, whose early to mid-twentieth-century publications about the necessities of local sovereignty, limited consumption, equality for all sentient life, compassion, ecological sustainability, and satyagraha were an inspiration to many, including the 1970s Chipko movement against logging in the Himalayas (Shiva *Staying Alive* 69–70). Although Gandhi's philosophy represented a turn to the self-sufficient village rather than the wilderness (Arnold and Guha 19), his work was extremely influential upon the Norwegian founder of deep ecology, Arne Naess—who wrote his PhD dissertation on Gandhism—and inspired many other theorists of environmental ethics (Guha *Environmentalism* 8, 19–24).[31] In fact if we are taking on a larger context of environmental thought we might also consider the important developments of ecotheology, which has been centrally concerned with the ethical and ecological implications of reading, interpreting, and transmitting foundational stories. Although ecotheology is a formal and institutional development since the 1970s that includes concerns raised recently by world religious leaders, it draws its inspiration from ancient thinkers, indigenous and non-Western traditions, and from foundational sacred texts of the major world religions.[32]

If we continue to expand our definitions and genealogies of ecocriticism, we see that there are other philosophical models that are closely aligned with the methods and concerns of postcolonial theory, a body of work that is complex in itself. For instance, most genealogies of ecocriticism neglect the long history of socialist ecology, which draws from Karl Marx and Friedrich Engel's nineteenth-century theorization of the political economy under capitalism and its exploitation of nature. The Frankfurt School's critique of the ideology of Enlightenment reason and domination over nature also has close theoretical ties to postcolonial thought.[33] In shifting from the Marxist focus on class to a framework that examined nature as an internal and external figure of conflict for the modern subject, Max Horkheimer and Theodor Adorno's 1945 *Dialectic of Enlightenment* theorized how the domination of nature translates into the domination of other humans. Writing amidst the horrific state violence of World War II, their work was crucial to outlining the relationship between concepts of alterity and power. Their discussion of the ideological production of dominance over the other and their destabilization of the Enlightenment discourse of reason have been tremendously influential upon the generations of Marxist, postcolonial, and/or ecofeminist scholars to follow. Our intention here is not to replace one singular founding figure or methodology with another, but rather to broaden the historical, theoretical, and geographic scope of contributions to ecocritical thought. We wish to foreground the ways in which, to borrow from Said, ecocritical discourses are "traveling theories" rather than national products, and are irreducible to one geographical, national, or methodological origin.

In short, critiques of capitalism, technology, neoliberalism, modernization, biopiracy, and empire demonstrate that environmental concerns are not the exclusive prerogative of the privileged north. In fact, given the history of international models of development that restructure national space, postcolonial subjects have not had the luxury of being oblivious to environmental pressures. Modernization schemes enforced by the IMF and World Bank such as the construction of hydroelectric dams, the use of agrichemical fertilizers and patented seeds, as well as other resource extraction initiatives like deforestation, mining, and the liberalization of internal markets have all radically altered postcolonial environments. The concept of the environment, as David Harvey notes, is an impossibly large term to define and varies radically between peoples and places; therefore we must not expect that dominant American articulations of ecocriticism are immediately conversant with postcolonial ones. Ecology as a concept always demands multiple acts of translation, from nature to human, and from human to human. While we want to foreground the fact that postcolonial environments are already internally complex and demand a necessarily flexible approach, generally speaking we could argue that postcolonial ecology's concerns are differently inflected than mainstream American environmentalism and tend to emphasize access to arable land and potable water, public health, the threats of militarism and national debt, and reflect social planning for cultural, economic, and national sovereignty.[34] Postcolonial and decolonizing nations have debated these particular issues for decades in ways that firmly place the human in nature, a significant difference from dominant Anglo-American environmental trajectories. Moreover, postcolonial ecology has presented some of the most important critiques of American empire, positioning, as do Huggan and Tiffin, the U.S. as "a country that has actively and aggressively contributed to what many now acknowledge to be the chronic endangerment of the contemporary late-capitalist world" (*Postcolonial Ecocriticism* 1).

Although rarely commented on by American ecocritics, the "chronic endangerment" posed by the United States to other countries derives from excessive consumption, pollution, and waste as well neocolonial forms of globalization, militarism, and development. Since the 1960s, ecological modernization has been a hotly debated issue as the roles of newly formed state agencies, NGOs, the World Bank, and international organizations were brought into a dialogue over this emergent concept of "human ecology."[35] Faced with progressive models of development from the colonial metropole, many emergent nations retrospectively turned to precolonial ecological models to help chart their futures. In fact, the impulse of postcolonial nationalism to recuperate precolonial (and often precapitalist) modes of thought and practice provides a compelling argument for the depth and complexity of non-European models of ecological sustainability.[36] This turn to precolonial models for guiding the future of the modern postcolonial state was apparent in Prime Minister Indira Gandhi's keynote address to the United Nations Conference on the Human Environment in Stockholm in 1972. She argued:

> People who are at cross-purposes with nature are cynical about mankind and ill-at-ease with themselves. Modern man must re-establish an unbroken link with nature and with life. He must again learn to invoke the energy of growing things and to recognize, as did the ancients in India centuries ago, that one can take from the earth and the atmosphere only so much as one puts back in them. (Quoted in Singh et al. *The World Charter for Nature* xiv)[37]

This was an era of extensive global discussion and activism about the fate of the planet, resulting in the Declaration of the United Nations Conference on the Human Environment (the Stockholm Declaration), which called attention to how technology was changing the earth, the necessity for resource conservation and placing limits on pollution, the close relationship between economic development and quality of life, and encouragement for postcolonial nations to pursue courses of development while asking industrialized nations to lend technology and expertise to ensure global equity in social and environmental stability.[38] With rising concerns about depleting the ozone layer and global warming, this UN discourse on the environment catalyzed a series of subsequent meetings throughout the 1970s on renewable energy, technology, food security, water access, and climatic desertification, and other topics which radically changed the "post-war perception of an open global space ... to an inter-related world system" (Sachs "Environment" 27). Importantly, this global discourse was always rooted in a *human environment*, and while anthropocentric, it suggested that there should be no decoupling of humanity from the natural world and it provided an international—albeit legally nonbinding—mandate for global environmental security.

Samar Singh has argued that this particular 1972 conference was a catalyst for a global response to environmental sustainability, a charge taken up by President Mobuto Sésé Seko of the Republic of Zaire (later renamed Democratic Republic of the Congo) during the 1975 UN General Assembly for the Conservation of Nature and Natural Resources, which was hosted in Kinshasa. He advised:

> The seas, the oceans, the upper atmosphere belong to the human community . . . one cannot freely overuse (such) international resources. . . . I would suggest the establishment of a Charter for Nature . . . If we were asked to be a pilgrim for environmental protection, this we would be willing to be. (Quoted in Singh et. al. *World Charter* xvi)

By 1982, the UN established the World Charter for Nature, modeled largely on the UN Declaration on Human Rights, an important albeit ironic history if we consider Seko's dictatorial legacy. Like the Stockholm Declaration, the World Charter for Nature (WCN) declared all life forms as unique and deserving respect and emphasized resource conservation, the interdependence of humanity and nature, and the need for environmental education. The WCN differed, however, in its insistence on the inherent value of nature "regardless of its worth to man," in its call for a moral code to guide natural resource use, in linking warfare directly to natural resources, in explicitly calling for the preservation of nature from military degradation, and in stating that individuals have a right "to redress when their environment has suffered" degradation by others.[39] While the WCN received strong support from postcolonial nations, objections were raised over the fact that the document did not sufficiently distinguish between the environmental challenges of developed countries versus those of newly decolonized and developing nations.

Similar to the debates over the concept of globally shared environmental governance during the UN Conference on the Law of the Sea (1973–1982), reservations were expressed in the WCN meetings that emergent postcolonial nations would be forced into environmental policies that would limit their economic development.[40] This question about the economics of human ecology has been a vital historical aspect of postcolonialism, yet has been largely overlooked by dominant forms of Anglo-American environmental thought. Indeed, biologist Wangari Maathai and many others have argued persuasively that national debt to "first-world" agencies such as the IMF and World Bank is one of the biggest obstacles to environmental sustainability in postcolonial nations today.[41] Discussions over what characterizes postcolonial ecological concerns can be traced back through these international debates over environmental, economic, and state sovereignty. Far from being oblivious to environmental issues, postcolonial subjects have had to mitigate and contest what Larry Lohman has described as "Green Orientalism," which he defines as a "postwar narrative of 'development'" that "sets up and enforces, in fine Orientalist style, a dichotomy between hungry, expectant, tradition-shackled Southern peoples and a modern, scientific, democratic North under whose progressive leadership they will gradually be freed for better things" (202). This binarism is implicitly foundational to the discourse of ecocriticism as an exportable American intellectual development.

Since nearly 100 new nations were established between World War II and the ratification of the WCN and the UN Convention on the Law of the Sea, we need to recognize this particular era as ushering in an unprecedented global discourse on the environment and the global commons. Yet the discourse of these new and still emergent nations has been largely submerged by economic powers that have redefined the concept of nature as merely an "environment" that can be "managed" (Sachs "Environment" 34), a post–World War II turn in which the global became "defined according to a perception of the world shared by those who rule it" (Escobar "Constructing Nature" 51). In this process the poor have been admonished for their presence, euphemistically called "overpopulation,"[42] or for their "lack of environmental consciousness" ("Constructing Nature" 51), a legacy that is visible in dominant ecocritical studies today. Strikingly, this purported lack of environmental consciousness was increasingly positioned as the fundamental *cause* for global degradation and thereby justified economic schemes of modernization and progress. By 1983 the World Commission on Environment and Development (the Brundtland Report), was turning to capitalist development as a global model for the ecological future (Sachs "Environment" 29). This is how capital, rather than being called into question, enters an "ecological phase," to incorporate new spaces and knowledges of nature (Escobar "Constructing" 47).[43] In this naturalization of capitalism, a transnational corporation such as Shell Oil might refer to itself, without irony, as a "responsible energy" business, a "greenwashing" that erases the fact that its gas flaring in Nigeria, along with ExxonMobil and Chevron Corporation, contribute disproportionately to global warming.[44]

Certainly postcolonial ecology must engage the complexity of global environmental knowledges, traditions, and histories in a way that moves far beyond the discourses of modernization theory on the one hand, which relegates the global south to a space of natural poverty, and the discourse of colonial exploitation on the other, which relegates the global south to a place without agency, bereft of complicity or resistance. Our conviction that dominant ecocritical methodologies that make universalist claims (from the unmarked Anglophone viewpoint of the United States) must address colonial legacies and postcolonial contexts is in concert with critics who have cautioned against turning to indigenous and postcolonial ecologies to simply provide moral, spiritual, or financial redemption for the capitalist metropole. Donna Haraway has warned of the "cannibalistic western logic that readily constructs other cultural possibilities as resources for western needs and actions" (*Primate Visions* 247).

While we argue for the necessity to map the diversity of ecological discourse and its representations of alterity, an uncritical turn to other spaces of natural knowledge can also produce "environmental orientalism" (Sawyer and Agrawal). This tendency often arises from the ways in which dominant American forms of ecocriticism have sidestepped questions of empire and privilege in the fashioning of a sense of place. Without considering these structural, historical, and methodological issues, a shallow green transnationalism may romanticize "primitive ecological wisdom" as a ready substitute or displacement of "the hues of radical red" (Moore, Pandian, and Kosek 39).

As we have tried to emphasize in this section, the mutually constitutive relationship between nature and empire over the past few centuries has produced a rich legacy of interpretive lenses for postcolonial ecology, and a long global conversation about how to define and attain environmental sovereignty at local, regional, national, and planetary scales. To separate the history of empire from ecocritical thought dehistoricizes nature and often contributes to a discourse of green orientalism. This is unfortunate not only for its misrepresentation of the past, but also for our ecological futures, as we all have much to learn from this long and complex history. Consequently, our intention here is not to fall into the trap of constructing rigid national and geographical differences, but rather to point to how postcolonial and other aligned methodologies of ecocriticism provide a rich and nuanced discussion of the normative ecological subject and that subject's relation to environmental history, economics, and politics.

IV. POSTCOLONIAL ECOCRITICISM: BRIDGING THE DIVIDE

In 2004 the Nobel Peace Prize was awarded to Wangari Maathai for establishing the Green Belt Movement, a predominantly women's grassroots organization that, commencing with World Environment Day 1977, has planted millions of trees in Kenya and beyond to stop desertification and the process of what Rob Nixon calls "slow violence." This momentous event inspired hopes that European and Anglo-American ecocritics would engage more thoroughly with global environmental dialogues and would broaden the language and practices of our ecological stewardship.[45] Those hopes have not been entirely realized for the reasons we've already outlined—the segregation of the history of empire from concepts of nature, the tendency to homogenize ecocritical genealogies, and the differently inflected concerns of postcolonial ecology such as debt and the threat of U.S. militarism, unlike mainstream American environmentalism which focuses on wilderness and conservation. This communication barrier between the realm of the "postcolonial" and the field of "ecocriticism" might also be attributed to the predominantly national framework for literary studies in general, the persistence of a lingering insular and/or exceptional vision of American Studies, and a difficulty in reconciling

Introduction

poststructural methodologies, utilized in many postcolonial approaches, with ecocritical models.[46] In this section we turn to postcolonial critiques of Anglo-American environmental thought to query these epistemological gaps and to suggest that these critiques, while important for a preliminary engagement, have also homogenized the complex body of ecocriticism itself.

Much has been made of the irreconcilable differences between postcolonial concerns and the environmentalism of the privileged north in terms of their approaches to issues such as the economy, development, conservation, biopiracy, sovereignty, consumption, militarism, and (over)population. This segregation of postcolonial studies and its allied scholarship from the dominant story of ecocriticism is not particularly surprising when we consider the extent of mutual critique. Since hierarchical notions of nature were key to justifying colonial expansion and the repression of nonnormative others, postcolonialists have been understandably wary about calls to "return to nature," or attempts to collapse the concern with the human inequalities that resulted from colonialism into a universalizing focus on the future of the nonhuman environment. This has generated a debate between those who tend to prioritize the environment over all human needs, like many deep ecologists, and those in the social justice movement who insist that human equity must precede green conservation and preservation.[47]

This debate has become a flashpoint for those exploring the connection between postcolonial and ecocritical thought, tracing back to historian Ramachandra Guha's 1989 article which outlined the central divisions between the fields. Guha critiqued Arne Naess and the deep ecology movement for their biocentricity, their emphasis on wilderness preservation, and their romanticism of Asian religious traditions. He contended that deep ecology demonstrated a "lack of concern with inequalities *within* human society," dehistoricized nature (72), and overlooked more pressing environmental issues such as global militarization and the growing "overconsumption by industrial nations and by urban elites in the Third World" (74).[48] Guha pointed out that the biocentrism/anthrocentrism dualism, as adopted by Project Tiger and the World Wildlife Fund in South Asia to conserve animals and their habitats, contributed to the displacement of poor communities who happened to live in the targeted conservation wilderness areas. As recent scholarship has demonstrated, international pressure on postcolonial states to conserve charismatic megafauna has catalyzed human alienation from the land, notoriously in the case of the Marichjhapi massacre in the Indian Sundarbans, an event inscribed by novelist Amitav Ghosh and explored by Jonathan Steinwand later in this volume.[49] Guha points out that the construction of pristine (read: nonhuman) wilderness areas benefits elite tourists rather than local peoples, and positions "the enjoyment of nature (as) an integral part of the consumer society" (79) rather than challenging the capitalist logic of consumption that creates the need for conservation to begin with.

He concludes, "despite its claims to universality, deep ecology is firmly rooted in American environmental and cultural history and is inappropriate when applied to the Third World" (71).[50]

Guha's critique of deep ecology has been a touchstone and catalyst for scholars seeking to bring postcolonial and ecological modes of thought into dialogue. While not detracting from his argument, which we support, we find the terms of this twenty-year-old debate have not deepened substantially until very recently. Because northern environmental discourse in this dialogue has become synonymous with deep ecology (which itself does not represent mainstream environmentalism), it has become difficult to foreground the complexity of environmental thought in Anglo-American discourse, and to highlight other modes such as ecosocialist, ecofeminist, and environmental justice approaches, which are often in concert with the concerns of postcolonial ecology. Here we'd like to encourage a broader range of participation for postcolonial engagement and critique beyond the thorny issue of wilderness conservation.

We seek to foreground here that ecocritical discourses, as they have been produced in the United States, are exceedingly complex and have taken on critiques of capitalism, the normative production of the ecological subject, and the segregation of culture and nature. The work of Patrick Murphy, for instance, has long questioned normative models of American ecological thought through an ecofeminist lens, and his edited collection, *Literature of Nature: An International Sourcebook* (1998), is perhaps the earliest collection of ecocritical essays with a truly global scope. There is also a neglected body of ecocritical scholarship that has responded to Guha's critique of American environmentalism. For instance, Deane Curtin's *Chinnagounder's Challenge: The Question of Ecological Citizenship* (1999) has directly engaged Guha's work to argue for the "disastrous consequences" of first-world claims to the universality of natural and conservation discourse (5) and has outlined epistemological assumptions held by dominant Euro-American modes of environmental thought that are not easily applicable to communities in the global south such as the "universalism of ethical claims," the individualism of the ethical subject, and notions of progress that uphold an ethically "neutral" model of reason (10).[51] Building upon Guha and Curtin's call for a more globally engaged ecological citizenship, Graham Huggan has turned to South Asian and African texts to counter the assumption that "ecocriticism, at present, is a predominantly white movement, arguably lacking the institutional support-base to engage fully with multicultural and cross-cultural concerns" ("Greening" 703). He has argued that "postcolonial criticism . . . offers a valuable corrective to a variety of universalist ecological claims—the unexamined claim of equivalence among all 'ecological beings' (Naess), irrespective of material circumstances" and the presumption "that global ethical considerations should override local cultural concerns" (720). In doing so, he has also pointed to the complexity of ecofeminist, ecosocialist, and even deep ecology's approaches to the entanglement of nature and culture, suggesting that postcolonial critiques "of First World environmental practice suffer from similar tendencies toward overstatement."[52]

In fact, we might turn to Rob Nixon's 2005 article "Environmentalism and Postcolonialism," which details four epistemological gaps between these fields that have contributed to the mutual lack of engagement and "reciprocal mistrust" and build upon them to suggest new directions for the future. In drawing comparisons between methodologies, Nixon has argued that the vast body of postcolonial theorists from Homi Bhabha to Glissant foreground hybridity and cross-cultural exchange as constitutive of history and literary discourse, whereas mainstream American ecocritics often emphasize a desire for a primordial natural purity in the wilderness, a retreat from the social and environmental pollution of modernity. This is an argument that builds upon Guha's important critique of deep ecology and reflects some general trends. However, we might reconsider this division by foregrounding the complexity of other forms of American ecocriticism, particularly ecofeminist and environmental justice movements that have critiqued or avoided discourses of wilderness and natural purity and have turned particularly to poststructural, urban, cybernetic, and even microscopic spaces of the ecological imaginary.[53] Or we might consider the ways in which postcolonial texts, from novels such as Patricia Grace's *Potiki* and Indra Sinha's *Animal's People* to Ken Saro-Wiwa's nonfiction *Genocide in Nigeria*, all strategically rely upon some type of discourse of precolonial purity and unity that was eroded through exposure to modernization, capitalism, colonialism, and/or toxic pollutants. Thus we might note that hybridity and purity may not be mutually exclusive nor are their political meanings inflexible. In both American and postcolonial texts, appeals to an uncomplicated concept of nature might often serve the rhetorical function of a critique of modernity, even when the texts themselves might belie, consciously or not, history's hybridizing effects.

Second, Nixon has argued that postcolonial frameworks focus on the diaspora and displacement created through colonialism and globalization, whereas ecocriticism generally foregrounds human continuity and the ethics of place and belonging.[54] While this has contributed to their lack of sustained dialogue, we can see that both positions are integral to speaking about the history and phenomenology of the environment. In fact, this helps explain why ecocriticism has been far more attentive to indigenous literatures than postcolonial studies has been. If we reflect back upon the postcolonial literary texts that opened this essay that demonstrated that "the land is recoverable at first only through imagination" (Said), we might foreground the ways in which the longing for that continuity might also demonstrate a constitutive element of the literatures of postcolonial ecology.

Third, Nixon points out that postcolonial studies is embedded in cosmopolitan discourses of the city and in the production of transnational literatures, whereas mainstream ecocriticism favors wilderness narratives and national literary frames, particularly of the United States. While again we would agree that this is largely accurate, we would like to follow the lead of Raymond Williams and Leo Marx to suggest a dialectic between city and country, culture and nature, and metropole and colony. We might turn to the many postcolonial coming-of-age narratives from Tsitsi Dangarembga's *Nervous Conditions* (Zimbabwe) to Merle Hodge's *Crick Crack, Monkey* (Trinidad) that suggest that migration from rural to urban space replicates the alienation of the postcolonial subject from a naturalized homeland, and that while urbanization offers educational opportunities to the protagonist, the very spatial structures of the city often replicate the alienating racial hierarchies of colonialism itself.

Finally, Nixon points out different models of historiography in which postcolonialists have focused on excavating the precolonial past and have sought to expose the machinations of colonialism and its attendant historical erasures,[55] whereas mainstream ecocritics often employ a "timeless history" of nature that supersedes human hierarchies. We agree that any formulation of an environmental ethic that is not attentive to history is problematic but would add that so is any conception of history that is not contextualized by deep time. Aldo Leopold's famous dictum to "think like a mountain" is not necessarily incompatible with postcolonial concerns and with the task of historicizing the earth. Indeed, in Leopold's discussion of the axe as a method of reading tree rings, he insists that an environmental ethic begins with nature's previous human history. Grounded in the layering of history, Leopold's call for a land ethic can be invoked to temper the anti-ecological tendencies of Western individualism and presentism that are often associated with the pastoral and the picturesque. In sum, Nixon's distinctions are exceedingly useful in pointing us toward general differences between postcolonial and ecocritical methodologies, but we can interpret a land ethic in ways that are not irreconcilable with a historicization of nature.

We feel a sustained dialogue is needed between postcolonial and ecocritical studies, particularly as these questions of representation are vital to our current environmental crisis as well as to the discursive contours of literary studies as a whole. While we recognize epistemological gaps between the two fields, we foreground four important areas of overlap. First, an ecological frame is vital to understanding how geography has been and still is radically altered by colonialism, including resource use, stewardship, and sovereignty—issues that have been crucial to independence movements and their constitutive literatures. As explained earlier, by turning to precolonial epistemologies of place, postcolonial studies is well suited to explore how these knowledges survive and are transformed and translated through narrative, particularly in modern genres such as the novel. Second, Enlightenment dualisms of culture/nature, white/black, and male/female were constituted through the colonial process, and postcolonialists (and ecofeminists) have long been engaged in disentangling the hierarchies that derive from these interpellations of non-European nature. Thus the "cultivation" that presumably constituted the post-Enlightenment European male subject was increasingly distanced from women, the poor, and peoples of color. Likewise, these naturalized others were likened to a construction of nature that was increasingly seen to require masculine European management. Therefore we suggest that this turn to nature is not so much an epistemological break in postcolonial studies as a continuity with the historical scrutiny of social hierarchies that has characterized the field. As Huggan observes, "postcolonial criticism has effectively renewed, rather than belatedly discovered, its commitment to the environment" (Greening 702).

Third, the ecocritical interrogation of anthropocentrism offers the persistent reminder that human political and social inequities cannot be successfully and sustainably resolved without some engagement with the more-than-human world and with deep time. Although this challenge to anthropocentrism is often assumed to directly challenge the human social concerns of postcolonialism, both fields have made it clear that sustainability is a mutual enterprise that pertains as much to human social well-being as to the health of the physical world. If they are at odds, it is only because of our failure to consider their interdependencies. Although it is never clear how we know if we have escaped our anthropocentrism, ecocritical postcolonialism attempts to imagine something beyond the confines of our human story, an imagination that is essential to modes of sustainability.

Finally, the field of postcolonial studies has long been engaged with questions of agency and representation of the nonspeaking or subaltern subject, foregrounding the ways in which narrative and language effectively displace the production of difference and alterity. Consequently, postcolonial ecocriticism importantly theorizes the question of who can "speak for nature" or speak for the subaltern subject in a narrative mode that does not privilege dualist thought or naturalize the hierarchies between the human and nonhuman.

V. PLANETARITY AND THE "AESTHETICS OF THE EARTH"

Postcolonial ecocriticism has a challenge to find a way to speak in ethical terms about the global and the local without reducing difference and without instituting old structural hierarchies; indeed we might say that this is the same challenge posed by global climate change. Global climate justice asks us how to move toward radical corrective measures while maintaining the delicate balance between global and local difference. While approaching a global ethics might be fraught with risk, the extent of our current crisis motivates thought that goes beyond simple dualisms in the interest of the survival of a new collectivity, even if that collectivity has been threatened disproportionately by American consumption, emissions, and waste. Just as we can no longer afford to eschew the concept of the global, neither can we risk erasing local particulars or bypassing a recognition of the alterity of human and nonhuman others. Global climate change is an all too threatening reminder to American critics, activists, and consumers that they can no longer afford to dismiss postcolonial concerns about the environment, or to argue that these concerns do not exist. Although postcolonial nations are the lowest in terms of carbon emissions, they are the most vulnerable to climate change, a point made all the more poignant by the prime minister of the Republic of Maldives, who hosted his 2009 cabinet meeting under the ocean to highlight the fate of this island nation which will be uninhabitable by 2100 due to sea level rising.[56] Virtually every model of global climate change indicates that the global south is particularly vulnerable to the predicted increases in weather extremes, such as more prolonged droughts, more intensified but less frequent rainfall and flooding, rising sea levels, shifting migrations of flora and fauna due to temperature increases, and even earthquakes.[57] For this reason, Michael Northcott argues that the ethics of climate change must respond to our modern history of colonial relations that have created "structural injustices and forms of economic coercion resulting in extreme poverty and even famine"(*Moral Climate* 58). A recent report of the UN's Global Humanitarian Forum, for example, calculates that global climate disruption causes 300,000 deaths a year due to increased drought, flooding, and other environmental consequences, a figure that will dramatically increase if mitigation against climate change is not pursued. Ninety-eight percent of all such deaths are occurring in postcolonial nations; in stark contrast, only one of the twelve least vulnerable nations is a developing country. Sub-Saharan Africa, the Middle East, South Asia, and the island states of the Pacific and Indian Oceans have been specifically identified as the most at risk.[58]

As William McKibben and others have argued, global climate change has raised the stakes for modernity. McKibben explains that because the effects of global climate change and other global environmental degradation are sometimes difficult to distinguish from natural processes and because they nevertheless have a direct impact on the environment, we can no longer trust in the Enlightenment division that places nature outside of human history and experience. This new era of human impact on the globe known as the Anthropocene has made it possible for countless individual perpetrators of environmental wrong to hide their actions in the midst of the complexity and collectivity of global processes and thus escape accountability. Nevertheless, global climate science suggests that despite the claims of the Enlightenment, nature is not outside of modernity and that Western thought can no longer afford the freedom from accountability that a facile nature/culture dualism affords. Adorno and Horkheimer, like the ecofeminists who followed, presciently argued that the Enlightenment bifurcation between internal and external nature was a rhetorical and ideological method for sustaining humanity's domination of the material world as well as provoking nature's eventual revolt. Our era of global climate change, then, presents a challenge and an opportunity that a postcolonial ecology is well suited to address.

Since postcolonialism is already familiar with the challenge of articulating otherness without reinforcing the very binaries that undergird hegemony in the first place, speaking of global climate change does not present an entirely new problem. Indeed, we can consider Michel Serres's articulation of this dilemma as a restatement of postcolonial principle. Serres writes that global climate change calls for new epistemologies that no longer imagine themselves as separate specializations because we need a "collective ethics in the face of the world's fragility" (78). Serres describes a kind of restoration of banished knowledges as a response to this challenge, one that understands the importance of the local while acting in response to the important ecological demands of the global. He writes, "Never forget the place from which you depart, but leave it behind and join the universal. Love the bond that unites your plot of earth with the Earth, the bond that make kin and stranger resemble each other" (50). This ethic of care has been extensively theorized in feminist philosophy and ecotheology and remains an important component of postcolonial and ecocritical thought.[59]

Serres's approach here echoes the "poetics of Relation" that Glissant describes as a way of responding to the fragmentations of history by "conceiv[ing] of totality but willingly renounc[ing] any claims to sum it up or to possess it" (*Poetics of Relation* 21). This poetics of Relation has particular importance for a postcolonial ecology. With Renée Gosson, in *Caribbean Literature and the Environment: Between Nature and Culture*, we built upon Glissant's contention that the Caribbean's violent "irruption into modernity"(*Caribbean Discourse* 146) created a schism between nature and culture in the region that its literature sought to bridge. We noted that Glissant called for an "aesthetics of the earth" that moved beyond an "obsolete mysticism" of place (*Poetics* 150) and engaged a form of "ecology" that criticized homogenizing models of consumption, "exclusiveness," and "territorial thought" (146). He suggests that "passion for the land where one lives is a start, an action we must endlessly risk" (151). We are particularly struck by his use of the word "risk" here. Passion for land is a risk because if internecine conflicts over land teach us anything, it is the ease with which devotion to the local can lead to exceptionalism and violent expulsion of difference. So why the imperative? Because without undying passion for place, the values of the global and the "affective standardization of peoples" and nature will encounter no resistance and local ecology, no allies (148). At the same time, however, this aesthetics must resist the reactionary and "obsolete mysticism" of much environmentalism, which yearns for the sacred root, or the "sectarian exclusiveness" of atavistic cultures (147). An "aesthetics of the earth" for Glissant rises to the challenge of appreciating beauty even when the land and sea have been ravaged by colonial violence. The seeming inappropriateness of aesthetics in the context of waste and rupture can enable a regenerative response. By reorienting a people to a "love of the earth so ridiculously inadequate or else frequently the basis for sectarian intolerance," Glissant hopes that literature can teach the political force of ecology (151); that is, literature can recapture ecology's radical articulation of "the relational interdependence of all lands, of the whole Earth" (147). In this sense, it's an "aesthetics of disruption and intrusion" the homogenizing market of consumption itself (151).

Glissant raises the specter of the reader's incredulity, asking "an aesthetics of the earth? In the half-starved dust of Africa? In the mud of flooded Asia? . . . In city sewers?. . . In mud huts crowning gold mines?" (151). His questions anticipate ecocritical challenges to whether "an environmentalism of the poor" might provide both an aesthetics and a politics that we might draw from as a model of postcolonial ecology. Yet by foregrounding the "aesthetics of rupture and connection" (151) as constitutive parts of ecology (particularly chaos theory, which he borrows from), Glissant critiques the discourse of totality that drives the homogenizing reach of globalization.[60] Like Spivak's theory of "planetarity," an approach that shifts away from the all-knowing discourse of globalization in order to "embrace an inexhaustible taxonomy" of alterity through multiple figures, including nature (*Death* 77), Glissant argues that "not knowing this totality is not a weakness" (154). He contends that we must turn to a poetics that not merely thinks of the other, addressing alterity, but rather creates "the other of Thought," a more radically transforming move that through "an aesthetics of turbulence" (155), creates change of thought and generates action, which in turn generates more change and more action.

Our intention in this collection is to foreground this complex theory of an "aesthetics of the earth"—a discourse of transformative self-conscious disruption that calls attention to the universalizing impulses of the global—as a key aspect of postcolonial ecocriticism. We must note that any effort to shift ecocritical discourse toward a more global framework, particularly for us writing from the United States, is fraught with dangers. We hope to heed Susie O'Brien's warning that ecocritical models should not replicate the consumptive drive of empire, in which the "environmentalist expertise emanating from the United States outward," reproduces an "implicit imperialism in this globalizing move" ("Garden" 168). Thus a postcolonial wariness of "globalizing impulses" is necessary to ensure that "the global and local come together, not by way of simple synecdoche . . . but in a way such that each interrupts and distorts the other" to refuse homogenization (O'Brien "Articulating" 143). Similar to the poetics of Relation Glissant and Serres articulate between the particular and the general and between the local and the global, O'Brien argues that foregrounding the limitations of representation and translation, and engaging the local and often inassimilable aspects of culture and history, help to uphold a sense of alterity while still engaging a global imaginary.

We already know enough about the dangers of a discourse that ignores the specificities of the local. Stopping global environmental degradation, for example, requires more than a "one-size-fits-all" approach to sustainability. However, a planet so thoroughly humanized by the forces of modernity requires a recognition of the ways in which place has already been conditioned by global processes of change. This is much the same way that a postcolonial poetics attends to the fragmented conditions of colonial displacement or diaspora without either idealizing fragmentation or yearning nostalgically for wholeness; it is instead an exercise in imagining relations in new ways in order to forge new epistemologies. This postcolonial exercise relies on the power of figural language to describe and redress the fragmentation of memory. In such strategies, identity is not static or predetermined but poetically created by the imagination's virtual and cross-cultural journey across geographies of difference. These methods avoid facile generalizations about the world's diverse peoples and places that a collective ethos might otherwise produce, but they also don't shy away from the task of seeking a culture's imagined relation to the global. We would argue that this tempering of a postcolonial environmental imagination is part of its strength and is one reason that postcolonial ecologies can stimulate an adequate and collective response to the challenges global environmental change poses.

The subaltern historian Dipesh Chakrabarty argues that global climate change "spell[s] the collapse of the age-old humanist distinction between natural history and human history," a distinction upon which postcolonial critiques of capitalism and globalization have relied ("The Climate and History" 201). This necessitates for Chakrabarty a more nuanced consideration of how we can critique the logic of capital and act in the interest of better futures while also being aware of how our evolution in deep time renders our knowledge contingent. A truly ecological postcolonialism, in other words, must be assiduously critical and rigorously aware of the dangers that lie ahead but also aware of our always contingent grasp on the role we play in predicting and determining a knowable future. He suggests that we still need the hermeneutics of suspicion that postcolonialism offers but that we must not conclude that our human experience and our human responsibilities can be reduced to the self-understanding that historical knowledge produces for us. This is because knowledge of our role as "geological agents" capable of disrupting the climate of the planet is not phenomenological but is rather the vision that deep historical and evolutionary explanations of human existence have produced. In other words, because our role as geological agents is not always readily discernable to us even if it is no longer deniable, a more contingent, collective, and cautious hermeneutics becomes necessary, one that emphasizes the importance of our agency and accepts the limits of what we can know—contra Hegel—about universal human experience. While it is obvious that science often still aspires to a totalizing and explanatory narrative that seeks to replace previous mythologies of universal human experience, Chakrabarty wishes to push the contingent and interdependent implications of these new ecological narratives. Similar to Glissant's notion of the poetics of Relation, Chakrabarty calls for an acceptance of our belonging in "a negative universal history," one which we accept that we are irrevocably a part of but which we can never know in its totality (222).

VI. POSTCOLONIAL ECOLOGIES: LITERATURES OF THE ENVIRONMENT

In mapping the always-shifting terrain of postcolonial ecologies, we've chosen to organize this volume into four thematic sections. The first, "Cultivating Place," foregrounds the ways in which colonialism created a complex history of displacement and exile and how contemporary postcolonial writers have sought to establish an aesthetics of belonging through language and literature. Since our relationship to place is often mediated by metaphysical concepts of soil and roots, particularly the plants that we often assume are natural and prior inhabitants, the first section disentangles the relationship between place, soil, belonging, and displacement across multiple genres such as the novel, poetry, and the visual arts. Our contributors Jill Didur and Elaine Savory turn to the European history of plant collecting and exchange between the colonies and the ways in which this history has connected the global south, particularly as this has been imagined in Kiran Desai's novel *The Inheritance of Loss* and in the poetry of St Lucian Derek Walcott. Didur argues that the British "hill stations" of the Himalayas were depicted by colonials as Gardens of Eden, jumbled colonial spaces that were tamed through form, most notably through the picturesque and the sublime. Desai transforms these representations in her 2006 novel to provide a "counterlandscaping" (Casid 241) of colonial fantasies as well as the separatist demands of the Gorkha National Liberation Front. She positions the Himalayan landscape as a generative and hybrid botanical space, an alternative to the Anglophilia of elite South Asian and expatriate communities, the Hinducentrism of the Indian state, and the patriarchal identity associated with the GNLF movement. This queering of the landscape cultivates a postcolonial ecology in terms of a contingent model of community. Savory explores creolized landscapes in her close reading of Walcott's poem "The Bounty" and explores how he inscribes the Caribbean relationship to plants, arguing that the garden has become globalized through British trade networks and continues to have relevance to the region's construction as an Edenic refuge for tourists. By turning to the work of English poet John Clare, an important influence on Walcott, Savory demonstrates that an environmental imagination not only informs Walcott's thematic concerns as a poet but, more importantly, so profoundly shapes his aesthetic strategies that for Walcott the work of metaphor is necessarily an ecopoetics. LeGrace Benson shifts the focus from literature to the visual arts in her analysis of how the tremendous environmental and economic devastation of Haiti has been refracted through, paradoxically, the ubiquitous trope of the Edenic garden in which local artists merge African and New World ecologies in their visual mapping of place. Although the rise of these idealized landscape paintings is closely tied to global tourism in Haiti, Benson outlines the ways in which these works encode sacred epistemologies of place derived from both Christian and Vodou traditions that were also central influences on the literary production. Her argument shows an emergent syncretic theology that is telluric and earthbound in its ethical orientation. All of the essays in this section engage with the representation of the garden as a hybrid space of nature and culture, historicizing the ways in which European colonialism configured utopian narratives of floral abundance in a dystopian era of slavery and exploitation.

Ecocritical literature has often inscribed the forest wilderness as a geographical and imaginative space where the Western individual subject might retreat from the social pressures of urbanization and modernity (see Garrard). In our second section, "Forest Fictions," our contributors demonstrate the intense human acculturation of the forest in postcolonial histories, particularly the ways in which these literatures complicate the representation of a "natural" or primordial forest outside of modernity. Lizabeth Paravisini-Gebert draws from an extensive body of Caribbean literature and history in the major language areas of the region (Spanish, English, and French) to demonstrate how the forest has been a site of multiple power struggles over time and how it has shifted significance. In the early colonial days forests represented spaces of fear, but in more recent times the forest and rural spaces in general have been recuperated as sites of refuge for the escaped slave and places of folk authenticity in nationalist movements. In an essay that ranges from the travel narratives of Sir Walter Raleigh and Bartolomé de Las Casas to the environmental activism of Puerto Rican poet Juan Antonio Corretjer, whose work on ecological toxicity predated Carson's *Silent Spring*, Paravisini-Gebert traces out the ways in which forests and spaces outside the plantation complex signify the cultural continuities of diasporic and indigenous populations in the Caribbean.

Jennifer Wenzel examines the Bengali writer Mahasweta Devi and her inscription of arboriculture in India, drawing from Vandana Shiva's argument that the privatization of natural resources under the mantle of economic development means the "exclusion of the right to survival"—or "genocide"—for a significant section of India's population. Devi's short stories have long been concerned with the privatization of the forest and its impact on India's indigenous and subaltern communities, particularly women. In her reading of how Devi depicts the exchange of trees and women's bodies for capital, Wenzel posits sex work as the rationalized equivalent to the privatization of nature and as the alternative to its genocidal consequences. Wenzel suggests that nature's complete indifference to the protagonist's plight at the end of the story allows us to move beyond the expected trope of pathetic fallacy to the more pressing question of how an absence of the register of ecological crisis works to dilate the temporal relationship between cause and effect, foregrounding our persistent misreading and even naturalization of crisis. George Handley turns to the literature of the Americas, examining Alejo Carpentier's novel *The Lost Steps* to suggest that Carpentier's theory of the New World Baroque, derived from his experiences in the Amazonian interior of Venezuela, undermines the anthropocentric assumptions of much cultural theory while also interrogating facile assumptions about biocentrism. Although Carpentier's encounter with the tropics is fraught with the various masculinist and neocolonial impulses of the West, the indeterminacy of his aesthetics suggests how ecology might serve to deconstruct the colonial order.

Our third section, "The Lives of (Nonhuman) Animals," shifts from this discussion of place and figures of natural belonging to examine the relationship between human and nonhuman animals. Animal studies and postcolonial studies have developed a close relationship in recent scholarship. As Martha Nussbaum has written, "the pursuit of global justice requires the inclusion of many people and groups not previously included as fully equal subjects of justice" such as women, the poor, and marginalized religious and ethnic groups. "But a truly global justice requires. . . . the other sentient beings with whose lives our own are inextricably and complexly intertwined" ("The Moral Status of Animals" B6). The contributors to this section expand the relationship to animal studies to encompass postcolonial questions of justice, representation, conservation, and biomythic narratives. Rob Nixon considers the temporal and spatial contradictions of the postapartheid game reserve as a place of managed stasis on the one hand and, on the other, a place of transnational transit for tourists and human migrants, particularly Mozambican refugees. Examining how African wildlife functions as a sign of the "ecological archaic," Nixon examines how black tourists at the game reserve trouble the racial politics of what he terms "ecological spectatorship." Turning to South African writers like Njabulo Ndebele and Nadine Gordimer, he focuses on the Kruger National Park as a buffer zone between South Africa and Mozambique and between the human and the animal.

Jonathan Steinwand explores the notable emergence in postcolonial literature of inscribing the relationship between humans and charismatic megafauna such as whales in the novels of Amitav Ghosh (India), Linda Hogan (United States) Witi Ihimaera (Aotearoa/New Zealand), and Zakes Mda (South Africa). In shifting our attention from the land to the sea and its propensity for universalizing metaphors, his essay examines how recent postcolonial novels press our conceptual boundaries of bioregional ecologies. The large body of work produced by postcolonial writers about the sea (or the land-sea relationship) suggests that ecocriticism's reliance on a "land ethic" might be reconfigured to include maritime spaces.[61] Steinwand draws upon the ecofeminist work of Mette Bryld and Nina Lykke to demonstrate that this cetacean turn is in a large part a post–Cold War exploration of "extraterrestrial" space and yet also tied closely to postcolonial concerns in which biomythic narratives that position nonhuman animals as ancestors or companion species are crucial to resisting the disenchantments of secular modernity.

Allison Carruth turns to the ethics of animal domestication in the novels of J. M. Coetzee (South Africa), particularly the way the human treatment of animals reflects on a larger discourse of citizenship and rights. Her analysis of Coetzee's recent fiction, particularly his novel *The Lives of Animals*, suggests that the human compassion necessary to act on behalf of other animals might come at the expense of human affinities with other human beings. Because animals in these novels are almost always consumed, Coetzee foregrounds a vital component of postcolonial ecocriticism: that of the human consumption of the other-than-human world and, by extension, human complicity in perpetuating those systems. Pablo Mukherjee examines Indra Sinha's *Animal's People* (India), a novel that tests the human/animal divide by representing one of the children poisoned and disabled by the Union Carbide Corporation's 1984 gas leak in Bhopal as a self-professed "Animal." In foregrounding the lack of medical, legal, and financial compensation and treatment for the hundreds of thousands of Bhopalis who were poisoned by the pesticide leak, the novel calls into question the uneven distribution of universal human rights in the global south and "the spatial politics of environmental toxicity." Mukherjee argues that this turn to the animal reconfigures our ideas about communality, relationality, and universality, and that paradoxically, the very postcolonial context that allowed Union Carbide to create environmental toxicity with impunity will be utilized as the catalyst for an ethics of resistance.

Our final section examines "Militourism," a term coined by American Indian writer Louis Owens and theorized by Teresia Teaiwa to explain the mutual constitution of the tourist and military industries, particularly in the island tropics, and how "the tourist industry masks the military force behind it" (Teaiwa "Reading" 249). The stereotype of the peaceful and exotic Pacific Islands has been created through centuries of colonialism and a tourist industry that has mystified the region's militarization and nuclearization. In her important work on the displacement of Pacific nuclearization by the sexualized two-piece garment, Teaiwa asks, "what does the word bikini evoke for you? . . .A bikini-clad woman invigorated by solar radiation or Bikini Islanders cancer-ridden by nuclear radiation?" ("bikinis" 91). The irradiation of the Marshall Islands, paradoxically, has been generative to ecological thought. Elizabeth DeLoughrey's essay traces out how the field of ecology was constituted by the Atomic Energy Commission in its radiological surveys of the Pacific Islands, suggesting that concepts of global ecology are derivative of the literal fallout from the Cold War, and positioning solar and military forms of radiation as key indicators of globalization. Exploring how atomic discourse was naturalized by likening nuclear weapons to the sun, her essay demonstrates how natural figures of solar radiation have been used in Pacific Island literature to articulate a heliocentric global modernity. In connecting radiation to ecological thought, her essay foregrounds the close connections between militarism and ecological violence and their representation by indigenous writers of the Pacific. Dina El Dessouky builds upon these questions of sovereignty in the era of military neocolonialism in her examination of contemporary indigenous literatures from Hawai'i and Tahiti, turning to literary representations of the fifty years of U.S. military weapons testing on Kaho'olawe and the thirty-year French nuclear weapons testing program on Moruroa and Fangataufa atolls. Drawing from the work of Chantal Spitz and Michou Chaze, she argues that these authors articulate island space in terms of the indigenous body, advocating a discourse of inalienable rights for human and nonhuman ecological communities.

Anthony Carrigan examines the work of Chandani Lokugé (Sri Lanka) to explore the ways in which the wartime violence of Sri Lanka bolsters the gendered and racialized hierarchies of the tourist trade, and asks how imaginative portrayals of tourism and disaster might shed light on interdisciplinary debates concerning more sustainable cultural, environmental, and economic futures. He turns to how the social and environmental legacies of the 2004 tsunami are anticipated in Lokugé's pre-tsunami novel *Turtle Nest*, which depicts links between child sex tourism and animal abuse, highlighting the fact that ecological disasters are never isolated but are part of the ongoing crises of civil war, chronic poverty, and ecological degradation.

Byron Caminero-Santangelo similarly critiques the neocolonial presumption of economic well-being that tourist development in South Africa brings. In the novel *The Heart of Redness*, by Zakes Mda, Caminero-Santangelo sees an interrogation and revision of the concept of bioregionalism, offering a postcolonial paradigm that avoids the pitfalls of what Rob Nixon has called "ecoparochialism." Mda shows the effectiveness of a nuanced and dynamic understanding of the interpenetration between urban and rural, local and global, regional and national differences that allows for an ethics of place within spaces compromised by globalization.

Postcolonial Ecologies: Literatures of the Environment is the first collection of essays to engage literatures from Africa, the Caribbean, South Asia, and the Pacific Islands in their postcolonial constructions of the environment. We position postcolonial ecology as a critical engagement with an "aesthetics of the earth," which, as Glissant explains, is also an imagining of alterity, a politics, and an impossible "aesthetics of chaos" (*Poetics* 155). As we have become increasingly dependent on epistemologies of the social and hard sciences that offer the often misleading reassurance of reliable and measurable outcomes, global environmental degradation and the disproportion of that degradation suffered by the world's poor would seem to suggest the need to put more faith in the performance of such inexact sciences as listening, interpretation, reading, and ethics. In other words, we need to recover an appreciation for the relevance of the humanities in the face of the global environmental challenges of the twenty-first century, something we very much hope this volume helps to accomplish.

NOTES

1. Later in the book Fanon would argue "imperialism . . . sows seeds of decay here and there that must be mercilessly rooted out from our land and from our minds" (181), a point that connects the land directly to the psychological impact of colonialism.

2. In Ghosh's inscription of the dynamic tidal country of the Sundarbans, he writes, "the speciality of mangroves is that they do not merely recolonize land; they erase time. Every generation creates its own population of ghosts" (*Hungry Tide* 43).

3. In this sense we follow Lorraine Code's model of "ecological thinking" which "reconfigures relationships all the way down: epistemological, ethical, scientific, political, rational, and other relationships between and among living beings and the inanimate parts of the world" (47).

4. See Williams, *The Country and the City*.

5. Plumwood argues, "'Living close to the land' may under the right conditions help generate knowledge of and concern for ecological effects of production and consumption within a local community, but neither this closeness nor the local ecological literacy it might help generate is sufficient to guarantee knowledge of ecological effects and relationships in the larger global community or even a larger regional one" (*Environmental Culture* 77).

6. For more on ecomimesis, see Morton's *Ecology without Nature*, especially chapter 1.

7. This work on human and nonhuman alterity/otherness has been explored by ecofeminist critics such as Haraway in *Simians, Cyborgs, and Women: The Reinvention of Nature*, and Murphy, *Literature, Nature, and the Other*.

8. These points are expanded in our introduction to *Caribbean Literature and the Environment*. Our thanks to Renée Gosson for her work on this argument and Glissant's translation.

9. See also Martinez-Alier, *The Environmentalism of the Poor*.

10. See Murphy, *Literature, Nature, and Other*, and Escobar, "Difference and Conflict in the Struggle over Natural Resources."

11. ASLE: The Association for Study of Literature and Environment sponsors a biannual conference and the journal *ISLE: Interdisciplinary Studies of Literature and the Environment*. More recent journals have been established such as the *Journal of Ecocriticism: Nature, Society, Literature*. A substantive list can be found here: http://www.asle.org/site/papers/manuscripts/journals/.

12. See the *PMLA* discussion in the Forum on Literatures of the Environment. See Parini, "Greening the Humanities," Nixon, "Environmentalism and Postcolonialism" (233–34), and Saro-Wiwa, *Genocide in Nigeria*.

13. To engage postcolonial ecocriticism is to recognize that, for example, the western landscape of the United States that has become a vital site of wilderness discourse has also been constituted by European expansion and white-settler nation building. See Kolodny, *The Lay of the Land*, Alaimo, *Undomesticated Ground*, and West, "Wallace Stegner's West: Wilderness and History." For a poststructural approach to the construction of western wilderness, see Cronon's "The Trouble with Wilderness or Getting Back to the Wrong Nature."

14. See Foucault's *The Order of Things*.

15. See also Brockaway, *Science and Colonial Expansion*, Grove, *Green Imperialism*, Miller and Reill, *Visions of Empire*, Drayton, *Nature's Government*, and Cañizares-Esguerra, *Nature, Empire, and Nation*.

16. Arnold, *The Problem of Nature*, Livingstone, "Tropical Hermeneutics," Stepan, *Picturing Tropical Nature*, Browne, *The Secular Ark*, Moore, Pandian, and Kosek, "Introduction: The Cultural Politics of Race and Nature," Eze, *Race and the Enlightenment*.

17. The Australian Flora and Fauna Act was finally changed in the 1967 referendum, which granted citizenship to aboriginal peoples.

18. For a different history, see Rajan, *Modernizing Nature*.

19. See also Carolyn Merchant, who connects the rise in nostalgia for a feminized and passive Eden to the mechanization of industrial capitalism in *The Death of Nature* and *Reinventing Eden*.

20. See Arnold, *Famine*.

21. The shift to "green" is a deliberate deflection from the social revolution of the "red." William Gaud, Director of the U.S. Agency for International Development, famously coined the term in 1968 by commenting: "Developments in the field of agriculture contain the makings of a new revolution. It is not a violent Red Revolution like that of the Soviets, nor is it a White Revolution like that of the shah of Iran. I call it the Green Revolution" (Gaud). See Shiva, *The Violence of the Green Revolution*, and Peet and Watts, *Liberation Ecologies*.

22. See von Braun and Meinzen-Dick, "'Land Grabbing' by Foreign Investors in Developing Countries."

23. Crosby, *The Columbian Exchange* and *Ecological Imperialism*. See also Tiffin, "Introduction," *Five Emus to the King of Siam: Environment and Empire*, xii.

24. See, for instance, Lawrence Buell's *The Future of Environmental Criticism*, which argues that to "first wave ecocriticism" the environment meant "the natural environment" (21) while only later "second wave ecocriticism" challenged this "organicism" (22). If one includes the work of ecofeminist, environmental justice, and postcolonial scholars from the very beginning, this genealogy is not possible.

25. While scholars such as Murphy and Curtin have consistently contributed to postcolonial ecocriticism, more recent collections on the topic include DeLoughrey, Gosson, and Handley, *Caribbean Literature and the Environment* (2005); the special issue of *Interventions* (9.1), on "Green Postcolonialism," edited by Graham Huggan and Helen Tiffin (2007); the special cluster on postcolonial ecocriticism in *ISLE: Interdisciplinary Studies of Literature and the Environment* 14.1 (2007), edited by Cilano and DeLoughrey; the special double issue of the *Journal of Commonwealth and Postcolonial Studies*, on postcolonial studies and ecocriticism (13.2 and 14.1: 2007). See also recent books by authors in this collection such as Pablo Mukherjee's *Postcolonial Environments: Nature, Culture and the Contemporary Indian Novel in English* (Palgrave, 2010) and Anthony Carrigan's *Postcolonial Tourism: Literature, Culture, and Environment* (Routledge, 2011). Forthcoming books include Byron Camerino-Santagelo's coedited volume with Garth Myers, *Environment at the Margins: Literary and Environmental Studies in Africa* (University of Ohio Press) and Rob Nixon's *Slow Violence and Environmental Time* (Harvard University Press).

26. Nixon observes, "Lawrence Buell, Cheryll Glotfelty, Harold Fromm, Daniel Payne, Scott Slovic, and many others . . . canonize the same self-selecting genealogy of American writers: Ralph Waldo Emerson, Henry David Thoreau, John Muir, Aldo Leopold, Edward Abbey, Annie Dillard, Terry Tempest Williams, Wendell Berry, and Gary Snyder" ("Environmentalism" 234).

27. Ecofeminism remains strangely absent from much ecocritical scholarship and its legacies have been largely ignored, in a large part because it has been incorrectly reduced to a dated essentialist methodology. See Sturgeon, *Ecofeminist Natures*, for a compelling genealogy of the multiple and complex strands of thought that contribute to ecofeminist critique, and the work of Haraway, Merchant, Plumwood, Code, Mies and Shiva, and Shiva, for ecofeminism with a particularly global and anticolonial approach. See Young, *Postcolonialism*, 100–108, for a discussion of ecofeminism and postcolonialism.

28. Heise's recent book makes an important call for an "ecocosmopolitanism" that strikes a more nuanced balance between localism and globalism, even though it does not engage postcolonial literature as part of this globalizing move.

29. On nature and universalizing discourse, see Tsing, "Transitions as Translations," Sturgeon, *Ecofeminist Natures*, O'Brien, "Articulating a World of Difference."

30. On this interdisciplinary influence, see Cohen, "Blues in the Green."

31. See discussion in Misra, *Environmental Ethics: A Dialogue of Cultures*, Guha, *Environmentalism: A Global History*, Hill; and *South Asia: An Environmental History*, and Young, *Postcolonialism: A Very Short Introduction*, 100–105, one of the few texts to address ecofeminism in relation to postcolonial studies. See also Curtin's discussion of Gandhi in *Environmental Ethics*, 98–130.

32. See, for instance, Berkes, *Sacred Ecology: Traditional Ecological Knowledge and Resource Management*; and Gottlieb, *This Sacred Earth: Religion, Nature, and the Environment*. See also the Yale Forum on Religion and Ecology, http://fore.research.yale.edu/.

33. The field of ecosocialism is enormous. Merchant's *Ecology: Key Concepts in Critical Theory* gives an excellent overview of both Marxist ecology and the Frankfurt School and includes extracts from key thinkers. Bookchin's *Our Synthetic Environment*, published just before Carson's *Silent Spring*, examined the impact of pesticides and radiation, whereas his later work, *The Ecology of Freedom: The Emergence and Dissolution of Hierarchy* (first published in 1982) turned to social hierarchies, including patriarchy, and their impact on nature. See also the work of O'Connor, *Natural Causes: Essays in Ecological Marxism*, and Foster, *Ecology against Capitalism*, and the archives of the journal *Capitalism, Nature, Socialism*. In addition to Merchant, other scholars who have drawn from the Frankfurt school include Harvey, *Justice, Nature and the Geography of Difference*.

34. See Martinez-Alier, *The Environmentalism of the Poor*, all the works of Vandana Shiva, Maathai's *The Challenge for Africa*, and Peet and Watts, *Liberation Ecologies*.

35. The First Commonwealth Conference on Development and Human Ecology was hosted in Malta in 1970; see Bowen-Jones, *Human Ecology in the Commonwealth*.

36. Some have argued that the ideology of the Chipko movement can be traced back for hundreds of years in Indian history. See Pal, "Chipko Movement Is 300 Years Old," in Misra, *Environmental Ethics*, who cites a communal protest against tree felling in Rajastan in 1720.

37. At the Non-Aligned Conference in 1983 she argued, "some people still consider concern for the environment an expensive and perhaps unnecessary luxury. But the preservation of the environment is an economic consideration since it is closely related to the depletion, restoration and increase of resources" (quoted in Misra, *Environmental Ethics*, 16).

38. The Stockholm Declaration is available here: http://www.unep.org/Documents.Multilingual/Default.asp?DocumentID=97&ArticleID=1503.

39. See http://www.un-documents.net/wcn.htm.
40. The UN Convention on the Law of the Sea and its impact on postcolonial literature has been discussed in DeLoughrey, *Routes and Roots*.
41. See Maathai, *The Challenge for Africa*, 83–110. See Taylor and Buttel, who argue that debt, "the South-North capital drain, and the international monetary order (the World Bank and IMF)" are "fundamental contributors to environmental degradation" (412). See also Martinez-Alier, *The Environmentalism of the Poor*.
42. See Amartya Sen, "Population: Delusion and Reality," and Curtin, *Environmental Ethics*, 74–97. Zygmunt Bauman argues that the construction of human waste, termed "overpopulation," is a byproduct of modernity. "Rich nations can afford a high density of population because they are 'high entropy' centres, drawing resources, most notably the sources of energy, from the rest of the world, and returning in exchange the polluting, often toxic waste of industrial processing that uses up, annihilates and destroys a large part of the worldwide supplies of energy"(*Wasted Lives* 43).
43. Escobar, "Constructing Nature: Elements for a Poststructuralist Political Ecology," 46–68. In this development discourse, poor nations are also reprimanded for their overpopulation, a discourse initiated by the Club of Rome reports such as *The Limits to Growth* (1972).
44. Shell was admonished for "greenwashing" by the British Advertising Standards Authority, http://www.asa.org.uk/asa/adjudications/Public/TF_ADJ_43476.htm. For more on the Nigerian context, in addition to Saro-Wiwa, see *The Curse of the Black Gold*, by Kashi and Watts. For more on natural capitalism, see Plumwood, *Environmental Culture*.
45. See Mwangi, "Nobel Prize: A Shot in the Arm to African Ecocriticism." On Maathai's contribution to environmental discourse, see Nixon, "Slow Violence, Gender, and the Environmentalism of the Poor" which foregrounds Maathai's "intersectional environmentalism" that interlinks human, women's, and environmental rights (23). This might be linked to other ecojustice writers such as Vandana Shiva, who argues powerfully for what she terms "earth democracy."
46. There has been a vigorous discussion of the role of post-structural thought in environmental and ecocritical studies. In addition to Escobar, see Conley, *Ecopolitics*, and Zimmerman, *Contesting Earth's Future*.
47. Some ecocentric frameworks have alienated postcolonialists, such as Edward Abbey's stance against Mexican migration to the United States (Nixon, "Environmentalism" 236). Critiques of deep ecology have come from many quarters, including ecosocialists, ecofeminists, and the postcolonialists discussed here.
48. This division, Plumwood argued in *Feminism and the Mastery of Nature*, generally overlooked feminist thought and thereby missed a third epistemological position between social ecologists and deep ecologists (*Feminism* 2; see also her *Environmental Culture*). See also Code, *Ecological Thinking*. The Guha and Naess debate is explored in Curtin, *Chinnagounder's Challenge*, and also in Cilano and DeLoughrey.
49. Guha, "Radical American Environmentalism," and Mallick, "Refugee Resettlement in Forest Reserves."
50. See Naess's response, "The Third World, Wilderness, and Deep Ecology."
51. Plumwood points out that Western classical logic with its emphasis on instrumental reason produces a hierarchical dualism in which the concept of reason provides the unifying and defining contrast for the concept of nature (*Environmental Culture* 5). For more on otherness and the decentering of humanism, see Head.

Introduction   39

52. Huggan cites Guha and Martinez-Alier's *Varieties of Environmentalism* as an example of this tendency toward overstatement. See Head "The (Im)Possibility of Ecocriticism." Cilano and DeLoughrey, in a special postcolonial cluster of the journal *Isle* (2007), also used Guha's critique as a starting point to examine the contested ground between dominant American conceptions of ecocriticism and postcolonial critique, arguing that:

> postcolonial topics should not be viewed as entirely *new directions* in the field of ecocriticism as much as they represent *increased visibility* to a western-based audience who is rethinking the limitations of U.S. national frameworks that had occluded other perspectives. To suggest that *postcolonial* ecocriticism is *new* is to give a normative status to ecocriticism's institutional origins without questioning the limitations of its foundational methodologies and focus. (73)

53. See, for instance, the work of Haraway, Code, Conley, and Bullard. Although the body of environmental justice work is immense, we recommend two of the more globally inclined collections: Filomina Chioma Steady's *Environmental Justice in the New Millennium* and Joni Adamson, Mei Mei Evans, and Rachel Stein's *The Environmental Justice Reader*.

54. See also Buell, who remarks on the "xenophobic stigmatization of outsiders and wanderers" (*Future* 68).

55. See, for instance, Nandy and Chakrabarty.

56. See http://www.guardian.co.uk/environment/2009/may/29/1.

57. See the online scholarship at the Caribbean Community Climate Change Centre (CCCCC), http://www.caricom.org/jsp/community/ccccc.jsp?menu=community

58. "Global warming causes 300,000 deaths a year, says Kofi Annan thinktank," http://www.guardian.co.uk/environment/2009/may/29/1. The source is the Global Humanitarian Forum: http://ghfgeneva.org/Media/PressReleases/tabid/265/EntryId/40/Climate-Change-responsible-for-300-000-deaths-a-year.aspx.

59. Aldo Leopold, for example, in 1949 called for "an extension of the social conscience from people to land" and noted that "we can be ethical only in relation to something we can see, feel, understand, love, or otherwise have faith in" (214). This need for nature as a kind of subjective presence is one reason why ecotheology has paid so much attention to the ways in which nature can be construed to have what Northcott calls "intelligible order and moral value" (254). One of the earliest feminist theorizations of an ethic of care, which foregrounded relationships as a constitutive component of ethical behavior was Gilligan's *In A Different Voice: Psychological Theory and Women's Development* (1982). See also Held, *The Ethics of Care*, and Merchant, *Earthcare: Women and the Environment*.

60. Chaos theory has played an important role in theorizing ecology in the humanities. Worster has argued that ecology has shifted to become "a study of disturbance, disharmony, and chaos" (*Wealth of Nature* 158). The deeper we venture into the operations of complexly interconnected systems, we learn that "change is without any determinable direction and goes on forever, never reaching a point of stability" (162). See also Zimmerman, *Contesting Earth's Future*, Conley, *Ecopolitics*, and Prigogine and Stengers, *Order Out of Chaos*.

61. See note 40 and Cilano and DeLoughrey's "Against Authenticity" on the land-sea relationship in postcolonial ecocriticsm.

PART I

CULTIVATING PLACE

1

Cultivating Community

Counterlandscaping in Kiran Desai's *The Inheritance of Loss*

Jill Didur

The Indian "hill station" is a British creation partially fueled by fantasies of virgin landscapes and the possible recovery of or retreat to the Garden of Eden. Nowhere is this association with the landscape more prominent than in the Darjeeling region of West Bengal. Darjeeling first attracted the attention of the East Indian Company in 1827, when its representatives recommended it as an ideal spot for a sanitarium, later built and named Eden Sanitarium (Kennedy 22). It is this same general geographical location that Kiran Desai has chosen for the Indian setting of *The Inheritance of Loss* (2006), during the 1986–88 escalation of the Gorkhaland movement, just prior to the signing of the Darjeeling Hill Accord (DHA). In this essay I argue that the hill station, as a place of retreat, a recovery of the Garden of Eden, and an appropriate subject for the picturesque, is a colonial imagining taken up by Kiran Desai's novel as a countercolonial approach to representing the Himalayan landscape. Rather than disavow the strategies used in colonial travel writing and fiction for representing the environment and local communities of the Kalimpong and Darjeeling region, I argue that Desai's narrative displaces normalized notions of the land, gardens, and nature, mobilizing what art historian Jill Casid has called "counterlandscaping practices of resignification and transformation" (241).

Following Casid, my reading of Desai's depiction of the Himalayan environment tracks how colonial landscapes are not only produced through material practices but also "through forms of reproductive print, visual and textual, that were to serve as prototypical models of colonial relandscaping" (2). Furthermore, I read Desai's *Inheritance* as alert to how "different cultural understandings of society and nature have been deployed in specific historical moments," and aware of "ecology's value for a postcolonial environmental concern, one attuned to histories of unequal development and varieties of discrimination, including, of course, racism and sexism" (Vital "Toward an African Ecocriticism" 90).[1] My reading of *Inheritance*, therefore, begins the process of articulating what Anthony Vital describes as a "historicity of ecology" that draws "critical attention . . . to histories of change, which would link the discursive to cultural, social, and environmental factors, clarifying the situations through which a language has evolved" (90). This reading practice takes for granted that "all understanding of the world . . . is always delivered through language" and that "different languages (and discourses within a language) . . . permit varieties of understanding with unequal value" (90). With these assumptions in mind, I offer a "double reading" of Desai's depiction of landscape in and around the hill stations of Darjeeling and Kalimpong that "turn[s] the colonial natural and descriptive histories" of the Himalayas "against themselves . . . [and] gather[s] how landscaping or the master's garden tools could be used against the master" (Casid 197). Desai's novel, I suggest, remakes the Himalayan landscape (especially its assigned picturesque and sublime qualities), investigates the cultural and environmental effects of these modes of seeing, and challenges colonial notions of retreat and innocence associated with hill station environments and communities in a postcolonial context.

In order to understand how Desai's text remakes the colonial tropes associated with the landscapes of hill stations, it is important to take into account how places like Darjeeling and Kalimpong came to be represented in literature and culture in India during colonialism. Like many hill stations, the Darjeeling area was viewed by the British as an ideal location for retreat from the heat of the plains, something that in the first half of the nineteenth century was believed to have serious health consequences for Europeans and was equated with "disease, decay and death" (Kennedy 19).[2] Retreat to the cooler climate associated with places like the Eden Sanitarium in Darjeeling was seen as "especially suited for patients suffering from [what the army medical officer described as] 'general debility, whether arising from a long residence in the plains or depending on tardy convalescence from fevers and other acute disease'" (Kennedy 29).[3] Apart from health and strategic political reasons, the other overwhelming attraction the hill stations had for colonial subjects was the way in which their landscapes could be assimilated to British notions of the picturesque, a trope that pervades travel writing of the nineteenth century when these areas were first settled by Europeans.

As Indira Ghose, among others, has argued, "the aesthetics of the picturesque were enormously influential in moulding nineteenth-century travellers' perceptions of India" (38). Partha Mitter describes the picturesque as "an attack on classical notions of beauty as it advocated 'disorder' and 'irregularity' in landscape in both art and nature and suggested that even artificial rudeness was to be preferred to order and neatness" (122). Casid describes the term picturesque as an "eighteenth-century neologism" that "occupies the space of translation" (45). The "picturesque," she explains, "most obviously mediates between nature and art. When applied to paintings, it often meant that the scene or handling of it was somehow faithful to nature. When applied to "nature" or to physical terrain, *picturesque* primarily signified that a select "view" was "like a picture" (original emphasis 45). I find Casid's definition particularly useful because it stresses that it is not simply roughness or "disorder" that defines this aesthetic style but also an attempt to balance or augment these irregular scenes with a frame that unifies their elements (thus involving an aesthetic "improvement" of nature). Casid's analysis of the term underscores how the picturesque is not a description of the quality of a certain view of nature "but rather a process of recognition," a zone of translation, where the viewer constructs a scene in nature according to certain aesthetic conventions (45).[4] The emergence of an interest in the picturesque among the wealthy classes in nineteenth-century Britain "led to a displacement of both history painting and portraits by landscape painting as the most valorized mode of art" (Ghose 38). "At the same time" Ghose explains, "classical literature was being challenged in the field of poetry, where a shift towards a celebration of national rather than classical scenery reflected the project of cultural and national self-definition" (38–39). While earlier versions of the picturesque focused on the English landscape, and worked to unify this with representations of nature in the rest of the British Isles, the use of the picturesque in written and visual accounts of travel in India (and other colonial locations) extended the "project of cultural and national self-definition" to colonial regions. As Casid suggests, colonial travel narratives "depended on the picturesque as a discourse of aesthetic and political control for the translation and forcible reshaping of the foreign and exotic into the familiar and tamed" (47). The exercise of representing India in picturesque terms gave the colonial artist the opportunity to define India—and in the case of Darjeeling and the surrounding Himalayan landscape—in a particular way.

Casid's discussion of how picturesque notions of landscape take on a particular salience in the colonial context suggests that the picturesque also served as a way to reconcile two conflicting desires that are important to my reading of *Inheritance*; on the one hand, the remaking of the colonized space involved a deliberate hybridization of the physical and natural world, or what she describes as a "highly controlled intermixture" (14), that positioned colonial intervention as improving the landscape. Writing about French and British colonial practices of "relandscaping" in the Caribbean, Casid argues that the process of environmental hybridization, "through the material transplantation of plants, enslaved African people, and machines," should be understood as "a symbolic, material and geopolitical colonization" (1). This claim positions her analysis slightly at odds with Homi Bhabha's view of hybridity as "the subversive product of colonial systems," and questions the process of hybridization as simply "an effect of colonial power, but rather as one of the main technologies by which colonial power was produced as discursive and material effect" (1). In other words, hybridization of colonized landscapes might also be justified as a program for improving the environment. On the other hand, in order to balance this diversification of plants and transformation of landscape, the discourse of what Casid suggests is better described as the "imperial picturesque" (14), helped to unify and naturalize this transformation as well as erase evidence of the labor required in its achievement. As Casid's *Sowing Empire* shows, in the material and textual practices that went into establishing plantations in Jamaica, "colonial intermixing and imperial picturesque worked together to make a visual argument for rightful possession to land in actuality worked by slave labour" (14). Casid adapts Mary Louise Pratt's notion of "anti-conquest," which reflects "the strategies of representation whereby European bourgeois subjects seek to secure their innocence in the same moment as they assert European hegemony" (Pratt 1992 7), to coin the phrase "anti-empire" (Casid 28). "Anti-empire," in Casid's view, refers to colonial landscaping "as a site of nature improved . . . to reproduce empire as its opposite" (28). In my reading of *Inheritance*, I track how the narrative makes visible the power relations that went into constructing hill stations as "anti-empire," unsettles the innocence associated with their cultural and material maintenance, and restores an awareness of the cultural transformation that normalized their political culture in the post-colonial era.

As Dane Kennedy notes, however, British representations of hill stations alternated between the rhetoric of the picturesque and the sublime, especially when writing about the Himalayas, and this dynamic also informs Desai's representation of the Darjeeling and Kalimpong areas in *Inheritance*. Mitter explains "the feeling for sublime was aroused by the size of the subject. It had to be so large that the human mind failed to comprehend it" (121). In Edmund Burke's well-known view, the "essential ingredients of the sublime" included the obscurity of the subject arousing fear induced by ignorance. The subject had also to express a certain power, greatness, and a dimension of infinite magnitude. The atmosphere of darkness, solitude, and silence enveloping the subject increased the feeling of terror (Mitter 122).

Kennedy observes that while hill stations like Ootacamund, in southern India, are surrounded by "gently rolling, sparsely wooded plateaus bounded by steep escarpments . . . [and] fitted easily within the pastoral conventions of the picturesque" (41), the immense mountain ranges of the Himalayas resisted attempts to *fully* domesticate their appearance. "By the early nineteenth century, the British knew that the highest peaks in the world could be found here, although their full measure remained underestimated" (Kennedy 45). In fact, Kanchenjunga, which figures prominently in the landscape of Desai's novel, was considered to be the highest peak in the world until 1856 when Indian mathematician Radhanath Sikdar used data collected by the British trigonometric survey to establish that Everest and K2 are higher. Early British travelers to the Himalayas, such as George Francis White, emphasized how the "wild," "overpowering," and "raw" quality of the natural world induced "a sensation allied to fear" and a diminished sense of human significance (White in Kennedy 45). White refers to the size of the Himalayas as "a salutary reminder of how puny human beings were," and Barron observed in the 1840s, "what an atom in its system a human being appears" (Barron in Kennedy 47). The general qualities of the sublime, first articulated in the eighteenth century, seemed tailor made, in some respects, for this landscape.

This sense of the British traveler's insignificance in the face of the Himalayan mountain range presented a problem for the colonial settler seeking a sense of respite from authority over a colonized population. "To feel dwarfed and overawed by the untamed forces of nature," Kennedy points out,

> may have been emotionally edifying for the passing traveler, but it was intensely disturbing to the invalid or other sojourner trying to find sanctuary from the plains. Such respite necessitated a landscape that had been tamed of its danger and reduced to human proportions, which is to say a landscape that had been made picturesque. (46)

This taming of the Himalayan landscape and its people involved a "selectivity of . . . vision" (Kennedy 40) in representations of these places in literature and visual art, a physical remaking of the landscape through the transplantation of plants and trees associated with the English countryside, and a stereotyping of its indigenous groups.[5] In colonial travel writing, the indigenous Lepcha community in Sikkim and West Bengal became "tokens of the secluded and Edenic character of the places they inhabited" (Kennedy 227), portrayed as noble savages, children of nature and, most important, "represented [as] a moral antithesis to the intractable and unfathomable subjects who occupied the plains" (69). Similarly, private gardens, government nurseries, botanical gardens, and artificial lakes were common additions to hill station environments, all of which contributed to an assimilation of the landscape to British aesthetics, topography, economic desires and botanical familiarity. By "domesticat[ing] the disorderly" (51), Kennedy suggests, "over time, hill stations were drawn so tightly within the aesthetic confines of British landscape traditions that they became divorced from the surrounding environment, particularly when that environment was as intimidating as the Himalayas" (52).

Significantly, Desai's *Inheritance* debunks this history of translating and taming the Himalayan landscape and people through the picturesque by offering a view that suggests a more complicated postcolonial ecology is in place.⁶ The colonial legacy of environmental and anthropological refashioning of the Himalayan landscape is rendered unstable even as it is shown to be taken for granted by most of the fictional postcolonial inhabitants of Kalimpong and Darjeeling. Unlike the literary and material practices that characterized British colonial encounters with the Himalayas, Desai's representation of the environment unsettles picturesque portrayals of the so-called hill stations and deploys the rhetoric of the sublime in a manner that estranges historical attempts to colonize the landscape. Moreover, the novel's reference to colonial tropes used in other narratives about the Himalayas, such as Elizabeth Sarah Mazuchelli's *The Indian Alps and How We Crossed Them* (1876) (mentioned as firing the imagination of the Scotsman who built the judge's residence) (12), and indigenous narratives like A. R. Foning's, *Lepcha, My Vanishing Tribe* (1987) (a book Sai takes out of the Darjeeling Gymkhana library), draws attention to the limits of representation and reminds readers that no one "view" of the Himalayas can adequately portray the environmental truth of the region.

The novel opens with a description of the view from the veranda of Cho Oyu (named after the sixth highest peak in the world), the house the protagonist Sai's broken and reclusive grandfather bought in 1957 from a Scotsman "on his way back to Aberdeen" (28). This description epitomizes Desai's counterlandscaping practice in its subversion of colonial aesthetics. Desai's omniscient narrator describes the judge's attraction to the house and the Kalimpong area as driven by his desire to retreat from society while he struggles to cope with an overwhelming sense of self hatred and acquired distaste for all things Indian. We are told that thirty years earlier, when the judge first surveyed the property before deciding to buy it, "passionately colored birds swooped and whistled, and the Himalayas rose layer upon layer until those gleaming peaks proved a man to be so small that it made sense to give it all up, empty it all out" (29). Here the rhetoric of the sublime is inverted, given a positive spin, stressing how the landscape might help humble, obliterate, or unravel the judge's identity, and provide him with an avenue for escape from his troubled past.

Descriptions of impenetrable fog, vapor, or mist, are a standard aspect of colonial accounts of the life in Darjeeling, including Mazuchelli's book where she describes that, upon arrival, her party is "overtaken by one of those dense fogs of which we had ample experience during our residence in Darjeeling" (48). Such descriptions are also the subject of the opening sentences of *Inheritance* and the narrative begins with a description of how "mist moving like a water creature across the great flanks of mountains possessed of ocean shadows and depths" is so thick that it had obscured the sun, making it seem like dusk "all day" (1). The smoke from the cook's cooking fire in the house is described as:

> Mingl[ing] with the mist that was gathering speed, sweeping in thicker and thicker, obscuring things in parts—half a hill, then the other half.

> The trees turned into silhouettes, loomed forth, were submerged again. Gradually the vapour replaced everything with itself, solid objects with shadow, and nothing remained that did not seem molded from or inspired by it. (2)

This is a threatening landscape, untamed by the picturesque, even in the space of the garden where the discourse is commonly used. As Sai reads an old *National Geographic* about an elusive giant squid, her environment takes on the appearance of a murky sea and trees at the end of Cho Oyu's garden are described as "moss-slung giants, bunioned and misshapen, tentacled with the roots of orchids" (2). The house also fails to be a refuge from these influences, as we are told "the grey had permeated inside, as well, settling on the silverware, nosing the corners, turning the mirror in the passageway to cloud" (2). As the human figures in Desai's landscape are obliterated, the environment is anthropomorphized, and reaches out to "caress" Sai (2), dissolve solid objects, and invade the house.

Raj nostalgia and romance associated with colonial homes like Cho Oyu are quickly undermined in the opening pages of the novel. As Kennedy has argued, unlike colonial architecture in the plains, in the hill stations the "traffic with exotic traditions [such as Indo-Saracenic style] was intentionally shunned" (106). Instead, "the British turned exclusively to European models where they erected and embellished their highland cottages, and they did so not only to re-create something of the physical appearance of their homeland but to recover elements of its moral meaning as well" (Kennedy 106). The narrator of *Inheritance*, however, does not allow the underside of the "moral meanings" associated with these structures to remain unexamined. "As always," recounts the narrator,

> the price for such romance had been high and paid for by others. Porters had carried boulders from the riverbed—legs growing bandy, ribs curving into caves, backs into U's, faces being bent slowly to look always at the ground—up to this site chosen for a view that could raise the human heart to spiritual heights. (12)

The narrator's description emphasizes how the colonized workers' bodies and faces were curved downward with labor so that the colonist might gaze upward in a disembodied and leisurely fashion. Here, Desai scratches away the veneer of "anti-empire" that inflects romantic images of the hill station (often reproduced in contemporary nostalgic collections of Raj photography), contrasting the forgotten physical labor of colonial subjects with the transcendent and self-absorbed outlook of the colonizer. In postcolonial Kalimpong, structures built at the expense of others are figured as decaying while plants, animals, and the environment reappropriate the colonized space. The cook's hut is described as "buried under a ferocious tangle of nightshade" (13); in the garage, the judge's car is "sunk low, nose to the ground, grass through the floor" (12);

and a pair of snakes have been granted the one "weedless corner" of the garden as their own private domain (12–13). Similarly, during the first night Sai spends at Cho Oyu, "she could sense the swollen presence of the forest," while the house seems "fragile in the balance of this night—just a husk" (34). The fragility of the house versus the fecundity of the environment is no mere illusion; as Sai's toes push through the rotting table cloth she has been given to sleep under as a makeshift sheet, she becomes "aware of the sound of microscopic jaws slowly milling the house to sawdust" (34).

Desai's counterlandscaping narrative positions the Himalayan environment as a generative and queer botanical space, an alternative to the monoculture associated with the Anglophilia of the elite South Asian and expatriate communities, the majoritarianism of the Indian state, and the exclusionary and patriarchal collective identity associated with the Gorkha National Liberation Front (GNLF). As mentioned above, colonial practices of hybridization involved a "highly controlled intermixture such that elements mingle and yet remain distinct" (Casid 14) re-presented through "picturesque aesthetics" that framed "transplantation not as violent relandscaping but as an organic outgrowth in harmony with the place" (9). Desai's narrative rejects the anthropocentric, heteronormative, hybridizing, and domesticating impulses associated with this colonial mode of representing space offering instead a description of the landscape in and around Kalimpong as an "unsettling" and "queer" place (xvi) of beauty *and* exploitation. While making visible how "the dominant refashions itself as nature" (xiv), Desai's narrative also imagines alternative, queer, postcolonial ways of dwelling in the Himalayas that break with the colonial, national, and botanical practices of "segmentation, distinction, and separation" (9). The status of this alternative—queer nature, the more-than-human—is not something that *Inheritance* presents as static, outside history, and therefore unsullied by human contact, but rather as something more akin to Haraway's notion of "situated naturecultures, in which all the actors become who they are *in the dance of relating*, not from scratch, not ex nihilo, but full of the patterns of their sometimes-joined, sometimes-separate heritages both before and lateral to this encounter" (original emphasis, *When Species Meet* 25). For instance, Desai's narrative radically undermines notions of the Himalayas as an unchanging, physical location when in response to Noni's daydreams about living by the sea, where unlike the mountains that surround her, "the waves are never still," Sai reminds Noni that "the Himalayas were once underwater" and "there are ammonite fossils on Mt. Everest" (69). Similarly, as historians of the environment have established, "that exquisite scent of pine that people like Lola and Noni came [to the Himalayas] from Calcutta to sample" (84) is partially the result of a history of deforestation during the nineteenth century that took place at the height of the hill stations' popularity.[7] As Kennedy notes, tea estates, other agricultural crops, the railway and construction gobbled up forest areas in the region to the point that an 1876 report by the Darjeeling district gazetteer commented that "'the forest has almost entirely disappeared in many parts, owing to the spread of cultivation'" (53). Conservationist measures undertaken in the second half of the nineteenth century involved the replanting of indigenous species, but also the introduction of foreign trees such as *Pinus Petula* and *Cryptomeria Japonica*. These foreign transplants are now, ironically, a defining "natural" feature of the Darjeeling landscape. Parallels in the history of tree transplantation here and in other hill stations in the south of India[8] make it difficult to distinguish in Desai's novel where the concept of the garden—as something reflecting human intervention and cultural control of the environment—ends, and the wilderness begins.

The constant references to the presence of Kanchenjunga throughout *Inheritance*, from the first to the last page on the novel, paint it as a shifting emblem of cultural significance, sometimes sacred, as in the precolonial Lepcha cosmology described in Foning's *Lepcha, My Vanishing Tribe*, and sometimes sexual, as when it is described as "glowing a last brazen pornographic pink" (223) in the eyes of melancholic friends, Sai, Father Booty, and Uncle Potty. Desai's chameleon-like representations of Kanchenjunga throughout *Inheritance*, coupled with her passing reference to Foning's text rejects the primacy of an indigenous view of the land, even while it prompts us to remember that this land has already been landscaped by the Lepcha community prior to the arrival of the British. As already mentioned, colonial accounts of encounters with aboriginal Lepcha are characterized by paternalist admiration for their childlike nature. For example in his *Himalayan Journals* (1854), Joseph Dalton Hooker refers to the Lepcha as "exceedingly picturesque" (128) and describes their "disposition" as "amiable and obliging, frank, humorous, and polite, without the servility of the Hindoos; and their address is free and unrestrained" (129). Hooker and other colonial figures offer an image of the Lepcha as innocent children of nature, a quality that is emphasized in opposition to the more aggressive attributes associated with the Nepalese Gorkha community:

> An attentive examination of the Lepcha in one respect entirely contradicts our preconceived notions of a mountaineer, as he is timid, peaceful and no brawler; qualities which are all the more remarkable from contrasting so strongly with those of his neighbours to the east and west: of whom the Ghorkas are brave and warlike to a proverb, and the Bhotanese quarrelsome, cowardly, and cruel. (Hooker 128)

In the postcolonial time frame Desai chooses for her novel, the Lepcha are portrayed as a demoralized group, a forgotten minority in a community whose majority members, the Gorkhas, have internalized their colonial identity as a martial race and are pushing for greater autonomy from central government and increased control of the economy. The idea of the Himalayas as a "homeland" for the Gorkhas, a major theme in the GNLF political rhetoric, is continually unsettled in the novel through references to the Lepcha population: the town drunk, who is identified as a Lepcha, is wrongly arrested for the robbery at Cho Oyu and then beaten by the local police; when the wife of the beaten man visits Sai's grandfather, the judge, to plead for charity (her husband is left blind by the police beating), she asks, "'What will we do?' . . . 'We are not even Nepalis, we are Lepcha . . .'" (263), emphasizing their marginal status in relation to the Gorkhas. The "innocence" and "trustworthiness" associated with Lepcha "nature" in colonial travel narratives like Hooker's is also contradicted in Desai's narrative when, after the judge twice refuses to extend any charity to the tortured man's wife and father, they steal the judge's dog with the desperate hope of later selling it in the market (283). When Sai locates and reads Foning's *Lepcha, My Vanishing Tribe* in the Gymkhana library, she realizes she "knew nothing of the people who had belonged here first" (199).[9] The Lepcha's subaltern status is emphasized throughout the novel, and their aboriginal identity is consistently excluded from the GNLF political rhetoric and speeches.

While it might seem obvious to assume this book would provide Sai with a more authentic ecological perspective on the region, I feel it is necessary to extend Anthony Vital's view of the historicity of all ecology even to this indigenous description of the environment. In the preamble to the book, Foning describes his study as a "quasi-autobiography wherein most of the matters contained have been recorded in the light of my own personal experiences in my normal walk of life as a man of the tribe and touching upon my family and relations" (xxii). Framed in this way, Foning's book resembles what Mary Louise Pratt describes as an "autoethnographic expression" in which "colonized subjects undertake to represent themselves in ways that *engage with* the colonizer's own terms" (original emphasis 7–9). Pratt elaborates:

> Autoethnographic texts are not, then, what are usually thought of as "authentic" or autochothonous forms of self-representation . . . rather autoethnography involves partial collaboration with and appropriation of the idioms of the conqueror . . . and will become important in unravelling the histories of imperial subjugation and resistance as seen from the site of their occurrence. (7)

Foning deliberately and unwittingly seems to adhere to this autoethnographic agenda, offering on the one hand, an important alternative view to the colonial picturesque, and on the other, casting himself as a native informant caught within those same picturesque tropes. Foning describes his study as an "unacademic" account of Lepcha "primitive beliefs, superstitions and convictions" (xxi) that he hopes might help "qualified men to bring to light some of these unfathomed, hidden and often misconceived notions in some segments of our Lepcha life" (xx). Foning later describes Mount Kanchenjunga as

> the eternally pure white, awe-inspiring, inexplicable structure that we see constantly standing before us. Just as with any other primitive

people, to our simple minds, this was it. It not only provided us with a tangible shape for our conception of God, it provided us with a meaning for our life itself. It is He who sends down the rivers from which we collect our food, such as fish and other creatures. It gives us rain for our crops and for the forests to grow where we get fruit, roots, creepers, and other food, including animal food and thus sustain ourselves. In fact, if one probes deeper into Lepcha life, one finds the whole being, the whole community and the whole tribe depending upon and revolving round this wondrous object of nature. (43)

While Foning's description offers insight into a non-modern Lepcha conception of ecology, or what Vital calls a "people-centred environmentalism" (90), it is one that must be read under erasure; Foning's reference to his community's "primitive" beliefs and "simple minds" suggests that even this view of the environment romanticizes the Lepcha people, folding them into the childlike outlook imposed on the community by colonial history, and reducing their cosmology to a somewhat generalized animistic attitude toward nature.

Likewise, the agricultural activities of the Europeans in Kalimpong cannot be read in a simple binary fashion to an indigenous world view, as simply compromising or colonizing the landscape. Father Booty's dairy operation and related homemade cheese business is characterized as a positive intervention into the local economy that does not follow the colonial script of hybridization from Europe as the only avenue for improvement. As one of two gay men identified in the novel (the narrator recalls how Uncle Potty "remembered the time he and Father Booty had first met ... their admiring eyes on the same monk in the market ... the start of a grand friendship" [197]), it might be more appropriate to describe Father Booty's horticultural activities and Swiss dairy operation as queering rather than hybridizing the landscape. If, as Casid argues, British writing about the colonies often represented it as "a global botanical garden that becomes the scene of torrid romance, particularly of those sexual practices disavowed at home" (2), Desai's text inverts this practice. Father Booty's character is marked as queer and embedded in a hyper-fertile and sexualized botanical world, as he travels to Darjeeling with a plan to lure prospective customers away from the plastic taste of mass produced but popular Amul processed cheese in favor of his locally produced artisanal cheese. "Father Booty" the narrator states, "was with hope, anyway, whizzing through the spring, every flower, every creature preening, flinging forth its pheromones. The garden at St. Joseph's Convent was abuzz with such fecundity that Sai wondered ... if it discomfited the nuns" (193–94). In *Inheritance*, Desai defies the colonial practice of confining "sexual practices disavowed at home" to the plant world, but also suggests that the kind of "queer self-inscription" (Casid xiv) Father Booty's unofficial migration to India represents still cannot be accommodated for by either the Indian state or a minority-based ethnic movement like the GNLF.

When Father Booty neglects to renew his foreign residency visa and is ordered to leave India by the local authorities in the midst of the GNLF escalation, the loss of his wider contributions to horticultural heritage are underlined. As he searches for someone with influence to try to reverse the government order, we learn that Father Booty's dairy products, "made by local farmers" (193), have been enjoyed by many Kalimpong and Darjeeling residents. Additionally, his much-coveted oyster mushrooms are given to him as a gift from a local forest official who later bought the seeds of his rare flowering bamboo and gave him new seedlings when the exhausted bush died (221).

Father Booty demonstrates his contingent sense of belonging as he imagines his home, *Sukhtara*, Bengali for "Star of Happiness," and land, being confiscated by the army in his absence:

> Father Booty felt his heart fail at the thought of his cows being turned out in favour of army tanks; looked about at his craggy bit of mountainside—violet bamboo orchids and pale ginger lilies spicing the air; a glimpse of the Teesta far below that was no color at all right now, just a dark light shining on its way to join the Brahmaputra. Such wilderness could not incite a gentle love—he loved it fiercely, intensely. (222)

In this passage, Father Booty's view (like Foning's in *Lepcha, My Vanishing Tribe*) privileges indigenous plant species like bamboo orchids (*Arundina graminifolia*) and ginger lilies (perhaps *Hedychium gardnerianum*) and a river that crosses through Tibet, India, and Bangladesh and across national borders without passports, visas, or foreign residency requirements.[10] The notion of property or ownership of *Sukhtara* and the surrounding land, however, is also uncoupled from the idea of "home" and belonging, as the narrative tells us that Father Booty's dairy "was actually in the name of Uncle Potty" because of the rules concerning foreign nationals owning land (221). Here, Father Booty's relation to the landscape could be said to resemble what Catriona Mortimer-Sandilands describes as characteristic of American expatriate lesbian writer Jane Rule's anti-pastoral fiction—a "*mindfulness*, a pragmatic and earthbound but deeply respectful sensitivity to the complexities of Human attachments to nature" (original emphasis 463). Both Ruth in Rule's *The Young in One Another's Arms* and Father Booty in *Inheritance* can be read as "wounded people coming to 'belong' in a rural nature by physically experiencing and embracing *its and their* fragility, and by thus mindfully and daily recognizing the contingencies and tensions of their web of attachments, including their implications on other-than-human-communities" (original emphasis 464). In a novel preoccupied with what is sacrificed and lost in the pursuit of normative economic, cultural, and social values, Father Booty's queer relationship to the Himalayan landscape displaces ideas of essentialist belonging with a more contingent awareness of dwelling.

While Father Booty's residence, activities, and outlook are allied with the surrounding fragile but bountiful landscape, the representatives of the

Indian state are associated with its destruction and sterility. As the Kalimpong neighbors travel to Darjeeling to exchange their books at the Gymkhana library, Indian soldiers jog by a "grand sign" that reads "FLOWERS . . . part of the Army Beautification Program, though it was the only spot on the hill where there were none" (195). The absent presence of blooms in this state-sanctioned garden plot is tied synecdochally to the increased military presence in the region resulting from the Sino-Indian war in 1962. If representatives of the state are positioned at odds with the prolific quality of the natural world, the successful cultivation and enjoyment of flowers is figured as cutting across class lines in the private lives of community residents. When, for example, Sai goes to Bong Busti to apologize to Gyan for mocking his attraction to the GNLF movement, she is deeply troubled by the signs of residents' abject poverty, but also finds repeated plantings of "fuchsia and roses—for everyone in Kalimpong," the narrator reminds us, "loved flowers and even amid botanical profusion added to it" (254). Similarly, though Sai is shocked by the condition of Gyan's family home, (a "slime-slicked cube . . . made with cement corrupted by sand"), plantings of "marigolds and zinnias [that] edged the veranda" remind her that despite its crumbling condition, "it was someone's precious home" (255).

The conflation of biology and ethnicity that characterized colonial discourse on indigenous groups like the Lepcha's was also a structuring aspect of the formation of racial theories concerning Gorkha identity. *Inheritance* hints at an unwitting and ironic reproduction of this colonial racial logic in the nationalist rhetoric driving the GNLF. As Rajat Ganguly has argued, the Gorkha community in the Himalayan region of West Bengal could be described as an "entrapped minority," as "linguistically and culturally different from and politically and economically subordinate to the majority ethnolinguistic communities that wielded power in the states" (470). The construction of the Gorkha community as a minority in essentialist terms has a long history that Lionel Caplan argues constitutes "a particular mode of 'orientalist discourse'" (571). In British military writings about the "Gurkhas," there is "less concern" with distancing them from their colonial masters and more attention "to represent[ing] them as being, in certain fundamental respects, quintessentially like those very Europeans who produce the discourse" (571). Caplan explains:

> The term 'Gurkha' . . . derives from the place name of Gorkha, which was a small principality to the west of Kathmandu, whose king, around 1765, sent an army against the Newar rulers of the Valley of Kathmandu and after his victory made it the capital of his newly constituted kingdom. . . . The creators of this discourse see the Gurkhas as the descendants of the fighting men who conquered the Valley and created the modern Nepalese state. They apply the term to those sections of the population whom they regard as suitable for military service. (571)

The practice of recruiting Gorkhas for military service began under the British with the "discovery of Nepalese fighting qualities" (578) during the Anglo-Nepal war in 1814–16, and continued into the postcolonial era with the Gorkha community overrepresented in the Indian Army, providing 100,000 soldiers (572). While native Indian recruits to the British East Indian Company's armies were viewed as "incompetent" (578), "the Nepalese forces who fought against the Company's army are portrayed in glowing terms" (578). What is stressed in colonial accounts of this period is the Nepali ability to "meet them [the British] and beat them on equal terms" (Northey and Morris in Caplan 578). The "'formulaic [and essentialist] quality'" of writings about Gorkhas in British military texts from this time onward is evident in the way "'certain formulas, stock phrases and ideas are repeated time and again'" (Padel in Caplan 572). Colonial ideas about the "Gurkha race" emphasized their "martiality and loyalty," qualities that were seen as best cultivated "under the tutelage, supervision and control of British officers" (579). The main stereotypical qualities ascribed to Nepalis were their "warlike" and "masculine" outlook that was principally attributed to their residence in the cooler climate of the Himalayan regions (582). As Caplan explains, the belief that these qualities were somehow literally in the "blood" or the result of the "physical make-up" of the Nepalis was first put forward in 1833 by the British Resident in Kathmandu, Brian Hodgson. Hodgson, Caplan argues, was "probably the first to label particular tribal groups within Nepal as 'martial classes'" (581). This is significant in terms of Desai's use of nature imagery to frame and comment on the GNLF. In addition to his political and diplomatic work, Hodgson was also an extremely important figure in Himalayan natural history; having settled in Darjeeling in 1845, he exerted a considerable influence on Hooker when he first visited the region to write his *Himalayan Journals*. The embeddedness of Gorkha culture in the writings of one of Britain's earliest and influential Orientalist scholars of Nepalese language, culture and natural history signals the convergence of nineteenth-century theories of race, botany and biology that Desai's depiction of the "natural" landscape in *Inheritance* seeks to unsettle.

Desai frames the subplot of the GNLF uprising as a minority/majority confrontation but also seeks to trouble the normalization of this modern nationalist construct and highlight some of the ways it has been naturalized. The novel opens with the arrival of three young Nepali men at the judge's home in Kalimpong. We quickly learn that they are looking for guns to steal, and the depiction of this incident both invokes and questions the Gorkha stereotypes discussed above. The men are described as "creeping across the grass" wearing "leather jackets from the Kathmandu black market, khaki pants, bandanas—universal guerrilla fashion" (4). While it appears the young men are attempting to exude the hypermasculine image associated with Gorkha men in colonial and postcolonial writing, they are described as "unconvincing" and screaming "like a bunch of schoolgirls" when Mutt, the judge's dog, barks at them upon their arrival (4). The narrator emphasizes the theatrical quality of the robbers' behavior, through descriptions of how they fall into familiar "roles," follow "lines" and a "script" (6) and refers to how "they laughed a movie laugh" (5) and generally emulate the conduct of macho Bollywood heroes. The instability of the young GNLF supporters' masculine, nationalist identities, therefore, disrupts the larger essentialist discourse of Gorkhas as a martial race and the broader colonial practice of communalizing Indian subjects. Furthermore, when the GNLF robbers intimidate the judge, Biju, and Sai into repeating the Gorkha movement slogans, "Jai Gorkha" and "Gorkhaland for Gorkhas," they unwittingly undermine the conviction associated with these chants, emptying them of political or nationalist significance.

Desai's novel explores the dynamics of the minority/majority binary through her depiction of the GNLF movement and its relationship to the community in Kalimpong and Darjeeling. At the conclusion of the robbery scene described above, the narrator identifies the date as February 1986 and provides a summary of stories printed in national newspapers around that time:

> In Kalimpong, high in the northeastern Himalayas where they lived ... there was a report of new dissatisfaction in the hills, gathering insurgency, men and guns. It was the Indian-Nepalese this time, fed up with being treated like the minority in a place where they were the majority. They wanted their own country, or at least their own state, in which to manage their own affairs. (9)

This brief news report captures the Gorkhas' easy identification with the minority/majority binary and their recourse to Enlightenment notions of autonomy and a universally shared sense of national community in the formulation of their separatist demands. When the narrator comments that "this time" it is the Indian-Nepalese demanding a separate state, s/he suggests that there have been other demands that have fitted this profile in the past. Desai's portrayal of such demands for separation and exclusion of outsiders (both in India and in the U.S.-based portions of the novel) capture something of what Aamir Mufti describes as the paradoxical-natural and arbitrary quality of these movements in relation to the modern state (50); "The crisis of modern subjectivity," Mufti suggests, "is ... the threat of artificiality and arbitrariness that hangs over it, its implicit imitativeness and protean nature" (50). The narrator in *Inheritance* foregrounds the arbitrariness of the GNLF's sense of primacy in the region when s/he declares "Here, where India blurred into Bhutan and Sikkim, and the army did pull-ups and push-ups maintaining their tanks with khaki paint in case the Chinese grew hungry for more territory than Tibet, it had always been a messy map" (9). Similarly, the descriptions of the military presence required to maintain India's sovereignty in the region are followed by additional references to the "great amount of warring, betraying, [and] bartering" that had occurred between "Nepal, England, Tibet, India, Sikkim, [and] Bhutan" (9) before the territory became part of West Bengal. Ultimately, however, the narrator returns to an earlier description of the ubiquitous fog "charging down like a dragon, dissolving, undoing, making ridiculous the drawing of borders" (9). The mist described in the opening paragraphs of the novel as obscuring and destabilizing the view of the surrounding landscape, as well as enveloping and penetrating the house, is here compared to the figure of a ferocious dragon, capable of overriding any division of the landscape or national community suggested by the state or its minority opponents.

Throughout the novel, Desai's relandscaped view of the Himalayan environment presents it as a fecund and queer alternative to the conservative political struggle between the Indian state and the GNLF movement, as well as the stagnant colonial attitudes of Sai's elite Bengali neighbors. When part of Lola and Noni's garden is occupied by families connected with the Gorkha movement, the sisters are forced to confront the implications of their privileged landholding status. Noni curses herself for earlier

> feeling they were doing something exciting just by occupying this picturesque cottage, by seducing themselves with those old travel books in the library, searching for a certain angled light with which to romance themselves, to locate what had been conjured only as a tale to tell before the Royal Geographic Society, when the author returned to give a talk accompanied by sherry and scrolled certificate of honor spritzed with gold for an exploration of the far Himalayan kingdoms—but far from what? Exotic to whom? It was the center for the sisters, but they had never treated it as such (247).

Significantly, Desai ties this moment to an engagement with how the region has been imagined in terms of colonial travel narratives and the picturesque, and the sisters' growing realization of how they have internalized this colonial script. Ironically, despite Sai's neighbors' loss of their comforting view of the landscape, the rise of the GNLF political fortunes leads the neighbors to become more intimately tied to the regional ecology for their survival, as food imports from the plains and beyond dry up and they come to rely, more than ever, on their garden and local agriculture goods for their meals. The narrator reports:

> For the first time, they in Cho Oyu were eating the real food of the hillside. *Dalda saag*, pink flowers, flat leafed; *bhutiya dhaniya* growing copiously around the cook's quarter; the new tendrils of squash or pumpkin vine; curled *ningro* fiddleheads, *churbi* cheese and bamboo shoots sold by women who appeared from behind bushes on forest paths with the cheese wrapped in ferns and the yellow slices of bamboo shoots in buckets of water. After the rains, mushrooms pushed their way up, sweet as chicken and glorious as Kanchenjunga, so big, fanning out.

People collected the oyster mushrooms in Father Booty's abandoned garden. For a while the smell of them cooking gave the town the surprising air of wealth and comfort. (281–82)

The turn to local vegetables and plants for food by this otherwise privileged group of residents in Kalimpong is not characterized as a hardship. Indigenous plants and fungi are presented as desirable, abundant, and readily available. As in the earlier reference to mushrooms, the fruits of Father Booty's garden are described as enriching the community's diet, and are compared with the sacred presence of Kanchenjunga. While the GNLF asserts its dominance in the community by taking over major government and private buildings and intimidating local non-Gorkha residents like Lola and Noni, the local human and nonhuman actors are brought closer together in a "natureculture" "dance of relating" (Haraway *When Species Meet* 25) with transitory and unassuming women, unmarked by political affiliations, who appear fleetingly on "forest pathways" selling their locally cultivated food stuffs.

In conclusion, I want to suggest that Desai's narrative offers an alternative mode for imagining the Himalayan landscape that takes up essentializing colonial tropes and subverts their naturalized status. While the colonial process of reimaging the Indian landscape, and in particular the Himalayas, largely seemed focused on reproducing aspects of British social, cultural, horticultural, architectural, and environmental experiences, it is not a process that could ever be understood as complete. Desai's queering of nature, and related majority, minority, and indigenous community relationships, questions the essentialist outlooks of privileged *and* marginalized groups in the novel. With attention to the ways in which colonial aesthetics of the picturesque and the sublime have previously impinged on representations of the Himalayan landscape and its inhabitants, Desai's narrative offers a counterlandscaped view of the region, and cultivates a contingent sense of community—a literary postcolonial ecology—where decentered notions of belonging and localized modes of existence might thrive.

NOTES

1. There are two versions of Anthony Vital's article (as listed in the works cited). The original appears in print in the 2008 issue of *Research in African Literatures*. A "corrected" version appears online on a special webpage set up by Vital after learning about the unauthorized publication of his essay. The page numbers given are from the original article and they are also cross referenced with the corrected online version.

2. For further discussion of assumptions concerning the link between hill station climate and European health, see Mark Harrison's "Climates and Constitutions: Health, Race, Environment and British Imperialism in India 1600–1850."

3. It is, of course, ironic that the establishment of hill stations like Darjeeling had a negative environmental impact on the region that included things like

deforestation, water contamination and shortages, soil erosion, and the extinction of various species of wildlife. See Kennedy's *The Magic Mountains* for an overview of sources of the environmental impact of hill stations during the colonial era, especially pages 47–59, 60–62.

4. Casid's *Sowing Empire* offers a fuller description of how this way of seeing was shaped by sketches and paintings associated with the grand tour and in particular the travel journals of Reverend William Gilpin in the late eighteenth century. See especially pages 45–48. For a more general history of the picturesque, see Andrews's *The Search for the Picturesque*.

5. Kennedy argues that the initial choice of the word "hill" versus "mountain" to describe areas like Darjeeling may have been the result of "an etymological effort to minimize the disturbing implications of the sublime" (46). He also notes that "the Nilgiris [another hill station in the south of India] were initially described as 'mountains' in official reports, but once John Sullivan and others had established permanent residence there, they quickly became 'hills'" (47).

6. The *Oxford English Dictionary* explains that the term "ecology" was first coined by German biologist Ernest Haeckel in the 1876 preface to the English translation of his book *The History of Creation*, a text intended to popularize the theories of Charles Darwin. Haeckel, however, was also heavily influenced by Lamarckism, a now discredited theory that argued behaviors learned by one generation in a particular environment would be biologically inherited by subsequent generations. Thus the original definition of ecology suggests a biological relationship between race and environment. The contemporary definition of ecology is "[t]he branch of biology that deals with the relationships between living organisms and their environment," a definition that gestures toward this etymological history but dispenses with its colonial connotations. Part of this essay highlights the history of racist assumptions about the effects of climate and the natural world on different human communities in the Himalayan region that fit in nicely with a Lamarckian view of ecology. However, the dual emphasis in contemporary definitions of (postcolonial) ecology on the *interrelatedness* of "organisms and their environment," of human culture and the natural world, enables my reading of how some of these same colonial ideas about the Himalayas inflect aesthetic perceptions of the area, and are rearticulated in postcolonial literature and culture.

7. The problem of deforestation has escalated in the postcolonial context and is linked to landslides and drought in the region. As Ganguly notes, "while in 1951 about 45% of the total area of Darjeeling was under forest cover, by 1986 the number had fallen to 23%. Besides destroying the region's aesthetic beauty, deforestation caused additional problems such as soil erosion, heavy landslides, drinking water scarcity and social tensions" (474). See Jessie Patrick Ferguson's essay "Violent Dis-Placements" for a discussion of how *Inheritance* links "natural and human violence" through representations of landslides (35).

8. This "naturalization" of foreign species to the Himalayan area parallels a similar story of the Eucalyptus in the Nilgiri hills, recently discussed by Paul Sharrad, who argues that the eucalyptus, which often serves as a self-explanatory symbol of "Australianness" in Australian settler fiction, is estranged in the context of India and in particular the Nilgiri hills. In the Nilgiri hills, Sharrad argues, the eucalyptus is "literally and figuratively, part of the landscape" (32).

9. It should be noted that Foning's book was first published in 1987 in the midst of the events of the GNLF uprising, making its presence in the library collection a potentially anachronistic reference in Desai's novel.

10. Desai does not represent Father Booty's privileged carelessness without comment. As the time arrives for him to depart he chides himself, "why hadn't he applied for an Indian passport? Because it was just as silly as NOT applying for an American or a Swiss? He felt a lack in himself, despised his conformity to ideas of the world even as he disagreed with them" (222–23).

2

Haiti's Elusive Paradise

LeGrace Benson

The artists who painted the first of the Earthly Paradise and "jungle" landscapes so prominent in Haitian art from about 1950 to the present came into Port-au-Prince from the countryside, the *andeyo*. Like hundreds of other rural Haitians migrating into the city in search of work, they were separating themselves from intimate daily contact with the cycle of the rainy season and the dry, with the soil and the water, with plants and animals, and from the living material within which and by which they coexisted. Thus distanced from the mother environment, in the city they would learn to paint pictures of a recollected place. *Andeyo* would become a "landscape" object available for sale. Although commodified, the images bore the marks of memory and the desire for the distant home. To reflect upon this art is to arrive at understanding something of the complex relationships Haitians have with the social and material environment of Haiti and the world beyond. Because the paintings became popular in the international art market and as souvenirs for tourists, there is something to be learned about what landscape objects reveal regarding a fundamental human yearning for what scientists call "a sustainable ecosystem" and popular discourse refers to as "paradise."

An unbridgeable chasm seems to lie between the beauties of the painted tropical paradise and the wretchedness of a failing ecosystem.[1] Considering the relationships between visual works of art and the ecological systems within which the artists create requires attention to history of the locality together with attitudes of the inhabitants. Economics, politics, linguistics and religious sensibilities all come into play. Two unusual conditions shaped the particular circumstances of the "paradise" painters. One was their language, Kreyol, instead of the French of the government, educational institutions, and the leading class. The other was their religious practice that encompassed Protestant and Roman Catholic Christianity and Afro-creole Vodou (Bellegarde-Smith).

In comprehensive ecosystems, visual works operate differently from literary productions. Artists create palpable visibilities that take place as new environmental givens, fashioned from matter in the environment. Art enters into the general conversation as an object before giving rise to exchanges of signifying words. Thus painting and writing have distinctive modes of mediating the nature of the universe and the nature of its human inhabitants.

The visualizations of the perfect ecology, Earthly Paradise, devised by these Kreyol artists (*moun andeyo*) evidence their environmental circumstances: the oral history of physical dislocation from Africa to Haiti; their translocation from rural to urban; divergent meanings of the stories heard in the Christian churches; and the unique Centre d'Art in Port-au-Prince with its studios, its library of art books, and its commingling of French speaking, European-style artists and writers with the Kreyol *moun andeyo*. At the Centre d'Art artists saw book illustrations of the Garden of Eden as conceived by Europeans adventuring into the world to search for paradise, richness, and power (Scafi 84–124). In Christian missions the artists heard the Genesis Creation story and the agricultural parables and metaphors of the Gospel since childhood, hence Christian Renaissance narrative paintings were immediately meaningful. The chief characters in the paintings were the saints that the artist's great-grandparents had copied on the walls and sacred tables of Vodou temples as images of the divine *lwa* (Desmangles 11, 99–130). The stories and ceremonial tradition of blessed African homelands from which the ancestors had been forcibly exiled contrasted with actualities of the struggle to live in Haiti's devastated ecosystem. The painters from *andeyo* were in triple exile from any paradise ecology: from the beginning of the world from Eden; from the time of the great-great grandparents from Africa; and themselves only yesterday from the cycles of the dry season and the rainy, and from rural plants and animals. The elite artists and writers lived in walled gardens on the cool slopes above the city and conversed in flawless Parisian French.

In a post–World War II Haiti tied to the international political and economic system, Kreyol artists engaged in dual roles as intermediaries of a personally-apprehended numinous on the one hand, and as vendors of works into the cosmopolitan art market on the other. The tourists and art collectors who purchased the works usually had little knowledge of the traditions or life circumstances from within which the artists created. Yet superficial enjoyment of a pretty object linked to deeper longing of the primordial search for a glorious land, recognition of loss and the image of return, a search for order and harmony, and the hope of pure delight. The artists generated the paradise and "jungle" themes out of this complex milieu, the works then returning to these tropes to serve as figures of merit,[2] that is, as criterion images displaying the attributes of a balanced ecosystem. The desires embedded in that figure of merit were and are simultaneously individual and universal, Haitian and international.

There is a growing literature on how experience or views of open space with greenery affect well being.[3] The earliest global seafaring adventurers and colonizers returned home with sketches, and J. M. W. Turner's sublime views of Chamonix in the French Alps were surely enticing factors in the success of the Thomas Cook Tours that followed on the heels of British mountaineering.[4] The literature and media presentations of every environmental conservation organization strongly evidence the profound attraction and structural importance of views and images reckoned to be beautiful, suggesting there may be aesthetic values tied to human perceptual systems that transcend local times and spaces. The increase of books and scholarly papers concerning paradise concepts tracks a rise in environmental consciousness (DeLoughrey, Gosson, and Handley 1–30). The bright Haitian paradise paintings exemplify the use of visual images as delights to the spirit and blandishments for the tourist industry, thus on both counts marketable commodities. Tropical paradise as a desired view from a window or a painting serves the same function. As a magnet of tourism it ultimately relates to an apprehension of harmonious environment that seems essential to human well-being.

Beautiful environmental images served the political agenda of the Paris-educated intellectuals of Port-au-Prince, thus setting the stage for a dramatic entrance on the art scene of the Kreyol painters. Jean Price-Mars, whom Aimé Césaire would call the "father of Négritude," had celebrated the rural population—the *moun andeyo*—as the Haiti that still held on to African traditions. There was new acceptance of their language, Kreyol, its stories and songs, crafts and life ways, and religion, Vodou, with its belief in an environment inhabited by intentional spiritual forces. Price-Mars in his widely read book, *Ainsi parla l'oncle* (1928), had initiated a riposte from the urban, intellectual elites to the nineteen years of indignity suffered under the 1915–1934 United States Occupation. Certain literary figures, historians, and artists took up his nationalist call for revalorization of African heritage, forming a movement, *Indigénism*, creating a new Bureau of Ethnography, and producing novels, poetry, treatises, and paintings that brought a romanticized *Aiti Toma* to the forefront of attention (Pompilus). And there was a rejuvenated Department of Agriculture. For many, the revalorization concerned the land itself as well as the life-ways of the Haitian people, since both had suffered under the occupation.[5]

Lightly schooled Haitian artists from the eroded and deforested *andeyo* arrived on the international art scene with sudden prominence after 1946 (Lerebours 233–35 & 309-44). Called "naïve" or "primitive" in the art press, and "Vodou" or "popular" painters by some of the Port-au-Prince intellectuals, the vision of Haiti they brought to light in little paintings on salvaged scraps of hardboard, wood, or cloth interested the *Indigènist* movement.

For the intellectuals wishing to reconnect with *Aiti Toma*—the supposedly less Europeanized *moun andeyo* (equivalent to "hillbillies" in U.S. slang), the paintings served as a link that required only looking, not putting their hands to the hoe or placing their bodies into the gritty, sweaty, and mysterious peasant life. The writers' appreciation of Kreyol art was in part confirmation of their own Afro-creole identity, by now highly urbanized and secularized, but in part what has been called a "folklorization" and "idealization" of the African presence in the Caribbean.[6]

Among those engaged in the revalorization efforts were brothers Philippe Thoby-Marcelin and Pierre Marcelin. Pierre grew up enjoying the *andeyo*, eventually serving as a technical expert in the agriculture department. Philippe spent more time with books and writing. Both participated in the energetic Price-Mars retort to United States' racist and ecologically denigrating attitudes. Together they wrote several novels threaded through with environmental concerns, uniting Pierre's practical knowledge and Philippe's literary insights and skill. Philippe, especially interested in Kreyol art, in 1945 led Dewitt Peters, the director of the newly established Centre d'Art, up the main coastal highway to a settlement near Montrouis. There, Hector Hyppolite eked out a living selling sodas and sundries when he was not painting houses or his remarkable tableaus or designs for the walls of the Vodou temple where he worshipped. Soon this Kreyol artist's works were on display at the Centre. Surrealist André Breton would view them there during his consequential visit in December 1946–January 1947.

Breton's purchase of several paintings by this *andeyo* painter created contention. At issue were the merits of the works by the immigrants from the countryside as opposed to paintings and sculpture by educated modernist artists. Breton's public lecture (Breton "Discours"), his purchases, and his 1947 essay on Hyppolite (Breton *Surrealism*) weighed heavily in changing the direction, mode, and content of Haitian art (Benson "Long Bilingual" 99–109). The insights and opinions of this influential surrealist and his specific allusions to Vodou in Hyppolite's works accorded with the revalorizing of African traditions slowly gaining concurrence among urban intellectuals, although in ill favor with the light-skinned elite in political control or with certain modernist artists.

In an essay about Hyppolite written not long after his visit, Breton wrote that his first sight of one of the paintings in the Centre d'Art "evoked the same sensation of a beautiful sunny day in the country, gently waving grass, sprouting seeds, buttercups, the iridescence of insect's wings, the tiny clashing cymbals of the flowering creepers." He describes further that from this nature subject there emerged the vision of the Virgin Mary (Breton *Surrealism* 308). In a single image Hyppolite pictured the lush world of lovely leaves and blossoms, the Blessed Virgin and Christ Child as the sacred route joining heaven and Earth, and *lwa* Ezili, the spirit and force of love. Hyppolite's brush strokes were the track of a man working rapidly and passionately, marking total and unifying engagement with the matter of "matter" and the matter of "spirit." Devout Vodouisant Hyppolite's *Adoration* captured an environmental meaning of the *Incarnation* that is obscured in the usual Christian teaching and discourse of the last four centuries (White). At the compositional and spatial center of the painting the Virgin Mary stands worshipfully over the Infant Jesus, her arms outstretched in the ancient Christian receptive prayer position "orans," also a major gesture in Vodou. The Christ Child lies on the ground rather than in a manger, in direct contact with the earth as is prescribed for barefoot participants in the Vodou temple. Exactly as though Virgin and Child were the sacred *poto-mitan* (central pole) of a temple, angels and saints, many in the white garments of Vodou *ounsi* (initiated devotees) circle around them. Environing all is, as Breton described, the great swirling ring of tropical flowers and leaves, including Ezili-Virgin Mary's roses. A later Hyppolite *Adoration* shows the crucified Christ centered like the *poto-mitan* surrounded by kneeling, white clad *ounsi*. In both the Nativity *Adoration* and the Crucifixion *Adoration*, Hyppolite positions the Christian's embodied God into a Vodou sacred space locating Him both *at* and *as* the juncture of earth and sky, human and divine, just as the Roman Catholic Mass describes. The composition echoes the sacred space arrangement of the *ounfo* (Vodou temple) that in turn reiterates the Yoruba and Congo cosmogram. The artist mediates the connection.

Many Christians over the centuries have asserted that a good God could not partake of the evil of the material world. Hyppolite held no such beliefs. His Jesus figure is also the *lwa* Legba who opens the communicating gate between the divinities in the sky and trees above and the earthly congregation just below. This attitude recognizes and adores a divine presence fully participating in flesh, consequentially honoring all earthly creation. Recognizing the presence of the Vodou religion in the works exhibited and Hyppolite's averred initiation into Vodou in a ceremony in Dahomey, Breton wrote of the artist's unification of matter and spirit. "Hyppolite's vision succeeds in reconciling superb realism with exuberant supernaturalism. He has an extraordinary capacity for expressing the sense of anguish which pervades the Haitian climate" (Breton *Surrealism* 312). Had Breton been the contemporaneous Lutheran theologian, Paul Tillich, he might have quoted from the letter of Paul to the Romans: "All creation groans until His coming again," or from the prophet Jeremiah (Tillich 1).

Another Breton purchase was *Une dees represent met gron bras* (A goddess representing Gran Bwa), a feminine representation, or better, *emanation*, of the forest *lwa* Gran Bwa, usually imaged as a male anthropomorphic tree. Hyppolite brushed this landscape in tender greens, ochers, grays, and Ezili's rose hues. Foliage of two large trees nearly covers the surface except for a rayed sun shining through an opening in the branches and a nude figure of a woman with dark hair and pale skin in the bottom foreground. The *"dees"* seems to be growing out of the lowest branch of a tree and in the process of descending from it: anthropomorphic tree/arborimorphic woman. At left the holy serpent Danballah Wedo ascends the tree trunk. A peacock, another symbol for Ezili, hovers at the base of the opposite tree. The woman looks directly at the viewer, her left hand cradling Ezili's roses. This work arises from an understanding of the power of sun, trees, flowering plants, and living creatures, and of the co-presence of the potent male forest *lwa*, Gran Bwa, with the feminine spirit of all forms of love, Ezili. The female emanation of the male Gran Bwa can occupy the body of Hyppolite or a tree with equal ease (Hurbon "L'arbre"). The ecology is terrestrial, strong, explicitly erotic, here/now and demonstrates a reciprocal and respectful relationship of artist to environment.

Hyppolite lived outside direct engagement with church schools, although, like any good Vodouisant, he attended Mass. His work arose out of his being-in-the-world deeply imbued with a religious faith and practice that continued African traditions reconstructed and evolving to meet conditions arising in the Caribbean, including the appropriation of Christian imagery. His works are prime examples of a Kreyol *moun andeyo* creation that put Western art materials at the service of a vision rooted in the Afro-creole religious consciousness of the forces of nature as personified divinities who exercise moral agency. Hyppolite's art was cut short by early death, but the later works even of this quintessentially *Aiti Toma* artist begin to show modifications in the direction of what would become a new stage of *creolité*, responding to Haiti's rapidly increasing urbanism and its traffic with the global economy and world-power politics.

In the art galleries of Paris, London, and New York, at the 1946 UNESCO exhibition in Paris as well as at the Centre d'Art in Port-au-Prince, Kreyol works by Hyppolite and other artists from the *andeyo* took the lion's share of attention. At the Washington International Exposition of 1950, Wilson Bigaud received a prize for his painting *Paradis Terrestre*. Hyppolite had recognized his young neighbor and fellow Vodouisant's talent and brought him to Centre d'Art and Peters's attention.

It was Peters who suggested that Bigaud have a look at the art books in the Centre library as preparation for an entry into the competition for the Episcopal Cathedral murals. Bigaud's entry would be *Paradis Terrestre*. From among dozens of images Bigaud selected, a theme prominent in European painting from the middle Renaissance (and "Age of Exploration") era came forward: Earthly Paradise about to be lost as Eve succumbs to the serpent's temptation and accepts the fatal apple from the sacred tree of knowledge. An illustration of the *Temptation of Adam and Eve* (1526) by Northern Renaissance painter Lucas Cranach shares visual motifs, compositional arrangement and, perhaps, even a sensibility with what Bigaud would soon paint.

There is an interesting parallel between the environmental philosophy of Cranach, who like Hyppolite began his career as a house painter in a rural village, and Bigaud's. Cranach connected to the things of this world with an attitude that is at once that of the burgeoning natural science of his

Figure 2.1 Paradis Terrestre

time with its emphasis on exact observation and that of a viewer who regards his environment with delight and even affection. Cranach's precision is both that of the naturalist seeking to know the world descriptively and the peasant whose livelihood depended on knowing the environment intimately enough to make a living from it. Cranach reintroduces and revalues the pagan view of the environment and the "animal" sexuality of the natural human that had been suppressed by the Christian Church. Out in the country European peasants maintained their empathetic arrangements with the forces of nature, just as would the *moun andeyo* of Haiti. On the high seas Europeans were busy laying claims to colonies, altering ecosystems everywhere and attempting to create botanical garden paradises in their colonies (see Prest) and at their metropolitan universities (Stearn).

Cranach, like Bigaud, had to negotiate a path that would lead to gaining a living and attaining status as an artist by avoiding the displeasures of patrons in a society rent asunder with religious, linguistic, and cultural contentions. Catholics and Protestants of both eras did agree upon the dogma of God's instruction to Adam to "have dominion over" the earth, infecting even the science of the day (see White). Moreover, in Bigaud's Haiti reentry into the world economy slammed traditional rural awareness of inspirited trees and water into the metropolitan, instrumentalist view that scourging the landscape into crop fields and logging operations could make the global presence profitable.

This collision of beliefs had a history in Haiti. As Saint Domingue, Haiti's cane fields had made it the richest of all colonies and probably the most altered ecosystem on earth (de Wimpffen 165). Toussaint, appointed governor of the colony, continued the plantation system in vigor. After declaring independence in 1804, when Haiti became the first plantation colony to liberate the slaves and enter postcolonial statehood, King Henri Christophe meant to ensure the success of the new nation through exports to Europe and the United States from restored cane, cotton, coffee and indigo production (Christophe and Clarkson). A return to precolonial ecological equilibrium was unimaginable and impossible. The Taíno population that had achieved this equilibrium was decimated before the Africans arrived. Furthermore, the role of Vodou in the struggle to abolish slavery had emphasized social solidarity rather than the relationship to the forces and conditions of environment. Haiti's early initiation into the postcolonial era entailed skillful appropriation of European social stratifications and the continuation of European agricultural and environmental practices. Two results were the marginalization of the former slaves now peasants, and the inhibition of Vodou environmental attitudes in favor of profit-centered agriculture.[7]

The United States Occupation insulted the Haitian people with the institution of Jim Crow laws and labor corvées (Schmidt 137) and insulted the land and peasant agricultural practices with policies of land appropriation and aggregations for export-oriented agricultural production (Plummer). Some claim that occupation-era environmental damage was the greatest in Haitian history. Postoccupation Haiti repeated the ecological choices of postcolonial Haiti because import-export trade relations seemed essential. The prevailing ethic of land use was and still is shaped by and subordinated to the desired outcomes of profitable engagement in trade conducted by and primarily on behalf of individuals.

It would not be until 1986 that ecologically-oriented projects would begin to enter political and economic conversations at the cabinet and presidential levels (Smarth and Balutansky 54–55). Haitian agronomy, forestry, and land conservation experts produced numerous documented, thoughtful reports for the government, many of them multidisciplinary in scope. There were, in addition, dozens of environmental, agricultural, and economic proposals from religious and secular nongovernmental organizations. Sadly, this conversation dissipated after the coup d'état in 1991 (Smarth and Balutansky 17). In subsequent political regimes, the ecological sensibilities of intellectuals, of the religion of *Aiti Toma*, of the secular technology of the Haitian foresters, ecologists, and agronomists, or the mediations of artists of *andeyo* all remain outside official discussion. In hundreds of environmental projects this conversation is silent.

Although attenuated, the land ethic that proceeds from a supposition that the forces of nature are intentional sacred beings requiring respect, and that certain trees, hills, rocks or waterfalls are especially imbued with the sacred or are inhabited by sacred personages, remarkably survived the French plantation system, the postrevolutionary need for the new nation to garner significant income, and the agri-business projects of the American occupation and after. The Afro-creole notion of the individual (Kimmerle) as necessarily a participant in an extended family, and community also survived, as could be seen in the *konbit*, a practice of multifamily collaboration in the planting and harvesting of crops, the construction of fish weirs, arrangements for milling grain, and similar labor-intensive projects. Yet the concept of human dominion taught in Christian churches coupled with the characteristic secular individualism of European and North American societies prevails in politics, in business, in agriculture and forestry, and in the art of the academies.

The Vodou and peasant farmer comprehension of milieu does not utterly disappear. Such concepts can reside in a single image, sensibly but wordlessly, and can be apprehended by another artist attuned to pick up the subtle visual information that specifies the choice of subject, the selection of narrative and symbolic, allusive devices, the physical meaning of illusion, of placement and compositional relationships, of all the complexities of color, and of the facture that evidences how the artist made the work. Breton picked up this entire range of information from the Hyppolite images. It is likely that Bigaud apprehended similar perceptual information in the Cranach illustration and recognized its resonance with the peasant beliefs about environment that each had observed in his particular milieu.

Young Wilson Bigaud had encountered the teachings of ordinary Christian parishes: overt or tacit messages about the relationship of human to environment essentially unchanged from Cranach's time. It was at odds with *andeyo* Kreyol attitudes pervading family and community life of himself, his mentor Hyppolite, and the other artists of the Kreyol coterie active in the Centre d'Art. The old Latin word, *pagani*—pagans—meaning country people and, by extension, those who worshipped animistic nature deities, could describe Cranach's rural folk or Bigaud's peasant relatives:

> The Black judges that in every natural phenomenon and in every being that encloses a harmful or latent life, there exists a spiritual power or dynamic or efficacious spirit (*niâma* in Mandingue) that is able to act by itself [and] from the cult of spirits personifying natural forces and the souls of the dead, spirits who by death are liberated from their momentary human receptacle. (Price-Mars 19–25, translation mine)

Urban writers and artists listened equally to Price-Mars and to Breton. They defended the religion and worldview of the peasants and even celebrated it in their novels, their poetry, and their professional duties as ethnographers and professors (Benson 106–9), but as sympathetic observers, not as participant believers. Urban painters saw in Bigaud's *Earthly Paradise* a cleverly devised underlying geometrical composition, a richness of entertaining detail, and a pleasing harmony of vivid colors. They appreciated the presumed "innocent vision" comparable to the unschooled, "primitive" African and South Asian and peasant art much in vogue among modernists of that era (Gombrich). Their acceptance of the artist and of his work would have been in part aesthetic and in part politically programmatic: he was of that newly championed population who were understood to be the living receptacles of the now-esteemed African heritage. For these writers and artists, to take up the cause of African heritage, to assert the value of African identity, and to call attention to the land attached was to broaden their scope of observation. They remained like modern Europeans in point of view: "land" was "landscape." With few exceptions, they did not truly espouse the Kreyol life ways or the Kreyol religion, Vodou.

The work of the Haitian writer Jacques Roumain exemplifies this intellectual distancing. Notably, with Jean Price-Mars, he founded the Bureau of Ethnography and his writings perceptively portray the lives and religion of *moun andeyo*. He attended Vodou ceremonies but without initiation into that religion. The passages of his well-known novel *Gouverneurs de la Rosée* (*Masters of the Dew*) of 1946 that describe the farms and fields and forests are as accurately detailed as Cranach's landscape and as modern European in their mode of attention. His peasants, like Price-Mars's, are as romantically viewed as those in the poetry of William Wordsworth.

Likewise, the brothers Pierre Marcelin and Philippe Thoby-Marcelin, to whom Breton attributed the discovery of Hector Hyppolite, could include a sacred mapou tree as a central figure in their 1946 novel, *La bête de Musseau* (*The Beast of the Haitian Hills*), with intimate understanding of the peasants' beliefs. An observant agronomist, Pierre could recognize a Vodou sensibility that understands the tree to be inhabited with spirits. Yet the brothers kept as emotionally distant from the religion itself as would an anthropologist (Thoby-Marcelin xv–xxi). In a telling poem, "Croix-des-Missions, Port-au-Prince of 1928," Philippe turns his back on the boring chatter of peasants riding with him in the "broken down bus that recites: / "Bayahondes / Bayahondes / Bayahondes"[8] ... / The road arches its back, /opens out, and what a beautiful landscape! A sea of Mango trees spread out like a large bed/ alongside the green river of sugar cane fields" (Thoby-Marcellin 1386).

Bigaud participated directly in the same Kreyol *andeyo* as Hyppolite, and also in the French-speaking city, its competitive commercial and political daily life, its school lessons, and its Christian services. At home with family and in the Vodou services, the language was Kreyol. He experienced two conflicting worldviews, two distinct linguistic milieus, two different presumptions about the relationship of individual to family and neighborhood, and two contrasting implications for the Haitian ecosystem. His drawing lessons at the parish school and later at the Centre d'Art were in the European mode. Neither contained anything to inform him about environment or ecosystems except as externally "other" to be recorded as landscape. His understanding of the environment as inhabited by the same flow of spirits that could enter into his own personhood came from home, from Vodou.

Christianity exposed Bigaud to the belief that one God created the universe and humankind, giving humans dominion over all living things (Genesis 1:28). He learned that Adam and Eve committed the Original Sin by disobediently eating fruit from the forbidden tree, were condemned to leave the Garden of Eden—the Earthly Paradise—and doomed to harsh labor-he in the fields, she in childbirth. In the Second Coming those saved would rise in glory to high Heaven with God forever. He learned that wars and conflagrations would destroy the earthly environment in an ultimate rejection—Damnation—by their Creator.

In contrast, Vodou presented the young artist with a fundamentally different view of the nature of divinity, the nature of humanity and the nature of nature. There is for the Vodouisant a single Creator, *Bondye* (*Bon Dieu*, Good God), and divine *lwa* and *zanzet* (ancestors) who visit the quotidian community. Both *lwa* and *zanzet* can arrive in a Vodou ceremony to possess the believer who becomes a communicating vessel to deliver their message to the community. The *lwa* and *zanzet* of Vodou accompanied the captives as they journeyed the Middle Passage to Haiti (then Saint-Domingue), fated to work as slaves on French cane, indigo, and coffee plantations (Duval-Carrié). These African spirits became creoles, speaking a callaloo of old African languages, old Taíno, Church Latin, and French, but mostly Kreyol, and now inhabit the Haitian environment, dwelling in the clouds, trees and forests, rains, all waters, fields, and cemeteries. They assist the faithful in all aspects of quotidian life: raising crops and getting a good fish catch, finding love and a mate, healing sickness and discord, dealing with enemies, and serving as guides and companions during the dangerous passages into birth and death, the sojourn in Vilocan under the sea and thence to the beautiful and pleasant *Lan Giné*, mystical Africa. (Hyppolite claimed he had been privileged to do this while still living.) All takes place in the earthly realm between clouds and sea floor, exactly the environment in which human perceptions are competent. Misadventure, discord, and crimes are astutely recognized and dealt with in the *lakou* (the extended family and close neighbors) primarily through the *oungan* and *manbo*. The concept of Original Sin is absent from Vodou discourse. Absent as well is any sense of the material world as inherently unworthy or laced with evil. There are spirits who do evil but there is no Satan.

The dominant (but not exclusive) Christian view is of an individual and the environment that are separate and separable now and in eternity. Material environment passes away but the self, as nonmaterial soul, exists in eternity. Lynn White Jr. has described the importance of the prevailing doctrinal relationship to the environment and the inherent double sense of time in his essay on Christian myth and history. He sees this dogma as a broken mythology still operating in popular religion and leading to an instrumental, ultimately destructive relationship with the environment. Per Binde notes that Greco-Christian cosmology fundamentally separates mind and matter (hence the eternal Self from nature), but that there is a long history of popular cults of saints focused on sites on or near "features of the landscape that connote natural force of creation and life: the chthonic energies of the earth, the life-giving sources of water and the vegetal fecundity of pristine forest and trees" (Binde 21).

Differentiation of self (observer) and environment (observed) also shapes the predominating scientific view from the Renaissance forward, and further back into its Greek and Arabic prolegomena. It is this view that prevails in Haitian agronomy, forestry, and environmental conservation. Among Western secular scientists with alternative views, Nobel Prize–holder Barbara McClintock spoke of her discoveries about the nature of chromosomes to her biographer, Evelyn Fox Keller: "When I was really working with them I wasn't outside, I was down there. I was part of the system . . . these [chromosomes] were my friends." Later in the same interview session she averred, "As you look at these things, they become a part of you. And you forget yourself" (Keller 117). This relationship to scientific investigation is rare in Haiti, where instrumentalist values focus attention on immediately usable, profitable results.

The alternative view of geological, paleontologist scientist and Jesuit priest, Pierre Teilhard de Chardin, particularly in *The Divine Milieu*, presents what can be read as an extended meditation seeking to reconcile Western science, Roman Catholic theology, and his profound experiences of being there in a beloved world. His theological teachings are discussed in Haiti but with little influence in parish churches, none evident in the Department of Agriculture. The official church regards his work as too close to pagan sensibilities. Church-sponsored environmental projects prefer standard Western science. Nor is the work of Evangelical theologian Paul Tillich, with its participatory view of human and environment, promulgated in Haitian Protestant parishes.

The more popularly known of Christian exceptions to dualistic attitudes is the early Renaissance Saint Francis, who came to perceive himself on the one hand as physically identified with the crucified Jesus Christ, Son of God, and on the other with Brother Sun, Sister Moon, Sister Mother Earth, Sister Mortal Death; and in communication with birds and even a wolf. Almost the only aspect of alternative Christian or scientific attitudes concerning the relationship between human beings and environment that comes into Haitian awareness is the nativity scene with animals invented by Saint Francis and now repeated every Christmas in Christian parishes all over the country.

It is doubtful that either Hyppolite or Bigaud had any contact with Franciscan ecological thought, but both painted Franciscan nativities. The shift from Hyppolite's Nativity *Adoration* to Bigaud's *Nativity* signals a move from engagement—as in adoration—to observation of a dramatized narrative. Hyppolite was closer to the mysticism of Francis. The transit from Vodou sacred space where the viewer is drawn into an act of worship occurring in an environment inhabited simultaneously by ordinary worshipers and divinities to a drama taking place on a framed stage is radical. The move from Hyppolite's works to those of Bigaud is a passage from a sense of being in ineffable reciprocity with miscible visible and invisible worlds to a perception of surrounding nature as "out there" and "other." Deity is a transcending mystery to be observed as part of an even more distant "other."

Wilson Bigaud tried to come to terms with these fundamentally different suppositions about human beings and their relationship to one another and the environment. The shift from Hyppolite's unconflicted Vodou worldview to the unresolved tensions of Bigaud's double consciousness shows plainly enough in the *Paradis Terrestre*. Some of the powerful appeal of the work results from the artist's intuitive or deliberate structuring of the contending monotheistic and henotheistic stories into one forced and forceful harmony.

Bigaud's perspective alters the depiction of flora, fauna, and the space they inhabit from a representation of experienced environment to a quasi-representational symbolic stage set of two invented, juxtaposed "worlds": the first an Earthly Paradise about to be lost and the second the *Lan Giné* (Africa) from which Adam and Eve are in diaspora. In the recognizably Haitian foreground the Christian myth of sin and loss overlays and partly obscures the symbolized but truly lost African savannah. The distant giraffe and hippopotamus iconically specify *Lan Giné* from which slavers seized the ancestors of the population of Haiti to carry them across the Atlantic into exile and forced labor. The foreground Haitian foliage frames the symbolic animals like an inhabited initial in a mediaeval missal. "*Giné*" is the Expulsion: a sin against the Ancestors by enslaving colonial powers. There is a shift of spatial perspective that creates a chasm between the two universes hinged on the single sacred tree. Yet high in the overarching branches and foliage a spider spins a web between the two. This is the spirit, Anansi, one of the sacred *lwa* who came with the captives and maintains the liens between the homelands and Haiti, the ancestors and the living. The artist places her in his compound ecosystem ensconced in the upper branching of the sacred tree, dwelling place of the *lwa*, where her presence will be recognized and appreciated by initiates. *Anansi* for the uninitiated art collectors is an incidental creature with no essential role in the drama of abundance, beauty, love, depredations, and loss.

Bigaud's bricolage of Renaissance art and the tumbled, tangled imagery of Kreyol tales and religious symbols accorded with the often chaotic and conflicted aspects of everyday urban life. The profound alienation of people from a land given over to profitability was surely a factor in his sense of a third exile—his own and that of his family and friends. His work emerged as a public revelation from his witness and his insights into the underlying meaning of daily circumstances. Rich with disclosures, the painting served as the wordless artistic figure of merit for the hundreds and hundreds of Paradise tableaux that followed.

The artists who took up this theme may well have wished to repeat Bigaud's fame and financial success and more. Many of the subsequent works, even those lined up on the streets as gaudy trinkets for sale to tourists, have something more to them. The humble works are recollections of a paradise gone missing for Haitians and for the visiting travelers.

Bigaud's painting that became the criterion model—the figure of merit—for those to follow received its honors in an art market environment that was alert to what would later be called "outsider" art, but then "primitive" or "naïve" or "peasant" art with a concurrent and related fashion for children's art. The implications for a dismissive amusement are apparent: "other" as entertainment. From the beginning the fashion had a relationship with the long string of European and, later, North American efforts that proceed out of natural history investigations, tightly bound to the expansion of empires. One secondary consequence of the naturalist's ventures, along with botanical gardens, was the tourism industry (Ring). When the Haitian government began to encourage tourism soon after the end of World War II, the art of Haiti quickly became a primary feature. The Centre d'Art participated in these efforts, and several persons associated with it sharply focused on continuing international art market attention to the Kreyol artists' works. Collectors soon arrived to enjoy sunshine, rest easy in tropical gardens, and buy colorful paintings at a risible price.

The paintings ranged in quality from exceptional, like those of Hyppolite and Bigaud, to proficient variations on the theme, to drabbles of tyros suddenly aware that the profession of "artist" netted enough income to buy a bicycle or maybe even an automobile. Questions of quality aside, there remains the question of what factors in addition to the hope of making a living were operating in the choices made by the artists and in the choices from among those works made by the art entrepreneurs, the collectors, and the tourists. Is there some particular importance attached to the special theme of paradise or *Lan Giné* lost that can inform notions of the ecology of people and environment in Haiti and generally? Is the religious element of paradise or *Lan Giné* incidental or is it aligned with some fundamental stratum of human consciousness of being in the world now and here? What do the innumerable tourist magazines and brochures or the 137,000,000 hits on web search engines (Google 2009) for the word "paradise" reveal?

A generation after Bigaud's exemplary Earthly Paradise, an anonymous artist at the Centre d'Art created his personal version of the theme, eerily illuminating the nourishing tree of beauty with a bright nimbus.[9] Everything revolves around the glowing tree, the *poto-mitan* path of the *lwa*. A pink-winged avenging angel wields a sword on the left as Adam and Eve, derived from Masaccio's Renaissance Brancacci Chapel, depart weeping. Quitting Earthly Paradise with them are Haitian and African animals. The birds stay, as do ascensions of butterflies circling arboreal paradise. The presence of so many butterflies is a signifier for the Christian Resurrection myth embedded in a myth of Haitian history that continues to make the rounds since the mid-eighteenth century. The proto-hero of the revolution, Makandal, told his followers that even were the French to capture him, he would escape. Though bound and burned at the stake, he would rise from his ashes transmogrified into butterflies and flying

Figure 2.2 Expulsion from Paradise

insects. He was indeed caught, escaped, captured again, and burned in the public square. A great clouding flight of butterflies ascended from the pyre, and the slaves knew he would be present with them until freedom was in hand. Resurrection bears multiple meanings in Haiti, joining religion, ecology, and political history. Such recombination of the religious and political symbols into a new narrative became typical among thoughtful followers of the original criterion image. Paradise lost-but-to-be-restored lends itself to a reading that the resurrection of Haiti, necessarily requiring restoration of environment, is a process of unification of flesh and spirit, person and world into a properly metabolizing ecological cycle.

The unknown artist brought together the theme of disobedience, exile, and hope of resurrection in a complex and disquieting visual staging. The figure of merit is pronounced in the gorgeous colors and the harmony of the underlying geometry, the "earth measure" and *axis mundi* centering on the Sacred Tree/Poto Mitan joining sky to earth. But the positive message is countered and even denied in the sorrowing couple departing the blissful garden. The artist repeats the narrative and draws upon the same symbolic and allusive devices as Hyppolite and Bigaud, including their composition. His facture, however, is put entirely at the service of narrative, suppressing signs of the hand of the artist. The finished work thus reveals little about the artist's personal engagement with the story, with his daily environment, or with earth, plants, and animals. The work is almost entirely "literary" painting with a carefully duplicated "primitive" facture. Vodou is present as symbols and the flora and fauna are icons selected from earlier paintings rather than representations from the artist's environment. The "naïve" work is curiously "modernist" in being a nearly autonomous piece that is art about other art rather than art expressing experiential ties to an environment and a belief system. While viewers can legitimately read the work as a call for an environmental as well as historical resurrection, the presentation of environment is more kin to Roumain's or Thoby-Marcelin's intellectual, observant distance than to Hyppolite's understanding of himself as participant in a seamless unity. Unlike Hyppolite who made paintings for the Vodou temple, this artist created a work for the external art market. The core meaning of an environmentally dependent religion is absent. What does remain is the beauty with its faint but insistent reminder that something terribly important is lost.

By the time this artist created his mournful exit from Eden, the U.S. railway linking the cane plantations with the export center at Port-au-Prince harbor was in disrepair. Outdoor patch-up shops stacked with salvaged auto parts, lumber, wire, conduits, and plumbing supplies encroached upon Boulevard Harry Truman bordering the quay. Trees and shrubs on heights above the western part of the city were giving way to hundreds of small shacks side by side, higher and higher up the slopes. On the highway toward Gonaïve and Cap Haïtien dry creeks poured bare cobbles of stone and earth into eroded declivities. Sugar and rice were beginning to be imported as the price for the refined product from subsidized farms outside the country fell lower than the Haitian farmers could ask and still make a living. Land freed from cane or rice production mostly lay fallow and subject to more flooding and erosion. Some large tracts did remain in production, and a few of the landowners did reinvest profits back into Haiti. Peasants, however, were finding it prohibitively expensive to establish legal claims to smaller and smaller divisions handed down from postrevolutionary distributions, or to grow enough to feed a family. Vodou was of little practical assistance.

The restorationist point of view, land-centered as it was, arose with special vigor in response to the identity denigration of the American occupation, and was as fully twined into the conversations, the tracts, the poetry, and the novels of the Indigènists as it was in the conversations of peasants who, like Hyppolite, had suffered the indignity of *corvée* work gangs so reminiscent of colonialism. Intellectuals and peasants seemed to bind together into an accord across métier and across class lines that might have resulted in stronger environmental restoration. However, it appears that while the scientists and writers revalorized Vodou, they did not enter into any significant degree of religious, mystical comprehension of and collaboration with the forces of nature. Nor did they materially participate in the daily life and spaces of the *moun andeyo*. The Kreyol artists belonged to socially and politically marginalized strata of society with no political influence.

Currently the Vodou religion itself, although surviving more than two centuries of attempted extirpations by political and religious leaders, shifts attention from ecological unity with the environment to more social interactions within the environment. While nongovernmental organizations led by Haitians or by international aid missions make vigorous efforts to save the beautiful ecological sites that remain and to restore what has been lost, comprehensive concerted action to save a visibly failing environment remains latent. With profitability the chief guiding figure of merit or constraining force for urban intellectuals, Kreyol artists, and aid organizations alike, the virtues of either religious or pure scientific exploration are secondary, attenuated, or obscured.

From his village east of Cap Haïtien, artist Henry Nickson views the result of two centuries of abusive dominion over the land. He knows what is happening and why. His divine companions Danballah, Gran Bwa, Aizan, Loco, Azaka, and even Legba are captive slaves to Mammon. Nickson knows where tiny pockets of bright vegetation flourish by sacred cascades watering the roots of the mapou tree joining water to sky. Sometimes he paints that. Those verdant remnants are a long walk from his tiny house. Huts made of industrial detritus give half shelter to a throng of poorly nourished residents; a swampy place once a rice field breeds mosquitoes; and where the land begins to rise toward the hills, the earth is cracked like an expanse of pottery shards. Streams of scarcely running water are opaque with topsoil runoff, and dry gullies trace the path of old hurricane floods. Nickson has an urge to display his indignant grief about the ugly surrounding devastation. His works are absent from the galleries in Port-au-Prince. Other artists do not follow his figure of demerit.

For now, the grand tableaus invested with expressive trails of the brushes of Hyppolite, of Bigaud, and of known and unknown Kreyol masters remain as marks of merits yet to be reached. The great works and vivid little tourist clichés are stealthy mediators of an enduring figure of

Figure 2.3 Henry Nickson, *Desolate Landscape*

ecological merit where water cascades through lush greenery over the living stones and continuous energies course through all.

NOTES

1. Reliable statistics for Haitian agriculture and environment are not available since such organizations as the United Nations Development Program or USAID depend in part on data provided by the country in question, with lags as much as a decade. USAID Country Studies (http://www.usaid.gov/pubs/cp97/countries/ht.htm 2009) states, "Environmental degradation undermines political and social stability, food security and sustainable economic growth. Deforestation in the past decade reached estimated levels of 30 million trees per year, 80% of the national watersheds are severely degraded, and the equivalent of 15,000 acres of arable land are eroded annually." Data from nongovernmental organizations vary by several percentage points. Estimates tend to present precolonial forest cover at over 90 percent with decline to between 5 percent and 3 percent. Arable land estimates range from 23 percent to 28 percent, mountainous terrain being the greater part of the total surface of the country.

2. "Figure of merit" is a term taken from thermal engineering in the familiar thermostat, where one sets a temperature for the system to reach and hold, and from Erich Auerbach's *Scenes from the Drama of European Literature* in which he traces the concept of *figura* from antiquity to Dante and forward, with special attention to how such criterion models as Jesus Christ developed over time—what the engineers would call an "advancing" figure of merit.

3. See Kaplan and Kaplan, *The Experience of Nature*; Kuo and Taylor, "A Potential Natural Treatment"; Wells, "At Home with Nature."

4. See Hansen, "Albert Smith, the Alpine Club"; and Rose, "English Artists."

5. See Balch, *Occupied Haiti*; Barros, *Haïti de 1804 à nos jours*; Fatton, *The Roots of Haitian Despotism*; Heinl, *Written in Blood*; Renda, *Taking Haiti*; Schmidt, *The United States Occupation of Haiti*.

6. See Godreau, "Changing Space"; Souffrant, *Littérature et Société*.

7. See Barros, op. cit; Madiou, *Histoire d'Haïti*.

8. Bayahonde (*Prosopis juliflora*) is a leguminous, flowering tree that can grow in dry, thin soil.

9. Attempts to identify the artist have so far yielded no name. The work was in a large bin of several dozens of similar paintings.

3

Toward a Caribbean Ecopoetics
Derek Walcott's Language of Plants

Elaine Savory

> I'm a wild golden apple
> that will burst with love . . .
> —Derek Walcott, "Sainte Lucie," *Collected Poems*, 314

> The noise my leaves make is my language.
> —Derek Walcott, "Isla Incognita," 57

Ecocriticism reads texts through a politically engaged lens for their representation of ecology, past, present, and looking forward to the future. It has begun to answer the charge that literary and cultural studies are not especially aware of the growing recognition of our planet as an increasingly fragile and threatened ecosystem, for which time might well be running out. As Lawrence Buell remarks, in his study of Thoreau and American nature writing, "an inquiry into the environmental imagination forces us to question the premises of literary theory whilst using its resources to expose the limitation of literature's representations" (*The Environmental Imagination* 5). Buell argues that a text that is environmentally orientated has to exhibit particular identities: the connection between human history and the nonhuman environment, empathy with the nonhuman, accountability on the part of humans toward the environment, and the idea that the environment is not fixed but constantly in process.[1] Cheryll Glotfelty argues that the purpose of ecocriticism has as its most important task consciousness raising about the environment ("Introduction" *The Ecocritical Imagination* xxiv).[2] But postcolonial ecocriticism is deeply concerned with the ways in which empire has abused and exploited both people and their environments. It is concerned with what Jill Casid has described in *Sowing Empire: Landscape and Colonization* as what "means were available to those displaced, subordinated, or terrorized by imperial landscaping" (241).[3]

Within postcolonial ecocriticism, scholars focused on the Caribbean have already made an important contribution. Ian Gregory Strachan speaks to a very urgent concern in the Caribbean, investigating the charge made by Frank Taylor that tourism is in effect constituting a "neoplantation."[4] Certainly developers have recently removed many beautiful places once accessible to Caribbean populations behind gates and walls.[5] Elizabeth DeLoughrey, Renée Gosson, and George Handley, in their introduction to *Caribbean Literature and the Environment*, trace out the long historical entanglement between transatlantic colonialism and landscape production, highlighting the mutually constitutive relationship between nature and violence. They point out the particular challenge Caribbean ecocriticism has in resisting the silencing effects of colonial legacies on Amerindian, African, and Asian peoples, as well as to what Derek Walcott calls nature's own "vegetal fury" (DeLoughrey et al., 3), as the environment itself erases human history.[6]

Whereas a postcolonial ecocriticism seeks to raise consciousness and even encourage activism with regard to the environment by means of exploring literary and cultural texts, my concern here is a postcolonial ecopoetics, a reading of literary texts not only in relation to ecological themes, but with regard to aesthetic strategies. This essay provides an ecopoetic reading of the poetry of Nobel Prize–winning author Derek Walcott. By this I mean to investigate how environmental or ecological consciousness manifests in his aesthetic decisions. Walcott's use of flora is extensive and various. But he is far from a late Romantic, finding inspiration in nature, for his ecological imagination is postcolonial. He finds in flora a richly nuanced source of his poetics, which comprehend plants through poetry and poetry through plants, in an aesthetic representation of the indissoluble bond between the fate of humans and the fate of flora. Walcott's almost obsessive representation of interplay between poetry and plants is of vital importance in raising consciousness about sustainable change appropriate for social and environmental conditions in the Caribbean. This is an urgent need given the long history of colonial and neocolonial degradation of human and nonhuman ecologies.

In "The Antilles: Fragments of Epic Memory," Walcott's Nobel address, he references the way vegetation is perceived in colonial perspectives as being subdued, ordered, submissive, and thus appearing as "proper palm trees . . . civilizing decency . . . colonized vegetation" (74). The imperial beholder saw landscape "furious with vegetation in the wrong light and with the wrong eye" (74). Walcott knows the outsider still misreads the Caribbean: a German tourist he remembered found he could not paint because it was "too *green*" (Montenegro "An Interview with

Derek Walcott" 136). Walcott, a skilled painter himself, has no trouble distinguishing the many shades of foliage around him. He argues that Caribbean culture defines itself as flora, "branch by branch, leaf by leaf" ("Antilles" 79), and the "sounds of leaves, palm fronds . . . are the sounds of fresh dialect" (79), the demotic language of Caribbean people. Creole names of Caribbean trees seem to Walcott to be "suppler, greener" than their English names (80). He sees Caribbean history in particular flora, as when the genocide of Amerindian people "bleeds in the scarlet of the immortelle" and the "lances of green cane" are a "green prison" for indentured Asians (81). Leaves are "illiterate" but "there to be read," for formal learning is not the only way to express intelligence and understanding (81), something Walcott has often demonstrated through characters in his plays and poetry. He has even projected himself as a tree, the oak, as Ned Thomas noted ("Interview" 68). Finally he reads plants carefully in their context: some are "literary" and not "agricultural," such as wheat, just as for Walcott, sugar "is not a pastoral," because of the blood and sweat in the Caribbean earth which produced it (Montenegro 146).

Most critically for my argument here, Walcott points out that an almond leaf is not an olive leaf, and the "only thing" that makes either of them important is literature (Brown and Johnson "Thinking Poetry" 183). Thus ecologically sensitive literature "reads" flora in critically important ways. Walcott's poetry, then, in its deeply thoughtful employment of plants, not only raises the reader's ecocritical awareness of the place and function of flora in Caribbean history, but also demonstrates that he owes some of his key poetic practices to his ecological consciousness, making his work importantly ecopoetic. This is crucial because it encourages the reader not to marginalize aesthetics for themes when thinking about ecology and the environment: form is philosophy and politics as well. It also encourages a more reflective and deeper engagement with the Caribbean, perhaps inspiring an environmental awareness of the region.

Through the sheer variety of type and location of plants in his work, Walcott identifies and critiques the long history of flora in empire and after. As Richard Drayton has excellently demonstrated (2000), British obsessions with exotic flora contributed centrally to the nature of British imperialism, visible in the trade of peoples and plants for colonial gardens and plantation agriculture.[7] Whether we examine literary texts written within the ideological imperatives of the British Empire, or texts that are written from an anti- or postcolonial response to British imperialism, plants appear often, employed for a variety of purposes.[8] In British literature, plants appear thematically in the portrayal of an idyllic natural world, an Eden, or as a pastoral space, nostalgic for a lost perfection. In these texts poetry and other arts nevertheless flourish because of their proximity to nature, a nature somehow outside the fallen world of human politics and greed.[9] In Caribbean literature, plants are also often centrally important, frequently metaphors or metonyms for aspects of the brutal history of colonialism and slavery.[10] Recent Caribbean writing has demonstrated a strong engagement with ecology, such as in the works of Jamaica Kincaid or Olive Senior.[11] For example, Senior consistently uses flora as allegories for human issues and conditions: an escaped slave wants "nothing more than to be / left alone, to live in peace" (*Gardening in the Tropics* 108) for the garden is a source of potential healing, and her avid modern gardener uses old remedies, often from plants, such as cowitch, to prevent human thieves robbing her prize crop (110). In her poem "Brief Lives," the gardener unearths "occasional skeletons" (83). Senior's ecological imagination encourages the reader to connect gardening and plant life with a history and a present that are not devoid of the social but rather register ongoing violence against people.

Walcott's employment of plants is far more pervasive, so it is surprising that this has received relatively little critical attention. John Thieme and Rei Terada, though only paying brief attention to this topic, see "greenness" in Walcott's work as having a rather romantic and positive significance. Terada thinks greenness in his poetry is "conventionally metonymic of natural purity" (*Derek Walcott's Poetry* 61), and Thieme believes that references to vegetation in the Caribbean are allusions to rural land and folk custom (*Derek Walcott*). Katie Jones argues that Walcott, in his early collections, *The Castaway* and *The Gulf*, contributes to "the resurrection of landscape poetry" ("Land and Sea" 37), and demonstrates how in "The Almond Trees," Walcott identifies the trees with both sunbathers' burnt bodies and "seared writhing bodies of slaves brought from Africa" (39). Jana Evans Braziel thinks Walcott, Kincaid, and Glissant all refute a "static Eden" (Idem 112), and critique the idea of Eden ("Caribbean Genesis" 123). They offer ecocritical resistance to capitalism's exploitative relation to Caribbean ecology (11). George Handley's work on Walcott's "poetics of the environment" provides a vital frame for my argument here. Handley points out the immense importance of Walcott's birthplace, St. Lucia, in the development of an ecological consciousness, but that his sense of nature is well aware that, as he says, "beneath its virginal untamed appeal" might lie an indifference to human pain (*New World Poetics* 285). He explores Walcott's ethical agony in his poem "The Bounty" over the proper use of poetry to mourn his mother's death, asking what value it has for an environmental ethic, concluding, "Walcott's nature is neither a sign of the Eternal Garden nor the inevitable victim of human destruction. It becomes a sign of an always ending, always dying present that paradoxically makes poetic language potentially always new and new futures always possible" ("Derek Walcott's Poetics of the Environment" 201).

At the outset of his argument, Handley discusses Octavio Paz's hopes for poetry's positive intervention in protecting the environment, via ethical values that poetry possesses in its metaphorical imagination. He quotes Walcott to demonstrate how the poet understands that those who profess love for nature "really hate it," whereas those who work in it, often violently, such as fishermen or hunters, "become nature" (207). When this happens, loving nature is loving the self. Walcott's point is crucial, for it can be paralleled by the liberal patronage to which postcolonial subjects are subjected by those who "hate racism" but do not see it as having anything to do with their most inner selves. In an interview, Walcott demonstrates a sense of the importance of naming both "objects and plants" to reclaim them from colonial identity, aware *both* of the "degradation" brought about by history *and* the possibilities at the dawning of each new Caribbean day (Handley "Argument of the Outboard Motor" 135).[12] He resists simple pastoral romanticization of plants, because despite its beauty, the Caribbean's history erases the nostalgia for originary perfection found in pastoral, even while Walcott equally resists a facile rejection of Europe (Handley "Derek Walcott's Poetics of the Environment" 206).

I want to begin with "The Bounty," because it is a special case within Walcott's work written to mourn his mother and reflect on the ethical purpose of poetry in the face of death. Walcott had declared suspicion of eulogies after being asked to write one for W. H. Auden's New York funeral, even though this was a chance to pay respect publicly to a poet he deeply admired as an influence.[13] There was much at stake therefore for Walcott in the composition of "The Bounty." This was to be both a family elegy, recording the grief of the bereaved and reflecting on the relationship with the deceased and a poem suitably demonstrating the prowess of a newly wreathed Nobel Laureate. The destructive vehemence of grief and the anxiety for aesthetic achievement would battle with each other, providing the tension that drives the poem, if at times threatening to tear it apart. This tension, so important to Walcott's aesthetics, is deeply connected to his awareness both of the colonial and postcolonial in the Caribbean, and of its environmental history, as I intend to demonstrate.

One important clue as to Walcott's purpose in both the poem "The Bounty" and the collection of the same title, both of which often employ plants, is in his employment of the English poet John Clare (1793–1864). Greg Garrard argues that Clare "has a much better claim to be the true poet of nature" than Wordsworth (*Ecocriticism* 44). Clare was a farm laborer, the son of farm laborers. As a young man, he earned a meager and exhausting living, but, as do the laborers and fishermen in Walcott's work, he could observe the life of plants and creatures closely as the seasons passed. But Clare was more than a nature poet: what makes him unusual among English elegists is that his grief was political over enclosure, the seizure of common lands on the claim of best usage being larger, more profitable, industrialized farming.[14] He directly connected enclosure to enslavement, confinement, and alienation. He saw that those who commit crimes against nature and powerless humans are often the same people given to pontificating about liberty. His "The Fallen Elm" is a sad witness to the loss of an old and much loved tree, destroyed by someone with power who ironically "barked of freedom" (*I Am: The Selected Poetry of John Clare* 142). He grieves for places that were once collectively enjoyed, and are now taken away into private ownership. "Swordy Well" is an elegy for the loss of a piece of open public land to enclosure (135). "The

Lament of Swordy Well" gives voice to a piece of common land which has fallen into the clutches of town authorities who are working it to death: "His feelings wither branch and root/That falls in parish hands" (212). So the wild creatures who used to enjoy Swordy Well (bees, rabbits, butterflies, beetles) are driven away from what they need to survive. Clare gives Swordy Well a human identity, worked to exhaustion and then crushed further when too weak to resist. The workhouse that in Clare's day the poor dreaded, and the parish that administers it parsimoniously are both part of the complaints of Swordy Well: "Parish allowance gaunt and dread / Had it the earth to keep / Would even pine the bees to dead / To save an extra keep" (213). If a wild plant, clover, arrives in spring, the "next day brings the hasty plough / And makes me misery's bed" (214). Trees are cut down on Swordy Well to facilitate profit from crops, and Swordy Well complains that if the price of corn goes up, encouraging more planting, ". . . I shan't possess a single fly/Or get a weed to grow" (216). Weeds are thus subversive, vital elements in a free space, a space that before enclosure "made freemen of the slave" (218), but now even Swordy Well itself is made into "a parish slave" (218). Thus Clare's response to nature, although rooted in England, the imperial center, apprehends the connection between oppression of the poor by the wealthy and the eradication of wild and self-reliant flora, something that is strongly relatable to Walcott's employment of flora.

There is much debate about the meaning of enclosure and its impact on agriculture and the poor. Jonathan Bate explains that the open-field system that preceded enclosure fostered an "intimate relationship between society and environment" (*John Clare* 47). But he also remarks that the economic effects of enclosure have been greatly debated, with those thinking enclosure favored only the wealthy on one side and those arguing that enclosure improved the land's productivity and also employment in rural areas (48). Regardless of this, for Clare enclosure was a tragedy for himself and his community. Robert Marzec's work on enclosure is critical here: he identifies the connection between imperialism and enclosure, the latter serving the expansion of the former because "the idea of a singular uncommodified territory of land stands on the stage of modernity like an outlaw" (*An Ecological and Postcolonial Study* 22). In an essay on enclosure and colonization, Marzec points out that Daniel Defoe was a "great believer in the power of enclosures to establish a radically new mode of enlightened (imperial) existence ("Enclosures, Colonization" 130). Relevant to this discussion is Marzec's careful separation of ecocriticism's desire to think of colonialism and globalization erasing "the spirit of the place" and postcolonialism's frequent reading of nature as "raw materiality" (41). Clare certainly revered the spirit of place, but in his formation of it, it is both vulnerable and resisting, and has a complex and intensely ethical intelligence. Thus Clare's apprehension that nature is as complex as the human world he knew can be read productively in conjunction with Walcott's complicated apprehension of nature as well as the Caribbean.

This mixture of lament, even agony, and pastoral admiration for the beauty of nature also marks Walcott's "The Bounty." St Lucia and other Caribbean countries are losing beautiful places, previously accessible by all, to developers, somewhat parallel to the brutal loss caused by enclosure as Clare perceived it.[15] Though Walcott's grief in "The Bounty" is primarily for his mother, Alix, she is strongly associated with nature, specifically with flora. Handley rightly explains the reference to John Clare and "Tom" in "The Bounty" in terms of the poet's mad grief that threatens to destroy his ability to even respect poetry, let alone write it. "As the poet approaches the muteness of a mad Tom and moves further and further away from the generative function of language, his poetry becomes obeisant to the natural world and nature therefore functions as an emanation of God because it creates the Word ("Derek Walcott's Poetics of the Environment" 9).

But the relation of insanity and expressive language is complicated: all poetry that destabilizes language and meaning is on one level a rejection of rationality, refusing the imperative of direct communication. However, Tom and Clare are useful avatars for Walcott in this moment of intense grief, because they are each both mad and intensely sensible in the same moment. Tom, Shakespeare's wise fool in *King Lear* and a beloved figure of English folklore, is both insightful and crazy, and Clare was an asylum inmate for many years, yet productively writing perfectly coherent poems there: indeed, Clare's life demonstrated how the opposition of mad and sane is always problematic.

Walcott's introduction of Clare comes very close to the beginning of "The Bounty," making Clare a part of a list that is not immediately comprehensible. The lovely image of the breadfruit opening its palms in praise is followed by a number of descriptions of this fecund tree, including "tree of bread" in both English and St. Lucian creole, and "slave food," which is what the English colonial apparatus was trying to bring to the planters when they transported the breadfruit from the Pacific to the Caribbean.[16] Right after "slave food," "the bliss of John Clare," introduces the poet, a Clare "lacing his boots with vines" (3), signifying his closeness to nature. In the poet's imagination, the breadfruit, which is exploited by unfeeling imperialist greed, praises Clare, whose empathies for Nature were so great that he cried for "a beetle's loss," for the "weight /of the world in a bead of dew on clematis or vetch" (5). Clare's sensitivity was so intense that it warns Walcott that whilst "there is grief, there will always be," (5), it must no madden. The poem contrasts Clare's tender feelings with "these tinder-dry lines of this poem that I hate" (5). This is the intense expression of a crisis in Walcott's faith in his poetic ability, which in the context of his mother's death seems merely facile and almost shameful. The success of a poem that is about painful emotions has much to do with the delicate balance between agonized sensitivity and an absolute virtuoso control of the music of language, bending it to the poet's will and purpose.

In parts of "The Bounty," poetic ambition and success are represented as dangerous precisely because they can be pursued sanely. The poet must demonstrate technical proficiency, which usually means the crafter controls the making of the craft, but deeper levels of grief and mourning, both personal and communal, are powerfully inchoate. The employment of Clare and his closeness to abused nature, juxtaposed with a disgust with his own facility to create achieved verse, demonstrates order and pattern. In this way, Walcott contrasts raw emotion, ethically admirable, with emotion controlled for effect. Nature cultivated is likely to serve power and be rewarded by becoming more abundant, as in the case of crops that make a profit. When Walcott asks forgiveness from Clare right after his reference to "a crowning wreath of false laurel," signifying the Nobel Prize for Literature he had recently won, he is likely referencing Clare's courage in expressing responsiveness to a marginalized and vulnerable nature. If poetry is successful in a world that is ruled by power intent on harming the environment as much as it hurts people, it might be allying itself with that kind of power. Thus Walcott's crisis is not just about his ability to let intense feeling into his work, but, by extension, about his anxiety that he is somehow contributing to the degradation of the environment by being a successful poet. The way out of this is to follow Clare's example and really listen to nature. Thus he references Clare hearing a "murmur" in nature "of bounty abiding," which precedes the "clear language" that Alix Walcott taught her children. Clare then becomes a kind of pathway not just back to a sensitive apprehension of nature but even back to Alix Walcott. He is visualized in his northern climate, up to his ankles in freezing ('iron") streams, associated with plants such as clematis and vetch, and, directly referencing his poem "The Progress of Rhyme," enjoying birds, "these thin musicians" (*The Bounty* 15). In Clare's poem, bird songs are powerful teachers of music, closely related to poetry.

If Clare is a very important presence, Walcott's relation to nature, and especially flora, is also intensely connected to the loss of his mother. The poem expresses anxiety that his poetic voice is either going to fail him or, worse, that by not failing him, it will make his grief for his mother shallow. Plants reflect the tempestuousness of his grief. He feels "nettles of remorse," vividly imaging the common wish of the bereaved that they had loved more expressively while they had the chance. Walcott's voice in the poem expresses experiencing his grief in terms of a powerful surge of life-giving water coming up under plants that are vital and rambunctious. "Swollen gulches" not only "babble" but loosen the roots of plants, until "hairy clods" are "like unclenching fists" (7). Crocuses stutter but also "choir" (15), a tropical cedar is "voluble" (13), and the pomme-arac "purples its floor," as if intentionally (11). New growth is dynamic: green lances "spring / from the melting fields" (15). Lances appear often as an image of new plant growth in Walcott's poetry: they are distinctly phallic and associated with aggressive manhood and warfare. The energy a lance-like young plant seems to display is a strong defeat of the "death" of dormancy.

This makes something new here of the age-old use of cycles of nature by poets to signify cycles of human life. But in the Caribbean, tropical cycles are different from those giving rise to myths such as Demeter and Persephone, where winter is explained; in the tropics, climate and flora are far more subtle in their changes. Temperate plants, such as pines and roses, can often adapt to the tropics, paralleling European settlement in the tropics. Walcott chooses the rose, an ancient image of love and women, to signify Alix Walcott, his mother (*The Bounty* 3). She was a devout woman, and Walcott pays her homage by direct reference to Dante's thirty-third canto of the *Paradiso*. St Lucia does not have temperate seasons, so it seems like a "viridian Eden," yet what happened in Eden "engendered decay" (*The Bounty* 15). Alix Walcott has taken even tropical "seasons" with her, like a contemporary Persephone (but a mother Demeter as well). By the end of the poem, the beloved dead are "part of earth's vegetal fury," and "their veins grow/with the wild mammy-apple, the open-handed breadfruit / their heart in the open pomegranate, the sliced avocado" (*The Bounty* 14). They are part of what the living eat, and so the earth rejoices in receiving what will fuel more life in the future. By this Walcott manages his grief in accepting the cycles of life and death: the living eat fruits and plants and in death contribute to the next generations of plant life; thus the individual literally becomes part of nature, and nature requires death to contribute to future life.

Through the association of several particular plants with Alix Walcott, marigolds on an altar, the bougainvillea with its thorns, the imperial lilac, and the feathery palms associated with Palm Sunday, we learn that plants were key in Walcott's most originary memories. However intensely personal Walcott's use of flora becomes, he contextualizes plants in a larger frame of religion, history, and myth. It appears that Alix Walcott knew the mutiny on the *Bounty* story and passed it on to her children, though it is not clear which version she had read. It occupies the heart of the poem as plants occupy the heart of this story. The breadfruit plants on the *Bounty* "will be heaved aboard" and "bob in the ocean's furrows" (*The Bounty* 9). Plants are even associated with the hymn she loved, "There Is a Green Hill Far Away" (10). Her shade or soul is aligned with trees, both temperate and tropical, poplars and casuarinas, as well as "the in-and-out light of almonds" (11). At the end of the poem, as acceptance of the loss develops, there is mention of the "nailed and thorn-riddled tree" on which Christ died, with the suggestion of course of resurrection, in which Alix Walcott, a devout Christian, presumably believed. The use of flora strongly references the brutal history of Caribbean colonialism and slavery: "the breadfruit opens its palms in praise of the bounty, / *bois-pain*, tree of bread, slave food" (*The Bounty* 3), as well as that of the economically exploited, rural working class in Britain. Walcott thus works through his fear that poetry can be too self-serving by employing plants as ethical reminders of Caribbean history.

Walcott has been accused at times of being too willing to embrace European poetic tradition, but his inclusion of Clare in "The Bounty" establishes a parallel between Clare's ecological imagination and experience with the violence of enclosure and Walcott's own sense of nature and place in the Caribbean context. Walcott expresses the cosmopolitan nature of the Caribbean and its human and environmental diasporas, and his employment of plants illuminates not only his reading of Caribbean history and culture, but that of the colonial center. He conceives Caribbean culture as reworking and combining aspects of cultures from across the world, a kind of ecological regeneration of previous lives, and for this reason his poetry about the most local and personal of places often takes the reader out of the Caribbean to travel into new environments.

Thus both tropical and temperate plants contribute to Walcott's poetic environment, just as the Caribbean's people trace ancestry to many parts of the world. In the epic poem, *Omeros* (1990), the Caribbean has both the wild trees used for making fishermen's canoes on the beach or the plants that Maud Plunkett treasures in her colonial garden. The world of *Omeros* includes Africa's calabash and mangroves, America's Pacific pines, and Ireland's "wiry hedgerows" (200) and cypress. For Walcott, flora include enduring and strong trees, fragile and ephemeral flowers, and many identities in between. In his references to a wide variety of plants in a wide variety of places, Walcott constantly reminds the reader that people must learn strategies of adaptation just as plants have done, though the circumstances of that travel and that relocation are of many kinds, from the brutal experience of the Middle Passage for slaves to the drift to the Caribbean of the Plunketts in *Omeros*.

The sheer quantity and variety of Walcott's references to plants demonstrate his considerable botanical interest and knowledge. For example, in his *Collected Poems 1948–1984*, there are over forty references to palm trees, some appearing generically as palms, but many more specifically described, as cabbage, yellow, copper, yellow dwarf, gold, and brown. The very repetition provides a melody within the poetry, where the reiteration of sameness and difference illuminates Walcott's vision of culture. Plants inform Walcott's early titles for poem collections (*In a Green Night* 1962, *Sea Grapes* (first published in 1976), *The Star-Apple Kingdom* first published in 1979). Titles for individual poems that reference flora, such as "Orient and Immortal Wheat," "The Banyan Tree, Old Year's Night," "Nights in the Gardens of Port of Spain," "Sea Canes," and "To Return to the Trees," reflect his wide-ranging consciousness of plants. They may be flowers, shrubs, or trees, regarded as weeds or highly treasured by people, found in forests, on beaches, in meadows, or on mountains. But they are rarely set into deliberate gardens or any other kind of rationalized and controlled space of nature such as the lawn. Instead they convey a sense of eclecticism and diasporic wildness. Walcott, like Clare, sees plants as struggling to live in an often harsh or indifferent landscape, as people have to do, and contending with cruel or at least oppressive power, as Caribbean people have had to do.

Walcott's images make sure that the reader conflates human with plant life, as when death, wielding the conventional but "wild" scythe, blindly cuts "friends, flowers and grass" (*The Bounty* 19). Human grief can be assuaged by nature: getting beyond the "self-importance of despair" requires turning to "water, leaves and air," which can take you "beyond happiness" (*The Bounty* 27). Human qualities are bestowed on plants by the use of evocative adjectives ("shattered," "helmeted," "bent," "spiked," "ragged," "scraping"). The life of man "is grass," presumably to be walked upon by indifferent others (*Collected Poems* 81), and thoughts fall from a man "like leaves" (116). Walcott's Crusoe sees a "rotting nut" (coconut) rolling in the ocean surf, and it becomes "his own brain rotting from the guilt" (69). Plants also have human qualities, often strikingly uncommon. In "The Bounty," the breadfruit tree is imaged as "opening its palms" and later, being "open-handed," since the large leaf has a number of prominent lobes, vaguely looking like "fingers."

The sexual life of plants is observed in the language of human reproduction. Plants can be phallic, and the tiger orchid has a "speckled vulva" (*Collected Poems* 60). When the tree is "branched with cries," it is uttering inarticulate emotion, on the way to speech. The pomegranate is christened "with a careful tongue" (14). There is an *"alphabet of . . . aloe"* (15). The human witness attributes capacity for speech to a dying leaf, "When a bronze leaf glints, I hear again / the torn throat in the torn shade," (415). There is the "green-leaved uproar of the century" (428). In the quotation that opens this essay, the speaker claims to be a "wild golden apple," a fruit that is sweet but laced internally with sinuous woody threads: this fruit does not deliver an easy enjoyment, and is indisputably local, but loved by Caribbean children and adults alike. Walcott's attribution of human language to plants, and his particular reference to Caribbean flora, suggests also that his poetry has learned a kind of environmental witness that makes it both ecocritical and postcolonial.

Plants contribute to Walcott's poetics in several important ways. Plant names that are sonorous, like frangipani or ginger lily, are often key to Walcott's use of heightened patterns of sound: he turns to these names for particular sound effects in his poetic music.[17] For instance, "Sainte Lucie" (*Collected Poems* 310) has a celebratory list of plant names in St. Lucian patois that reverberates the French name for apple: "Pomme-arac/otaheite apple / pomme cythère /, pomme granate / moubain, / z'ananas". His use of lists of plants is interesting: they convey the rich variety of plant life, comparable to the diversity of human life, but their variety in the Caribbean is often due to British imperial intervention in bringing plants from the Pacific to the Caribbean, and their names therefore invoke a history that saw all Caribbean islands as recipients of imperial "improvement," despite the different names for the same plant within the region.

Reflecting the complexity of Caribbean history and languages, Walcott employs both standard West Indian/English and Creole plant names, often heightening them by alliteration or assonance (all these references are from *Selected Poems*): "The last leaves fell." (142), "white lilies stiffen" (177), "leathery sea-grape leaves" (54). Caribbean plants are, in Walcott's work, frequently metonymic, recalling aspects of hidden history or present experience, whether it be a remedy for healing (such as bush teas) in a time when medical help was available only for elites, or a fruit associated with childhood joy and sometimes childhood pranks (dunks), or a necessity for the building of boats (great trees).[18]

The other major role that plants play is as illustration of the writing process, which represents Walcott's poetry as a part of nature as well as culture. Indeed, the frangipani flower is Walcott's image for Caribbean literature itself: "what delight and privilege there was in watching a literature . . . bud and open island after island in the early morning of a culture, not timid, not derivative, any more than the hard petals of the frangipani are derivative and timid" ("The Antilles" 73). In its dormant season, the frangipani presents a peculiarly ugly leaflessness, with homely looking gray branches, but even when leaved it is not in its full glory. Its sap is disturbingly viscous. The beauty of the frangipani is in its stiff, slightly satiny flowers, perhaps white or pink or apricot, richly fragrant, but notoriously reluctant to be cut and made into a house decoration. This tree has learned how to survive a tough environment for a flowering shrub, which mostly includes by turns too much hot sun and too little rain as well as a thin and parched soil. It is a native of central America, a kind of botanical neighbor, not included in Jamaica Kincaid's list of plants imported to the Caribbean from far away (among which are hibiscus, flamboyant, casuarina, mango, tamarind, and of course breadfruit), all staples of the Caribbean garden and park (Kincaid *My Garden (Book)*: 135).

So how does this plant assist Walcott to convey his sense of the growth of Caribbean literature? On an obvious level, the first writers had as encouragement only the sparse examples of local writing in the colonial period and the overlay of colonial literary culture, the parallel of poor soil. Those who did not go overseas to find audience, Walcott among them, had to deal with a difficult climate for writing, where scribal literature was not bought or read by the majority of people. The expected flowers that resulted, the first canonical works, Walcott likens to the frangipani flower on two counts, originality and courage. Thus he uses local Caribbean knowledge of flora to enhance the reader's understanding that the way flora have learned to deal with their environment in the Caribbean is comparable to ways Caribbean writers have refused to be defeated by inhospitable circumstances. The frangipani also suggests a strategy for survival in colonialism, through its quiet, self-strengthening inertia for part of each year, which is part of its stubborn refusal to be eradicated by adversity.

In *Tiepolo's Hound* (2000), plants are often arranged in clusters to display them more emphatically, by the use of rhyme, assonance, and alliteration: "The gommier in flower did not mimic the dogwood / Or snow at the roots of white cedar, or Queen Anne's lace, // an apple orchard, or April's autumnal firewood; / they were, like the breadfruit, true to their sense of place." (92) It should be noticed that these are plants from both temperate and tropical climates, once more referencing plants in relation to movement and relocation. Some commonplace nouns and adjectives that generically denote flora (such as "green," "grass," "trees," "forests," "leaves"), draw attention by sustained repetition. In *Omeros* (1990), we can track a long list of leaves of various kinds, often simply left unspecified, though sometimes named (for example, "grape," "yam," "black"). Leaves have a metapoetic quality as in the leaves of a book, so their prevalence helps to connect Walcott's poetics and the life of the environment which inspires it. In *Tiepolo's Hound*, his lines have usually between ten and twelve syllables, but the tone is relaxed and conversational as he employs his own adaptation of European couplets, just as in *Omeros*, he utilized his own version of triplet stanzas, vaguely reminiscent of Dante's *terza rima*. The couplets make *Tiepolo's Hound* run along quite quickly, especially given the presence of repetition and rhyme, but Walcott avoids the closure of the heroic couplet, both in terms of rhyme and regular meter. He does employ an occasional interlocking rhyme (abab). When we consider this alongside the clustering of plants in the poem, we can see parallel demonstrations of ebullient energies of growth defying the gardener/poet's control. Walcott's Caribbean imagination uses but is not contained by European poetics, any more than plants translated from one climate zone cultural environment to another can be the same as they were originally.

Walcott's imagery is sometimes fantastical, so that the reader is stopped by the effort of trying to imagine. The flow of the poetry is interrupted while the reader tries to imagine what can be slightly sinister or at least unsettling or almost unbelievable. There are many examples, but a few will suffice (all from *Collected Poems*). They range from vividly original but directly imaginable, such as "the wood's crude hair" (5), bougainvillea thorns "moult like old fingernails," (156), the leaf "insists on its oval echo." (197), to the really elaborate, as when a "serpentine" mangrove sapling has roots like a hand with six fingers, and clutches, among other things, a toad (59). In *The Arkansas Testament* (1987), we find "gusty wicks / of black sea grapes" (3). Soldiers have "the sugar-apples / of grenades growing on their belts" ("The Hotel Normandie Pool," *Collected Poems* 443).

Paul de Man's discussion of John Locke's condemnation of "mixed modes," or abuse of language, is relevant here:

> [abuse of language is] itself the name of a trope: catachresis . . . capable of inventing the most fantastic entities by dint of the positional power inherent in language. . . . Something monstrous lurks in the most innocent of catachreses: when one speaks of the legs of a table or the face of the mountain, catachresis is already turning into prosopopoeia, and one begins to perceive a world of potential ghosts and monsters. (De Man, "The Epistemology of Metaphor" 19)

Locke was condemning of catachresis, thinking, as de Man shows, that it resulted in chimeras being substituted for true knowledge (19), and de Man also seems at root suspicious of an aesthetic that allows itself to be overgrown, much as Eve in Milton's *Paradise Lost* worried about plants becoming too overgrown and escaping the control of pruning.[19] But for Walcott, accepting that nature is at times not under human control is an act of not only resistance to colonial control but an affirmation of inventive and subversive energies. At the other extreme from outlandishly unusual metaphors, he pointedly revives dead metaphors using plants, such as "leaves were paper" (*Collected Poems* 6), reminding us how long people have intertwined plants and human activities. Then he can stretch a familiar comparison almost pedantically, "the sound / of papers" is "shuffled by an inquiry / into the parasitism of poetry by the dry-lipped leaves" (*The Prodigal* 38). For like vegetation, language can be overgrown, withered, lush, fragile or full of new life, conventional, repetitive, or newly apprehended despite familiarity.

A further development of this is Walcott being distractingly metapoetic, which makes more sense when we think of the way language can become overgrown, shapeless, feeding on its own energies, producing a dysfunctional effect: examples include "vines of syntax" (*Collected Poems*, 116), "spreading lianas of syntax" (119), and "bitter almonds of consonants" (14). In *The Prodigal* (2004), small farms are "conjugating Horace" (17) and olive trees are "as twisted as Ovid's syntax" (17). Poetry is aligned with a plant that washes up from the ocean like some perpetual traveler who writes, "a universal metre / piles up these signatures like inscriptions of seaweed" (*The Bounty* 11). Playfully, but also seriously, in "The Castaway," Crusoe is a writer who iconoclastically destroys what has become too familiar and safe, imaged via plants: "Godlike, annihilating godhead, art / And self, I abandon / Dead metaphors: the almond's leaf-like heart, // The ripe brain rotting like a yellow nut" (*Collected Poems* 58).

Through his poetic use of plants, Walcott teaches not only a sensitivity to their presence in the Caribbean and elsewhere but their ethical role in a world scarred by violent histories. By means of an aesthetic approach to the ecology of plants, Walcott glosses Coleridge's sense of the organic nature of poetry by reminding us that like a poem a postcolonial environment might be degraded but proves resilient and vibrant. Within the poetry that seeks to praise a damaged world, there will be failures, formal and ethical, as well as the risk of facile betrayals of the harsh complexities of the aftermath of colonial degradation and facile representations of the joy of each morning as the Caribbean awakes. There will be excesses, too, like metaphors that embrace catechresis or unlikely survivals, or metaphors that are coaxed back from the dead, like an abused plant that lies dormant and then surprisingly produces new shoots. In light of the hope such accidents signify, Walcott's ecopoetics encourages us to embrace failure (both deliberate and incidental) as much as we hope and work for achievement. This element of chance and unpredictable change is fundamental to nature, and confronting it makes poetry emotionally honest and rigorous: only such a poetry can be of any use in pursuing the goal of inspiring readers with a deeper commitment to save a potentially dying earth.

NOTES

1. Lawrence Buell rightly points out how much self-deception exists in the love of nature in the United States, where it "calls us to think ecocentrically" but at the same time encourages "the readerly temptation to cordon off scenery into pretty ghettoes" (4).

2. She argues that literary studies are constantly being rethought in our time, as are the terms associated with ecological approaches to literature (ecopoetics, ecocritical, green cultural studies, and so on) (xx). Poetics can be used broadly, to signify *poeisis*, as Terry Threadgold determines, "a making" (*Feminist Poetics* 1) not just of poetry but of the performance of a critique of texts, or it can signify the nature of poetic technique in the writing of poetry. It is the latter meaning that I use here.

3. Casid brilliantly shows how what happened in the colonies and on the plantations also became an important part of British culture at home. In her chapter on "imperial picturesque," she discusses the attempt to "transplant and transvalue a West Indian fortune back into an idyllic vision of England's green and rolling hills," namely through the example of the Harewood estate in Yorkshire, owned by the first Baron Harewood, born in Barbados, an investor in the slave trade (53). This is pertinent to the discussion later of Walcott's inclusion of temperate and tropical flora: his vision of both poetry and flora understand the deeply interconnectedness of imperial colony and imperial center, and the cultures that developed from them both over time.

4. Frank Taylor's *To Hell with Paradise* (1993) is a history of the tourist industry in Jamaica that establishes a direct connection between mores established on the plantation, such as slaves/servants who were pleasant to visitors, and the mores of the contemporary tourist industry.

5. Derek Walcott commented to George Handley that the construction of the Hilton Jalousie Hotel between the Pitons in St. Lucia was a complex political issue, because local people needed jobs, but he also felt that something "spiritual" should be left for St. Lucians, for the Pitons seem like a sacred space (Handley, "The Argument of the Outboard Motor" 129).

6. The editors draw attention to the colonial legacies of the Caribbean facilitating writers' perceptions of their own limitations, so that "nature's dynamism" is more apparent: thus ecocritical approaches to Caribbean literature should identify that dynamism and thus strengthen resistance to environmental indifference (*Caribbean Literature and the Environment* 28). This sense of limitations is relevant to my later argument that Walcott takes risks with his poetic achievement in order to avoid controlling either nature or his own cultural work.

7. Drayton's remarkable book, *Nature's Government*, began my interest in ecocriticism, because in its outstanding scholarship, it expresses in detail how the history of plant migrations and domestication and the history of human migrations (forced and voluntary) are deeply intertwined. He explores the coming of

industrial agricultural techniques in England as well as the "improving" of the empire via Kew Gardens.

8. See, for example, the role of plants and their fruits in Mrs Carmichael's anti-emancipation account of Caribbean plantation life (*Domestic Manners and Social Condition of the White. Coloured and Negro Populations of the West Indies* 1833). Her close observations of flora serve to try to establish readerly trust in her highly distorted rendition of slavery on the plantation.

9. John Milton's *Paradise Lost* is a foundational example, for Milton's descriptions of the Garden of Eden and of the gardening of Adam and Eve are remarkably detailed: "The roof / of thickest covert was inwoven shade, / Laurel and myrtle, and what higher grew / Of firm and fragrant leaf. On either side / Acanthus and each odorous bushy shrub / Fenced up the verdant wall. Each beauteous flower, / Iris all hues, roses and jessamine / Reared high their flourished heads . . ." (*Paradise Lost*, ed. Teskey, Book Four, 96). It is Eve's anxiety that the garden may become "wanton," "Tending to wild" (202) that leads her to argue that they should work in separate places so as not to distract each other from toil during the day: this makes her vulnerable to the serpent.

10. See, for example, Elizabeth Nunez's *Prospero's Daughter*, in which a garden becomes an allegorical representation of the invasion of colonialism into the natural world of the Caribbean: an artificially bred flower becomes a parody of its original self, suggesting ways in which colonization distorted human identity and behavior.

11. Jamaica Kincaid has produced three books on gardening and botany, two entirely her own *My Garden (Book)*: and *Among Flowers*, an edited collection, *My Favorite Plant*. The first two map tensions between an "innocent" pleasure in gardening or plant collecting and the sinister role both have played in colonial and neocolonial history and culture.

12. "Sainte Lucie" (*Collected Poems* 309–23) is a praise poem to St. Lucia, and like many praise poems, has lists of aspects of the subject to be celebrated, including flora.

13. Walcott discusses this and the eulogy at length in an interview with William Baer (Baer "Interview"). He remarked, "The thing about eulogies and elegies is that they're sometimes suspicious because they so often focus on the person writing them than on the subject" ("Interview" 196). Usually elegies are considered poems of mourning and eulogies praise for the dead: elegies are often far more conflicted. Walcott wrote the Auden elegy in response to a request by Joseph Brodsky, who had benefited from Auden's kindness: it is not one of his best poems, though technically very accomplished.

14. Greg Garrard, *Ecocriticism*, offers a very interesting survey of critical readings of Clare's response to the environment, ranging from Raymond Williams to Bate. Garrard says that despite the fact that Williams sees Clare as "an environmentalist with leftist inclinations" and Bate sees him as a "deep ecologist," neither proves that enclosure was in fact ecologically damaging (*Ecocriticism*, 47). Clare's identification with wounded and displaced nature clearly was an extension of his own sense of being displaced and hurt by powerful class interests.

15. In recent years, gated communities have been springing up in the Caribbean, which not only shut off access to particular areas by the general populace but also greatly inflate the price of land plots, which in turn confines even the middle class to land of lower value. Governments argue that revenue from property taxes and maintenance fees provide urgently needed national income and also jobs. Issues

from the use of too much water by golf courses to the development of expensive organic food and products only for the use of affluent visitors are deeply connected to environmental concerns.

16. On the history of how this "fruit of liberty" was utilized by British planters to suppress actual slave emancipation in the Caribbean, see DeLoughrey, "Globalizing the Routes of Breadfruit and Other Bounties."

17. Reducing Walcott's plants to a list is reductive, but it does help us to understand how wide-ranging and numerous his plant references are. He includes plants, shrubs and trees, some fifteen tropical, eighteen temperate, seven ubiquitous (like onions or vines), twenty-four useful to humans as fruits, vegetables, aromatic leaves, and a couple that represent stubborn survival in harsh conditions (such as sea grape).

18. Also called June plum, dunks originates in the Pacific but is much loved in the Caribbean, especially by children. The late Alfred Pragnell, Barbadian performer of monologues and dialogues, termed tea made by pouring boiling water on fresh garden herbs "we tea" and the imported tea from England (breakfast, Earl Grey etc.), "white people tea." Bush teas are metonymic of cultural survivals, means by which slaves and indentured laborers sustained collective memory in the face of colonialism's desire to erase it. Bush teas also played a critical role in societies where the poor were mostly excluded from Western health care offered to whites.

19. Eve makes a major speech to Adam, persuading him to let them work separately in the Garden. This not only gives Eve an elevated sense of her own powers of persuasion, but provides the serpent with a perfect opportunity to practice his own, and so recruit her to his design. Eve's reason for making her argument is her worry that the Garden is too much for herself and Adam to keep under control: ". . . what we by day/Lop overgrown or prune or prop or bind/One night or two with wanton growth derides,/ Tending to wild . . ." (*Paradise Lost*, ed. Teskey, Book Nine, 202).

PART II

FOREST FICTIONS

4

Deforestation and the Yearning for Lost Landscapes in Caribbean Literatures

Lizabeth Paravisini-Gebert

Early descriptions of the West Indies speak of a region of exotic and bounteous beauty, with its profusion of dense tropical forests, abundance of fresh water, and diverse and wondrous fauna. The notion of the Caribbean as new Eden, drawn from biblical and classical iterations of the *locus amoenus*,[1] found its earliest expression in Christopher Columbus's own letters and ship logs, where he describes the islands as "most beautiful, of a thousand shapes," noting, above all, how they were "filled with trees of a thousand kinds and tall, so that they seem to touch the sky" (Columbus). For sailors like Columbus, accustomed to an increasingly deforested Europe, the densely wooded islands of the Caribbean recalled a primeval, pre-Adamic world. The encounters with wild landscapes seemingly little altered by man, along with the variety and abundance of new plant species, meant that the region entered the European imaginary as a virginal space vulnerable to "colonisation by an ever-expanding and ambitious imaginative symbolism" (Grove *Green Imperialism* 5). Embracing the "cultured nature" they found in the Indies as a "natural landscape," as Emanuele Amodio explains, the conquistadors "naturalized" the environment they found, an assumption that allowed them to claim the land without due recognition of prior indigenous rights.

At the center of this "naturalized landscape" were the region's ostensibly inexhaustible forests. "Before sugar, before tobacco, before livestock," Manuel Moreno Fraginals has argued, "precious woods were the very symbol of the Far Antilles" (quoted in Funes Monzote 20). The history of how these once dense forests moved from abundance to scarcity can be traced through the development of Caribbean literatures. From a very early stage in the development of the region's literature, its writers have explored the relationship between colonialism and the environment, unveiling the threat posed by continued colonial exploitation. Historically, Caribbean writing has continuously addressed "rather than belatedly discovered, its commitment to the environment, reiterating its insistence on the inseparability of current crises of ecological mismanagement from historical legacies of imperialistic exploitation and authoritarian abuse" (Huggan "Green Post-Colonialism" 702). This is a point also argued by Elizabeth DeLoughrey, Renée Gosson, and George Handley in their introduction to *Caribbean Literature and the Environment*, where they write that "unlike the white settler culture of nature writing, Caribbean writers refuse to depict the natural world in terms that erase the relationship between landscape and power" (4). In the work of these writers, the fate of the Caribbean forests—as they move from fertile symbols to dwindling realities—is inextricably linked to colonialism and its metaphors. It stands for the environmental burden colonialism has placed on the islands of the Caribbean and points to the challenges facing the region's island nations as they confront the compromised deforested environments that have been one of the chief legacies of colonialism.

My analysis of the ways in which the literatures of the Caribbean have addressed the forests—and the waves of deforestation that came in the wake of the Columbian encounter—underscores their centrality to any discussion of environmental colonialism in the region. As Vandana Swami writes about the history of forestry in colonial India, the fate of the forests can serve as "more than a subtext" in the narrative of the consolidation of power in colonial societies—it can "itself enable a reassessment of the nature of imperial power" and "provide insights into issues of wider historical significance" (Swami 118). The discussion that follows explores a number of recurring approaches and themes: the connection between the forests and notions of indigeneity throughout the Caribbean basin; the related theme of the immersion in the forests as the means of recovering a cultural authenticity that was lost on contact with the plantation; the idealization of the plot system of agriculture (especially of the small farm on the edge of the forest or bush) as an alternative to the plantation system; the threat that deforestation during the colonial period poses to present-day Caribbean nations; and the importance of the forests as symbols and realities in postindependence national formations. These themes underscore a central focus of postcolonial environmentalism—that the social and political framework of colonial administration was anchored in the assumption that the colonies' natural resources were subject to the demands of the colonial powers. The forests of the Caribbean were "the sites on which several conflicting relationships of power were enacted" (Swami 124) and where the violence of colonial environmentalism left its most profound mark. As one of the most salient casualties of colonial expansion, they emerge in the literatures of the Caribbean as both tangible presences and multivalent, protean symbols—as new Edens, as alternatives to the sugar plantation, as vital elements in environmental sustainability, as sites of indigeneity, or as ghostly remnants of ancestral presences.

The Caribbean's colonizers brought to the new world a set of cultural assumptions regarding forests, their meanings, and their uses that would impact significantly the ways in which the new territories would fare under colonial control. Michael Williams, in *Deforesting the Earth*, argues that "from the time of the first farmers, almost anywhere in the world, forests had been seen as wild and hostile, and human progress had seemed to be viewed in some proportion to the amount of woodland cleared, or at least used" (145). In the Caribbean, the preference for cleared, usable land was linked to prevailing European notions of economic profit in an age of mercantilistic expansion. Sailing into the interior of Guiana in 1594 through what he feared were endlessly dense and forbidding forests, Sir Walter Raleigh saves his delight for his first encounter with extensive grassy plains: "On both sides of the river, we passed the most beautiful countrie that ever mine eies beheld . . . plaines of twenty miles in length, the grasse short and greene, and in divers parts groves of trees by themselves, as if they had been by all the art and labour in the world so made of purpose" (Raleigh 57). Raleigh's culture-bound appreciation of a natural beauty that appears created by "art and labour" is not only an expression of English aesthetic sensibilities *vis à vis* the landscape, but voiced an impulse to reform the landscape by turning it into a space of agricultural production that recreated the known British model.

Between British expansionism and this potential for exploitation stand not only the forests, which emerge from the descriptions in Raleigh's *The Discovery of Guiana* as dark, eerie spaces into which his men venture gingerly, but those very indigenous inhabitants who the "naturalization" of the landscape sought to erase. His sensitivity to landscape rooted in British agrarian economy, Raleigh cannot intuit the importance of the forest as a habitat and place of refuge to indigenous peoples and native fauna in the way, for example, that we find in the writings of Bartolomé de Las Casas. Las Casas, who arrived in the Indies in 1502, wrote in his *A Short Account of the Destruction of the Indies* of how those among the Taíno Indians of the Antilles "who could flee would seek refuge in the forests or climb to the mountains to escape the Spanish soldier's inhumanity" (Las Casas 19). His account recognizes that as early as the first decade of the sixteenth century, the need to control the indigenous population had joined the pursuit of profit as an important motivation for the clearing of the Caribbean's forests. His writings are imbued with his apprehension that full control of the colonies—which meant "that the world was to be used and its products could be exploited, sold, and traded" (Grove *Green Imperialism* 144)—required an ecological revolution of the "natural" landscape. As Beth Fowkes Tobin argues in *Colonizing Nature*, "the vast plantations devoted to the monoculture of sugar in the Caribbean and

Pacific, and the cotton, tea, and indigo estates of India not only transformed these regions but also radically altered their populations through genocidal policies and the massive movements of people from one region of the globe to the another" (10).

The forests "discovered" in the Caribbean region had already been impacted by the indigenous population, but the newcomers' arrival would bring radical and irrevocable changes to the environment. Françoise Hatzenberger argues convincingly that "with the European conquest, humans become an important factor in the (Caribbean) environment" (66). The assault on the Caribbean forests was a major contributor to the ecological revolution—the "abrupt and qualitative break with the process of environmental and social change that had developed *in situ*" (Melville 12)—that followed the colonization process. Portions of the coastal forests were cleared to establish settlements, as well as for fuel and ship repairs. As the first century of the European conquest progressed, wood was used in large quantities for the construction and repair of the fleets that moved goods and people between the Latin American mainland, the Caribbean, Africa, North America, and Europe. Land quickly began to be cleared for the planting of provisions to feed a growing population, and the forest fauna came under pressure from the intensification of hunting. The forest ecology was transformed within years of the arrival of the Spaniards in many of the Caribbean islands by the release of hundreds of pigs meant to assure that the Europeans would have plenty of protein available on return trips. With the dawn of the seventeenth century, shipments of precious woods to Europe grew frequent as West Indian woods became prized materials for the construction of the palaces and manor houses of those involved in the Indies trade. Exports of Brazilian wood, coveted for their red dye, Mauro Agnoletti reported, "reduced the coastal forests of this species to a very small area by the 18th century" (15). Despite an early recognition of the role the mangroves played in the organization of the islands' defenses, mangroves were cleared to expand ship landing facilities and trees were debarked for tanning extracts, a procedure that killed extensive portions of mangrove forests.

By far the greatest damage to the forests, however, was done by the development of the plantation economy. Throughout the Caribbean, coastal mahogany forests were completely cleared to make room for sugarcane plantations. In Haiti, coffee plantations were created "on previously forested territories" whose rapid deforestation led to "the destruction of certain tree species" (Agnoletti 15). Timber was used for housing and for the daily fuel requirements of the boiling machines in the sugar mills, which led to endemic species becoming scarce as early as the mid-seventeenth century. The assault on the forests can be measured in terms of biodiversity losses that have led to the disappearance of countless species in the region, which so far number in the hundreds. Such was the environmental impact of the production of sugar in the region that by the time Aphra Behn visited the English colony of Surinam in 1663, the geographies of Caribbean territories were clearly divided between plantations that were home to colonists and enslaved Africans and forests that remained the embattled domain of those among the indigenous populations to have survived the violence and epidemiological assault of the European encounter.

Behn's months in Surinam coincided with what has been called "the Great Clearing," the period between 1650 and 1665, marked by devastating deforestation throughout the British and French Caribbean that resulted in significant soil erosion and "the scarcity and high price of timber for construction and fuel wood, particularly for refining the sugar" (Williams *Deforesting* 102). Behn novelized the events she had witnessed during her sojourn in the Royalist colony in *Oroonoko*, published in 1688. The geography of Behn's novel reflects the history of the development of the plantation economy in British-held territories in the first half of the seventeenth century. Behn underscores the historic interdependence between the plantation and the forest-dwelling indigenous inhabitants who "supply us with that 'tis impossible for us to get" (12) and are therefore vital to the Europeans' survival. She, however, also recognizes that their continued control of the forests is threatened by their having "an intrinsic value above common timber; for they are, when cut, of different colors, glorious to behold, and bear a price considerable, to inlay withal" (51). The forests also represent a psychologically liminal terrain that the indigenous people navigate easily but which remains as much a barrier to the cowardly European soldiers that support Governor Byam in the text as it had seemed to Raleigh's men. Of those dwelling on the plantation side, only the African protagonist Oroonoko and his wife Imoinda embrace the forest as offering an approximation to a return to Africa, a transitional space onto a death they embrace as their only escape.

By the time of Behn's visit to Surinam, descriptions of the Caribbean had shifted from broad depictions of *the islands* as generic paradise to island-specific accounts, underscoring not only shifts in European sovereignty over the territories but the first glimmers of a Creole consciousness that begins to assess colonial policies in terms of how they use or abuse the colony's environment. Such is the case of the 1647 "*Descripción de la Isla de Puerto Rico*," a proto-literary text by a Catholic prebendary, Diego de Torres Vargas, a native of the island and the first to express in writing his *criollo* pride in its beauty and the density of its forests. In his *Descripción*, the young writer exults in the richness and variety of the island's wood preserves, equating them with the land's identity as a self-contained natural and political space. His concern for the preservation of the local forests offers one of the earliest indications of a developing region-wide concern— that of a coherent region-wide acknowledgment of the problems posed by environmental degradation. Although the earliest Spanish legislation for the protection of mangroves and forests dates from the beginning of the eighteenth century, observations of microclimate changes, erosion, and reductions in the supply of fresh water had already been noted in the mid-seventeenth century. As Richard Grove argues in *Green Imperialism*, the "full flowering of what one might term the Edenic island discourse during the mid-seventeenth century closely coincided with the realization that the economic demands of colonial rule over ... island colonies threatened their imminent and comprehensive degradation" (5).

For Torres Vargas, writing from an island that was still marginal to the plantation economy, the Puerto Rican forests, dense and rich, represent a complex space, penetrable and rich in possibilities, both botanical and cultural. In his text, he is responding to new assessments of the utility of the forests that stemmed from medical expeditions like that of Francisco Hernández in 1570, which revealed a "living forest" that contained indigenous people with knowledge of "vegetable substances" that could treat medical problems and edible fruits and vegetables unknown to newcomers. Some of these representations of the forests, as Amodio has argued, "derived their identification from a complex system of representations, in which the forest was seen as a place inhabited by protective spirits" (56). "This 'living forest' and its associated spirits," as Amodio explains, "were not very different from those imagined by the Spanish peasants, who also believed in spiritual guardians of the forests and of the springs" (56). Torres Vargas, moreover, belonged to a peasant culture that had already witnessed its first religious miracle: a child had been lost in the woods, "which in that part of the island are most dense and frightfully steep," and when found reported "that a woman had given her to eat during all that time, pampering and caressing her like a mother, whom we understood to be Our Lady of Montserrat, to whom her father was devoted" (185–86). Torres Vargas's miracle underscores the social and economic realities of the relationship between the Puerto Rican peasantry and the woods in the mid-seventeenth century, when the islands had lost their centrality in Spain's colonial enterprise, and large numbers of colonizers had resettled in the mainland. Subordinated to a peripheral way station for the Spanish fleet, the island had developed a subsistence economy in which the peasantry lived on small farms on the edge of the forests. Villagers like those of Hormigueros, where the miracle occurs, lived on the crops they planted, which they supplemented with fruit and game from the surrounding forests. Hormigueros, moreover, was then a village settled on the site of Horomico, an earlier Taíno village that, according to archeological remains, dated back to 820 B.C.—an ideal space for the syncretism of cultural elements Amodio describes. The creolized Catholicism that had evolved amidst this peasant population, syncretized with Amerindian practices as Spanish and Taíno populations intermarried, offered a blend of animism and the miraculous, both elements that Torres Vargas reflects in the narratives he inserts in his *Descripción*. His "miraculous" narrative offers the reader an entry into the central role of the forests in a different type of agrarian development than that represented by the plantation.

Los infortunios de Alonso Ramírez, by Carlos de Sigüenza y Góngora, published in 1690, evidences a similar affirmation of Creole identity. The testimonial narrative of a young man who circumnavigates the world, as narrated to Sigüenza y Góngora, it opens with what is perhaps the earliest pronouncement of a Puerto Rican nationhood in literature: "My name is Alonso Ramírez and my country is the city of San Juan de Puerto Rico, capital of the island" (Buscaglia-Salgado). Ramírez disassociates his narrative from that of the *locus amoenus* of the encounter narratives, underscoring instead the travails of the local population in their struggle to escape the lives mired in poverty of which Torres Vargas had written just a few decades earlier. In *Los infortunios*, as José Buscaglia Salgado argues, "the island world is not . . . the placeless site where the ideal is shaped in the most elaborate moral or utopian versions of the (nation) state, or the space of adventure where the human condition is defined from the perspective of a European subject who has free reign of action in an exotic realm. . . . Quite the contrary, in the *Misfortunes* the island, specifically the fortified harbor town of San Juan, is a very real place that holds no promise and that must be fled at the earliest possible age. It is as if the island placed a curse on the native-born" (Buscaglia-Salgado).

The "curse" Buscaglia Salgado identifies in the text is linked by its narrator to two environment-related concerns; the depopulation of the island, which Torres Vargas had already identified as linked to war, epidemics, and the departure of so many of its inhabitants to the mainland, and the natural hazards to which the island forests were vulnerable, both its virginal woods and its domesticated species: "The wealth . . . today has been transformed into poverty, due to the absence of the original inhabitants to work them, and because of the force with which the tempestuous hurricanes cleared the cacao trees that in the absence of gold provided those engaged in the business, and consequently the rest of the islanders, with the bare necessities" (Buscaglia-Salgado). His allusion to the cacao trees is particularly significant in our context, as it confirms Torres Vargas's assessment of the role of the forests in the peasants' ability to eke out a living through sustainable farming in the unfortunate colony. As an understory tree, cacao grows best within the overhead shade provided by the forests and as a cash crop was ideally suited to the symbiotic relationship between subsistence farming and the woods on which the peasantry depended for their livelihood before the widespread entrenchment of the plantation.

In the eighteenth-century histories and descriptions of the islands that pave the way for the emergence of a Creole literature in the Caribbean in the nineteenth century, the narrative of the domestication and planting of cacao for profit—which Ramírez highlights as central to the seventeenth-century Puerto Rican economy—will parallel that of the destructive intensification of sugar cultivation in the region. As we enter the eighteenth century, sugar moves into the ascendancy while cacao is pushed to the fringes of commercial production. In the highly profitable sugar-producing colony of St. Domingue, for example, it was relegated to being planted "in the middle of the forests, in the interior," whereas in Martinique it was grown on cleared forest lands on steep hills unsuitable for the cultivation of sugar (Clarence-Smith 121). The marginalization of cacao also signals the loss of the possibilities it opened to indigenous peoples, smallholders, freed slaves, and people of mixed race to incorporate themselves into the life of commercial agrarian development as an alternative to the plantation (Clarence Smith 129–131).

These tensions between a commercial crop that grew within the protection of the forests and the deforestation needed for the growth of the sugar plantation becomes a thematic strain in the histories and descriptions of the islands in which we begin to glean the foundations of Creole literary traditions, as it does in Père Labat's *Nouveau voyage aux isles de l'Amerique*. In his memoirs, Labat finds himself straddling the vanishing world of the indigenous inhabitants and the developing world of the plantation. It is a struggle waged against the backdrop of the Caribbean's disappearing forests, as we see most clearly in his discussion of the culture and habits of the Caribs in Martinique and Dominica and the inroads of plantation development in Barbados. Labat's voyage through the Caribbean takes place between 1693 and 1705, several decades after "the Great Clearing" and at a time when climate changes and species extinctions associated with deforestation had already begun to be registered. Labat records both the growing human presence encroaching on the forest reserves and the price exacted from nature and the indigenous population in the form of habitat losses and vanishing species of trees and fauna. In Labat's narrative, the sustainability of Carib culture is connected as much to the surrounding plenty as to the small size of their communities. With villages located primarily on the coast or alongside rivers, seventeenth-century indigenous communities had put little strain on the island's forests. However, at the time of Labat's writing, the Caribs had joined the ranks of the endangered species in Martinique, and he writes poignantly of visiting "the last Carib carbet remaining in Martinique." Their rapid disappearance is portrayed in the text against the growing number of African slaves that accompanied the development of the plantation. Of Barbados he writes that "the number of black slaves in the island is very great. I was told that there are more than 60,000. . . . This is a large number for so small an island" (126).[2] Labat's text offers a snapshot of a Caribbean in flux. As the disappearing forests take with them the region's original inhabitants, attention shifts to the struggle against the plantation, which will be waged, not by the remnants of the indigenous populations, but by those among the newcomers who "go native" and find in their Creole identity the resolve to defend their environment against the forces of colonialism.

We see this emerging Creolité most clearly in José Martín Félix de Arrate y Acosta's *Llave del Nuevo Mundo* (*Key to the New World* 1761), where it is linked to a literary celebration of the environmental richness of his native Cuba. It is also linked to an implicit project for the conservation of this diversity against the forces of the Spanish empire, which, deep into the eighteenth century, seek to move toward a mono-crop system, following the successful example of the French and British Caribbean colonies. The focus of his text, which he expects will be read by Crown officials in Spain, is to underscore the difference, diversity, and implied self-sufficiency and sustainability of the island as an environmental system different from that of Spain. His text is both a description and a boast of an enviable abundance that is the foundation for a proto-national identification, of an expression of an incipient *cubanía* that will begin the separation (of which twentieth-century Cuban anthropologist Fernando Ortiz will write in *Cuban Counterpoint*) between producers of sugar living in the deforested plains and those able to plant and profit—yet still conserve and live—on the edge of the abundance and protection of the forests, planting cacao, coffee, and tobacco. Arrate, in his effort to emphasize this difference, establishes a clear distinction between these lands of natural abundance and the "tierras de labor" (literally, "lands of labor," or plantations that require a labor force) that produce "besides tobacco and sweet cane, which are the most useful crops, a profusion of manioc, sweet potatoes, ginger, corn, rice, cocoa and coffee." In his narrative, Arrate implies the existence of three distinct groups in Cuban society—all with a different relationship to the landscape: the Spaniards who have brought irreversible changes to the landscape in the form of new crops and animals; the *isleños*, or islanders (the peasantry that represents both Spanish and indigenous ethnicities), whom he sees as belonging to the landscape in an especially authentic way as they live off the bounty of the forests and sea; and those like him—upper-class and Cuban-born but not indigenous—inextricably connected to a new definition of the landscape, seeking to profit from the landscape without altering it inexorably.

Arrate wrote with an understanding that although Cuba was moving rapidly toward capital intensive plantation agriculture, which would form the basis of its path toward nationhood, this type of agriculture, "based on slave labour, promoted very rapid environmental change in terms of deforestation and subsequent soil erosion, flooding, gullying, local aridification and drying up of the streams and rivers" (Grove "The Culture of Islands"). The experience of Spanish and Portuguese sugar producers in early cane plantations in the Canary Islands and Madeira was that these islands "were devastated in this way by the effects of deforestation for sugar cultivation as early as the fifteenth century" (Grove "The Culture of Islands"). This potential devastation was also evident, as far as the Caribbean region itself was concerned, in the writings of Martinican historian Médéric Louis Élie Moreau de Saint-Méry in his two books on Hispaniola, *Description topographique, physique, civile, politique et historique de la partie française de l'isle Saint Domingue* and *Description topographique et politique de la partie espagnole de l'isle Saint-Domingue*, published in 1796. Moreau de Saint-Méry's texts offer the most comprehensive account of the impact of the intensification of sugar production on a Caribbean island in the eighteenth century. His text chronicles the impact of deforestation on threatened or vanishing species and is particularly eloquent on the nature and fate of the forests of Hispaniola, noting not only their beauty and "inexhaustible fecundity" but also the forces that threaten their very inexhaustibility. "Their utility is proved by continual experience, though their distance from the places where they might be advantageously employed, is often the cause of their remaining in tranquility" (31). Moreover, he explicitly notes the environmental impact of the island's too-rapid deforestation, especially on the intensification of soil erosion and the reduction in rain levels. In Haiti, the French colonists "who have aided these depredations by the cultivation of coffee, and by a system which counts the time to come as nothing," he writes, "have cut down even the trees that covered the summits of the mountains and attracted the rains, insomuch that a diminution of the rains is now perceivable in the French part, where they were formerly very considerable and regular" (20).

Moreau de Saint-Méry's observations on the state of the forests of Hispaniola are of particular interest here because of the backdrop they offer to one of the most salient literary traditions in Haiti—that of the celebration of the beauty and extension of the island's deep forests, which becomes an essential element in the development of the national literature following the revolution. It is a thematic strand that emerges in Haitian poetry from the earliest literary efforts in the nineteenth century and includes a rich vein of poetry on the topic of Haiti's "musician trees." Alcibiade Fleury-Battier, in his *Sous Les Bambous: Poésies* (1881), writes of how he "love[s] the deep forests quivering with the songs / of those winged bards we mistook for flowers" (32) and celebrates Haiti's centuries-old *mapous*, sacred trees of Haitian Vodou, in a poem in French that includes lines in Haitian Creole. Likewise, Massillon Coicou, the novelist, poet, dramatist, and politician executed in 1908, writes in the poem "Vents et Flots" about Haiti's musical trees: "his path / vibrates, in endless hymns, the wild music / of the trees, of the birds, of all the voices / that make up the dazzling fanfare of the forest" (Coicou 95). This love for the forests and delight in the coolness of its groves and musical quality of their presence stands in dramatic contrast to the rapid disappearance of the trees that Haitian novelists like Jacques Roumain or Marie Chauvet will mourn in the twentieth century.

Throughout the nineteenth century, the idealization of the diminishing forest environment in the emerging literatures of the Caribbean responds to Romantic sensibilities and the adaptation of European models that turned the forests into highly symbolic spaces. Romanticism was linked—especially in Haiti and the Hispanic Caribbean—to processes of national definition in islands that had already gained their independence in the early nineteenth century and were, literally, postcolonial (such as Haiti and the Dominican Republic) or were engaged in protracted ideological battles against continued colonial control and functioned as pre-independent political spaces (such as Cuba and Puerto Rico). In the literatures of these islands, the celebration of the forests as significant national spaces acknowledges their symbolic role in preserving the integrity of the nation (or proto-nation), a role based on an acknowledgment of scientific notions of climate change and land preservation. It is true that many Caribbean writers of the nineteenth century, most of them emerging from the Creole elites, "naturalized" the social and ecological landscape of the plantation, waxing nostalgic about the flower of the sugarcane tree (as Puerto Rican poet José Gautier Benítez does in his 1879 poem "Puerto Rico") or returning to old notions of the forest as the mysterious environment for Obeahmen, healers, or Vodou spirits.[3] It is also true, however, that this "naturalization" was in the service of identifying the developing national character with notions of the indigenous or autochthonous in which the "primeval" forest stands for a precolonial space of "national" authenticity.

The importance of the forests in the discourse of national and cultural formation in the Caribbean is most clearly seen in the twentieth century, as the islands begin to articulate the parameters of their postindependence identities. They also begin to measure the forests in terms of what natural resources have survived the colonial onslaught, looking environmentally at how the remaining woods fit into the overall pattern of national development—economically as well as culturally. This process is evident most clearly in Haiti, where the literary role of the forests moves from the depiction as places of reflection and inspiration (the poet's *locus amoenus* with its musician trees) to the symbols for the rapacious nature of the postindependence exploitation hoisted on the Haitian people by the alliance between foreign powers and the local elites. Following the 1914–36 U.S. Occupation, the intensified destruction of the Haitian forests becomes the most serious threat to the viability of the nation. Haiti's forests, already depleted for lumber to be sold in the international market in the early twentieth century, have in recent decades been cut down in catastrophic numbers for the charcoal used everywhere for cooking. With forest coverage below 1.5 percent of the national territory, topsoil has been washed to sea, where it threatens marine habitats. The loss of topsoil—"as much a nonrenewable resource as oil," as Wes Jackson reminds us—has rendered large portions of the Haitian land permanently unproductive, exacerbating already serious levels of food insecurity.

The literature of Haiti has bemoaned the environmental calamity that has befallen its people, denounced the practices that led to this catastrophe, and offered inspiration and ideas for solving the nation's most central problem. It has counseled, above all, political action against exploitative governments as a path toward environmental safety, focusing on the state's inaction as evidence of the slow violence of environmental neglect. Jacques Roumain's 1944 *Gouverneurs de la rosée* (*Masters of the Dew*), Jacques-Stephen Alexis's 1957 *Les Arbres musiciens* (*The Musician Trees*), Marie Chauvet's 1968 *Amour* (from *Amour, Colère et Folie*), and Pierre Clitandre's 1979 *Cathédrale du mois d'août* (*The Cathedral of the August Heat*) all demonstrate that the Haitian novel has been, above all, a chronicle of the nation's unimaginable ecological catastrophe.

Because the Caribbean shares Haiti's history of colonial exploitation and subordinate economic development, the Haitian experience with deforestation echoes across the archipelago. As events have proven convincingly to the world that Haiti's ills could not be cured through foreign aid, investment, or technology, we have witnessed growing levels of popular engagement in local environmental movements elsewhere in the Caribbean islands, many of them led by writers, artists, and musicians ready to use their local fame and reputation in the service of stemming the tide of deforestation and environmental degradation in their home nations. Haitian concerns over the damages of deforestation are echoed, for example, in the "agrarian" poetry of noted Puerto Rican poet Juan Antonio Corretjer (1908–85), known for his celebration of the richness and diversity of Puerto Rico's mountain ecology and its history of subsistence agriculture. Corretjer wrote of his delight at entering "the moist fields with their crisp grassy greenness / through which the river traces its sinuous geometry" ("Pared de la soledad") and of penetrating forest groves where he could rub against the bark of the trees and "inhale the sacred smoke / that makes the mouth capable of prophecy" ("Yerba bruja"). His environmental activism—which evolved in the 1950s, predating by some years the similar concerns expressed by Rachel Carson in *Silent Spring* (1962)—aimed at counterbalancing the violence that had been perpetrated on the environment by American agricultural corporations, had focused on the impact of agribusiness on the island's interior. In essays, poems, and interviews he decried "the overwhelming encroachment of concrete and the use of poisonous chemicals [insecticides and synthetic fertilizers] in Puerto Rican farming" that had led not only to massive deforestation in the interior, but also to the disappearance of bird, lizard, and butterfly species that had been plentiful in the landscape of his youth and young adulthood (Ruiz Marrero).

What Corretjer's poetry unveils, in its concern for the preservation of the Puerto Rican woods, is how wedded his notion of the relationship between the Caribbean peasantry and the woods remains to the ideal of agrarian development described by both Alonso Ramírez and Diego de Torres Vargas in the seventeenth century, when the most desirable plot of land went from seashore to the wooded hills, with the planted fields providing a variety of subsistence crops to complement the protein from the sea's fish and the animals that graze at the edge of the forest.[4] This peasant ideal, present already in the earliest literary texts produced in the Caribbean region, persisted into the twentieth century through its inclusion in the "counter-plantation system" that was part of most of the region's decolonizing projects. It became the cornerstone of theories of the nation that gave root to land reform programs such as that of Governor Luis Muñoz Marín in Puerto Rico (1898–1980) and Prime Minister Eric Williams in Trinidad and Tobago (1911–1981). Williams, as Teruyuki

Tsuji has argued, expanded this idea "into a cultural theory" that made free peasant villages "autonomous of either urban-based or plantation-based colonial modes of production" the "prototypes of his imagined nation of Trinidad and Tobago" (Tsuji 1150). Williams's project involved a process of "villaging the nation" that was responsive to articulations of national identity built on the ideal symbiosis between the plot system of agriculture and the bush (see Wynter).

These processes of national formation—defined and narrated in our earliest literary texts—also proposed a more environmentally benevolent role for the Creole planter away from the cane fields and into the production of coffee, tobacco, or cacao as alternatives to the oppressive foreign-controlled sugar plantation. This redefinition of the Creole planter is explored in Enrique Laguerre's 1935 novel *La Llamarada*, a work that examines the contrasting spaces of the Creole coffee producing regions and the U.S. corporation-controlled cane fields. Its protagonist—the agronomist son of a local coffee producer who gets seduced into the patterns of exploitation of the American *central*—must be awakened from his stupor into an understanding of a just and environmentally sound alternative for the island's economic development. The novel returns us to notions of the symbiotic relationship between coffee production and forest preservation that we had found in Arrate's *Llave del Nuevo mundo* and had formed the basis of Torres Vargas's ideal of a new nation. In *La Llamarada*, the protagonist's growing awareness of the price that the island's environment had paid for its plantation development includes an acknowledgment of the problems posed by deforestation. Early in the text, when invited to a hunt, he observes the dwindling forest coverage and relates it directly to the production of sugarcane:

> Juan Pedro took us to the site of an ancient ausubo forest. There remained only a very few ausubos, a resistant and haughty tree, and, as Moreau told me, these had already been 'marked for the ax, to make way for cane.' The harsh announcement pained me, and despite my being head of production at the mill, I stared rancorously at the cane-field, with its flexible and wounding leaves, like a million swords. (58)

The concern for the island's deforestation is woven throughout the novel to the idea that the Puerto Rican peasant is "natural" to the subsistence plot cleared on the edge of the forest. The peasant "places the seed in its furrow and feels he is witnessing a religious feast," he explains, echoing the descriptions of Taíno agricultural rites described by Ramón Pané in the early sixteenth century, and therefore his "unnatural" work of the plantation is tantamount to "the chain of slavery" (137). The disillusion with the environmental consequences of the development of agribusiness throughout the Caribbean in the mid-twentieth century—of which *La Llamarada* is a salient example—is echoed in works as varied as Herbert De Lisser's *The White Witch of Rose Hall* (1928), Édouard Glissant's *La Lézarde* (1958), Juan Bosch's *Cuentos escritos en el exilio* (1962), Pedro Mir's *Hay un* país en el mundo (1949), Michelle Cliff's *Abeng* (1974), and Maryse Condé's *Traversée de la mangrove*, among numerous others.

Condé's novel portrays a community settled between the sea and the forest that has turned away from the enslavement of the cane fields to build cultural traditions centered on the woods. "Traditionally," Condé writes, "the people of Rivière du Sel worked with wood," looking among the "giants of the dense forest" for materials to build their homes—Caribbean burwood or *gommiers blancs*—or for cashews and rosewoods to make fine cabinets, or oleanders from which to carve delicate tables inlaid with magnolia" (*Traversée* 38). Condé's community is imagined as grounded in the peasantry's "natural" relationship with the trees, as we see in her character Aristide's description of the sense of peace he finds in the forest: "It was only among the big trees that he felt a sense of well-being, among the *marbri*, the big-leafed chestnut, the *gommier blanc*, the burwood, the *bois la soie* bush. He glided among their serene and silent shadows, barely pierced by the chirping of the birds" (70). In the forest he recalls how his father spoke to him of the time "before jealousy and hatred poisoned the air around them . . . when the brutal hands of man had not deflowered the trees and the forests of Guadeloupe were bursting with all sorts of birds" (70). Aristide knew about these birds from the pages of a book his father often perused with him, Père Labat's *Nouveau voyage aux Isles de l'Amerique*. Condé acknowledges, through his reference to Labat's seminal text, the priest's early realization of the losses the plantation system would bring to Guadeloupe as measured in deforestation and habitat destruction, and builds her fictional community as one anchored by the notion of a possible return to that idealized preplantation time.

Labat, in his *Nouveau voyage*, wrote of a moment when the Caribbean forests were succumbing to the push for an incipient capitalist premodernity in which the plantation represented the colony's entry into a mercantile economy. In postcolonial Caribbean literature, this symbolic relationship between the forests and modernity continues to be articulated through the representation of the forests as the "natural" domain of the indigenous or the Creole. Jean Rhys, in *Wide Sargasso Sea*, addresses this understanding of this cultural role of the forest when she immerses Rochester in the dark and (to him) hostile world of Dominica's dense forests as the means of narrating his discomfort in his Creole wife's world. The forests' capacity to exclude those not belonging to the national space has become a common motif in recent texts by Caribbean writers—it appears prominently, for example, in texts like Mayra Montero's *In the Palm of Darkness* (1995) and Eunice Richards-Pillot's *Les Terres noyées* (2006)—a development that appears to respond to the growing importance of the forests as places of reflection and leisure for Caribbean peoples as the tourist industry continues to exclude them from beaches and coastal lands.

This return to the age-old theme of the forests' capacity to exclude those who do not belong—which entered the region's literature with the earliest writings of explorers and visitors—is linked in more recent texts to that of the forest's potential for obliterating the remnants of colonial history, a subject the region's photographers and painters have rendered in response to the common sight of plantation buildings and machinery partially obliterated by the bush. Derek Walcott, in *The Prodigal*, reflects on the potential for historical amnesia in this power of the forest to erase history; he ponders what would happen "if our history [were] so rapidly enclosed / in bush, devoured by green / that there are no signals . . . and our forests shut / their mouths, sworn to ancestral silence" (99).[5]

In recent decades, as environmental concerns have moved to the forefront of social and political debates in the Caribbean region, concerns with the obliteration of the plantation have given way to the need to protect the forests from continued attack by international and local forces that see in the exploitation of the forests an opportunity for regional development. As a result, recent literature draws on the growing understanding that deforestation is the Caribbean basin's primary environmental threat. In Trinidadian writer Lakshmi Persaud's *For the Love of My Name* (2000), which follows the story of the fictional Caribbean island of Maya before it sinks beneath the sea, the text focuses on the clearing of the forests as the historical event most responsible for the nation's decline, as it has been in Haiti and threatens to be in other Caribbean nations if deforestation is not halted:

> "Hinterland Development" involved the cultivation of land cleared of its rainforest, then furrowed, its loose top soil open to the coming of the first heavy tropical rains. Our inexperienced, urban youths were being asked to repeat the destructive plunder of eighteenth and nineteenth century colonial 'developers' on tropical lands. And so it was that Maya was being governed by a system that was blind to the fact that it was digging the country's grave. (211)

Persaud's text is firmly anchored on a new understanding of the interrelation between environmental protection and economic development that has been extremely critical of continued deforestation throughout the region, focusing instead on integrative conservation approaches that rely "on the enhanced participation of local populations to achieve a sustainable management of natural resources" (Esposito 53).

This integrative conservation approach has been particularly critical of continued reliance on the use of wood as fuel for cooking or for the production of charcoal as contributing factors in the Caribbean region's postplantation deforestation. Texts like Trinidadian-born Ismith Khan's semi-autobiographical novel *The Jumbie Bird* (1985) acknowledge the centrality of coal as a source of fuel in Caribbean societies, mourning for the trees destroyed in this process. In this tale of three generations of Indian men trying to make their way from the plantation to a modest measure of financial stability, the use of a coal shop as a setting allows the young grandson to soulfully meditate on the processes through which the environment has been ravaged to sustain life on his adopted homeland:

And a feeling of sadness, of vast loneliness fell upon him as Binti raked away the fine metallic dust of coal that had come and gone. He thought of the coal men and of the silence of the jungles; he thought of the thick long vines that hung from the tall trees to the ground; he thought of the shafts of sunlight cutting through the trees; he thought of how they fell in a forest silence that no one heard; he thought of the long journey of the trees that went to coal. (184–85)

Khan's imagination integrates coal men, coal-bound trees, and the young man raking away the coal dust into one single tragedy that is personal as well as national, seeking in his sadness a way out of the cycle of coal production that can free the trees, the coal men, and himself from the ecocolonial bind in which they seem caught.[6]

The yearning for the lost forests in Caribbean literature—and the reiterated emphasis on finding a way to conserve and restore forested areas throughout the region—has as its core the possibility of recapturing the potential for a cultural maroonage that has, since the earliest texts of the region's literature, offered an alternative to colonialism in the region's imaginary. Aphra Behn's Oroonoko, the little girls in Torres Vargas's miraculous tale, Ramírez's cacao planting peasants, Arrate's Cuban Creoles, Labat's Caribs, Gómez de Avellaneda's Sab, and Laguerre's troubled agronomist are just a few of the characters who have found in the forest a symbolic space for cultural identification and national affirmation.

I started this discussion with a historical event—that of Columbus's discovery of the islands of the Antilles, a moment that initiated an assault on the forests from which the region is still struggling to recover. His "naturalization" of the deeply forested lands he "discovered" was instrumental in the attempt at dispossession of the indigenous inhabitants, many of whom appear in the pages of the books I've discussed here as ghosts of a past that seems irretrievable. I want to end with a tale of recovery and affirmation involving the remarkable forests of Surinam and Guyana, nations whose forest coverage remains the highest in the world, with 92 percent and 88 percent, respectively. The forests of Surinam and Guyana, which we first encounter in the literatures of the Caribbean in Walter Raleigh's *The Discovery of Guiana* and Aphra Behn's *Oroonoko*, were central to a precedent-breaking 1997 case involving the Saramaka people of Surinam, the descendants of the indigenous people of Behn's narrative—and of the African slaves brought to the territory to work the sugar and coffee plantations and who, like Oroonoko, fled into the forest. Since 1762, following a treaty with the Dutch colonizers, this community of maroons had been living in their state-within-a-state in the forests of Surinam. In the 1980s, however, the pressures of Surinamese development began to be felt in their territory. A civil war between maroons—among them the Saramakas—and Surinam's government led to thousands of them seeking refuge in French Guiana. Large timber and mining concessions were granted to foreign multinational corporations (Chinese, Indonesian,

Malaysian, and others) in Saramaka territory without consultation. Peace Corps volunteers descended upon the territory in numbers that threatened the cultural practices of the Saramakas. Brazilian gold miners began operating in indigenous-controlled territories, bringing prostitution, gambling, and drug smuggling to the region. The pressures led the Saramaka to submit a complaint before the Inter-American Commission of Human Rights to validate their land rights. In November 2007, in a landmark decision, the commission ruled in favor of the Saramaka people, who were granted collective rights to the lands in which their ancestors had lived since the eighteenth century, including full control over their natural resources (which in the region include timber and gold), and compensation from the Suriname government for damages caused by previous timber grants issued to foreign companies.

The continuities between the indigenous peoples we encounter in the works of Walter Raleigh and Aphra Behn, living in the deeply forested domain they controlled, and the success of the Saramakas' struggle to retain those still-forested lands, point to the symbiotic relationships established through a long history of colonial and postcolonial writings between the rights of the region's peoples and their presence in our texts. The myriad ways in which writing from and about the Caribbean has addressed its forests—whether as earthly Eden in Columbus's letters and diaries or as nightmarish absences in contemporary works like Mayra Montero's *In the Palm of Darkness*—always return to the articulation of a deep connection between the woods and what Derek Walcott, in "The Myth of History," called the indissoluble "ego of the race" (354). This connection, in an era of postcolonial environmental activism, now transcends the page, as the peoples of the Caribbean region, which astoundingly still possesses nearly a quarter of the world's extant forests, come together to defend their patrimony in the name of connections that our literatures have articulated and fostered through the centuries.

NOTES

1. The *locus amoenus*, perhaps the most familiar and typical landscape topos in the classical world, formed "the principal motif of all nature descriptions" from the Roman Empire to the sixteenth century (Barasch 309). The quintessential idyllic space, the *locus amoenus*, is an environment that includes a variety of elements—a grove of trees, a meadow, a spring or brook, birdsong, and a warm breeze.

2. Barbados, he noted, was severely deforested, a fact that a planter had noted as far back as 1653, when he wrote that "this island of Barbados cannot last in an height of trade three years longer especially for sugar, the wood being almost already spent" (quoted in Kurlansky 161).

3. See, for example, the 1827 Jamaican novel by Cynric R. Williams *Hamel, the Obeah Man* and Cuban novelist Emilio Bobadilla's 1903 work *A fuego lento* (At Low Heat).

4. This ideal forms the core of peasant aspirations in novels like Jan Carew's *Black Midas* (1962), where his gold-panning characters dream of returning to their

"natural" life of subsistence farming in the shadow of the forests. As one character comments, "I'm going to buy . . . a piece of land that will stretch from the sea to the forest and I'm going to grow coconuts and rice and ground provisions. I'm a village boy, and I know the land just like my grandpa knew it" (Carew 272).

5. On the subject of landscape and amnesia, see also DeLoughrey et al. The connection is also explored in Jan Lowe Shinebourne's *The Last English Plantation* (1988), where the trees retain the power to exclude as well as to erase a history of the plantation, as one of her characters explains as he points to the forests that have engulfed former plantations: "They used to have plenty Dutch plantation up the river. African slave rebellion and river finish them off one by one. This is the last plantation left here in Canefields" (40).

6. It is a concern echoed by Patrick Chamoiseau, in his 2002 novel *Biblique des derniers gestes*, which sets the stage for its exploration of Martinique's environmental quandary by linking the problems the island is facing to the deforestation caused by ecocolonial policies, what he calls the "deforestation caused by Progress." As a mass of clouds drops massive amounts of rain on the communities near Mont Pelée, the narrator comments that "the annoying thing about this is that, because of the deforestation caused by Progress, the water in the clouds has free rein to tear down the hills. The deluge can roll down any hillside, rushing through houses, dropping loads of mud on the most unexpected places" (19).

5

The Postcolonial Ecology of the New World Baroque

Alejo Carpentier's *The Lost Steps*

George B. Handley

In the late nineteenth and early twentieth centuries, primitivism was a widespread and vital artistic strategy of postcolonial resistance for Latin American writers. This essentially white and urban appeal to give representation to the nonwhite and rural populations of various Latin American nations marked a rhetorical turn to regional, local, and racial differences as signs of new Latin American cultural possibility in the wake of political independence. Of course, the rhetoric didn't always match the political reality, especially since much of Latin America's political changes in the early decades of the twentieth century failed to redress its persistent colonial structures. White patriarchal and paternalistic oligarchies continued to control land and political power, while millions of yeoman workers continued to work land they didn't own. These were largely indigenous and/or Afro-Latin American subjects, unlettered and with little or no social mobility. The majority of indigenist and other regionalist artists during this period of Latin American modernism were part of a white urban and lettered elite whose work often served the interests of national consolidation at the expense of those very peoples and places on the margins that their fiction sought to rescue. One thinks of the indigenism of Guatemala's Miguel Angel Asturias, the negritude of Puerto Rico's Luis Pales Matos, or the regionalism of Rómulo Gallegos, for example. Mary Louise Pratt has called the self-contradiction of this failed postcolonialism "creole self-fashioning," a kind of unrecognized neocolonial desire to assume the position of the colonizer within one's own nation. Primitivism, in this way, silences even as it attempts to give voice to the Other.

The work of scholar Erik Camayd-Freixas, however, points to an important characteristic of some more nuanced forms of primitivism that perhaps warrant our reconsideration. He insists that when primitivism is used to critically examine "*self*-representation" as opposed to mere representation of a non-Western otherness, it can "expose the contradictions of cultural myths and . . . deconstruct the instrumental concepts of identity construction," particularly in response to the positivist and industrial legacies of Latin America's experience of modernity (xviii). As various strategies of primitivism began to expose their own neocolonial paternalism, new and more ironic and self-reflexive strategies emerged, laying bare the gaps between the city and the country, between white and nonwhite populations, and between gendered social positions. What Camayd-Freixas implies is that by the middle of the twentieth century primitivism produced works that investigated and interrogated the very terms of identity—the quintessentiality of such figures as the Indian, the black slave, the guajiro, the gaucho, the mestizo, or the mulatto—upon which modern Latin American nations had sought to found themselves.

For the purposes of this essay, it is important to note that the desire for the voice of "the primitive" marks early attempts to give voice also to nature in Latin America, since the primitive non-Western figure—either indigenous or black, and not infrequently female—was often conflated with the space of wilderness and the jungle. And this means, of course, that the neocolonial trappings of such desires for otherness were not uncommon in relation to nature either. Deep ecologists have insisted on the possibility of an unmediated access to nature's subjectivity and therefore of a biocentric understanding that would redress the violence of anthropocentrism. But as Jorge Marcone reminds us, in the context of Latin America especially, the desire for ecological wisdom cannot be so easily disassociated from a Western desire for the primitive other: "the myth of primitive ecological wisdom is, indeed, a version of the Western myth of the 'noble savage'" (159).[1] The privileging of animism and the essentializing of the native or the black subject can lead to a categorical dismissal of the diasporic subject and of hybridity, and the valorization of wilderness can lead to an unfruitful dismissal of history, technology, and culture.[2]

But if Camayd-Freixas is to be believed, there is a certain power and effectiveness, too, to arguments within cultures seeking postcolonial independence for a thorough reorientation toward those spaces and people who remain on the margins of modernity *as long as these subjects are not rendered ahistorical*. As James Clifford has suggested, Western forms of primitivism fail to challenge the prevailing assumptions and values of colonial culture when the primitive subject is reduced to an ahistorical object, which happens when "the historical relations of power in the work of acquisition are occulted" ("On Collecting" 624). This results in the West's bourgeois desire for fetishized objects, tokens, souvenirs, and other commodities that serve to tame the otherness of the non-Western subject. The hunger for the primitive commodity, whether it be an artifact—or we might argue the fetishized and ahistorical space of wilderness itself—is a false rendering of culture as "enduring, traditional, structural (rather than contingent, syncretic, historical)" (630). Postcolonialism's impulse, as a result, has been to restore historicity to colonialism's wide-ranging fetishes. But Clifford suggests that the Western desire for the primitive can produce new knowledge or new understanding, especially if it is critiqued with an eye toward restoring understanding of the contingency and syncretism of all cultures.

In the example of Alejo Carpentier's *Los pasos perdidos* [*The Lost Steps*], I wish to suggest that a key component to this postcolonial work of historicizing is not just reviving awareness of syncretism and the historical processes by which cultures have emerged in their present and contingent form but also of the ways in which human culture stands in dialectical relationship to ecology. As will become evident, I understand ecology as a space of indeterminacy and instability; it is, of course, the world of ecosystems and their myriad complexes of interdependencies, but as ecologists have argued, it is also a dynamic space of change, imbalance, and even chaos. Because it renders the static boundaries of the human perpetually porous and unstable, an ecologically centered imagination is paradoxically a renunciation of the very idea of a center. Moreover, in this essay I argue that Carpentier's aesthetic of the New World Baroque strikes a balance that is implied in the term "postcolonial ecology;" it is a balance between ecocriticism's important critique of anthropocentrism and postcolonialism's concern for social justice, what I have elsewhere called a "postcolonial sense of place."[3]

Carpentier revised over several years, beginning in 1949, his theory of *lo real maravilloso* or Latin America's marvelous reality, a belief in the region's fundamentally hybrid character, strange and surprising history, and extraordinary natural environment. He would later connect this marvelous reality to his conception of a New World Baroque, an "inclusive, syncretic, symbiotic" theory of "artistic expression" and of "history and culture" (Zamora "Magical" 96). Lois Parkinson Zamora has argued that his baroque aesthetic taps into a predominant characteristic of Latin American experience and sees with what she calls "the inordinate eye." The early manifestations of the New World Baroque in indigenous art and the indigenous and African transculturations evident in colonial architecture and in Latin American music and artistic expression evolved into the neo-baroque of twentieth-century Latin American narrative. Zamora characterizes this neo-baroque of Latin American fiction as a "self-conscious postcolonial ideology aimed at disrupting entrenched power structures and perceptual categories" (*Inordinate Eye* xvi). Examples of this New World Baroque include Carpentier's contemporary and compatriot José Lezama Lima, Mexico's Carlos Fuentes, and the magical realism of Gabriel

García Márquez. Because Carpentier's New World Baroque inherently recognizes nature's unpredictability and strangeness, it does not pretend to control nature but neither does it choose to ignore nature's relevance. Instead of forcing a choice between biocentrism and anthropocentrism, it offers a sense of ecology that is a kind of decentered humanism.

Such notions of ecology have been largely missing from prominent postcolonial critiques of discourses of nature. Thinkers such as Raymond Williams and Mary Louise Pratt have insisted on the historicization of nature in order to expose the human violence hidden by recourse to discourses of the pastoral, "wilderness," and "nature." Pratt, in the recent second edition of *Imperial Eyes*, adds a discussion of Carpentier's notion of *lo real maravilloso*, in which she argues that although he aims toward a more decolonized orientation of cultural authority, his celebration of Latin American marvels collapses into a neocolonial desire for control over cultural meaning on the American side of the Atlantic. Carpentier, she writes, "resolves the neocolonial predicament by re-imagining his relation with Europe as one not of otherness but of authenticity. Through this simultaneously decolonizing and recolonizing gesture, the destination for others becomes a home for a unified white, creole self" (229). Her suspicion toward discourses of "wonder" and the "marvelous," of course, is understandable, given how such praise of nature often disguised colonialism's violent ambition to exploit foreign natural resources.[4] When art praises nature, Williams explains, it does so by means of "a simple extraction of the existence of labourers" (32). To speak of the "innate bounty" and the "natural order" of the country, then, is "an abuse of language" because of the erasure of a laboring human presence (33). Robert Marzec extends the implications of Williams's thesis to insist that British colonialism's aim to rationalize, order, and control across the globe was a symptom of an "ontological dread of undisciplined land" (*Ecological* 31).

The risk of these arguments, however, is the ease of their own overgeneralization. Among other things, historicization also reveals that Williams's English dialectic of city and country or Pratt's imperial eyes are not always operative in the same fashion no matter where we are on the globe, nor with the same ideological and political meaning. If this were the case, historicization and careful interpretation within the context of distinct geographies, cultures, and historical moments would be unnecessary. Stephen Greenblatt warns in *Marvelous Possessions* against an "*a priori* ideological determinism, that is, the notion that particular modes of representation are inherently and necessarily bound to a given culture or class or belief system, and that their effects are unidirectional" (4). He suggests, moreover, that the alternative is not to imagine that representations are always neutral; he stresses the protagonism of cultures and individuals who have "fantastically powerful assimilative mechanisms, mechanisms that work like enzymes to change the ideological composition of foreign bodies" (4). This flexibility is particularly needed in relation to the question of ecology, lest nature disappear altogether in our critical frames as the ontological fact—separate from the human imagination—that Marzec reminds us it is. In short, nature's nature is that it should never be reduced or equated to its representations.

While it might be difficult to define what nature is, critical readers can at least learn to identify strategies of representation that attempt to respect this ontology. According to Édouard Glissant, successful strategies of this kind render nature dynamic, fluid, and resistant to naming; nature constitutes a character in the story and is never merely background staging for the human drama. It is *terre* not *territoire*. In this regard, Glissant sees something exemplary in Carpentier's novel;[5] we see a modern Western subject of New World history—an aspiring musicologist in New York City who moves to the South American tropics in pursuit of the origin of music—making a mythological journey backward in time from a known geography, *terra nostra*, to a kind of willed, self-consciously denoted unknown, *terra incognita*. It is, in other words, an abdication of the reductive and controlling impulses of naming that in turn liberates the poetic force of language. Glissant suspects that nature's dynamism will more likely exhibit itself in narratives where "landscape in the work stops being merely decorative or supportive and emerges as a full character. Describing the landscape is not enough. *The individual, the community, the land are inextricable in the process of creating history*" (Caribbean Discourse 105, emphasis added).

It is this last point that is vital. Glissant describes here a poetic, oneiric function of art that paradoxically emerges from an attempt to mimetically describe and represent a New World reality. This "aesthetics of disruption and intrusion" imagines the shape of overlapping histories of violence *and* the force of ecology itself but in so doing becomes not a copy of the world but a poetics, a world-(re)making. This means that representation attributes meaning to human experience and to the environment without making a summative or totalized claim on that meaning (*Poetics* 151); human experience and ecology are instead imagined in meaningful yet tentative relation. To insist that nature is "always a form of social knowledge," though true, is also, as Nancy Stepan points out, "almost a cliché" because critics have wanted to reduce nature merely to its social meaning. To fail to see, or to refuse belief in, anything at work in culture beyond social meaning means we have condemned ourselves to a solipsistic and anthropocentric theory of culture. It would seem we are condemned only and always to see ourselves in the mirror of nature we create. What is needed is an added consideration of the fact that nature is not *only* a form of social knowledge but also always performing a challenge to social knowledge.[6]

THE MARVELOUS REALITY OF LATIN AMERICAN NATURE

Ironically, the fact that nature appeared Edenic to scientists, authors, and other members of the literate elite in nineteenth-century Latin America was itself already a symptom of human-caused environmental cataclysms in the age of Conquest. These events included widespread, unprecedented, and exceptional disease, enforced labor and enslavement, violent displacement of peoples and cultures, and the transplantation of Africans, Europeans, European flora and fauna, and Asian plants and peoples. As Shawn Miller points out, the population of the Americas wouldn't reach pre-1492 levels until the twentieth century; Latin America was more forested in 1800 than it was in 1492, and it saw greater biodiversity than its precolonial past until its rapid demise in the age of modernization in the late nineteenth and early twentieth centuries. Environmental history like Miller's not only insists on the historicity of nature; it also makes the case for the ecological foundations of human history and, for my purposes here, for the ecological dimensions of *literary* history. Latin American modernism's varied attempts to ground Latin American authenticity in regional soils resulted in ironic portrayals of the limits of representation; nature's ontology—its dynamic ecology—proved consistently resistant to its capture in language or image.

The modernism of Alejo Carpentier (1904–80) is characterized by a sustained argument against European modernism and its discontents.[7] Born in Cuba to a French father and a mother of Russian descent, Carpentier was a polyglot, a world traveler, and a man of extraordinary erudition regarding Western art, literature, and music history. But he was also devoted to the cause of a cultural and political liberation of Latin America and his native Cuba. As evident in his theory of *lo real maravilloso* [the marvelous reality of Latin America] and the New World Baroque, his profound awareness of the particular racial, political, geographical, and cultural history of his region of the world convinced him that the postcoloniality of Latin American culture lay in its willingness to give form and shape to its lived experience.

It was accepted wisdom, at least since the nineteenth century, that Latin America's liberation turned on this willingness to engage in the praxis of mimesis. The colonial condition of Latin American culture, as many saw it, was most evident in a patent disregard for the local particulars of the Americas and a preference for the patterns and precedents set by European and U.S. trends. By the late nineteenth century, artists had begun to experiment with a kind of hermeneutics of recovery, scanning local landscapes, histories, and peoples for signs of difference from this colonial legacy. This would culminate in the movements of regionalism, indigenism, and negritude of the early twentieth century and the staunch insistence that Latin America, as a transnational entity, was inherently mestizo. This new Latin Americanism sought to be more authentic and overtly postcolonial than the earlier attempts of cultural liberation in the nineteenth century even though it resulted at times in a well-documented paternalism and continued marginalization of more radical voices of regional and racial difference. Carpentier's theory of *lo real maravilloso*, first articulated in his 1949 prologue to his novel about the Haitian Revolution, *El reino de este mundo* [*The Kingdom of This World*], took this project to capture and valorize the local to a more nuanced and much-needed level of poetic self-ironizing.

The marvelous, for Carpentier, is the experience of surprise and wonder in an encounter with utter strangeness; it is "the awareness of being Other, of being new, of being symbiotic, of being a *criollo*; and the *criollo* spirit is itself a baroque spirit" ("Baroque" 100). This, of course, was akin to the pursuit of much of European modernism and surrealism in particular, but Carpentier insists, "if Surrealism pursued the marvelous, one would have to say that it very rarely looked for it in reality" (103). For Carpentier and his compatriot Wifredo Lam, surrealism was not wrong to want to counterpose a "soul-less, urban modernity" with a "natural frenzy," a "living, animated jungle" (Wilson 78); the problem was that this jungle for the European was more imagined than experienced and therefore a mere rhetorical trick, a first-world fantasy about the third world. The Latin American's closer proximity to the jungle, of course, doesn't guarantee an escape from fantasies of primitivism. To experience wonder is to experience eccentricity, to be outside of the center of phenomena one experiences.

The perhaps unintended consequence of Carpentier's theory is that even though it produces the same eccentricity that surrealism couldn't overcome, because it more overtly commits itself to the objective of mimesis—of direct confrontation and experience with the tropics—human consciousness is understood as eccentric in relation to an unnamed but dynamically present biological center. The saving grace of this relationship is how ecology is a world without a center, as I already indicated, and therefore disrupts and renders perpetually contingent the binary of center and periphery. For Carpentier, surrealism's effect of strangeness was calculated and prefabricated (Salvador Dalí's melting clocks, for example); it did not start with the intention to be mimetic since European modernism did not have the confidence that reality itself would provide the experience of strangeness.[8] Carpentier's theory, on the other hand, was inherently mundane; it found its greatest potency and, as I will argue, its richest ironies, in what in *The Lost Steps* Carpentier refers to as "Adam's task of giving things their names." This is direct experience with the "raw state" of the "commonplace" and in the "untamed" and "unruly complexities of [New World] nature and its vegetation, the many colors that surround us, the telluric pulse of the phenomena that we still feel" ("Baroque" 104, 105). As opposed to the Old World Baroque that was born out of the Counter-Reformation and was so closely allied with Catholic aesthetics, José Lezama Lima similarly saw the New World baroque as more centered in, and hence decentered by, nature: the Old World baroque was fashioned to facilitate "a rationalistic elaboration of the city" whereas the American baroque "raised . . . the wealth of nature over and above monetary wealth . . . in such a way, that even within Hispanic poverty, lies the wealth of American matter [material]" (50).[9] The resistant force of the New World baroque "is nourished, in its very purity, by the gusts of the true American forest" (56).[10]

This mimeticism of the New World Baroque did not produce naïve neo-Romantic nature writing, however. Although centered on a description on the physical world, what emerges is not a copy but a new world made by "a new vocabulary" and "a new optic" required to see the environment one inhabits (Carpentier "Baroque" 105). In this sense, a baroque response to the world is both faithful and treacherous; it centers and decenters the self. For Carpentier, it helps that tropical nature itself appears to be characterized by the baroque "horror of the vacuum, the naked surface, the harmony of lineary geometry." The New World baroque is eccentric in that it "moves outward and away from the center, [it] somehow breaks through its own borders," and it is only because so too does the biological world (93). As he explains, "If our duty is to depict the world, we must uncover and interpret it ourselves. Our reality will appear new to our own eyes. Description is inescapable, and the description of a baroque world is necessarily baroque, that is, in this case the *what* and the *how* coincide in a baroque reality" (106). Baroque representation leaves us with two worlds, linked but apart—the world and a represented world and a split awareness that poiesis and mimesis are intertwined and inseparable but never identical.[11] While this is arguably true of all representation, baroque forms seem to offer a particularly self-reflective method of assessing one's eccentricity, or outsideness, vis-à-vis an extravagant ecological reality within which one is nevertheless embedded.

In her description of the differences in the role of representation in indigenous and European art, Lois Parkinson Zamora notes that European tradition has favored the control of the observing "I/eye," a subject that remains separate from and not participatory in the world that is represented, whereas indigenous forms of representation seek to be *"image-as-presence,"* inseparable from the seeing subject (*Inordinate* 15). In the former, mimesis predominates, in the latter poiesis. She writes, "the conventions of Western perspective . . . remind viewers of the image's *likeness to* nature and, hence, our *separation from* nature. Western perspective frames what is seen from outside the framed scene, thus encoding the seer's detachment from the visible world" (15). Ecocriticism has sought to identify ways of seeing that do not result in this separation but that also do not erase or obscure the human agency in giving representative form to nature. It would seem that Zamora's definition of the "inordinate eye" works as one such method.

As Amaryll Chanady notes, in its aggressive inclusiveness of different orders of seeing, Carpentier's notion of America's marvelous reality "does not occupy a distinct area of literary production separate from that of mimetic writing, as does the marvelous domain of fairy tales [or the fabricated methods of surrealism, for Carpentier]. . . . On the contrary, the mode challenges realistic representation in order to introduce *poiesis* into *mimesis*" (130). What accounts for this new method of representation is not "a naïve essentialist argument" that sees Latin American exceptionalism—its history of racial mixture, its political violence, its uneven development, or even its extraordinary geography—as the rule that determines this cultural outcome; after all, an environmentally determined culture can hardly be conceived to be liberatory. This new method is, rather, a combination of attentive description of the particulars of one's environment and of self-willed creation of a new world. This combination makes of a work of representation something both *of* nature and *like* nature. Ecologically centered art is ambiguously both separate from and part of the world and is the vehicle by which we explore and understand our belonging in the more-than-human cosmos. While one might insist on the postcolonial value of *lo real maravilloso*, this ambiguity makes it also ecologically valuable.

THE NATURE OF CARPENTIER'S BAROQUE WORLD

In 1947 and 1948, Carpentier made two voyages of several weeks in duration to the Amazonian interior of the Orinoco watershed, the same territory that had inspired Sir Alfred Conan Doyle and Jules Verne, the lands of El Dorado. These voyages would later find fictional form in *The Lost Steps*. What he came to appreciate was that culture has a tendency to grow impatient with and distant from the dynamism of the natural world, at its own peril. In a column he wrote for *El Nacional* in Venezuela months before the publication of *The Lost Steps* and after his voyages, he insists on a commitment to a dialectic contact and comparison between the space of the city and the space of nature:

> The tentacular cities—as the poet Verhaeren calls them—New York, Philadelphia . . . produce a kind of man, son of modern times, who inspires in me an infinite pity. He is the one who passes months of the year without having any contact with nature. . . . For me, such an existence—which is the existence of millions and millions in this world—is an intimation [prefiguración] of hell. Moreover, I cannot bring myself to believe that it is worth living in such a manner. Without frequent contact with nature, man forgets who he is, he is sterilized, loses his vital rhythms, he becomes distrustful of his own biology [se hace desconfiado ante la propia carne]. In his labyrinths of reinforced concrete, in his pathways of asphalt, he comes to forget, as well, the very sky that exists overhead—a round and true sky, not framed by the stony edges of buildings [la estereotomía de los edificios]. [This man] knows a little bit about everything . . . but he has forgotten the names of the stars." ("Presencia" August 23, 1952)[12]

Carpentier was intent on revising Romanticism for a modern Latin America whose natural wonders had made little difference in the formation of Latin American culture. As he suggests in another column, however, the difference in Latin America is the nature of the tropics, nature on a scale that defies description, shatters illusions of pastoral balance, and terrifies the onlooker into a kind of muted submission ("El turista").

He notes, "America still lives beneath the telluric sign of the great storms and great floods. There will always be some meteorological role, from Miami, Havana, the Grand Cayman islands, to remind us that our nature has not yet become so 'friendly,' so tranquil like Goethe would have wanted the whole world to be—in the image of his romantic Germany" ("Presencia" October 2, 1952).[13]

His expedition to the Amazonian interior of the Orinoco delta in 1947 fanned the flames of this desire to lay claim to a still relatively untamed and unknown natural world, but it also brought him into contact with the people and cultures of the region and the jungle's potent and defiant telluric ontology. One can hardly miss the ways in which *The Lost Steps* is a fable of a twentieth-century neocolonial and masculine conquest and mapping of *terrae incognitae*. His frequent use of the clichéd "virgin" nature both in his essays and in the novel attest to this masculinist temptation, as we will see. However, he is generally more drawn to the idea of nature as Genesis rather than Eden. That is, nature is not static or passive but is instead a kind of ongoing creation—what he calls a "perennial 'revelation of forms'" (*Visión* 33)—demonstrating an ecological dynamism that defies linguistic control. As we see, this generative force has the effect of destabilizing the tropic and neocolonial methods of the white, metropolitan man in *The Lost Steps*. As Timothy Morton notes, nature "keeps giving writers the slip" (2); that the mimetic attempt results in a poetics suggests, ultimately, that a more ecological understanding of human being requires a critical apparatus that is interested in critiquing more than just the socially-constructed self. Moreover, this human ecology becomes a cross-cultural poetics that is a mode of imagining the whole complex overlay of divergent mythologies, desires, and experiences with nature that inform Latin American experience. Inasmuch as *lo real maravilloso* relies on a position of outsidedness, it can play into the fantasies of the Western traveler whose externality relies on the privilege of travel, of mobility, and access to comparative cultural and geographical contexts. But its more profound implication is that ethical experience between diverse human subjects and the natural world should remain *intersubjective*, multiplied and decentered by an awareness of the contingencies of the singular seeing I/eye.

THE LOST STEPS TO AN UNNAMEABLE NATURE

Carpentier's unnamed male protagonist in *The Lost Steps* is the quintessence of the unhappy modern. A composer and academic, he is unhappy in marriage as well as in his liaison with a pseudo-intellectual mistress with whom he leaves the fatigue and "automatism" of a northern American city, presumably New York, and arrives among the tribes of the Amazonian interior of the upper Orinoco in order to prove that the foundations of music lie in the mimetic impulse to copy the sounds of nature (5). New York and Caracas, where he stays temporarily, are characterized by an architecture of the urban baroque, similar to Lezama Lima's description, where a rationalization "falsif[ies] the reality of proportions, establishing a scale of their own, like constructions designed for some unfamiliar use" despite the fact that "for hundreds of years a struggle had been going on with roots that pushed up the sidewalks and cracked the walls" (38). As he gets farther away from urban life, he is struck by the fact that the world's metropolitan centers are "museum cities," founded on commemorating what resists nature's ravaging erosions (65). This resembles, of course, the very opposition between city and country that Raymond Williams challenges, but in a Latin American context, "country" is not imagined to be the pastoral space of human harmony with the landscape but the barbarism the nineteenth-century writer and Argentine politician Domingo Faustino Sarmiento once associated with the untamed spaces outside the law. Carpentier wants to challenge Sarmiento's dichotomy between civilization and barbarism by exposing not only the marginalized nonurban subjects but the wild ecology that the rationality of the city has not learned to tolerate.

Initially, however, it seems his narrator has found in the jungle his ideal object of nonurban otherness. Once he arrives at the Amazonian interior, he falls under Rosario's spell, a simple, uneducated woman in whom "several races had met [varias razas se encontraban mezcladas] ... Indian in the hair and cheekbones, Mediterranean in brow and nose, Negro in the heavy shoulders and the breadth of the hips" (81/147).[14] In over-the-top primitivist and sexist rhetoric, he describes her as a veritable "living sum of races [viviente suma de razas]," the "great races of the world," which history had separated for centuries and which "had ignored the fact that they inhabited the same planet" (82/147). Unlike Mouche, his surrealist mistress, or Ruth, his actress wife, she seems to be the very emblem of a pastoral possibility because she always "established links with her surroundings [establecer con el ambiente ciertas relaciones]" (106/170); she is a "woman of the earth" (180). To the narrator, Rosario moves according to natural rhythms, is an avatar of ancient peoples and lifeways, and with her, sexual intimacy and work in a tropical pastoral village become a kind of sacrament (173). The protagonist sees her as the ultimate antidote to modern mobility, urbanity, and angst, the very trope of the receptive native woman who welcomes the Western outsider.

Significantly, as the protagonist advances into the jungle and into his relationship with Rosario, he begins to find this attributed symbolic meaning slipping from his control. This is concomitant with his growing awareness that nature's generative powers defy his capacity to give adequate representation to its various forms. The baroque qualities of the jungle are evident in its "disconcerting and new" forms, its "blind geometry" (119, 138). Unlike an easy German Romantic pastoral or the passive and static notion of an Eden discussed earlier, he insists the jungle is more akin to the pre-Edenic moment of genesis, the "diabolical vegetation that surrounded the Garden of Eden before the Fall." He finds himself observing a

> kind of crater in whose depths horrendous plants proliferated. They were like fleshy grasses whose morbid shoots were round like tentacles or arms. The huge leaves, open like hands, resembled submarine flora in their texture of coral and seaweed, with bulbous flowers like feather lanterns, birds suspended from a vein, ears of corn of larvae, bloodshot pistils bursting from their sides [por un proceso de erupción y desgarre] without the grace of a stem. And all this, there below, intertwined, tangled, in a grappling, coupling, monstrous and orgiastic, incests that represent the supreme confusion of forms. (205/265)

Note that the strange and almost terrifying proliferation of forms leads to a similarly "blind geometry" of proliferating similes and metaphors. Baroque nature leads to baroque prose, but this is not mere mimeticism at work, precisely because of the ways in which nature's monstrous biodiversity is its incestuousness; ecology does not promise facile, predictable, or measurable reproduction or classification to appease male desire, but instead confuses forms and eludes his desire, leaving him conscious of his own figural language. As he contemplates the hundreds of thousands of unnamed species, the narrator laments that "this fearful density of leaves [ese tremendo espesor de hojas] . . . would one day disappear from the planet without having been given a name, without having been re-created by the Word [por la palabra]" (206/266). Adam's task of naming is really re-creation, more like Noah after the deluge; unnameable nature—which he here compares to the same "blank *terra incognitae* of the old cartographers" in the colonial period—provides endless "stimuli to thought, motives for meditation, forms of art, poetry, myth, more helpful to the understanding of man than hundreds of books written by men who pride themselves on knowing Man" (208–9). The narrator's unmistakable male desire turns away from the ambition of naming as possession toward that of the poiesis of artistic expression.

Elsewhere the narrator insists that this confusion leads to "a kind of disorientation, and a dizziness of the eyes [mareo de los ojos]. It was no longer possible to say which was tree and which reflection of tree. Was the light coming from above or below? Was the sky or the earth water?" (161/223).[15] He remarks, "What amazed me most was the inexhaustible mimetism of virgin nature [el inacabable mimetismo de la naturaleza virgen]. Everything here seemed something else, thus creating a world of appearances that concealed reality, casting doubts on many truths" (165/227). One of the truths that the ecology of baroque nature confuses is the reliable and identifiable distinction between human and more-than-human meaning. At several junctures the narrator is confused about whether he is seeing evidence of human ruins or simply natural forms that mimic and mock memorials to a human past, "as though some strange civilization of people different from those we know had flourished there"

(138). So "virgin" nature starts to lose its gendered and sexualized meaning and takes on the attributes of a space of such regenerative force that the tropes aimed at controlling nature's meaning lose their structure. If nature is indeed hiding a human history (which, of course, it was), its fecundity marginalizes, decenters humanity; as a result, language takes on the character of hopeful and rhetorical guesswork. Moreover, Carpentier implies that a decentered humanity in a biological cosmos in which boundaries are uncertain presents an opportunity for a postcolonial inclusion of differences expelled by colonial desire. He asks "whether perhaps the role of these lands in the history of man might not be to make possible for the first time certain symbioses of cultures" (119–20).

Representation as probing and investigative guesswork means that it becomes more rhetorical, self-reflexive, and hence less about recovering the "primitive" and the "wild" but more about understanding and respecting the contours and limitations of human cultures in an intersubjective and more-than-human context. Carpentier's point is that nature's value is precisely that it delineates these limitations, but only *after*, paradoxically, the artist first aspires to escape the trappings of culture and recover nature's rawness.

Initially the protagonist believes that music was born of imitation of natural sound, but while watching a tribe of Indians mourning over the body of a fallen hunter, he alters his theory. Art, he concludes, is

> the earliest attempt [intento primordial] to combat the forces of annihilation which frustrate man's designs. . . . Before the stubbornness of Death, which refused to release its prey, the Word suddenly grew faint and disheartened. In the mouth of the shaman, the spell-working orifice, the *Threne*—for that was what this was—gasped and died away convulsively, blinding me with the realization [dejándome deslumbrado can la revelación] that I had just witnessed the Birth of Music. (184–85/245)

All forms of artistic representation come to represent a response to or an awareness of the reality of death, which he shows in the novel is a confrontation with the biological facts that underlie our existence and consciousness.[16] To merely love picturesque nature, to praise its beauty and believe in a facile harmony between humankind and nature, is a shallow Romanticism that denies the passage and ravages of time. Carpentier's tropical world is not merely surprising because it is beautiful; it is marvelous because it is "implacable, terrible, in spite of its beauty" (195). Carpentier seems to presciently anticipate conceptions of chaos in ecology since the 1960s; the horror that nature's violence inspires makes it hard to argue for a harmonious notion of biocentrism where all life forms are on an equal plane; humanity—or at least the narrator's white male and erudite version of humanity—uses artistic representation to see with Zamora's "inordinate eye." This is a way of temporarily stepping aside so as to see himself within this newfound, broader context. The baroque offers a contingent biocentrism, just as his is now a more contingent self-reflective male desire. Although nature's violence is not as fearsome to those who live with it, the pastoral dream of harmony between nature and culture is no longer possible since

> the plagues, the possible sufferings, the natural dangers [must be] accepted as a matter of course [de antemano]; they formed part of an Order that had its severity [sus rigores]. Creation is no laughing matter, and [those whose life is spent with it] all knew and accepted the role each of them had been assigned in the great tragedy of living [de lo creado]. But it was a tragedy with a unity of time, place, and action; in it, death itself operated under the direction of known masters, attired in poisons, scale, fire, miasmas, to the accompaniment of the thunder and lightning. (195/256)

By implication, then, anything that denies human biology or human locality in the physical world will not provide a sufficient confrontation with human contingency, temporality, and mortality and therefore cannot sufficiently nurture an awareness of ethics. Representation that accepts the biological reality of death, of unpredictable change, of surprising beauty and horror, is art attuned to the minute changes and formal dynamism of ecology, an ever-dying, regenerative, and hence baroque, world. This is the reason that this ecological awareness, although ostensibly focusing the eye and ear to the physical world and therefore mimetic in intention, is self-reflexive and poetic in result.

The narrator composes his own masterpiece, his own Threnody and expression of mourning over death, as a tribute to this new awareness. He feels that this work represents the very renewal of civilization the automatism of his former life needed, but his failure pertains to the very material contingencies of a physical, biological world that inspired him. Even the life of the music depends on the dead body of a tree: paper. He needs more paper than he can find in the jungle to make it into a transferable and communicable thing. When an opportunity presents itself to return to New York, he takes the trip, intending to return with paper to complete his notes, which he leaves with Rosario. Neither she nor his manuscript is ever seen again.

His artistic failure is the culmination of a growing awareness of Rosario's eluctability. She becomes more distant and, showing more self-possession than he had thought she had, ultimately refuses to marry him. This causes him to consider that his sexual desires are pornographic, which he defines as "the degradation and distortion of all that might contribute . . . to a man's finding compensation for his failures in the affirmation of his virility, achieving his fullest realization in the flesh he divides" (99). After witnessing the arrival to the village of a young girl raped by a leper, he is given the chance to shoot the leper in punishment. He declines and admits his own pornographic desire: "The disgust and indignation I felt at the outrage was unspeakable; it was as though I, a man, all men, were equally guilty of this revolting attempt because of the mere fact that possession, even willing [consentida], puts the male in the attitude of aggression" (230/288).

This admission of guilt comes after pages of elaborate descriptions of the sexual energy he discovers in Rosario's companionship and after his voyage into the jungle has already been cast in unmistakably sexual terms. Early in the novel when he first arrives in the jungle, the travelers who accompany him look for a passage—unmistakably cast as a vagina—through a forest of mangroves, "without sign of an opening, without a cleavage, without a crevice" until they find a tree marked with three vertical V's next to which lies the narrow passage into the womb-like interior jungle (159). At the novel's conclusion, when he comes back to the jungle to find Rosario, he cannot locate the entrance because the sign has been buried by the river's higher waters, much to his dismay at being obstructed by "such an absurd contingency [tan absurdo contratiempo]" (270/323). To add insult to injury, after Rosario had told him she wouldn't marry him because she wishes to remain free, he learns that she has married in the village while he has been gone. The protagonist's journey ends in resolute failure.

CONCLUSION

My reading is not meant to suggest that Carpentier's theory of Latin American culture is inoculated in some way against the pitfalls of neocolonialism. Carpentier's binary of the city and the jungle exhibits many of the trappings of male colonial desire, and his insistence on the return to the feminized primitive and the wild in order to escape the artificial city is at times environmentally naïve. An ecocritical reading of this structure therefore risks reinventing the very opposition between nature and culture that New World history has rendered ambiguous. But we have to take that ambiguity seriously, and that means that we cannot know for sure what is natural and what is cultural. If the nature/culture binary becomes an *important but rhetorical differentiation*, then ecocriticism's interest in a return to nature can be understood as an advocacy of a kind of ritualistic performance, a self-conscious re-creation of the world, that keeps the human subject and human representations answerable to a world that cannot be possessed.

If ecocriticism asks us to ontologize in the interest of determining the proper human relationship to nature, postcolonialism urges us to historicize. Perhaps they both point to a kind of contingent ontology, an awareness that, as Carpentier argues, no culture can escape from the pitfalls of colonialism's commodification and binarization of the world without at least risking an appeal to nature. And yet we cannot approach the jungle as anything but human subjects—male, female, white, black, European, native, members of a social class, and so on—so there is no escaping the ways in which these factors shape and inform our desire for nature's otherness. Culture needs nature in order to remain creative and alive, but culture needs also to remain apart and deferential, lest we render nature objectified, falsely believed to be known and possessed, by our human discourse. An ecological ethos renounces all claims to authenticity and stasis founded on historical continuity, tradition, and habit. Carpentier's poetics is not the possessive impulse of colonial cultures and museum cities that fetishize and commodify nature and "primitives" outside of time and change; instead it portrays a culture founded on the paradoxical acceptance of the fact that it will be perpetually transformed by nature's indifferent erosions. Such indifference forces Carpentier's protagonist to renounce Rosario and the jungle as the static answers to Latin America's postcolonial quest he thought they were. His postcolonialism is oriented to the ecological margins precisely to the degree that he accepts the paradox of this renunciation. His own appeal to an ecological imagination becomes "an aesthetics of disruption," to borrow from Glissant. The only possession taken from the jungle is not the protagonist's *magnum opus* of the Threnody; it is instead Carpentier's novel in our hands, what in the novel he suggests is really an urn, a work at least thrice removed from the natural order that inspired it—once by the narrator's parallel world he created in the music, twice by virtue of the narrative acting as the music's substitute, and thrice by virtue of its function as a rhetorical representation of a fictional narrator. Wendy Faris notes that Carpentier's novel, like William Faulkner's "The Bear," represents an attempt "at the appropriation of land by text that [is] ultimately unsatisfactory, not only because of flawed motivations but because of the impossibility of the task" (252). The failure, she explains, "is only mediated by the [text] we are reading. Words bridge the gap between the two realms, giving access to the truths of the heart and the rhythms of nature learned in the primordial realm so that they are remembered in the city." Because of the self-ironizing that results from the confrontation of the nature/culture divide, she insists that Carpentier's protagonist "comes to [an] explicit recognition of his delusions" (253). In this sense the novel, and perhaps any ecologically oriented postcolonial work, is a *memento mori*, an expression of mourning, or recompense, for the mortal facts of human biology.

Carpentier's novel feels timely in both senses; it is relevant for contemporary concerns with ecology even as it also feels dated. Carpentier was not able to fully transcend the reactionary naturalism of earlier primitivism in Latin America that invoked the tropics, women, Indians, and blacks as reified opposites to European metropolitanism, but perhaps we would do well to exercise our readerly agency and imagine, as Amaryll Chanady does, that *lo real maravilloso* is a territorialization of the marvelously real; that is, instead of offering essential racial or gender difference or essential nature as sites of postcolonial resistance, it is a *rhetorical* performance or localization of a postcolonial ethos that values difference *deferentially*. A sense of ecology becomes both mimetic *and* poetic when art temporarily territorializes nature—as a sign of value—but then renounces its ability to subsume and capture it—as a sign of respect. In this perpetual dialogue between the physical word and human consciousness, the pathologies of believing in radical human naturalism, on the one hand, and of believing in radical human separatism, on the other, are thus both kept at bay. In postcolonial terms, this means that Latin America's diversity, size, and the simultaneity of its various cultures and geographies can generate cultural difference and autonomy while it also delimits that very culture ecologically. If Latin America's reality cannot generate cultural difference, it can hardly be trusted to offer an adequate answer to the legacies of colonialism. But neither can we consider it adequate if it does not result in a sense of ecology, since colonialism degrades cultures and ecosystems alike. Only a postcolonial ecology, then, holds the key to New World originality.

NOTES

I would like to thank: Luisa Campuzano and her colleagues in Havana who attended my seminar on ecocriticism and provided stimulating feedback in July 2008; Jorge Marcone, my collaborator on the seminar; Araceli García-Carranza Bassetti at the Biblioteca Nacional in Havana; Lois Parkinson Zamora and Wendy Faris, who read drafts and offered careful criticism; Ursula Heise, a marvelous critic, and the Penn State Americanists who supported my visit to campus; Luis Valente and Rex Nielson, who invited a presentation on the topic at Brown University; and Elizabeth DeLoughrey, for her tough and important criticisms.

1. On the ways in which this desire is also informed by gender, see especially the works of Carolyn Merchant and Annette Kolodny.

2. In readings of such writers as Horacio Quiroga, Benito Lynch, and Eustasio Rivera, Jennifer French marks the persistence of neocolonial desire for the tropics among Latin American regionalists that parallels the structures of British colonialism in nineteenth- and early twentieth-century Latin America.

3. See my essay "A Postcolonial Sense of Place in the Work of Derek Walcott." This idea receives full treatment in my book, *New World Poetics* and represents a kind of ecological poetics of diaspora, a way of imagining the importance of place and of nature but that also attends to a mitigation of the social hierarchies that a sense of place often generates. This kind of dual critical attention is exemplified by Sarah Casteel in her book *Second Arrivals* and in Elizabeth DeLoughrey's *Routes and Roots*. Casteel warns that diaspora theory "tends . . . to polarize mobility and sedentarism, often celebrating the former while neglecting, or even disparaging, the latter" (2).

4. This is the particularly important contribution of French's aforementioned ecocritical study of Latin American literature, in which she assiduously identifies the mystifications of landscape that have served to erase the hand of British and U.S. neocolonialism in the region.

5. See in particular Glissant's *Caribbean Discourse*.

6. See my chapter, "New World Poetics" in *New World Poetics*.

7. For an examination of Carpentier's intricate response to Andre Breton and the surrealists, particularly the reasons for his adaptation of Breton's title, *Les Pas perdus*, see Jason Wilson. Wilson suggests that Carpentier was critical of surrealism's

denial of history and desire to "start the whole enterprise from a violent *tabula rasa*" (71).

8. A famous anecdote about the surrealism of Andre Breton tells of his debate with Roger Caillois about a Mexican jumping bean. Caillois insisted that one should cut open the bean and solve the mystery of its movement while Breton preferred to remain in ignorance of the science in order to let his poetic imagination run free. Breton has created a false dichotomy, assuming that the biological facts of existence could not themselves warrant poetry, wonder, and estrangement.

9. Translation mine. All translations not indicated in the bibliography are my translations.

10. In *New World Poetics*, I have elaborated on the ways in which nature renders this Christian and gendered notion of the poet as Adam contingent and the extent to which it manages to avoid the excesses of the colonialist desire for untamed nature.

11. Timothy Morton notes that ecology inherently challenges the very binaries of self and environment, human and natural, natural and supernatural, that are operative in much environmental thought. What is important to recognize, for Morton, is that we can never definitively name nature, or as he puts it, "we cannot point to it" (18). In our desire to find that place where we are no longer apart from it, we "go on generating binary pairs, and we would always *be coming down on one side or the other, missing the exact center*" (19 emphasis mine). By definition, then, biocentrism produces eccentricities indefinitely.

12. These columns are archived at the Biblioteca Nacional in Havana.

13. Carpentier is not above neocolonial desire to appropriate the marvelous—without irony—in the interest of a pure Latin American originality, of course, and this is his great temptation. One column reports on a recent publication of the explorations of Alain Gheerbrant, who discovered several large petroglyphs in the interior that left Gheerbrant speechless. Carpentier insists that Gheerbrant stood "before a new fact, absolutely original, in the history of primitive art" ("Gran Libro"). Another column expresses intense excitement and vindication since Angel Falls—the longest waterfall in the world in the Amazonian interior of Venezuela—had finally appeared in the *National Geographic* ("Misterios"). The spectacle of the falls promises mysteries yet to be named and discovered. Carpentier remarks, "It is a Lost World, more moving than all of the imagined worlds of Conan Doyle" ("Misterios"). Jules Vernes's 1898 novel, *The Mighty Orinoco*, is the subject of two other columns, and in both cases his purpose is to strike a contrast between the inauthenticity of European representations and the authentic reality that is Latin America's own inheritance. Margarita Mateo Palmer notes that in *Los pasos perdidos*, Carpentier demonstrates that such myths are not the sole property of the European imagination but have difference valences, origins, and meanings in indigenous contexts in Latin America, making something like El Dorado a "mobile, migratory myth" (153).

14. Where the original Spanish is indicated for added clarification, I have listed a second page number for the Spanish edition.

15. In Carpentier's papers at the Biblioteca Nacional in Havana, one finds a photo album of pictures that Carpentier took during his 1947 voyage to the Upper Orinoco and the Gran Sabana. Among the photos are several images of the river's still shoreline reflecting identical forms above and below, illustrating precisely his fascination with this sense of disorientation.

16. Robert Harrison's *Forests* suggests that the very forms of representation we use in language to structure meaning stand in a delicate and tenuous balance with the forests, the spaces of perpetual and indifferent ecological regeneration. And because the forest is the space against which language—and civilization itself—structures itself, it is the space of death and silence. "Nature knows how to die," he writes, "but human beings know mostly how to kill as a way of failing to become our ecology" (249). To become our ecology means to reorient civilization toward the forest, to use language to "speak our death to the world" or to approach an acceptance of the biological facts of our existence, including an embrace of human mortality.

6

Forest Fictions and Ecological Crises

Reading the Politics of Survival in Mahasweta Devi's "Dhowli"

Jennifer Wenzel

Bengali writer and activist Mahasweta Devi has long documented the plight of some of India's most marginalized citizens, low-caste communities and indigenous peoples caught between oppressive social dynamics and dependence upon scarce or degraded resources such as agricultural land, forests, water, and salt.[1] Devi's fiction shares the documentary impulse of her activist journalism, unflinchingly depicting what it means to be reduced to bare life on scorched earth. Narrative conflict and ecological crisis are often inextricably related in Devi's fiction, making her *oeuvre* ideally suited for an ecocriticism that "evaluate[s] texts and ideas in terms of their coherence and usefulness as responses to environmental crisis," in Richard Kerridge's definition (5). Indeed, Devi's novella *Pterodactyl, Puran Sahay, and Pirtha*, with its account of drought-induced famine jeopardizing the survival of an *adivasi* (tribal) community, anchors Lawrence Buell's attempt in *Writing for an Endangered World* to "provincialize," we might say, an ecocriticism institutionally and epistemologically centered in the United States and the United Kingdom.[2]

In Devi's writing and contemporary ecocriticism, ecological crisis plays an indispensable role—it is a *sine qua non*, the *raison d'être*, what have you, what you must work to mitigate and prevent. Another important voice articulating the socio-ecological plight of the world's poor is Vandana Shiva, who demonstrates how internationally sponsored neoliberal development in the global South is a source of violence and injustice because it threatens the millions who depend upon access to natural resources for their survival. Shiva's concern with the "politics of survival" is echoed in the title of my essay: business as usual, in Shiva's view, is a socio-ecological crisis of genocidal proportions. Both Shiva and Devi make visible otherwise obscured forms of violence: their work is important for scholars who would challenge the limitations of earlier ecocriticism and advocate a broader agenda of global environmental justice.

Yet the task of postcolonial ecocriticism does not consist merely in widening the lens to include previously overlooked geographical regions, historical experiences, cultural perspectives, and questions of race, class, and gender. The excavation of the politics of knowledge that, following the seminal work of Edward Said, has been one of postcolonial studies' most important contributions, might lead postcolonial ecocritics to question the very notion of what constitutes ecological crisis, rather than merely add more crises and texts to the list of ecocriticism's concerns.[3] Indeed, as Deane Curtin writes in *Environmental Ethics for a Postcolonial World*, "if we believe that environmental and social justice are intertwined, we need to adjust our understanding of what an environmental problem is" (114). In this essay, I examine Mahasweta Devi's short story "Dhowli," which initially seems at odds with the concerns of ecocriticism.

Compared with the spectacle of ecological crisis staged in texts like *Pterodactyl*, "Dhowli" reads as a run-of-the-mill tale of caste oppression in rural India, without much overt ecological concern: there is, at first glance, no ecological crisis in "Dhowli." Or, following Greg Garrard's distinction between ecology as a scientific discipline and its broader, sociocultural implications, "Dhowli" is concerned less with empirical, scientific "problems of ecology" and more with "ecological problems" emergent (or divergent) from "normative claims about how we would wish things to be" (5). "Dhowli" poses important questions for the emergent field of postcolonial ecocriticism that, for reasons of both political commitment and disciplinary investment, must recognize the imbrications of the social and the ecological without retreating in the face of unwarranted charges of anthropocentrism; such charges, however ironically, may be less the product of a meritorious *eco*centrism than of an unfortunate *ethno*centrism. While "Dhowli" offers readers a glimpse of what it means to be pushed to the brink of survival, it also subverts readers' assumptions about what constitutes a crisis—whether ecological, social, or narrative. Its counterintuitive engagements with forest fictions and ecological crises suggest the need for new practices of reading both literary texts and the place of humans in nature.

FOREST FICTIONS

Many of Mahasweta Devi's narratives depict the desperation of Indian forest dwellers and others dependent upon forest resources for their livelihoods. Stories such as "The Hunt" depict forests degraded by commercial logging, while "Strange Children" attends to problems associated with industrial mining. In "Salt," state-managed forests become inaccessible to local communities, while "Draupadi" stages forests as sites of refuge for Naxalite guerrillas and as state-militarized zones where boulders turn out to be soldiers. These forest fictions attend to the fact of deforestation in India—a "problem of ecology," in Garrard's terms, documented by a 1984 government finding that less than 10 percent of India remained under forest cover, with much of the damage having occurred in the past decade. In her attention to the long history of contests over Indian forests—contests that include but also significantly predate the British Raj, and that involve not only material control of forest resources but also their cultural significance—Mahasweta Devi understands forests as an "ecological problem," in Garrard's broader, interdisciplinary sense. Her forest fictions of the late 1970s and 1980s not only corroborate, in their own way, the 1984 declaration of a forest crisis by the postcolonial Indian state; they also serve as a kind of literary counterpart to the path-breaking "Citizen's Reports on the Environment" sponsored by the Centre for Science and Environment, an NGO in New Delhi, beginning in 1982.[4] These reports, which were written in an accessible style, combined the perspectives of scientists, policymakers, and citizens in order to articulate how specific environmental concerns were imbricated with questions of development and democracy.

Much of Mahasweta Devi's fiction helps to document Indian forest crises, but such problems of deforestation, degradation, or limited access to forest resources are nowhere to be seen in "Dhowli." This is not to say that "Dhowli" is not deeply concerned with relationships between people and nature and how such relationships are inflected by gender, caste, and class. Dhowli is a young low-caste Dusad widow from Tahad, a village in Bihar so remote that it is literally at the end of the road. After her husband's death, Dhowli leaves his family and returns to her mother, who loses the lease to her own husband's land after his death. Without access to land, the two widows depend for their survival on tending the goats and sweeping the courtyard of their former Brahman landlords, the Misras. Dhowli returns to her mother to escape the sexual advances of her late husband's brother, but she again finds herself to be an object of desire—now of the Misra's son, Misrilal. Dhowli avoids the Misra house and arranges to tend their goats in the forest, which functions as a refuge from sexual coercion. Far from being a site of conflict or deprivation, the forest is what helps to keep Dhowli and her mother alive. It is such an uncontested site that, unusually for Devi's fiction, we do not know who owns or manages it.

The forest is also the closest thing that Dhowli has to a room of her own, a place of peace and solitude where she can "be alone . . . with time to think one's own thoughts. . . . The forest felt so peaceful that the constant discomfort and fear she had after hearing the Misra boy speak so strangely to her was slowly going away. She was at peace again" (190). The forest allows Dhowli to escape more than the Misra boy: her thoughts are about her desire to escape the backbreaking labor and maternal responsibilities that seem to be her inevitable future. The narrator tells us, "Dhowli had no desire for that kind of life, the only kind of life for a Dusad girl" (190). The forest allows Dhowli to imagine an alternative life that the narrator tells us is impossible.

Moreover, the forest's protective space of alternative possibility leads Dhowli back into trouble when Misrilal finds her there: "In the solitude of the forest, the Misra boy was dauntless, telling her of his plans, and his words seemed to mingle with all the myths associated with the old forest, taking on an enchanted and dreamlike quality" (192). Dhowli is seduced as much by a folkloric tradition of forest idylls—the forest as the enchanted home of fairies, or the romantic refuge of illicit lovers—as by Misrilal's scandalous promises. Misrilal claims to be in love with her, and he promises to defy his family and break caste taboos by marrying her and leaving the village together. Their forest trysts become regular, and Dhowli becomes pregnant; Misrilal reveals their love to his family but cannot stand up to their defense of caste protocols. They marry him off and send him away from the village. Dhowli reflects:

> In that same forest, beside that stream, a Brahman youth once called a Dusad girl his little bird, his one and only bride-for-ever. Didn't they once lie on the carpet of fallen red flowers and become one body and soul? [. . .] It is hard to believe that these things ever happened. They now seem like made up stories. All that seems real is the baby sleeping in her lap and the constant worry about food. (198)

At work here are several kinds of forest fiction that do something other than document ecological crises: we see that cultural constructs of the forest as a refuge have two contradictory effects, allowing Dhowli to imagine an impossible life beyond sexual vulnerability and domestic drudgery, but also leading her to succumb to Misrilal's erotic advances that make her situation even more dire than a remarriage to a Dusad man. To invert Garrard's idea of the socially constituted "ecological problem" that reveals the normative, it is precisely because the forest is for Dhowli a more accessible and sustaining space than agricultural land and less fraught than domestic space that she is able to entertain subversive ideas of "how [she] would wish things should be"—ideas that the narrator and, ultimately, the narrative cannot countenance. Once Misrilal breaks his promises, even Dhowli's memories of their rendezvous in the forest come to resemble another kind of fiction—"made up stories" that are "hard to believe."

These forest fictions, ways of imagining the forest, have the power to make things happen. The forest offers at least temporary refuge, and it functions as an ecological commons for grazing goats and gathering roots and tubers when nearly every other source of livelihood and sustenance is blocked. Even in the absence (or seeming absence) of ecological crisis, it's worth thinking about the forest as a cultural construct with ideological and material effects: Dhowli's relationship to the forest is nothing if not an "imaginary relationship of individuals to real conditions of existence," in Louis Althusser's definition of ideology (1498). Dhowli's repeated invocation of the forest as a site of escape might seem more resonant with celebrations of Western wilderness or the New England woods characteristic of some early versions of U.S. ecocriticism than with an "environmentalism of the poor" emphasizing access to resources, articulated by writers in the Global South.[5] But the affective register of Dhowli's forest retreat is different from the sublimity evoked by wilderness on the American continent: it is specifically the *stories* of alternative forms of sociality possible in the forest—the forest as a thoroughly and self-consciously *cultural* space—rather than a pristine, *natural* alternative to sociality, that make it a site of safety (and dangerous temptation) for Dhowli. The forest's appeal is not that it is undisturbed or unpeopled, but rather that it has *always* been peopled by lovers, misfits, and fantastic creatures.

As readers, we see the forest through Dhowli's eyes; in turn, she views the forest through the lens of extant cultural narratives. We know that her view is ideological in the sense that it seems blind to "real conditions of existence" such as the late twentieth-century forest crises that Devi documents elsewhere. But it is ideological in another sense because it simultaneously evokes and suppresses layered histories of conquest in which forested hill zones became sites of refuge for indigenous *adivasi* communities fleeing the march of agriculture and pastoralism across the subcontinent. Madhav Gadgil and Ramachandra Guha read the precolonial environmental history of India as a conquest of "food gatherers" by "food producers"; they associate the rise of Brahmanism with fire sacrifice rituals that had the mundane effect of consuming wood and clearing forests for agriculture (71–90). Brahmans are "pioneers" in this initial conquest of the forest; when their meditations and sacrifices are molested by animals, demons, or human inhabitants of the untamed, menacing forest, they are defended by *kshatriya* warriors (Gadgil and Guha 79). Once domesticated, the forest remains a site of contemplation: in the third of the four stages of ideal Hindu life, the *vanaprastha* renounces material attachments for a life of meditation in the forest.

Here we encounter the first of many scandals in "Dhowli." When Dhowli takes refuge in the forest from the daily indignities of caste domination, we might read her plight in terms of this millennia-old history of flight from Hindu conquest. Yet what Dhowli actually does in the forest makes her resemble less the retreating *adivasi* communities than the Hindu *vanaprastha*: like these twice-born male elder hermits of caste tradition who leave behind the domestic life of the householder, the untouchable young woman protagonist of "Dhowli" goes to the forest to think her own thoughts and to imagine a life other than "the same routine of backbreaking work, with kids in your lap, kids following you around" (190). Although focused on Europe, Robert Pogue Harrison's account of the forest as "a place where the logic of distinction goes astray . . . an outlying realm of opacity which has allowed that civilization to estrange itself, enchant itself, terrify itself, ironize itself, in short to project into the forest's shadows its secret and innermost anxieties" (x–xi) can also describe a fundamental ambivalence regarding forests in India, an ambivalence laid bare in the gender, caste, and age reversals of Dhowli's subtle evocation of the *vanasprastha*'s forest retreat. This ambivalence derives from defining India as *aranya sanskriti*—a forest culture—while suppressing the constitutive history of *contests* over forests and the threat their liminality has posed to its civilization.[6] The tradition of forest idylls allows Dhowli to embrace the hegemonic version of this history while forgetting her own overdetermined, marginal position within it. The menacing aspect of the forest suddenly emerges when Misrilal fails to return as promised: "The woods looked horrible to her, the trees looked like ghoulish guards, and even the rocks seemed to be watching her" (194).

Dhowli's culturally mediated relationship to the forest is at odds with the narrative's muted depiction of it as a site of resource extraction. The Misras are traditional Brahman landlords and moneylenders who extract rent, labor, and usurious interest from low-caste tenants, but they are also business partners with a forest contractor who supervises a team of timber-felling "coolies."[7] When the Misras refuse to provide land, food, money, or work for Dhowli and her baby, she faces the prospect of prostituting herself to these forest workers in order to survive. It is no accident that the men to whom Dhowli must sell herself are those who commodify the forest; her romantic view eventually collides with the economic one when Dhowli encounters the contractor in the forest that is not only her refuge but also his workplace. Even though "Dhowli" acknowledges the fact of commercial forest extraction through these characters who "exploit" both the forest and Dhowli, their presence in the narrative is not explicitly connected to the urgent problem of Indian deforestation. The temporal horizon they introduce is not crisis, but rather what we might (scandalously) call *sustainability*: they "did not mind the wait" to see whether the Misras provide for Dhowli, because "the contract for cutting logs and splitting lumber was to continue for a while, and she was worth waiting for" (195–96).

ON SCANDAL

Before returning to the question of ecological crisis, I want to examine how "Dhowli" plays with ideas of crisis, scandal, and the counterintuitive. In my reading, the narrative anticipates and actively subverts readers' expectations about the situation that the characters inhabit, the conflict that they provoke, and how that conflict is resolved. The relationship between Dhowli and Misrilal provokes a crisis, as we might expect: a relationship between a Dusad woman and a Brahman man would disrupt the ritual ecology of regulated commensality and conviviality that generates either caste purity or pollution.[8] Yet the story makes clear that the Misra men have not "left untouched" (187) any of the untouchable young women of the village. What *is* scandalous within the narrative is that Misrilal courts Dhowli rather than forcing himself on her, that he wants to marry her. Both the Misras and Dhowli's Dusad community are appalled. Had she been raped, the Dusads would support her (so the narrator says); had Misrilal not confused a sexual outlet with a prospective bride, his family would support her and her child as they had done in previous cases. In this counterintuitive logic, the illegitimate children of Brahman men and low-caste women enjoy a certain kind of legitimacy so long as their fathers don't hatch crazy notions of marrying their mothers. Dhowli's early ruminations in the forest also reveal that the life of autonomy she imagines is itself scandalous for a Dusad woman. Her pregnancy and the crisis it provokes reveal both the ideological fiction of intercaste "untouchability" and the precedents and everyday practices regarding the sexual exploitation of low-caste women. Ideology and practice converge in the statements that "The fault is always the woman's," or that "all the blame goes to Dhowli." These consonant judgments are pronounced by Misrilal's mother and "village society," respectively; they are accepted by Dhowli, who "never even thought of protesting" (193). While the narrative implicates almost everyone in the village, it is indeed the woman who pays the price.

The solution Dhowli eventually finds to the crisis that threatens her survival also subverts expectations within the narrative and for the reader. The first half of "Dhowli," which begins *in medias res*, is suffused with a state of waiting that generalizes the expectancy of Dhowli's pregnancy: she waits for Misrilal to return and keep his promises; the villagers and forest workers wait to see if he will return or if an abandoned, shamed Dhowli will "end up opening her door at night when the pebbles strike"—the euphemism for this form of informal, coerced sex work (198). What no one expects is that Dhowli will find a way not merely to survive, but even thrive when she embraces her new role and refuses to be ashamed about selling herself to anyone who can pay. The Misras attempt to "kill [her], but not directly" by starving her, but when she "figure[s] out the means of survival [and . . .] defeats [their] revenge," they force her from the village (192, 202). Dhowli's plight and her response to it are the logical consequence of the Misras's exploitation of low-caste women; her scandalous exception reveals the deeper scandal of the ordinary in which women are one more resource at the Misras' disposal. Indeed, it is the sight of a well-fed, rested, carefully groomed, and glowing Dhowli that enrages Misrilal when he returns and recognizes what she has become; his anger at this sight is the narrative catalyst that breaks the impasse between Dhowli and the Misras and leads to her expulsion from the village. Misrilal finally seizes the prerogatives of "a man and a Brahman" that both his hard-hearted brother and the spurned, defiant Dhowli accuse him of being too weak to claim (204). The narrative exposes a multi-layered scandal: in her castigation of Misrilal's smitten behavior, Dhowli invokes as normative the very patriarchal and caste privileges that the narrative would have us recognize as the broader scandal.

Yet Dhowli ultimately embraces her fate, regretting what she sees as her previous stupidity in resisting the pressure to prostitute herself. As she leaves the village, her mother laments that Dhowli did not stay with her brother-in-law instead of returning, widowed, to Tahad. Dhowli thinks to herself, however, that had she remained in the household she married into so young that she cannot remember her own wedding, she would have been

> a whore individually, only in her private life. Now she is going to be a whore by occupation. She is going to be one of many whores, a member of a part of society. Isn't the society more powerful than the individual? Those who run the society, the very powerful—by making her a public whore—have made her a part of the society. Her mother is not going to understand this. (205)[9]

As she heads for Bihar's capital to register as a prostitute, Dhowli understands herself as an agent rather than a victim, perhaps hoping that she'll find in the city the kind of autonomous life she once imagined in the forest. Her powerful—if unvoiced—critique reflects a subaltern woman's recognition of her place within systemic injustice and the possibilities for negotiating it. This narrative strategy is common in Mahasweta Devi's fiction: subaltern characters perceive glimmers of the "deep truth" of systemic exploitation, but their insights are voiced fully only for the reader.[10] Dhowli's recognition of herself as a "member of society" echoes a moment in Devi's "Douloti the Bountiful," in which the bonded laborer (*kamiya*) Bono Nagesia remarks that before he left his village "I didn't know how large our kamiya society was. . . . That's why I no longer feel alone. Oh, the society of kamiyas is so large" (72, 75). Bono's epiphany reflects his experience traveling the country to document the practice of bonded labor: like Dhowli, he is empowered by recognizing the structural nature of his experience, even as the evidence-gathering project confirms, without hope of remedy, that bonded labor (including bonded prostitution) is "all over India" (93).[11] Dhowli grasps her societal position even before she leaves Tahad; unlike Bono, however, she has no way to articulate this knowledge, which brings her position somewhat closer to Bono's niece Douloti, who suffers fourteen grueling years of bonded prostitution yet cannot even formulate the terms of protest.

Unlike Douloti, Dhowli's perception of a society constituted through prostitution allows her to stop seeing her body as her enemy (189) and to recognize it as a means of production from which—unlike land or forest—she cannot be alienated. Yet the sense of autonomy and self-proprietorship that Dhowli sees in sexuality and sex work is unusual, or at least depicted as unsustainable, in Mahasweta Devi's other fiction:[12] Douloti is literally consumed by the years of servicing men, her putrid body finally setting the limit to her ordeal, while Mary Oraon of Devi's story "The Hunt" kills the predatory Tehsildar in the forest but then must leave her community. It is difficult to imagine what follows the spectacular moment at the end of

"Draupadi" when the bloodied, gang-raped Dopdi defiantly challenges the man who organized her sexual torture. Indeed, in the narrative's continuing manipulation of assumptions and appearances, the empowering epiphany about Dhowli being a "part of society," and thus her prospects for an autonomous life as a "public whore," turn out to be fragile and tenuous, as they are subverted in the story's closing moments. "Dhowli" ends by reframing the notions of crisis that drive its narrative conflict.

As Dhowli leaves the village behind, her perspective gives way to the narrator's:

> Dhowli watches the sky, blue as in other days, and the trees, as green as ever. She feels hurt, wounded by nature's indifference to her plight. Tears finally run from her eyes with the pain of this new injury. She never expected that the sky and the greens would be so impervious on the day of turning Dhowli into a public whore. Nothing in nature seems to be at all moved by the monstrosity of what is done to her. Has nature then accepted the disgracing of the Dhowlis as a matter of course? Has nature too gotten used to the Dhowlis being branded as whores and forced to leave home? Or is it that even the earth and the sky and the trees, the nature that was not made by the Misras, have now become their private property? (205)

This passage concludes the story; it situates Dhowli's earlier epiphany about being a "public whore" into broader social and ecological contexts. Nature serves as a limit to Dhowli's resolve: its indifference is an unexpected "new injury" that, remarkably, seems to elicit the first tears of her ordeal. While nature looks on unmoved by Dhowli's expulsion, neither the bus driver nor the forest contractor can bear to look at her: the forest contractor's shame presumably derives from his having been the first man to whom Dhowli opened her door. She eschews a last look back at her mother and son for fear that she will also glimpse "the brass trident atop the temple of the Misras" that symbolizes their cosmological rectitude and patriarchal dominance (205).

In this economy of looking and not looking upon a scene of injustice, only nature remains indifferent. The passage raises questions about how to reconfigure the notion of pathetic fallacy for an ecologically minded and culturally specific reading practice.[13] At two earlier moments, Dhowli's feelings about Misrilal are strikingly entangled with the forest: we have already seen how his failure to return gives the forest a menacing aspect. And near the beginning of the narrative, Dhowli seems to recall Misrilal's first pleading words that "still make the breeze waft in her mind, the leaves rustle, and the stream murmur" (188).[14] Memories of Misrilal evoke a peaceful forest, while his absence later in the narrative darkens her perception of it. These fleeting moments of pathos pass without narratorial comment, however. Something quite different happens in the narrative's closing moments, which, as occurs elsewhere in Devi's fiction, reflect a shift in register—whether in diction ("Douloti the Bountiful") or temporality ("Draupadi")—that creates a striking final tableau. The shift here is evident in the sudden distance between Dhowli and the narrator, as well as the abrupt focus on "nature" (rather than the forest)—a word absent in the text until this point. In the narrative's closing moments, Dhowli is "wounded by nature's indifference," by the fact that nature does not reflect her own individual emotional state or social plight. I don't think we're supposed to dismiss Dhowli's pained perception of an indifferent nature as an unfortunate cognitive error, a pathological symptom of overwrought emotion. Even the forest contractor is ashamed at what is happening to her.

Without doing too much violence to his argument, we can situate this moment in terms of John Ruskin's valorization of those who "feel strongly, think strongly, and see truly": poets who love nature enough to be moved by it, yet maintain the proper mental "command" and "government" that prevents them from making the error of imbuing nature with emotion or sentience (164, 169). In this moment of overwhelming emotion, Dhowli *wants* to find her plight reflected in nature, yet does not; this pathetic disjuncture leads her to contemplate the possible truth (Ruskin's lodestar) of nature's acceptance of injustice or its expropriation by the powerful. Note that these possibilities are presented as speculative alternatives. Nature appears unmoved; therefore, it may have become either resigned to "accept[ing] the disgracing of the Dhowlis" or expropriated as private property. The lack of correspondence between nature's appearance and Dhowli's emotional state raises the possibility that even if nature is understood to cast judgment on human social dynamics, its authority would be mooted by human ownership of nature. In this logic, nature-as-property lacks the standing to have emotions or cognition.

This implicit progression of human/nature relationships from emotional reflection to sentient judgment to deadening expropriation is reinforced if we read the passage not only in terms of Ruskin's pathetic fallacy but also in terms of more culturally proximate literary contexts. Indeed, I think that we are invited to compare this moment with those in the Hindu epics *Ramayana* and *Mahabharata* when faithful wives are publicly accused of sexual impropriety or whoredom: gods, nature, or both respond to such false charges with outraged horror.[15] Dhowli is a poor, late twentieth-century Dusad widow (and prostitute), not a twice-born epic heroine like Sita or Draupadi; yet even in this disenchanted, modern world, it's scandalous, this unflinchingly realist narrative suggests, that nature acts (or fails to act) as it does. The series of questions that close the narrative transport us from the last vestiges of an epic chronotope (in which nature serves as a warrant for justice) to a contemporary worldview in which property relations obviate any affective or ethical correspondence between nature and humans. The implications of Dhowli's story become larger, if not precisely epic, when the focus not only shifts from the forest to nature, but also expands to encompass a broader—perhaps even global—class conflict between "the Dhowlis" and "the Misras," who now may even have nature on their side.

The momentum of the final questions carries us far beyond Dhowli's pained recognition of nature's indifference to the even more scandalous possibility of its expropriation. Nature may no longer serve as the warrant for justice; its indifference, however, seems a product not of its autonomy but rather its subordination as the instrument of a greater injustice. Dhowli's recognition of nature's indifference might raise important ecocritical questions about the limits of forms of relation to nature that work through personification, so that her second epiphany might be a salutary invitation for readers to consider nature *qua* nature rather than as a mirror for the human. The thrust of the narrative, however, pulls us past such implicit questions to those it does voice about whether Dhowli's—and nature's—exploitation by the Misras has been writ large across the globe. To see nature's indifference as instructive is thus to read against the grain of the narrative: this tension may reflect the uneasy terrain that the ecocentric/anthropocentric binary aims to chart.

THE POLITICS OF SURVIVAL

The story closes with the question of private property hanging in the air, and it's difficult not to think of Indian physicist and ecofeminist Vandana Shiva's critique of the privatization of nature assumed by neoliberal economic development schemes. Shiva emphasizes the violence inherent in these seemingly abstract economic processes:

> the transformation of commons into commodities [. . .] common property rights into private property rights [. . .] implies the exclusion of the right to survival for large sections of society [. . . . and] it robs from nature its right to self-renewability and sustainability, by eliminating the social constraints on resource use that are the basis of common property management [. . . .] At a time when a quarter of the world's population is threatened by starvation due to the erosion of soil, water, and genetic diversity of living resources, chasing the mirage of unending growth, by spreading resource destruction technologies, becomes a major source of genocide. (*Ecology* 332, 334, 349)

Shiva published *Ecology and the Politics of Survival* in 1991; in her earlier book, *Staying Alive* (1988), she argued, "The killing of people by the murder of nature is an invisible form of violence which is today the biggest threat to justice and peace" (36).

Shiva articulated these claims about the unparalleled violence of economic development at the beginning of a decade of more conventional forms of genocide: the 1990s saw a series of well-publicized crises of spectacular ethnic violence in the former Yugoslavia, Rwanda, and the Congo. The definition of genocide—and the obligations consequent from invoking the term—became a matter of public debate in the United States.

In this context, Shiva's concern about the genocidal "killing of people by the murder of nature"—a kind of violence whose effects are communicated in Mahasweta Devi's writing, of which many English translations appeared in the 1990s—could hardly compete with the sensational images of man's (more direct) inhumanity to man crowding nightly newscasts. "Dhowli" begins by stressing that the road ends at Tahad, which is nearly "cut off from the outside world" during the monsoon (185). Dhowli and Tahad were literally nowhere on the crowded post–Cold War map of violent conflict: the geographical obscurity and particular form of violence staged in Mahasweta Devi's fiction made it difficult to follow Shiva all the way in her superlative, globalist claims—the *biggest threat* to justice and peace, a *major source* of genocide. Reading their work together during the 1990s decade of genocide, I was sympathetic to Shiva's claims, but also found them rather scandalous amidst the Balkan and African crises and the inadequacies of U.S. responses to them. As the conversations running through this volume attest, however, the crucial move that Shiva makes, particularly amidst the spectacular political violence of the 1990s, is to call our attention to violence waged against people through nature that is all the more insidious for being *invisible*, whether its tempo is accelerated or, in Rob Nixon's helpful term, "slow."[16]

In 2011, there is hardly anything scandalous in Shiva's claims, a shift that is itself scandalous. Forecasts of global climate change suggest that its effects will be not only catastrophic, but also unevenly distributed, threatening in particular the already fragile existence of the world's poor: those who have for decades been living out the "politics of survival" under the mantle of development. In India, the ascendancy of the World Bank and the recognition of a deforestation crisis by the state and civil society in the 1980s brought a new policy of social forestry, which claimed to reorient forest policy toward the needs of the people, after more than a century of India's forests being managed for commercial-industrial rather than popular-democratic or local interests.[17] Published in 1979, on the brink of the transition to social forestry, "Dhowli" raises questions about privatization that anticipate some of social forestry's actual effects: the spread of privatized, commercial plantations of ecologically harmful eucalyptus. The story's complexity, however, derives from its focalization through Dhowli, so that India's forest crisis *remains* all but invisible in the narrative. Another kind of "forest fiction" is at work in this historical context, in which the powerful expropriate not only nature but also the rhetoric of its protection: in her foreword to Shiva's *Staying Alive*, Rajni Kothari warns against the "recent appropriation of the environmental vocabulary and metaphors by governments and elites, and by international agencies like the World Bank, who [. . .] are succeeding in both depoliticising voices of protest and struggle and making environmental protection into a surrogate for the same old development project on which corporate interests and technocrats are so keen" (ix).

This post-colonial, neoliberal common sense that, in Neil Lazarus's phrase, "mostly spell[s] out exploitation in new letters," underwrites the seemingly timeless conflict generated by caste-crossing lovers in remote Tahad (36). While Dhowli is seduced by imagining herself as the protagonist of a forest tale, Misrilal invokes what we might call "fictions" of the post-Independence nation-state, in order to flesh out his dreams of a world in which caste discrimination is outlawed and "'Tahad is not the only place to live.'" "The laws are not for people like us," Dhowli retorts, and the story proves her right (192).[18] The narrative's two conclusions about Dhowli's fate—her counterintuitive pride at having become a member of society, on the one hand, and the angry despair about nature's indifference to the plight of "the Dhowlis," on the other—reveal the contradictory interstices of the politics of survival in the era of privatization. "Dhowli" makes unsubtle connections among dangers in the forest posed by wolves, forest workers, and procurers who force women into prostitution. We see that sex work can function simultaneously as a rationalized equivalent to the privatization of nature, as well as a means of survival: a canny alternative to privatization's genocidal consequences. As Fernando Coronil writes, "prostitution as a strategy of individual survival reveals a link between the naturalization of market rationality and the perverse commodification of human beings through the transformation of what are generally considered 'natural' functions or private activities into a marketed form of labor power" (75). Coronil identifies the fundamentally (if perversely) ecological logic of capitalism, in which

> people may "count more" or "less" than natural resources only in terms of a perspective that equates them; the value of people can be compared to the value of things only because both are reduced to capital. The definition of people as capital means that they are to be treated as capital—taken into account insofar as they contribute to the expansion of wealth, and marginalized if they do not. (77)

This objectification of humans, as opposed to the personification of nature in the pathetic fallacy, obviates questions of reciprocity, affect, and sentience by instrumentalizing humans and nature in the service of capital. By closing with the terrifying prospect of "the earth and the sky and the trees" in thrall to "the Misras," "Dhowli" opens up a gap between nature and culture only in order to close it again with the idea of nature reified as private property (205).

Mahasweta Devi's narrative attends to the gendered aspect of treating humans as capital: Misrilal's elder brother Kundan counts Dhowli as part of his vast "empire," constituted by "so much farm land and orchards, so many illegitimate children and so many fertile untouchable women, so huge a moneylending business" (203). Women like Dhowli are little more than fields to be ploughed and sown; if they make trouble, they can be eliminated like parasites.[19] Dhowli seems to have internalized this view when she considers ingesting pesticide but instead vows not to die "before seeing that betrayer once more face to face, eye to eye" (187). This reference to pesticide reminds us that the Misras's "empire" of land and women is "'not a feudal remnant but perfectly consistent with the play of market forces'" in the post–Green Revolution era, in which women's knowledge, authority, labor, and interests, Vandana Shiva argues, are displaced from agriculture (Bardhan quoted in Spivak, "Woman in Difference" 86; Shiva, *Staying Alive*, 96–178).

Mahasweta Devi's "Dhowli" offers us a sense of the lived experience of the politics of survival: what it means to be "human waste," in Zygmunt Bauman's horrific pun, disposable populations of "wasted humans" that are redundant as surplus labor or in the way of the ongoing primitive accumulation of vital resources (111).[20] Reading "Dhowli" pushes us beyond Shiva's critique of privatization, in two important ways. First, Shiva tells us that "the opening up of the village economy to large urban and industrial markets [. . .] initiated a process whereby the rich were no longer subject to the traditional social norms and this in turn led to the breakdown of the community" (*Ecology* 172).[21] The scandal that Devi's story stages is that while relations between people and between people and nature may have changed, "traditional" social norms in villages like Tahad were themselves often an affront to notions of equality and justice: for an untouchable woman, being raped (the "normal" social relation) is preferable to being seduced because "traditional social norms" (as Devi describes them) dictate that raped women's babies are entitled to support. The ecological corollary of such longer histories of social injustice is that, in moments of crisis when they are pushed to the brink, the poor may have no recourse to the ethical and political grounds upon which they might even *claim* the right to survival. Second, the story stages the impossible politics of survival even in a situation where privatization is incomplete and the forest still serves traditional cultural and ecological functions. Indeed, what's most surprising about the end of the story is the fact that *nature appears unchanged*—it is "as green as ever"—despite the suggestion that its expropriation by the powerful leaves it blind to, and unmoved by, injustice. Nature's indifference in the final scene is, paradoxically, the key to the narrative's pathetic appeal. The seeming absence of ecological crisis is the scandalous, counterintuitive clue to how deep the crisis really is.

The distinction between disaster and crisis articulated by Eric Cazdyn is helpful here: disaster is contingent, things gone awry, "that moment when the sustainable configuration of relations fails, when the relation between one thing and another breaks down" (647). Crises, on the other hand,

> occur when things go right, not when they go wrong. In other words, crises are built right into many systems themselves; systems are structured so that crises will occur, strengthening and reproducing the systems themselves [. . . .] things are structured in dominance

especially when they go right and are not simply corrupt when they go wrong. (649, 657)

Cazdyn's account of crisis as inherent to a system, rather than threatening it, echoes Walter Benjamin's critique of progress narratives: "The concept of progress should be grounded in the idea of catastrophe. That things 'just keep on going' *is* the catastrophe. Not something that is impending in any particular time ahead, but something that is always given.... Hell is not something that lies ahead of us, but this very life, here and now" (N9a,1).[22] What I have called the seeming absence of ecological crisis in Devi's short story reflects this sense of broader crisis built into the system: Nature is "as green as ever" when Dhowli is made a public whore because the exploitation of both of them is always already factored in. The forest workers are in no hurry for Dhowli to open her door precisely because their contract for extracting timber will "just keep on going."

CODA: ON READING, CRITICISM, AND CRISIS

This essay represents a return to Mahasweta Devi's fiction and the situation of Indian forests after a period of nearly a decade. In my earlier, unpublished reading of "Dhowli," I outlined detailed historical contexts involving the history of forest policy and World Bank–sponsored social forestry in India; reading the story in terms of the definition articulated in the United Nations' 1948 Convention on Genocide, I weighed Shiva's claim that the privatization of nature is a "major source of genocide." Like Dhowli herself, however, I missed some crucial things regarding imaginary relations and real conditions of existence. Just as Dhowli misses the fact that current socio-ecological relations undermine the cultural narratives through which she interprets the forest, I misread and mined Devi's narrative as a source of evidence to corroborate Shiva's critique of privatization. Focused on the story's seemingly matter-of-fact, even sardonic depiction of "real" conditions of existence, I missed how it stages imaginary relations in order to confound readers' expectations about crisis and scandal. I missed, in other words, the kernel of my present interpretation.

This is not an argument against activist, materialist, or deeply historicized criticism, nor a plea for what might be easily dismissed as "close reading" concerned with nothing but the "text itself." Indeed, quite the opposite, as will become clear below. Rather it is a plea, as we consider the ways in which postcolonial ecocriticism is an interventionist discourse,[23] that we distinguish and understand the relationship between the interventions of our critical acts and the interventions made by the literary texts we read. As I have tried to suggest with my consideration of Dhowli's embrace of romantic forest tales, or her collision with what in Anglo-American criticism goes by the name of pathetic fallacy, literary genres and aesthetic modes are deeply implicated in relationships between humans and nature, as well as in our understanding of those relationships. The texts we read make their interventions not as empirical evidence of ecological crisis nor as ready-made blueprints for action—which would assume a transparency so unliterary that it cannot even be dubbed "realist"—but rather through their particularly literary mediations. An attentiveness to such mediations (along with an awareness of the contested status of "the literary" itself) is an intervention that our training as literary critics should position us as uniquely suited to make—at the same time that we learn from and draw on the work of scientists, historians, anthropologists, policymakers, and activists. Postcolonial ecocritics' concern for critical intervention, in other words, is best realized by embracing, rather than disavowing, a concern for literary convention.[24]

This concern for literary convention can be worldly and engaged rather than hygienically formalist: not "close reading," but rather reading that measures the distances among what Edward Said distinguished as the text, the world, and the critic.[25] Indeed, I want to close by suggesting that "Dhowli"—although written three decades ago about a fictionalized Indian village cut off from the rest of the world—might now offer timely insight into the broader temporal structure of global ecological catastrophe that is vividly imagined, undeniably in process, but as yet not fully realized. This insight comes not from the referential aspects of the story, but rather from the temporal and social implications of its narrative structure. Devi's narrative opens with a generalized sense of expectation and closes with a provocative question about a nature that is at once "unchanged" and thoroughly imbricated in a system of exploitation. Pursuing its suggestion of a broader conflict between "the Dhowlis" and "the Misras," I cannot now read the end of Devi's story without thinking about the narrative implications of global climate change, which dilates the temporal relationship between cause and effect. The damage is already done yet still continues; the full effects are displaced into the future yet become ever more evident. And the Dhowlis will suffer more than, and because of, the Misras.

I have in mind a kind of haunting by a future devastation that appears each day to be a bit less distant; a prophetic memory that points toward the costs of the status quo, what nature accepts, in the story's terms, "as a matter of course." This structure of feeling is explicitly one of distance from the most devastating aspects of climate change: distance, in other words, from the front lines of the politics of survival. This distance is, to be sure, geographic and economic, in which the costs of development in the affluent North will be paid all over again by the poor in the underdeveloped South, but it is also temporal and cognitive. At this distance, many are driving around like nothing's up, water still comes out of the tap, and the lights still are on. The trees seem as green as ever, and the sky, blue as in other days. These are, I suggest, other modes of "forest fiction" in conflict with one another—the tension between imagined, imminent catastrophe and seeming normality, at least if one doesn't look around too carefully.[26] In Devi's narrative, Dhowli looks in vain for her plight to be reflected in nature, and the narrative raises an even bleaker possibility. Likewise, in the context of global climate change, the discrepancy between understanding what is happening to the Earth's climate and appreciating a beautiful day can evoke any number of responses: cognitive dissonance, melancholy, or angry skepticism.

Or we might see this tension another way, as the obverse of the situation at the end of "Dhowli": nature *is* responding to the monstrosity of what has been done, and it is we who are, for all practical purposes, scandalously unmoved. The shock of the story's conclusion, after all, derives not least from the fact that Dhowli's culturally informed, affective embrace of the forest as refuge goes a long way toward obscuring what is "actually" happening there: we see neither the act nor the effects of the ongoing logging of the forest. Crisis is what goes wrong when things go right. This scandalous, counterintuitive logic of the self-sustaining (yet ecologically unsustainable) status quo is increasingly evident in advertising campaigns of self-flagellating oil companies proclaiming their green *bona fides* and future relevance, or in marketing strategies that reassuringly shepherd the environmentally concerned and financially comfortable toward "green" consumerism. I want to suggest that, like the characters at the beginning of "Dhowli," we inhabit a time of waiting, a time of crisis no less profound for being as yet largely invisible.

NOTES

1. Many low-caste communities claim an oppositional identity as *Dalits*; while *Dalit* counterdiscourse complements Mahasweta Devi's concern with marginalization and social injustice, the term *Dalit* does not appear in most of her work. Instead, her activist engagements with *adivasis* (literally, "first inhabitants," or "tribals") emphasize questions of indigeneity and India's layered histories of conquest.

2. I borrow the term *provincialize* from Dipesh Chakrabarty's critique of the Eurocentric historiography of imperialism; see *Provincializing Europe*. In "Environmentalism and Postcolonialism," Rob Nixon examines the inadequacies of Buell's attempt to move beyond a U.S.-centric ecocriticism.

3. Although not concerned with postcolonialism, David Mazel's "American Literary Environmentalism as Domestic Orientalism" is an important attempt to bring Said's work to bear on how power and knowledge intersect in our very understanding of "the environment": "what comes to count as the environment is that which matters to the culturally dominant" (142).

4. See Agarwal et al.

5. For examples of wilderness/refuge discourse in U.S. ecocriticism, see *The Ecocriticism Reader* (eds. Glotfelty and Fromm) or Lawrence Buell's *The Environmental Imagination*. For reflections on the limitations of such discourse, see Buell, *Writing for an Endangered World* and *The Future of Environmental Criticism*; Garrard's *Ecocriticism* offers a helpful overview and more trenchant critique. For a postcolonial critique of all of the above, see Nixon, "Environmentalism

and Postcolonialism." On the "environmentalism of the poor," see Guha and Martinez-Alier, *Varieties of Environmentalism*.

6. For a more extensive discussion of the contradictions inherent in the "forest culture" idea and a reading of Mahasweta Devi's fiction in this context, see my "Epic Struggles over India's Forests."

7. The term *coolie* appears consistently throughout Kalpana Bardhan's translation; although the word has derogatory connotations in English, in many South Asian languages (including Bengali) it is a term for a hired laborer, particularly in a colonial context.

8. The traditional occupation of the Dusad *jati* (or caste) is to clear away corpses and to serve as executioners; such "polluting" work places the Dusads among the Shudras, the lowest of the four Hindu *varna* (classes). By "ritual ecology" I mean everyday practices that regulate caste purity and pollution, with consequences at scales ranging from the individual to the cosmos. Gadgil and Guha argue that traditional divisions of labor and nature among castes have played an important role in balancing human impacts upon the environment (91–110).

9. With regard to Anthony Carrigan's essay in this volume on Sri Lankan child sex workers, it's interesting to note the importance in both contexts of a critique that locates sex work within broader systems of injustice, rather than vilifying the sex workers or the johns. Dhowli's analysis of her situation implies that being an adult sex worker is preferable to being a child bride or young widow. Although both the village herbalist and her first client suggest that it would be better to become the exclusive consort of a wealthy client, Dhowli eschews the "respectability" of such an arrangement and accepts whoever can pay.

10. On "deep truth," see Devi, "Salt" (38).

11. Dhowli's late father became a bonded laborer because of debts incurred for her wedding, but this fact plays no role in the plot, even though such debts are often passed down through generations. Devi's interest is elsewhere—not on the "facts" of bonded labor or deforestation, but on the imaginative and cultural terrain that shapes Dhowli's experience.

12. I am grateful to Jill Didur for this insight.

13. The pathetic fallacy is an aesthetic phenomenon that belies unresolved philosophical tensions regarding "the nature of nature" and human relationships to it. Buell argues that the pathetic fallacy, or the personification of nature, is an ethical precondition for the emergence of "ecological care" (*Environmental Imagination* 187, 218). Yet nineteenth-century European discourse on the pathetic fallacy is not easily extricated from imperialist epistemologies, a point implicit in Buell's discussion of Wordsworth's descriptions of "rocks in civilized countries" (Buell's phrase, 188) and John Ruskin's 1856 distinctions between "great" and "smaller" men's propensity to succumb to "ignoble" irrationality in the face of emotion (164, 169). Claims for the intentional or emotional capacity of non-human entities can serve as the mark of either overwrought poetic emotion or the animist, "primitive" mind. If contemporary ecocritical impulses seek to redeem the truths within what has gone by the name of pathetic fallacy, then this line of thinking must also be subjected to postcolonial critique.

14. The temporality of this retrospective moment is complex: it is unclear whether Dhowli is remembering Misrilal's words in a moment contained within the diegesis or from some later moment beyond the narrative. In any case, the narrative contrasts the power of his *remembered* words to evoke an idyllic forest against their effect when she first heard them: a "terrible fear" (188).

15. This intertextual echo is audible precisely because Devi restages Draupadi's public shaming and rescue in the *Mahabharata* in her short story "Draupadi." In my essay "Epic Struggles over India's Forests," I read Douloti's plight in "Douloti the Bountiful" in terms of Sita's ordeal in the *Ramayana*.

16. See Rob Nixon, "Slow Violence."

17. See Gadgil and Guha, *This Fissured Land: An Ecological History of India*.

18. Spivak describes the aporia of decolonization: "there is always a space in the new nation that cannot share in the energy of this reversal. This space had no established agency of traffic with the culture of imperialism. . . . Conventionally, this space is described as the habitat of the *subproletariat* or the *subaltern*" ("Woman in Difference," 78). The bodies of subaltern women, Spivak demonstrates, are at once the epitome of, and displaced from, this space.

19. Devi's "Douloti the Bountiful," whose plot centers around bonded prostitution, features a similar critique of the sexual exploitation of women's bodies: "the boss has turned them into land / The boss ploughs and ploughs their land and raises the crop" (59). These bitter indictments of treating women as agricultural land contrast with Devi's suggestion that characters like Mary Oraon in "The Hunt" are related metonymically to the forest. Indeed, "Dhowli" reverses the plot of "The Hunt": whereas Mary slyly arranges to tryst with her tormentor in the forest in order to slay him there with her machete, Dhowli initially brandishes her knife at the forest contractor but then agrees to accept him as her first client. Unlike "Dhowli," "The Hunt" valorizes the link between women and nature in Mary's defense of herself in the forest. Dhowli's relation to the forest, by contrast, is self-consciously mediated through the cultural tradition of forest tales in which she briefly imagines herself as protagonist. I'm grateful to Elizabeth DeLoughrey for prompting me to articulate this comparison.

20. In *The New Imperialism*, David Harvey describes primitive accumulation as a recurrent process whose contemporary mode he dubs "accumulation by dispossession." Neil Smith reexamines the ways in which contemporary capitalism exploits "natural" disaster in his essay "Disastrous Accumulation."

21. Gadgil and Guha add that the ever-increasing control over Indian forests by the state means that "no social group has any stake in the long-term husbanding of forest resources" (196), so that what were once wise forest management practices are now obsolete; most forest resources are or can potentially be subsumed under state control for the purpose of production and revenue.

22. The logical extension of this understanding of history is Benjamin's famous revision of Marx's idea of revolutions as the "locomotive of world history": "perhaps revolutions are an attempt by the passengers on this train—namely, the human race—to activate the emergency brake" ("Paralipomena," 402).

23. The question of postcolonial ecocriticism as an interventionist discourse was first raised by Anthony Carrigan at the 2008 ACLA conference where the idea for this volume originated.

24. For an important (and witty) critique of ecocritics' wariness about acknowledging the *literariness* of their object of study, see Dana Phillips, *The Truth of Ecology*.

25. See Edward Said, *The World, The Text, and the Critic*.

26. In *From Apocalypse to Way of Life*, Frederick Buell traces a late twentieth century shift from warnings against future environmental apocalypse to awareness of inhabiting present crisis and "living on through loss" (78). This argument has important temporal implications for reordering the plot of human-nature relations as a dynamic, present unfolding of past environmental harm, but it overlooks the

possibility that we may inhabit present crisis *and* yet face future apocalypse (or at least catastrophe). In the energy and economic crises of 2008, something important seemed to shift in the *zeitgeist* of the United States, but I would argue that most Americans' perceptions of present crisis are fundamentally economic rather than ecological, and that the ecological losses associated with climate change still remain to be fully realized in a very possibly catastrophic future. There is also a difference between the psychic grief one might experience today at the sense of a lost future and other kinds of losses yet to be experienced in actually inhabiting the futures that remain.

PART III

THE LIVES OF (NONHUMAN) ANIMALS

7

Stranger in the Eco-Village
Environmental Time, Race, and Ecologies of Looking
Rob Nixon

> [Conservation biologists and political ecologists] tend to speak entirely past each other.... Conservation biologists segregate nonhumans; political ecologists too often take them for granted as resources for human use. Instead, we might want to look at how species and populations slip in and out of markets, in and out of cultural attention, and in and out of a whole spectrum of not-yet-fully-described interactions between humans and nonhumans.
>
> Tsing, *Friction*, 173

Anna Tsing may be writing about Indonesia, but her insights resonate with particular force in South Africa, where the segregations of humans from nonhumans have long been implicated in the violent segregations of humans from humans. South Africa's traumatic history of colonial conquest, land theft, racial partition, and racist conservation places particular pressure on those conservation biologists, political ecologists, writers and activists committed to reimagining, for a postapartheid era, their society's inherited cultures of nature.[1]

This transformative task is rendered more urgent by South Africa's rare environmental significance: only two nations, Brazil and Indonesia, surpass it in biodiversity. South Africa thus combines, in combustible form, extreme ecological wealth and a postapartheid legacy of extreme economic and territorial inequity. A major flashpoint for the tension between these extremes remains the game reserve, that contradictory, lucrative, historically troubled space that both promises encounters with the "timeless" Africa of charismatic megafauna and risks reinscribing the society's dominant culture of nature as racially exclusive and inimical to political transformation. It is in this context that I seek to elaborate what I call ecologies of looking in relation to the temporal enclave mentality of the eco-archaic, a dynamic that, while exemplified with unusual force by the game reserve, has a broad pertinence to the prospects for a postcolonial environmentalism that strives to reconcile social justice, ecological sustainability, and the international marketing of nature.

Across much of southern and East Africa, game reserves and "native" reserves have shadowed each other historically in the interdependent administrations of conservation, leisure, and labor. The noun "reserve" may refer to either a sanctuary or a place of involuntary confinement—a refuge or a cage. This double valence carries a special force in South Africa, suggesting both spaces reserved for environmental protection and the "native" reserves (precursors to the Bantustans) that served as holding pens in the circuits of migrant mine labor. Because South Africa's ecologies of enclosure are ghosted by traumas of forced removal, the destiny of the game reserve—within what Njabulo Ndebele calls the postapartheid "liberation of leisure" (1998, 12)—remains inextricably bound to the racial dynamics of sanctuary and trespass, to visibility and invisibility, to looking and looking away.

To illuminate these dynamics I have shaped this essay around four journeys: one autobiographical, two nonfictional, and one fictional. Collectively, these journeys track the temporal and racial performances of "wild Africa" through the transnational questions that contour them, not least the international tourist feedback loop whereby the lucrative global branding of charismatic megafauna as quintessentially South African shapes touristic expectations and the nature industry that greets them. Such circular expectations, I suggest, can inhibit expanded access to what have been painfully exclusive spaces and retard a broader commitment to biodiversity that isn't reducible to—and is sometimes incompatible with— the spectacular concentrations of megafauna that drive South Africa's nature industry.

JOURNEY ONE: CANNED LIONS AND AN ETERNITY OF BUSH

In the run up to Nelson Mandela's election in 1994, South Africa experienced considerable white flight. One of the less-noted side stories was a surge in megafauna for sale—lions, elephants, crocodiles, hippos, and the like—sent to market by emigrating whites who had shut down their circuses and private zoos. At the time, I was covering the election in the country's Eastern Province and heard word of a wildlife entrepreneur, J. P. Kleinhans, who had converted his sheep farm into a hybrid space—half game reserve, half hunting lodge. I sought him out upon hearing rumors that some of the seventy lions in his reserve had been purchased on the white-flight black market and that he was charging foreign trophy hunters top dollars to shoot dangerous African animals that were in fact "canned lions," circus retirees put out to the carnivore's equivalent of pasture.

Kleinhans greeted me with a hearty air of practiced informality—"J. P. Kleinhans, just call me J.P., Texas-style." His huge palm in the center of my back, he steered me into the lodge lobby, where I found myself surrounded by lion, buffalo, hippo, warthog, bush pig, and a dozen species of antelope, all in half-body mounts, stampeding toward me through whitewashed walls.

Following him through a door, I found myself standing amidst one of the world's most voracious master bedrooms. Mounted carnivores massed everywhere—across the floor, through the air, obscuring windows. The bed was surrounded. A leopard slunk by the pillow, as if waiting for man and wife to drop their guard and dip into sleep. A lioness pushed past some jackals squabbling over first rights to the kill. Above the bed hung a vulture with eight-foot wings, beak tilted down, glassy eyes wide, searching the duvet for any whiff of carrion or death. What kind of person, I wondered, would choose to wake to vulture talons, to stagger from some convulsive dream into a hyena's huge, mocking teeth?[2]

As we stepped outside, beyond his theater of risk, Kleinhans made a tentative allusion to the slur of domesticity that had adhered to his lions. "I've been to the States to hunt. But let me tell you, man, it's different there. Their animals, compared to ours, they're all so tame." We were soon bumping across the thornveld in his jeep, Kleinhans recounting how his son and a school friend had survived a recent mauling by some lions— "just over there." As he spoke, I felt an anxious determination in him that the tired, AARP lion that had spent its life leaping meekly through circus hoops be crushed by that other figurative lion, the untamable, almighty king of beasts, whose rule since time immemorial had terrorized the African bush. Kleinhans, as a wildlife image manager, was clearly fearful that the reputation of his lions (including his lionesses) was being feminized. It was, after all, the aura of explosive risk that would give his lions, male and female, their commercial teeth. His economic survival and male dignity depended on decommodifying the purportedly canned lions in order to recommodify them as a different product—pure, uncanned embodiments of a snarling, timeless African authenticity that couldn't be bought elsewhere.

"Almost anything Africa has got to offer," Kleinhans interjected, "you can kill it here, right here at Wolwekloof. The Americans love this place. One client, he told me, he'd traveled all over—Masai Mara, Zambia, Namibia, Kruger Park. But he said here at Wolwekloof, for the first time, he'd touched the real Africa."

Kleinhans had no blacks working at his game lodge: "My wife and me, we made enough sons to do the job. I don't need blacks here." (His wife and female relatives took care of domestic chores—the cleaning, cooking, and secretarial side of things.) At the very moment of black empowerment in the society at large, Kleinhans was creating a racial and temporal enclave, a timeless island outside a time of change. His brochure promised his American (and Russian, Italian, German, and Canadian) clients an "exclusive" experience—a word that resonated in complex ways in a country whose psychic and physical landscapes bore deep scars of enclosure and expulsion.

Many of his American clients, he noted, loved to bag their lions with crossbows. I pictured the scene as he described it: Kleinhans picks up his client at the airport, drives him to the lodge, where he acts out some ersatz bow-and-arrow hunt, half National Geographic pigmy, half Iron John, accruing, before being whisked back to the airport, both a trophy lion and an indelibly African adventure shielded from any inconveniencing encounter with living Africans.[3]

It would be easy to read Wolwekloof as a straightforward narrative of atavistic, Afrikaner self-enclosure, of a racially and historically threatened man barricading himself against history, democracy, and black empowerment. But to that narrative we must add a complicating twist. If the postapartheid turn disturbed Kleinhans, he also recognized in it fresh business opportunities. With foreign tourists and hunters pouring in under Mandela, Kleinhans could capitalize on resilient mythologies of international white masculinity for which the lion hunt could serve as seductive, profitable shorthand. In creating a racio-temporal island in a sea of black majority rule he was simultaneously reaching out to an oceanic white wildlife kill-or-consume culture that stretched beyond the nation. By internationalizing his parochialism, Kleinhans was articulating himself to the white call-and-response of the charismatic megafauna touristic feedback loop.

Foreign hunter-tourists could be fierce in their demands; and what they demanded was the prospect of an ancient African ferocity, embodied not only in the king of beasts but in the landscape's untamed visage as well. These projected desires had solidified around Kleinhans's alfalfa problems that were compounding his canned lion problems. His clients kept grumbling about an alfalfa field on a distant farm visible from one corner of the lodge. The field spoiled the experience, they said; it didn't look African. In order to expunge from view agriculture's domestic taint, Kleinhans was busy erecting new accommodations for his hunter-tourists— "Zulu" huts on a hillside that guaranteed panoramic vistas unsullied by labor, human necessity, or food production.[4] Like the reed baskets, masks, and beadwork that adorned the lodge, his "Zulu" huts would foster the ambience of a cultural village sans villagers. By swiveling the view, Kleinhans could now provide his tourists with the sight lines they demanded, guaranteeing them a genuine simulacrum of foreign visual expectations of an authentic Africa.

"Don't get me wrong," Kleinhans said, tipping back his Elk Lodge baseball cap. "I like the American. But the thing about the American is you have to speak his language. What the American wants when he comes here is an eternity of bush."

I stood with him at that hilltop "Zulu" hut looking down at the bushveld scene he'd laid out for his clients: a seemingly endless temporal panorama of undying purity that his hunters could enter to make their kills.

Six months after visiting the lodge, I read in a local newspaper that Kleinhans and a Texan client had heard a distant ruckus one night: two lions brawling. The men had driven to the fight, where Kleinhans attempted to distract the warring lions by throwing them some donkey meat. When that failed, he walked toward them, shouting, waving, before trying to part them with bare hands. The lions turned on him, mauling him to death.

He died a performer in the transnational theater of Wild Africa on a stage crowded with anxieties about race, white manhood, domesticity, class, risk, and authentic wilderness, a stage that was both "timeless" and suffused with the historical uncertainties of an emergent postapartheid order which he sought to stave off—and capitalize on—by aligning himself, economically and psychologically, with the eco-archaic expectations of the Pretoria–Fort Worth axis.

Kleinhans's eldest son, Adolf, made an announcement to the press: "We will not kill these lions that killed our father." (In other words, the lions would not be singled out for punitive execution but would be available, as per normal, for commercial killing.) Within this family tragedy, something else emerged: through his unwitting martyrdom, Kleinhans had left a legacy of killer lions. The ferocious manner of his death had cleansed his animals—and the enterprise his sons inherited—of any domestic taint. Who now would dare claim he was defrauding foreign hunters with toothless, circus retirees masquerading as Wild Africa?[5]

JOURNEY TWO: RACE, CLASS, AND ECOLOGIES OF LOOKING

Not long after my encounter with Kleinhans, in the newly democratic South Africa of the mid-1990s, the fiction writer and essayist Njabulo Ndebele visited a game lodge in his native land for the first time, a venture he reflects on in his essay "Game Lodges and Leisure Colonialists."[6] Ndebele describes entering the game lodge at a dynamic moment in his society's transformation, yet finding himself cocooned in a temporal enclave, sealed against the environment of political change. Intent on leisure, Ndebele is haunted instead by "the damning ambiguities of the black tourist" (12).[7]

The white game lodge is a classic instance of what Anne McClintock terms an anachronistic space, a space marked as noncoeval with the world around it and whose implication in modernity is suppressed (244–45). But here the spatial anachronism does not simply mark the game lodge as "backward" in a progress discourse indebted to a tendentiously selective imperial enlightenment; instead, the lodge's refusal to acknowledge the contemporary renders it an atavistic space in denial of South Africa's democratic transformation while simultaneously capitalizing on that transformation. We can read the game lodge, then, as a manifestation of the postapartheid nation's suddenly expansive modern tourist industry and as a racialized and naturalized fortress against that very modernity. It is into this contradictory temporal domain that Ndebele steps.

In its antimodern dimension the lodge exists as a temporal enclave in a double, layered sense: the temporal styles evoked are both historically colonial (self-effacing servants vanishing into the bush, white campfire camaraderie, male tales of derring-do) and eternally natural (a time outside of time, before and after the human, when megafauna rule—Kleinhans's "eternity of bush"). Crucially, for our purposes, the game lodge locates itself in the postapartheid marketplace by selling a blended aura of colonial time and prehuman natural time.

Ndebele arrives as a visitor from the future present, a postapartheid pioneer. As a white-collar black wildlife tourist, his arrival at the game lodge gates is a harbinger of change, an intimation that the racialized ideology of fortress conservation is pregnable. His presence is historical in an enclave from which history has been banished; he disturbs the sealed domain of white men playing games of bushveld risk, reminding them, implicitly, of risk in a wider form—those political transformations that may, however, come in tandem with opportunities. (Ndebele wonders whether the whites around the campfire view him as someone with usable political connections to the ascendant black power elite.)[8]

In class terms, Ndebele, too, now belongs at the lodge. But the politics of his belonging are fraught with temporal contradictions. As an indigenous tourist from a newly arrived future, he also bears in his person reminders of the past; his presence points forward and backward in time. Forward to the anticipated incursions of an excluded black majority into white nature enclaves and backward to an ancestral history of being territorially *dislodged* by game lodges and other conservation projects that, while modest in relation to the country's broader history of forced removal, nonetheless created, under the banner of wildlife conservation, dispossessed conservation refugees.[9] Ndebele's presence thus renders visibly political the apolitical posture of the game lodge as natural sanctuary from politics.

We can read Ndebele's position as that of a man who has ventured abroad in his own country, an inner émigré in a white nature industry whose marketing premise is the managed wildness of the eco-archaic. His complex pursuit of leisure in this environment—and his concomitant existential stresses—are linked to what I call the ecologies of looking, that is, the interconnected webs of looking and being seen in a context where the idea of the natural predominates. Ndebele has come to relax and look: to peer through his binoculars, alongside these other folk, at the charismatic megafauna, at the spectacles of the wild. But his own spectacular presence disrupts the smooth optics of tourism.

By inserting himself into a tableau of neo-apartheid time, amidst those he calls by turns "leisure colonialists" and "leisure refugees," Ndebele makes whiteness visible (1998, 11). He does so by unsettling the temporal and physical insularity of the archaic game lodge scene, which, as I've suggested, operates paradoxically as both a quintessentially modern expression of postapartheid South Africa's reintegration into global tourist networks and as a space of white South African resistance to apartheid's aftermath.

Ndebele himself, however, is also profoundly unsettled. We can read the layered self-consciousness into which he finds himself propelled as a kind of bushveld version of Fanon's "Look, a Negro"; that moment when, on encountering the white world, Fanon observes: "I took myself far off from my own presence. . . . It was no longer a question of being aware of my body in the third person but in a triple person . . . I was responsible for my body, for my race, for my ancestors" (90, 92). But inside the game lodge, a black tourist like Ndebele isn't just under observation and self-observation, he is paying to be observed. As he notes sardonically, "he pays to be the viewer who has to be viewed." (13). (It's rhetorically apposite—a measure of Ndebele's self-anthropologizing self-estrangement—that much of the essay is written as third-person autobiography.)

Ndebele has long been troubled by what is sacrificed, imaginatively, to the pressures of spectacle. In the 1980s, amidst a brutal apartheid state of emergency, he published two controversial essays that questioned what he saw as the subservience of much South African writing to the Manichean dictates of spectacular racial violence. Those essays—"The Rediscovery of the Ordinary" and "Redefining Relevance"—lamented a literary bias toward "the predictable drama between ruthless oppressors and the pitiful victims," a bias that contracted and calcified the imaginative "range of explorable experience" (1991, 67). This "hegemony of spectacle" seduced many writers into focusing on a predictable apartheid-antiapartheid agon that obscured a whole spectrum of ordinary experience, thereby producing a literature deficient in complex interiority, deficient in inflected historical awareness, and neglectful of the fabric of everyday life. Skewed by international pressures to produce a recognizable black-on-white agon, Ndebele argued, the prevailing literary imagination tended to marginalize black rural lives in communities that might never encounter a white person from one year to the next.

I read "Game Lodges and Leisure Colonialists" as an extension of Ndebele's early preoccupation with both the spectacular costs of spectacle and the rediscovery of the ordinary. The essay asks, at least implicitly, what would it take for a black South African to enter the game lodge as an unspectacular, unwatched, *ordinary* tourist, thereby transforming what I'm calling the ecologies of looking? Second, how can the temporal enclave of the rural game lodge be reintegrated into a postapartheid national imaginary? Third, just as the international market for the Manichean conventions of apartheid-antiapartheid showdowns may have narrowed the South African literary spectrum, in what ways does the international tourist feedback loop of demand and satisfied desire narrow, through repetitive reinforcement, South Africa's viable cultures of nature? Returning to Anna Tsing's call for reconciling the priorities of conservation biologists and political ecologists, we can recognize in Ndebele's essay a quest to rediscover the ecological ordinary—those quotidian interactions between humans and nonhumans that move beyond the racialized theater of the eco-archaic.

Like the Caribbean paradise, the game reserve is shaped as a sanctuary from labor and from history's brutality; here history's corrugations have been Botoxed from nature's visage. In the temporal enclaves of the island refuge, ringed by ocean, and the game reserve, ringed by electrified fences, the tourist is guaranteed full immersion in the eco-archaic, which is not to be confused with the historical. To enter this refuge is to enter a charmed space that is segregated, among other things, from the history of its own segregation.

For black tourist-writers, from June Jordan and Jamaica Kincaid to Ndebele, this stage-managed amnesia becomes a special source of disorientation and outrage. A direct relationship emerges between a suppressed history of dispossession and the black visitor's embattled self-possession. "How is it [Ndebele asks,] that a simple quest for peace and restoration turned into an unexpectedly painful journey into the self?" He finds himself "pushed into a state of simmering revolt" (10).[10]

What surfaces for Ndebele, like Jordan and Kincaid before him, is a vexed relationship to labor, both historically and in the present. The violent labor histories that shaped the colonial landscapes of the Caribbean and South Africa were inseparable from forced removals, whether trans-Atlantic or internal to the white settler nation-state (via first the native reserves and later the Bantustans). Given this anguished history, all these writers are angered by the labor-intensive production of labor's illusory absence, an absence critical to the eco-archaic's role in producing a sweat-free, soft-focus, natural tranquility that appears at once effortless and untouched by human history.[11]

In the touristic present, the fraught issue of labor resurfaces through the prism of class, which complicates whatever racial identification the vacationing writer may feel with those who tiptoe around him in roles of unobtrusive service. Ndebele is plunged into anguished inner debate on how to relate to paradise's servants: if he fraternizes with them, will his dignity be compromised in the eyes of the white tourists? How do the servants view him? How much is the correct amount to tip?[12]

At the heart of the history-labor-nature quandary stands the vexed issue of transport—as ancestral racial journey, as aesthetic convention, and as touristic affect. Ndebele, Jordan, and Kincaid, all shadowed by histories of forced removal, find themselves unable to enter, in any straightforward way, the sublime as portal to a "natural" state of transport. Given their ancestral histories—and given the suppression of those histories in the temporal enclaves of eco-archaic amnesia—Ndebele, Kincaid, and Jordan all find themselves resistant to being unself-consciously "carried away."

The uneasy circuits of sublime pleasure are directly related to another dilemma: what does it mean, in the fullest sense of the phrase, to be *absorbed* by nature? In terms of a post-Enlightenment ecology of spectatorship, how are Kincaid (an anticolonial botanical enthusiast) and Ndebele (an avid antiapartheid bird-watcher) to circumnavigate the repressive legacy of racial classification that figured their ancestors as "natural"? White nature tourists, I would suggest, have less troubled access to sublime natural absorption in a postcolonial environment because they can experience their whiteness as an unself-consciously unclassified state.[13] Ndebele, by contrast, is painfully alive to the problematics of natural union and a historically freighted politics of looking: "when [black tourists] go game viewing, it is difficult not to feel that, in the total scheme of things, perhaps they should be out there with the animals, being viewed" (12).

The presence of these animals is critical. In the tourist cultures of the Caribbean, Eden typically figures as a garden—a sanctuary from history and labor, but a sanctuary without predation.[14] By contrast, the African Edens of the southern and East African tourist industries are shaped around the presence—and managed threat—of charismatic megafauna, which become the primary guarantors of encounters with the timeless and the pristine.[15] This has profound gender implications: the African Eden must be scoured not only of history and labor but also (as we've seen in the case of Wolwekloof) of the taint of domesticity, the stigma of the tame. As a result, the cultural spectacle around African Edens has a strongly masculine tilt: the white game guides, the black trackers, the bush pilots all carry forward—adapted for the contemporary global marketplace—a neo-Victorian obsession with risk (or at least with the performance of risk's illusions).[16]

JOURNEY THREE: STRANGER IN THE VILLAGE

James Baldwin's "Stranger in the Village" may seem an unlikely text to enfold into an analysis of game reserves, racialized tourism, and environmental time. Yet in light of the foregoing discussion of Kleinhans and Ndebele, we can glean from Baldwin's justly classic essay productive insights into the ecologies of looking and the role that cultures of nature play in modernity's civilizational power plays.

Some forty years before Ndebele arrived as a solitary, improbable novelty at the game lodge gates, Baldwin spent the first of several sojourns in a Swiss Alpine village that he portrayed as a "white wilderness" (159). Baldwin had been forewarned that "he would probably be a 'sight' for the village," and his essay offers a far-reaching meditation on invisible visibility, on how it feels—and what it means culturally—to be a "sight" unseen. Baldwin, like Ndebele after him, is thrust by the stresses of racialized leisure into a state of spectacular self-consciousness.

Baldwin's anger and insight flow from his experience of what I would call empowered parochialism. The Swiss villagers have never encountered a black person before; they lead untraveled lives, holed up in their icy redoubt, severed from the world. Yet Baldwin recognizes that these hyperparochial people are powerfully connected in their severance, unconsciously emboldened by the broad currents of Western culture—Dante, Michelangelo, the cathedral at Chartres—that afford them an assumed racial superiority and ease.

What makes Baldwin's essay so suggestive in tandem with Ndebele's is the acuity with which both writers expose the profound resistance—locally, nationally, internationally—to the temporal and geographical incorporation of blackness into modernity. Baldwin is treated in the village as a "suspect latecomer"; despite his experiential cosmopolitanism, he is made to feel more tangential to the vast temporal and spatial flows of Western culture than the most illiterate, cut-off Swiss villager (164).

Unlike Baldwin in blindingly white rural Switzerland, Ndebele doesn't have to travel far—just assume the mantle of local time traveler—in order to be exoticized as an oddity in a blindingly white South African rural enclave. If Ndebele, too, remains, for now, alone and improbable, he is writing decades later than Baldwin, on a very different historical cusp. Yet, when Ndebele exclaims that "the entire world of contemporary tourism carries no intuitive familiarity" for him, we sense a kindred indignation to Baldwin's anger at the energy it takes to stake out for himself a space in a modernity organized around his anachronistic yet constitutive exclusion.[17] The challenge Ndebele faces is to reclaim—and ultimately reimagine—the game lodge's overdetermined modern nature, a modern nature in denial of its modernity. Ndebele's insights can be read as supplementing Baldwin's in this essential way: it is not only the architectural, literary, artistic, and musical cultures of the West that have historically been wielded as weapons of black exclusion (largely through denied coevalness and denied hybridity), but the cultures of nature as well, including the culture of wildlife tourism, whereby a provincial whiteness is fortified by white pilgrims from abroad.[18] The game lodge becomes, then, a site, to adapt Amitava Kumar's phase, of "cosmopolitan provincialism" (2002, 64). Thus Wild Africa, while purporting to represent civilization's antithesis, freights whiteness with another kind of cathedral ballast.

Both Baldwin's and Ndebele's "white wilderness" essays assail a diehard, historically dominant culture's determination to keep living in denial, to sustain an unsustainable condition of contorted innocence. For the Europe of the 1950s, black people—over there in the colonies—could remain at an abstract remove: "in effect," Baldwin notes, "the black man, as a man, did not exist for Europe" (169). American whites of that era, he adds, proved even greater contortionists, "still nourish[ing] the illusion that there is some means of recovering the European innocence, of returning to a state in which black men do not exist" (173). The postapartheid South African game lodge—as sanctuary of illusory innocence and eco-archaic return—depends on an even less plausible theatre of denial, given the accession of the black majority to political power.[19] Buoyed by performances of ecological elegy and arrested time, the game lodge serves as the last great hope of a monochromatic nostalgia that wishes away the cultural, economic, and political transformations of the society in which it is embedded. If, in Baldwin's closing assertion in his 1955 essay, "[t]his world is white no longer, and will never be white again," how much more decisively his voice echoes four decades later in a nation where a black majority, for the first time in history, had voted a white supremacist regime out of office (175).

JOURNEY FOUR: FROM LEISURE REFUGEES TO THE ULTIMATE SAFARI

Nadine Gordimer's short story "The Ultimate Safari" gives voice to invisible, traumatized cross-border travelers at the furthest remove from Ndebele's "leisure refugees" and Kleinhans's foreign tourists seeking their "eternity of bush." "The Ultimate Safari" carries forward my concern, on the one hand, with racialized ecologies of looking and, on the other, with the tension between an eco-archaic conservationist ideology that exempts itself from history and a society undergoing tumultuous historical changes.[20]

Gordimer's story follows a group of Mozambican refugees on a fugitive, perilous trek across South Africa's largest and most celebrated wildlife preserve, the Kruger National Park. The Kruger Park, over eighty years old and roughly the size of Israel, stretches for 220 miles along South Africa's eastern perimeter with Mozambique.[21] The megafauna-rich Kruger is symbolically central to South Africa's conservation history, wilderness mythology, and tourist industry yet is multiply liminal, serving, during the Mozambican civil war years (1975–91) as an overdetermined border zone: between a Marxist postcolonial state and its anticommunist apartheid neighbor, between black majority rule and white minority supremacy, between the cultures of migrant leisure and migrant labor, and between the animal and the human.[22] This liminal overdetermination has a profound temporal dimension as well, bringing into frictional proximity animal time, tourist time, refugee time, the spiritualized time of white supremacy, and revolutionary utopian time, all represented as noncoeval on this particular cusp of modernity. If Yellowstone were located at Nogales or El Paso, it would loosely approximate the convergence of charismatic megafauna, tourist leisure, cross-border desperation, militarization, and legal and clandestine immigration that have marked Kruger's history.

The Kruger Park of Gordimer's story—especially when read alongside her little known essay on the park as frontier—takes shape as a place of visible and ghosted movements of animal herds, herds of tourists, civil war refugees, conservation refugees, and migrant laborers shuttling back and forth between Mozambique and South Africa's gold mines.[23] By selecting as her narrator a ten-year-old refugee, Gordimer grants her story a potent affective energy and intimacy. But the little girl's perspective is necessarily limited in its grasp of the broader political implications of the journey, which we can productively situate in the ideological history of Kruger Park, a history that dramatizes the complicity between the rise of a white supremacist capitalism and an eco-archaic bushveld aesthetic.

Almost a century ago, the Transvaal legislature banned blacks from owning guns and hunting dogs, transforming game from "an economic resource available to everyone, to a commodity reserved for the ruling white group" (Carruthers 17). This ban—in the name of conservation—compounded the multipronged squeeze on rural African subsistence living, rendering it increasingly precarious. In the dominant colonial conservationist mythology, the nineteenth-century decimation of game resulted primarily from the cruel, uncontrolled slaughter of wildlife by rural Africans, whereas historically the prime culprit in that butchery was an imported European ethos of killing as an ennobling sport, an ethos that, backed by advanced weaponry that Africans lacked, severed hunting from the need for protein and hide clothing, and the need to safeguard crops, herds, and flocks from animal predation (Carruthers 31). The racially skewed hunting laws had a malign impact on African nutrition, subsistence livelihoods, and food security. Together with the creation of national parks like Kruger and (to a far greater extent) the creation of congested native reserves and the imposition of taxes, such laws drove more and more blacks into the capitalist economies of the mines and white agriculture.[24] The racialized discourse of wildlife scarcity (mapped in temporal terms as an ethical difference between "backward" and "advanced" peoples) was thus profoundly entwined with the discourse of labor scarcity in a rapidly modernizing economy.[25]

The colonial rescripting of wildlife scarcity as a black problem—which helped rationalize the early twentieth-century creation of national parks—depended on demonizing blacks as barbarous poachers whose relationship to wildlife was one of illegality and threat and, conversely, on mythologizing whites as stewards of nature whose conservationist principles evidenced a wider civilizational superiority. This explosive history of land theft and unequal access to wildlife as resource (whether for hunting or, later, tourist revenue) helped harden stereotypes of the white conservationist and the black poacher that continue to hamper environmental efforts today, with many black South Africans continuing to view wildlife as rivals for water, food, and grazing land.

South Africa's game reserves are thus historically ensnarled in a tangle of elegiac narratives around vanishing wildlife, vanishing land, vanishing livelihoods, and vanishing labor. Neither the game reserve nor the native reserve was represented as coeval with South Africa's white, mining-driven modernity, yet both were products of that modernization: the game reserve as a hyper-visible space of "ancient" wildness administered for touristic consumption, the native reserve as an anachronistic space structured around invisibility, where crowded human suffering and attendant ecological calamity were concentrated in "out of the way" places.[26] In terms of a national progress narrative, the mutually constitutive discourses of racial and natural purity were mapped onto both game reserves and native reserves. Game reserves were represented as positively archaic—unimproved places where whites could venture for spiritual renewal—whereas native reserves were negatively archaic, places set aside for the uncivilized.

As Jane Carruthers notes in her definitive history of Kruger Park, the white nationalist regime, confronted with international condemnation when apartheid was imposed in 1948, invoked its caring conservationist ethos—with Kruger Park as primary showpiece—as evidence that South Africa belonged to the community of civilized nations (86). Carruthers's most astute insight is her recognition that in the 1940s and '50s, before the ascent of international tourism to South Africa, the idea of the national park helped foster a unifying ideology of white nationalism between historically antagonistic Afrikaner and English South Africans. That ideology drew on two quite discrete, mutually distrustful traditions: British colonial conservation and the Afrikaner mythology of themselves as a chosen people in a God-given land. Post-1948, a trip to the Kruger National Park could be promoted as a spiritual pilgrimage for both Afrikaner and English whites, as in the words of National Parks Board public relations director, R. J. Labuschagne:

> Exalted personages of the past have ever fled to nature for meditation and solitude: Christ climbed the Mount of Olives . . . Solomon repeatedly exhorts mankind to return to nature; President Kruger [of the Transvaal Republic] spent three days on the Magaliesberg in silent meditation. . . . It is for this reason that the [white] South African nation undertakes the yearly pilgrimage to the Kruger National Park.[27]

We have here the well-established colonial trope of the topographically and socially elevated white male communing in solitude as the monarch of all he surveys. However, Labuschagne also mobilizes the religious archaic as a rationale for touristic modernity by extolling a "return" to nature as a white nation-building exercise, an individually and collectively elevating pilgrimage of renewal which gets routed through both a Christianized antiquity and a racially exclusive romantic sublime.[28]

In the late 1980s, when Mozambique was gripped by civil war and South Africa by antiapartheid uprisings, Gordimer visited the frontier zone formed by southern Mozambique, Kruger Park, and the neighboring Bantustan of Gazankulu.[29] In an astutely materialist account of her untouristic explorations, she reads that frontier wilderness as a cultural space shaped by land wars, militarization, and migrant labor. Since the late nineteenth century, Mozambique has remained the primary foreign labor reserve for South Africa's mines.[30] At the northern end of Kruger Park, a giant baobab tree served for decades as the primary recruiting station for tens of thousands of Mozambican men who were certified, dipped in disinfectant, and carted off to the mines. At this site the cultures of labor, militarism, tourism, and nature converged and interpenetrated: "Although it is within the Kruger Park," writes Gordimer:

> the road leading to the TEBA [The Employment Bureau of Africa] site is barred, like the many roads which now lead to concealed military camps rather than viewpoints for observing the animals. Nevertheless, I got there, passing buck and warthog along deserted tracks. High up overlooking the convergence of the three frontiers was a scene out of Conrad: buried in tropical trees, low buildings where men were received, fed, medically examined, signed up and transported. . . . [A] dark-browed thatched mansion surrounded by a moat of huge-leaved plants, with a magnificent wild fig tree thrust, like a tower, through the structure (61).

To this complex ecology of spectatorship we must add another invisible layer. When this northern region was incorporated into the Kruger Park in the 1930s, the Tsonga-speaking Makuleke were driven from their land. Some of these conservation refugees ended up, after decades of resistance, in the Shangaan-Tsonga "ethnic homeland" of Gazankulu, others fled to Mozambique. By the late 1970s and '80s a reverse border crossing was underway; this time the Shangaan were in flight not from conservation violence in South Africa but from South African–fomented military violence in Mozambique. By the late 1980s, refugees were streaming into Gazankulu at the rate of one thousand a month. To get there, most had to breach first the Kruger Park's 11,500-volt electric fence, then a backup razor-coiled fence, and then the park itself. In short, this "timeless" place has been repeatedly crisscrossed by the convulsive movements of desperate humans historically uprooted from their land, whether by conservation, war, or the ethnic engineering of the Bantustans.

It is one such convulsive movement that Gordimer imagines in "The Ultimate Safari" that we can read as a fictional companion piece to the sociopolitical frontier essay she published fourteen years earlier. The unnamed ten-year-old war orphan who recounts her group's *via dolorosa* across the Kruger Park tells a story that becomes, among other things, about tourism without tourists, the perspectival antithesis of Kleinhans's "Zulu" village without villagers. If Ndebele's essay focuses on the dilemmas of the hyper-visible black middle-class tourist encircled by a white nature industry, Gordimer's story dramatizes the fears of the ultra-poor whose lives depend on passing unseen through the commercialized zone of animals.

The girl's journey through time, megafauna, and the bush stands in blunt contrast to the pilgrimage toward a spiritually regenerative white race-time promulgated by Labuschagne and his ilk. "To get there," she recalls, we had to go through the Kruger Park. We knew about the Kruger Park. A kind of whole country of animals—elephants, lions, jackals, hyenas, hippos, crocodiles, all kinds of animals. We had some of them in our own country, before the war (our grandfather remembers; we children weren't born yet) but the bandits kill the elephants and sell their tusks, and the bandits and our soldiers have eaten all the buck. There was a man in our village without legs—a crocodile took them off, in our river; but all the same our country is a country of people, not animals. We knew about the Kruger Park because some of our men used to leave home to work there in the places where white people come to stay and look at the animals. (272)

The girl's great trek from her lost "country of people" to the "whole country of animals" gathers force from a potent, if implicit, contrast with the journey the tourists have undertaken. In the country of animals the girl is entering, humans remain unseen: the story alludes to the tourists who exist only as voices and cooking smells wafting through the animal night from the far side of the rest camp fence. Though constituted by the same modernity, these two contiguous groups live trespass, risk, and animal time in radically different modalities.

As I've argued, white tourists purchase the frisson of trespass into a "timeless" animal zone, a memorable, risk-simulating adventure in an eco-archaic world liberated from history. However, those other foreigners, thrust into the "whole country of animals" by history's convulsions, seek to survive risk and trespass by laboring to remain invisible in the historical present, by passing through the elephant grass undetected (by game wardens, border police, lions), by moving "like animals among the animals, away from the roads, away from the white people's camps." (273). If the Kruger Park is pitched to tourists as an opportunity to "get close" to wildlife, for the refugees human-animal intimacy depends on a deeper kind of interspecies recognition. The girl and her fellow travelers, in their transnational trespass, have also crossed over into the border zone of the human animal—where knowledge gleaned from other species can offer life-saving pointers to where water and food are and how to achieve a deeper camouflage, a safer invisibility.

As they traverse this border zone, the tourist and the refugee exist in different states of transport. The Kruger Park promises the tourist the excitement of a safely managed plunge into the deep time, the eco-archaic, of the purely animal. (Suspense typically hinges on seeing or not seeing one of the Big Five—lion, elephant, rhino, leopard, and buffalo—that have proven indispensable to the branding of South African tourism.) The refugee's temporal experience is quite different: the perilous passage through a time zone dedicated to tourists and animals doubles as a portal, not into a suspended past, but into a suspended future. These two groups of transients from opposite ends of the spectrum of voluntary and involuntary mobility pass each other like ships in the night, freighted with radically different hopes, radically different experiences of national park space-time, and radically different visions of what constitutes escape.

On their ultimate safari, the Mozambicans' collective egress represents a history-driven descent into the timeless, though one quite remote from the fenced, managed timelessness of the tourist domain. When right-wing bandits scorched their Mozambican village church and schools, the girl and her siblings began to lose their footing in the institutional rhythms of calendrical time. Thereafter, as they flee through "the country of animals," the days lose their names and traction, the old, structured rhythms of a now-destroyed village time giving way to an improvised survival dependent on reading sun, sky, and animal behavior.

The Mozambicans, their known world razed by civil war, are not so much moving toward as moving away. "Away" becomes the story's signature word: "We wanted to go where there were no bandits and there was food. We were glad to think there must be such a place; away," the girl declares (271). "We started to go away, again" (277). When they finally reach a refugee camp beyond the park, she fantasizes about living "in a real house again, with no war, no away" (281).

Away: between the lines the reader fills in the complexities of that abrupt, complex word, connecting it to a double discourse of escape that exposes the chasm between the tourist blurb and the little girl's voice. Away: as in getaway, sanctuary, refuge, retreat, terms that take on diametrically opposed valences depending on whether leisure or terror is the propulsive force, depending on whether you're in temporary flight from your white-collar workweek or intent on the hard labor of flight through a time that has lost all shape.

Having survived the wildlife sanctuary, the girl finds sanctuary in a refugee camp that (extrapolating from hints in Gordimer's short story and her essay) is located in the Gazankulu Bantustan. By story's end the girl has been living there for over two years, in a vast, overcrowded tent that rises in implicit counterpoint to the tented rest camps of the leisure colonialists. The refugees have thus exchanged the suspended time of transit through the national park for the suspended time of the refugee camp, a provisional place that, within the symbolic economy of the story, can never quite serve as resolution or destination.

Gloria Anzaldua has famously observed:

> borders are set up to define the places that are safe and unsafe, to distinguish us from them. A border is a dividing line, a narrow strip along a steep edge. A borderland is a vague and undetermined place created by the emotional residue of an unnatural boundary. It is in a constant state of transition. The prohibited and the forbidden are its inhabitants... those who cross over, pass over, or go through the confines of the normal. (3)

When, one should add, that "unnatural boundary" is marked by a national park that embodies a national culture of nature, the borderland can become a site of redoubled violence in its militarized severance of natural from unnatural and native from foreign.[31]

This fierce severance pertains powerfully to the Shangaan, the transfrontier people to whom Gordimer's narrator clearly belongs.[32] On entering the refugee camp in the bantusan, the girl:

> was surprised to find they speak our language; our grandmother told me.... Long ago, in the time of our fathers, there was no fence that kills you, there was no Kruger Park between them and us, we were the same people under our own king, right from our village we left to this place we've come to. (280)

The refugees' journey thus retraces a continuity that persists only in the unfenced past of oral memory, before this threshold people was culturally and territorially severed, first, by the map separating Portuguese colony from Boer Republic, and later by conservation's electrified fence that delimited the beginning of South Africa's national and national-nature space.[33] The Shangaan were left straddling the divide.[34]

As a transfrontier people—who can be capriciously designated by South Africans as either "us" or "them"—the Shangaan have suffered a new wave of vulnerability in recent years, becoming targets of brutal assaults and expulsions. During the wave of xenophobic killings and shack burnings that swept through the shantytowns of Johannesburg and other South African cities in 2008, Shangaan, both South African and Mozambican, were targeted as "foreigners," who (in the all-too-familiar-scapegoating that bedevils our planet of the slums) were "criminal elements" who "come over here" to steal our jobs, our women, our shacks, our things.

This often violently enforced postapartheid discrimination between the "authentically" national and the undesirable foreign is ironically waived when it comes to the commodified performances of memory and amnesia on which the tourist industry depends. The carved wooden animals, the soapstone sculptures, and the masks that American, European, and Japanese tourists carry home as authenticating mementos of their South African game park trip derive overwhelmingly from beyond South Africa's borders, especially from Mozambique and Zimbabwe, but also from Ghana, Congo, Senegal, Nigeria, and Cameroon.[35] Immigrants who risk everything crossing borders, fences, national parks, and hostile communities may be branded as undesirable Others in their persons, yet play an indispensable role in the circuits of desire of the international tourist feedback loop. For it is these artists and vendors from "away" who serve as the primary purveyors of an ersatz indigeneity through the rebranding of their artifacts as "South African" memorabilia. The carved elephants, lions, hippos, and other charismatic megafauna they sell in the condensed form of the commodity icon authenticate the tourist's "ultimate safari" into the eco-archaic.

CONCLUSION

Whether the space of the game reserve can be repossessed, imaginatively and experientially, will depend on at least four critical factors. First, how will the reserves be impacted by government policies toward land restitution? Second, what role will the ascent of black tourism play in reshaping South Africa's nature industry? Will game reserves become alluring destinations to black tourists or remain alienating reminders of racial entitlement, dispossession, and apartheid atavism? Third, how sustainable will rural ecotourism initiatives prove? Will they offer broad-based economic opportunities and draw on cultures of nature outside the purview of neocolonial conservation? Finally, how will international forces—the feedback loops of global tourism and the pressures exerted by European and American-based conservationist NGOs—shape South Africa's environmental priorities?

Hector Magome and James Murombedzi, two incisive analysts of these policy dilemmas, have expressed a profound skepticism toward the international role: "If the dominant agenda is conventional biodiversity conservation, the political expediency that facilitates the decolonization of nature at the national level will cause its re-colonization at the international level" (131). This remains a real, active risk. That said, however, the primary driver behind the South African conservation systems, both state-run and private, has tended to be the lucrative, easy sell of spectacular megafauna rather than biodiversity per se, which, from a tourist perspective, is often unspectacular and therefore "boring."[36] As Kleinhans's alfalfa problem suggests, for many foreign tourists, mixed usage—landscapes that blend agricultural or subsistence activities with conservation—are anathema, unappealing as spectacle, insufficiently severed from the domestic and the familiar. Yet, for all the complexities that the coexistence of pastoralists, agriculturalists, and wildlife entails, such hybrid uses of land may play an essential part, long term, in helping dissolve the resilient, Manichean perception of blacks as poachers (or encroachers) and white environmentalists as humane toward animals but inhumane toward people. Amidst the land squeeze, increased mixed usage will be a necessary component of efforts to reconcile water, food, and ecosystem security for humans and wildlife. The alternative is unsustainable: powerhouse international NGOs in cahoots with stereotypical tourist demands for Wild Africa driving subsistence farmers and those Ramachandra Guha calls "ecosystem people" off the land.

In its unevenly postapartheid mode, South Africa has to contend with the civilizational clout of ideologies of nature; mutable ideologies, to be sure, but nonetheless etched into the nation's physical, psychic, and economic landscapes. These lingering legacies of political subjugation and territorial appropriation (buttressed by the civilizational discriminations of colonial progress narratives) have been used to rationalize unequal access to land, wildlife, and leisure while erecting a vast international marketplace around charismatic megafauna and the eco-archaic. What is acutely at stake in understanding South Africa's environmental dilemmas is that they point, in critical form, toward more generalized global crises around land access, food security, resource wars, biodiversity, tourism, and the international wildlife marketplace.

In our quest to transform these temporal and spatial legacies, a profound tension often arises between economic, historical, and psychological impulses. How much change, how fast, at what cost to whom, and when? The strategic answers will vary from context to context according to the friction between global forces, local and national power structures, and what Tsing calls "the sticky materiality of practical encounters" (1). Let Ndebele, surveying the game lodge, have the final word: "The ambiguities and choices are difficult, even painful. Now we want to throw off the psychological burden of our painful past; now we want to hold on to it. . . . We think: there is no peace for those caught in the process of becoming" (14).

NOTES

1. My use of the term postapartheid in this essay comes with all the familiar caveats. The nation's democratic turn on April 27, 1994, was a critical marker in South African history. But "surely," Njabulo Ndebele correctly insists, "the death of apartheid is a social process not an event" (2007, 93). That process is uneven and ongoing. My essay is, in part, an attempt to explore from the angle of environmental justice the limits and pacing of that systemic transformation.

2. Taxidermy is located at the complex crossroads of Enlightenment science, colonial trophy hunting, and hyper-masculine interior design. Taxidermal time is, then, in multiple senses, suspended time: the mounted corpses are frozen in animated positions, usually (for predators) with fangs exposed. The period reference is anachronistic as is the craft itself, which projects a musty, neo-Victorian aura of white male risk management.

3. African culture, of whatever ethnicity, was present only in the interior atmospherics: the reed baskets and masks that afforded the game lodge lobby a decorative indigeneity.

4. The Eastern Province is primarily a Xhosa region. It has very few Zulu inhabitants. But Kleinhans understood that Zulu had greater international recognition value, in the push for African authenticity, than Xhosa. Besides, Zulu was easier for foreigners to pronounce.

5. Looking back at my encounter with Kleinhans on this volatile cusp of history, I'm returned to Donna Haraway's insights in her classic essay, "Teddy Bear Patriarchy," where she links the exclusive trophy hunting expeditions to central Africa undertaken by Teddy Roosevelt and Carl Akeley to censored performances (in the field and in taxidermal 'family' displays) of racial, class, and gender anxieties. I'm returned to her insights—not just to the cropping from photographs and dioramas of anything that threatened to complicate a narrative of individual white male hunter heroics—but also to the connection Haraway makes between the anxious representational artifice of the transnational African hunt as theater of risk and the racial and gender panics, mobilized in a

time of social upheaval, around eugenics, suffragette militancy, and immigrant threat.

6. The cultural histories of game lodges dedicated to game viewing, private reserves where hunting is part of the experience, and national parks are all differently inflected. While a full accounting of those differences is beyond the scope of this essay, performances of the eco-archaic and racialized ecologies of looking remain, I believe, a constitutive element in all those varied spaces.

7. Ndebele is not alone in writing about the leisurely stresses, the wrenching ambiguities, of the ancestrally colonized tourist vacationing in an erstwhile colony. The comparison with black travelers to the Caribbean—like Jamaica Kincaid and June Jordan—is particularly suggestive, given the pervasive marketing of the islands as, like the game lodges, free-floating Edenic enclaves of natural time, unmoored from historical memory, clock time, and the time of labor.

8. For an insightful examination of the spatial politics of Ndebele's essay, see Barnard, 2007, 171–72.

9. One of the most notorious of these forced removals in the name of conservation involved the Makuleke when the Kruger National Park was extended northward. (I discuss this case below, in my analysis of the Gordimer short story.) Another controversial case involved the Tonga, who were moved twice: in 1924 to make way for the Ndumo Game Reserve, and then again in the 1990s to create a corridor that would give elephants greater freedom of movement and access to water, which, accordingly, became more difficult for the Tonga to access (Honey, 367). For a broader, international perspective on conservation refugees, see especially Guha and Dowie.

10. On her flight back from her Bahamas vacation, Jordan, likewise, is "burning up," on the verge of what she calls "a West Indian fit" (326).

11. On the role of effaced labor in landscape aesthetics, Raymond Williams's *The Country and the City* and J. M. Coetzee's *White Writing* both remain invaluable. William Cronon's related work in an American context remains foundational, while Robert Marzec's analyses of effaced labor, landscape, and enclosures in British and postcolonial environments are rich and incisive.

12. In the Bahamas, Jordan, a Harlem-born daughter of Jamaican immigrants, finds herself veering between racial and gender identification and a discomfiting acknowledgment of the class chasm that separates her from the locals. Sharing a common racial adversary, she concludes, is an unstable, insufficient source of shared identity (327). The question of labor—past and present—renders Kincaid apoplectic. How, she exclaims, can the emancipated descendants of slaves celebrate the Hotel Training School "which teaches Antiguans how to be good servants?" (55).

13. As I've argued elsewhere, one of the primary obstacles to a fuller integration of postcolonial and environmental perspectives has been the tenacious attachment in many environmental quarters (even in cryptic guises) to preservationist discourses of purity that have exacerbated the unequal distribution of post-Enlightenment human rights, land rights, and civil liberties. See Nixon, 2005, 242.

14. The environmentalist literature on the construction of Caribbean Edens is rich and increasingly vast. See especially Elizabeth DeLoughrey et al. (eds.), *Caribbean Literature and the Environment*, George B. Handley, *New World Poetics*, and Sarah Phillips Casteel, *Second Arrivals*.

15. *South African Eden*, James Stevenson-Hamilton's influential memoir on his Kruger Park years, appeared in 1937, the same year as Karen Blixen's *Out of Africa*.

Both books invoked an Edenic and elegiac rhetoric to help mobilize a megafauna-centered conservationist movement whose legacy continues to shape contemporary South Africa and Kenya's economic and cultural landscapes. Stevenson-Hamilton, a Scottish immigrant (and first warden of the Kruger National Park) was arguably as pivotal a figure, through his actions and writings, in the shaping of South African conservation, as that other Scottish immigrant, John Muir, was in the United States.

16. See especially Elaine Freedgood, *Victorian Writing about Risk*.

17. Cf. Jordan on "The Native Show on the Patio" at the Sheraton British Colonial. Her racial and gender identification with the Bahamian women who perform in the "Native Show," who serve her, or hawk trinkets on the street is compromised by the structures of the tourist industry: "We are not particularly women anymore; we are parties to a transaction designed to set us against each other" (321).

18. This is not to suggest that the relationship between local white ideologies and foreign ones always dovetail. Ndebele mentions, for instance, an American family who remark on the oddity of cross-dressing as "leisure colonialists."

19. Clearly, the postapartheid redistribution of political, economic, and cultural power remains profoundly uneven.

20. Gordimer has a penchant for ironizing tourist industry boilerplate in the titles of her stories, calling, for example, her most brilliant expose of a racist consciousness "Good Climate, Friendly Inhabitants." "The Ultimate Safari" bears, as its epigraph, an advertising pitch that appeared in a British newspaper: "The African Adventure Lives On . . . You can do it! The ultimate safari or expedition with leaders who know Africa." Gordimer's story pivots on the ambiguity of "ultimate," which can imply either "nonpareil" or "final." The tourist-ad safari is pitched as nonpareil, unbeatable, the adventure of a lifetime, while the refugees' safari, which trades the frying pan of domestic civil war for the fire of foreign human and animal threat, risks becoming terminally ultimate.

21. The routine comparison of Kruger with Israel reaffirms the park's status, particularly in Afrikaner cultures of nature, as a place of spiritual pilgrimage, a chosen people's chosen land. Kruger Park was officially established under the 1926 National Parks Act, although it was then much smaller than its current size.

22. The status of the Kruger Park as an overdetermined buffer zone was intensified by the ascent to power of Marxist guerillas in 1975, an event that marked the end of Portuguese colonial control of Mozambique and served, in addition, as a partial revolutionary inspiration for the Soweto uprising the following year. During the ensuing Mozambican civil war, the apartheid regime deemed Mozambique (which served as a base for ANC guerillas) a terrorist state. The South African regime, with strong backing from the Reagan administration, funded, trained, harbored, and armed forces opposing the Mozambican government. By the late 1980s, the civil war had displaced two million of Mozambique's fourteen million people and killed one hundred thousand of them.

23. Gordimer's compelling essay on the Kruger Park-Mozambique border zone, "The Ingot and the Stick," seems to have passed under the critical radar. It goes unmentioned both in Stephen Clingman's extensive critical work on Gordimer and in Ronald Roberts's 750-page biography of her.

24. After the discovery of gold in 1877, white immigration to the Transvaal surged. The resultant rapid ascent of industrialization and urbanization in turn fed the rise of commercial agriculture. White mining magnates and white farmers were thrust into competition with each other for scarce black labor. Waves of

legislation were passed intent on making rural survival more precarious for black subsistence communities, thereby forcing increasing numbers into capitalist wage labor on the mines and farms. The 1913 Land Act was particularly devastating, barring blacks from buying or leasing land from whites except in the designated native reserves. From a white ruling class perspective, this land squeeze had the double advantage of forcing blacks into wage labor and removing a source of agricultural competition. (For a more textured history of these developments, see Beinart.) Although it is beyond the scope of this essay, a fuller accounting of the rise of game reserves in relation to colonial cultures of labor and leisure would engage J. M. Coetzee's essay on idleness in *White Writing* and Syed Hussein Alata's *The Myth of the Lazy Native*.

25. This poacher-conservationist dyad helps explain an erratic policy toward human habitation inside the Kruger National Park. After initially barring Africans from the park in the early twentieth century, white authorities allowed about three thousand Africans to reside there, but charged them rent (Carruthers 81).This rent provided a revenue stream and ensured that those residents would be forced to sell their labor for menial amounts. Black bodies—of African renters and, later, prison gangs—were dragooned into erecting fences, building roads and camps, and catching poachers. The invention and maintenance of a wild, Edenic purity is, after all, a labor-intensive business.

26. Relevant here is Johannes Fabian's account of the two primary colonial responses to the bodily contest over land: forced removal (whether through genocide or deportation) or manipulating "the other variable—Time. With the help of various devices of sequencing and distancing one assigns to the conquered populations a different Time" (29–30).

27. Labuschagne, pp. 26–27, 63–64. Quoted in Carruthers, p. 83.

28. For a brief, suggestive history of the marketing of the Grand Canyon to American tourists as a destination associated with the religious archaic, the sublime, and patriotic spiritual elevation, see Stephen J. Pyne, *How the Canyon Became Grand*.

29. Gordimer's essay "The Ingot and the Stick" is a companion piece to a BBC2 television documentary she presented as part of a series on frontiers.

30. "The principle of the agreements has never changed. Gold and other mining interests in South Africa are granted large-scale labour recruiting of Mozambiquan men in return for a portion of the men's wages to be paid in gold, to Portugal during colonial times, later to independent Mozambique" (Gordimer, 1990, 56).

31. In a broader theoretical context, Liisa Malkki's work on the pathologizing of refugees as "unnatural" has a particular resonance here.

32. The girl's ethnicity goes unmentioned, but the story contains plenty of geographical and linguistic indications that she is Shangaan. (The people's ethnic self-designation has varied historically and geographically. Shangaan are frequently called Tsonga in South Africa.)

33. Before Zimbabwe's descent into chaos shrank the ambitions of the project, a three-nation transfrontier park was in the works, joining Kruger to national parks in Mozambique and Zimbabwe and thereby affording the prospect of greater freedom of movement for humans (exclusive subspecies, tourist) and other mammalian herds. The project has been dogged by controversy, not least because it would entail further involuntary removals (notably in Mozambique), and the economic benefits to local inhabitants have been at best hazily sketched out. The status of this transfrontier park, dubbed an "African Super Park,"

remains uncertain, although the corridor linking Mozambique and Kruger appears to be going ahead.

34. From the Kruger Park's colonial beginnings, the "gate guards" were historically Shangaan. As David Bunn notes, these uniformed guards "dramatize[d] two orders of time and racial identity—one that of the 'improved' native and the other that of the customary, ethnic collective—that [could not] easily coexist outside the boundaries of the reserve" (11).

35. For a thoughtful contrastive analysis of the treatment of white tourists and African immigrants, see Mathers and Landau.

36. For instance, the range of endemics in the vast Kruger National Park cannot compare with that of a seldom-visited, much smaller reserve on the Namaqualand coast that is biodiversity-rich but megafauna-poor. Moreover, in a creative attempt to legitimate and market its expansion, the Greater Addo National Park has pitched itself as the only park to boast the Big Seven (adding Southern Right Whales and Great White Sharks to the conventional lion, elephant, rhino, buffalo, and leopard) while also boasting that it has the greatest variety of biomes of any South African national park.

8

What the Whales Would Tell Us

Cetacean Communication in Novels by Witi Ihimaera, Linda Hogan, Zakes Mda, and Amitav Ghosh

Jonathan Steinwand

> The animals "already know by instinct / we're not comfortably at home / in our translated world."
> —Rainer Maria Rilke, quoted in Ghosh, *The Hungry Tide* 206

Breathing air, yet at home in the water rather than on land, whales and dolphins have fascinated human beings all over the world for quite some time. So much like us in some ways and yet "uncannily other," cetaceans have come to represent both the human animal and a mysteriously "fascinating alterity" beyond terrestrial knowledge (Buell, *Writing for an Endangered World* 203). The recent cetacean turn in environmentalist iconography and in postcolonial literature looks to whales and dolphins for guidance in how human animals participate in postcolonial ecology. As we will see, the cetacean-human encounter calls attention to the liminal positions of both cetaceans and humans. And where the encounter attends to songs, chatter, and play, the limits of interspecies communication are approached. Postcolonial ecology works to honor these limits of interspecies understanding by means of an analogous respecting of the limits of intercultural understanding. In order to work at these limits, we need to be alert for where each narrative of postcolonial ecology, like the curious whale rising vertically to sneak a steady glance above the surface of the water, "spyhops" the reader with its irony.

Whales and dolphins became symbols for environmentalist pleas to save the world's ocean ecosystems once it became apparent that the planet's oceans are threatened by pollution, extraction, and catastrophe. In

Writing for an Endangered World, Lawrence Buell locates this shift in environmental thinking between Rachel Carson's *The Sea Around Us* in 1950 and her *Silent Spring* in 1962 (201). Buell's analysis of this shift from seeing oceans as the world's great, inexhaustible global commons to worrying about their endangerment should be considered in relation to Carolyn Merchant's depiction in *The Death of Nature* of how we mourn what we have killed in nature and the idea of "imperialist nostalgia" attributed to Renato Rosaldo, that we mourn what we have helped to destroy. In *Moby Dick*, Herman Melville invokes such nostalgia when he compares the whale hunting of his day to the near extermination of the buffalo on the plains (383). Later, when the deep frontier was being explored with imperialist vigor masked by modern scientific curiosity, it was alarming for many to learn that we may never have a chance to master what we have never even been able to fathom or see. As the endangered charismatic megafauna of the sea, then, whales and dolphins become the icons through which environmentalists hope to move people to care for the ocean ecosystems (see Buell, *Writing for an Endangered World* 201–2).

The neocolonial stakes of cold war cetology should not be underestimated. In *Cosmodolphins: Feminist Cultural Studies of Technology, Animals and the Sacred*, Mette Bryld and Nina Lykke argue that increased interest in dolphins and other cetaceans ought to be considered in relation to the cold war space race and the New Age movement's interest in astrology. As the superpowers scramble for dominion over Father Sky and Mother Ocean, scientists and adventurers seeking government funding turn toward exploration of cosmos (space) and ocean as new frontiers (19–21). The study credits ecofeminists including Merchant, Val Plumwood, and Donna Haraway for their attention to the nexus of woman, native, and nature. Building on a rich tradition of cetacean mythology that links dolphins to Apollo, the oracle at Delphi, and Aphrodite (185), Bryld and Lykke trace dolphins as "extra-terrestrial others" who function variously as noble savages, companion species, messengers of the sacred, tricksters, and cyborgs. Bryld and Lykke summarize:

> Since the 1960s, dolphins have occupied the cultural imaginary as bearers of alternative values such as collectivity, compassion, friendliness, creativity, joyful sexuality, androgyny, spiritual wisdom and intuitive intelligence. With their huge brains and legendary helpfulness towards humans, the enigmatic sea mammals have been cast by popular culture as well as by scientific discourse as our extraterrestrial *doppelgänger*. Like another double, the "noble savage" of early modernity, the dolphin and the whale will allegedly guide us to insight into the "true and sacred" pleasures of a simple life in harmony with the natural environment. (2–3)

In connecting the early modern colonial fascination with the noble savage to the late modern scientific and popular interest in cetaceans, Bryld and Lykke call attention to modernity's defining tendency to simultaneously "cannibalize" and "worship" the wild (22). They contend that this tendency persists, for example, in science fiction novels built on the "noble savage dolphin fable" in which "an alien figure convey[s] profound cosmic wisdom to humans in distress"—a distress that "stems from civilization that has severed the connections with the animal world" (63).[1]

Although they do not press the point, Bryld and Lykke's analysis of an indigenous Siberian story by Yuri Rytkheu (208) invites us to consider whether the postcolonial perspective may be the best position from which to appraise both the kinship between humans and cetaceans and the way in which cetaceans work as "jester[s] capable of carnivalesque acts of blurring boundaries and mocking genderized and ethnicized hierarchies and oppositions" (225). Dolphins and whales are compelling figures because of their liminality and ambiguity (Bryld and Lykke 184): as mammals they are most closely related to land dwellers and yet they swim in the sea among other animal kingdoms. Marginalized and indigenous peoples are also liminal figures negotiating the boundaries of the dominant "civilization" and wild nature, of traditional premodern and postmodern late capitalist lifestyles. With guidance from the persisting countermemory of their cultural values and traditions, the marginalized find that survivance strategies emerge through their liminality. "Survivance" is the word Gerald Vizenor uses to challenge the "white" idea that indigenous people of the Americas are mere survivors of colonization and victims. Survivance, therefore, invokes "an active resistance and repudiation of dominance, obtrusive themes of tragedy, nihilism, and victimry" (Vizenor, "Aesthetics of Survivance" 11). Such repudiation is much more about trickster teasing and innovative irony than it is commemorating the near cultural genocide imposed on "the indian" by colonizers.[2] Aware of the history and politics of representation, indigenous and postcolonial writers play with what Graham Huggan calls "strategic exoticism" to complicate those representations and ridicule the reductive instances of such representation.[3] Such play, I am suggesting, is not unlike the sportive bodily antics, vocal improvisations, and spyhopping glances of cetaceans that capture our imagination and blur the boundaries of our serious rational categories.[4] Furthermore, their awareness of the politics of representation puts indigenous and postcolonial writers in a position to be able to recognize and complicate how charismatic megafauna such as cetaceans are represented.

While science fiction novelists, fantasy writers, environmental organizations, marine biologists, New Age musicians, nature theme parks, and the nature television industry have been lured by the mysterious song of radical alterity and uncanny kinship that cetaceans sing, four postcolonial novelists tease and challenge readers to reflect further on our relationship with these charismatic megafauna. In *The Whale Rider* (1987), Witi Ihimaera updates a foundational Maori story of human arrival to Aotearoa (New Zealand) on the back of a whale. In *People of the Whale* (2008), Linda Hogan rewrites the Makah whale hunt to reveal how people are complete and whole to the degree that they are connected to the companion species of the ecosystems in which they dwell. In *The Whale Caller* (2005), Zakes Mda transforms the tourist bureau–sponsored whale crier into a postmodern South African shaman who communes with the whales through his kelp horn music. And in *The Hungry Tide* (2004), Amitav Ghosh attends to the dedication of an Indian-born American cetologist who finds she has a lot to learn from the river dolphins, the fisherman, and the idealists she meets upon her arrival to the Indian Sundarbans. This cetacean turn in postcolonial literature invites us to attend to the survivance strategies that provide localized challenges to environmentalist universalism, correctives to the sentimentalizing tendencies of environmentalism, and the caution that a sustainable future must avoid imperialist nostalgia. In each case, the people who dwell among the cetaceans in related ecosystems face similar or analogous endangerment. And, in each case, these novels honor the biomythic narratives, arts, and local knowledge that resist the disenchanting tendency of secular modernity to privilege the story of human "progress" away from other animals.

By characterizing these threatened animals as ancestors (Ihimaera and Hogan) and companion species (Mda and Ghosh), these novels provide guidance for thinking about nonhuman others in ways that risk but ironically resist domesticating or romanticizing the other by focusing attention on the lives, the knowledge, the arts, the values, and the beliefs of the people who dwell among these species. Environmental ethics must respect this rich interconnectedness and consider the historical, material, and political bonds between the human and the nonhuman other within their localized manifestations.

The novelists themselves negotiate their liminal positions as cosmopolitan global cultural ambassadors with specific connections that allow them access to the lives of the insiders who dwell more permanently in the locales. Their audiences also include cosmopolitan readers lured by the postcolonial and the ecopastoral exotic. At the border, on the limit, along the coast, and in the tides is where tricksters and cyborgs tease us out of our mythic and modern thinking.[5] We should be alert for openings and gaps where the novels, like spyhopping whales, turn back on readers to tease or challenge.

The step beyond human exceptionalism radically disrupts our comfortable definitions of what it means to be human. The cetacean-inspired transgressive characters we follow in each of these novels do not merely redraw the lines demarcating the human and the nonhuman.[6] Instead, they redeem the human animals as having a place—albeit liminal—in relation to other animals. Such a place can only be claimed through facing what Cora Diamond calls "the difficulty of reality," an embodied knowledge of "vulnerability to death, sheer animal vulnerability, the vulnerability we share with" other animals (74).[7] After all, as Haraway's work demonstrates, the separation between humans and animals no longer holds—if it ever did.

Both Ihimaera's *The Whale Rider* (1987)[8] and Hogan's *People of the Whale* (2008) focus on indigenous coastal people who have become disconnected from the whales who once were not only companion species but ancestors. In each case, the catalyst for ecological reconciliation and postcolonial survivance is the startling step beyond anthropocentrism taken by the main character of each story. Whether that step is taken through innocence or experience, it is guided by playful attunement to the innovative traditions of trickster survivance in each local environment.

Ihimaera frames his novel by reenacting the founding myth of Paikea, who rode a whale to Aotearoa/New Zealand in a prologue depicting the inseparability of human and whale as companion species. In the beginning, land and sea rejoice with the coming of the people in their canoes (4). The whales join in and an original oneness of humans and other beings is commemorated. After this prologue, the story diverges into two narrative threads: one cetacean and mythic and the other human, modern, tragicomic, and involving family and gender politics. The novel in its structure and resolution attempts to repair the separation between human and animal, between land and sea, between modern and mythic perspectives.[9] Yet, such reconciliation requires not merely respect and humility but also innovation and open-mindedness.

Interspersed between episodes in the human story is the cetacean story told in italics from the point of view of the whales. Such anthropomorphic focus on the whales is not merely a magical realist gesture but is consistent with the Pacific ethic of genealogical connection among living beings. This genealogical emphasis on the kinship of all living beings calls attention to a long tradition of a nonanthropocentric environmental ethic in which there is no great divide between animal and human, between nature and culture (Allen 131–33, DeLoughrey, *Routes and Roots*, 164–65). These whales are equated, with the mythic and with the ancestors—they belong to a different time and yet inhabit the same ocean that laps up against and constitutes the human world.

Narrated retrospectively with somewhat comic effect by Kahu's uncle Rawiri, the human story line, on the other hand, emphasizes the family's distance from the myth. Rawiri tells the story of the life of his niece Kahu, who seems destined—against her great-grandfather's wishes—to become chief of the clan. Great-grandfather Koro Apirana holds rigidly to patriarchal beliefs about Maori traditions of leadership, succession, and cultural authority. Nanny Flowers, his wife, teases him with the threat of divorce and unsettles his authority over the family, tradition, and the novel with allusions to her ancestors Muriwai (19–20) and Mihi Kotukutuku (81–82), women who defy tradition to take leadership and save the people. Tensions heighten as Koro repeatedly excludes Kahu from his list of potential successors to his leadership. But eight-year-old Kahu is gifted in precisely the Maori ways that will make her a viable leader: she loves and respects her great-grandfather, she is eager to learn the traditions, she is skilled in the water, she is patient, and she has an unusual connection to cetaceans.

More important, she has been nourished on the teasing of her great-grandmother and the disarming, irreverent humor of her uncle. When the whales strand themselves, Koro is on the brink of despair until Kahu overcomes the separation between animal and human, the myth and the present moment of need, the sacred Maori legend and the English-language novel, by riding the whale back out to sea. The whale stranding becomes the opportunity for a new leader to show the community the way to be Maori today. More important, her audacious and innovative resistance to authority aligns her with her maternal ancestors, relaxes the rigid hold of patriarchal power, and thus reconciles the generations. It is not incidental that Kahu's final words appeal teasingly through the epithet she took from Nanny Flowers and turns into a term of endearment for Koro: "Oh, Paka, can't you hear them? I've been listening to them for ages now. Oh, Paka, and the whales are still singing" (150). "Paka" means "old bugger" (15).

Such restoration is not merely a nostalgic return to a precolonial or an invented Maori past. Rather, for Ihimaera and for the Maori renaissance, this restoration revalues Maoritangi—Maori identity—as the dynamic interaction between land and sea, between local human cultures and the immediate natural world, between precolonial tradition and postcolonial survivance.[10] As Maori leaders work within a postmodern world context to address the legacy of colonialism, they are guided by the myths, stories, songs, and survivance strategies that have given them their bioregional identity, that have connected them to the ecosystem in which they dwell.

While Kahu connects the Maori world to the cetacean world primarily through her innocent curiosity, playfulness, teasing, courage, and unconditional love, Hogan's main character forges a bond to nature through the trauma, guilt, and grief of experience. Both approaches complicate the myth of the "ecological Indian"[11] by acknowledging indigenous complicity in environmental destruction and by avoiding any suggestion that the local people necessarily have exclusive access to nature. Both cetacean-inspired characters embolden their communities with their trickster survivance. For Ihimaera and Hogan, postcolonial ecology means the human animal must promote sustainable human cultures that avoid unreasonable anthropocentric exploitation or endangerment of other animals and ecosystems.

Set in Dark River, a coastal village where the "nearby fishing towns are abandoned ... the sawmill in disrepair, the forest missing" (9), *People of the Whale* is Hogan's story of the survivance of Thomas Witka Just, Ruth Small, and the fictional A'atsika people[12] of the Olympic peninsula of the state of Washington. The A'atsika people trace their ancestry to the whales, as the rock carvings show human beings "being born of the whales" (267). And they have a long history of reverence for the whale as a key source of their sustenance. Both Thomas and Ruth have inherited fantastic gifts linking them to the ocean and to the whales. Ruth is said to have been born with gill slits, and she hears more than others do (27). Thomas's birth was said to have been blessed by the visit of the octopus (15–17), connecting him to his grandfather Witka, who "was the last of those who could go under the sea holding his breath for long times and remain, so he had a great deal of knowledge about the ocean and all sea life. He was the last of a line of traditional men who loved and visited the whales to ensure a good whale hunt" (18). Thomas and Ruth marry, but Thomas is enticed by Dwight and his cronies—apparently by appeals to Americanism (30)—to enlist in the army to fight in the Vietnam War. Ruth, meanwhile, bears a son, Marco Polo, whose webbed feet suggest he is destined for "liv[ing] in two elements" (34). Marco is said to have been "born an old man," an "incarnation of an ancestor" (38). Seeing him as the link to the future, the elders take Marco to them to teach him the old ways.

Hogan presents the trauma of war and the story of return through shards of memory that haunt Thomas. The ebb and flow of the narrative works on readers as the memories of Thomas bring him home to himself. Gradually, as the cruelty of war wears on Thomas's fellow soldiers, they point out that Thomas looks more like the enemy than one of them (249). When he sees them make fun of the dead and when he grieves the destruction of plants and trees in the natural world of Vietnam,[13] his reactions prompt someone to call him "a sorry excuse for a man" (173). For the men who laugh this comment throws Thomas's masculinity into question, but for Thomas (and later for his daughter Lin [209]), it is a question of whether those who commit the crimes of war can be human. Thus, Thomas "with brother M16 and AK and grenades" can no longer be Thomas, the human animal, as an American soldier in Vietnam. He becomes "monster" (175, 178), the cyborg man with weapons of mass destruction, attacking the environment. For the monsters, "the water was the enemy. The trees were Cong. The earth was a bomb. The rain was dangerous" (171). When ordered to massacre an entire innocent village, Thomas feels "like it was happening to us Indians" (255), so he turns on his own men, kills them all, leaves his dog tags with the dead, and hides among the villagers for several years (177–78). Among these "people of the earth" (167), Thomas becomes the earth (122, 249). He joins in the work of the village, becoming a rice farmer, finding a companion, even fathering a child. He does not want to leave when they come for him. Thus, when he returns to Dark River many years later, he is a ghost, haunted by his war crimes and the ambiguous designation of "Vietnam war hero."

About the time of Thomas's return, the tribe decides that "whale-hunting . . . will bring us back to ourselves" (69). Thomas joins in, perhaps to redeem himself as worthy of his lineage. Ruth leads the protest against whaling. The elders send Marco to show the whalers how to paddle (87) and to ensure that the traditional prayers (86), purification rituals, and rites of reverence are included. When Marco declares they have "the wrong whale to kill" (93), the "hunters" are too excited and even Thomas shoots to kill it. In the commotion, the whale upends the canoes and Marco is lost in the bloody ocean. Marco's mysterious disappearance and the dead whale haunt the rest of the novel and hang like two more albatrosses around Thomas's neck. But by reentering the sea and learning its ways, by meeting Lin and reconciling with Ruth, and by visiting the Vietnam memorial and giving his medals back to the Department of the Army, Thomas gradually returns to himself. He recognizes that "he has violated laws beneath the laws of men and countries, something deeper, the earth and the sea, the explosion of trees. He has to care again. He has to be water again, rock, earth with its new spring wildflowers and its beautiful, complex mosses" (268). He joins the elders and learns the old songs (279). And through this process, the albatrosses drop from his neck and "he is whole" (286). He is "not one of the conquered any longer but whatever was deep in him all along and precious" (286). He finds he is able even to sing "an old whale song he has never learned. He looks toward the ocean, and the song, it comes to him from out of a hole opened in time" (284). When, in the midst of a song, Dwight shoots him with a pistol, everyone thinks Dwight has killed Thomas, but "Thomas is thinking, Ha, there is no death" (287). The laughter of survivance is stronger than Dwight's desperate attempt at mere survival. As Thomas enters the legends of the people of the whale, some will say he was carried "by the whale who heard his song and recalled it and knew his intentions" (289), others will say it was the octopus who "took him to those who could help" (290).

The fictional return to whaling parallels the Makah whale hunt, which was arguably one of the most dramatic controversies of postcolonial ecology in North America. The Makah voluntarily gave up their traditional hunting of the gray whale in 1915, while other nations continued until the International Whaling Commission banned the killing in 1946 (Peterson, "Who Will Speak" paragraphs 8–9). Enticed by the idea of a symbolic return to the whale hunt as the path to spiritual and cultural renewal (Gaard 6–7), the Makah in 1994 rally around the idea of exercising their treaty right of hunting a gray whale, which had just been removed from the endangered species list.[14] Hogan's complaint against the Makah whale hunt is that it broke "the sacred agreement . . . where the whale is welcomed, sung to, and given back to the sea with prayers" (Peterson and Hogan 104). She goes on to say that "in the traditional and historic past, we recognized the sovereignty of other species, animal and plant. We held treaties with the animals, treaties shaped by mutual respect and knowledge of the complex workings of the world, and these were laws the legal system will never come close to" (153).[15] European settlers, according to Hogan, fail to recognize this Native American ecological ethic, and "perhaps history might have unfolded differently if they had known there was an ethic in dealing with animals" (277). For Hogan, the human animal lives and suffers in relationship to other animals and any violation of this relationship disrupts and damages the system and especially those who cut themselves off. The purification rituals, the prayers, the daily interaction with other species, and especially the songs, the tears, and the laughter restore us to be worthy of this relationship.

While both Ihimaera and Hogan reconnect their people to the cetacean ancestors through song and laughter, Mda's Whale Caller draws our attention even more to the mystery of the whale song and our fascination with it. Amidst the transnational migrations of whales and tourists, Mda turns in *The Whale Caller* to those who watch and attend to such arrivals and departures—those who inhabit the place where tourists go longing for a magical return to nature without commitment or responsibility. Although he refers to how in the "mists of time" Khoikhoi ancestors danced to celebrate occasional whale strandings as divine gifts (4), Mda draws our attention to the marginalized figures of the New South Africa who are largely cut off from such historical links. Through their music and their rituals of transgressing boundaries, each of the main characters tries to connect with the community but meets with minimal success. This novel presents no simple formula for harmony among those of land and sea, the rich and the poor. While there is something magical, transcendental, and sacred about the connection the Whale Caller makes with the whales, it seems that this connection, as Hein Viljoen puts it, "prove[s] impossible to translate into a new society. Human caprice, human willfulness seems to translate them rather into disaster" (207). Nevertheless, the attention the novel gives to the marginalized of the community and to the mysterious music of whales and children, of kelp horns and the blues, hints at where we might look for transformation and reattunement. Furthermore, we need to watch for where Mda's story spyhops us whale-watching readers with its satirical and ironic twists back on us to unsettle our comfortable complicity in postcolonial and environmental injustice.

Mda's story is both humorous and profound in how it blurs the boundaries between routine and ritual, the wild and the tame, the sublime and the ridiculous. Love, addiction, sex, confession, eating, and worship are not the same after Mda's satire. Haunted as it is by the impending violent death of the whale and by the ridiculous distance between the local people and the tourists,[16] Mda's peculiar love story emulates the longing and sad, yet playful and enigmatic song of the whales. *The Whale Caller* brings us to one of the prime tourist destinations in South Africa: the whale-watching mecca of Hermanus. The official Whale Crier of Hermanus works for the tourism office and walks around the town wearing a sandwich board explaining the code he blows through his kelp horn to indicate for tourists where they can find whales at any particular time. Mda transforms this popular tourist attraction of the Whale Crier into his Whale Caller. As a boy, the Whale Caller was fascinated by an old man blowing a kelp horn to accompany the hymns at church. The boy learns to play the horn and succeeds the old man, playing so well, in fact, that the bishop establishes a new church "known as the Church of the Sacred Kelp Horn" (8). The kelp horn and the new church "brought the worshippers closer to nature, and in greater communion with the spirits of the forebears that were hovering above the tall cliffs and in the cave" (9). This combination of fascination with nature and respect for the divine is further explored, undermined, challenged, ridiculed, and defended throughout the novel. Once he recognizes that "through his kelp horn he had the power to communicate with" the whales, he drifts away from the church and spends most of his time with the whales (11). Unlike the Whale Crier, the Whale Caller calls whales in their own language not tourists in mere codes. Pressing the tendency of nature lovers to get a little carried away, Mda tells of one southern right whale in particular, with whom the Whale Caller has a special relationship. When Saluni, the town drunk, falls in love with the Whale Caller, she negotiates for position in what she calls "the eternal triangle: man, woman, and whale" (81). The result is a ridiculous, yet strangely sublime, triangulated love story in which routines become rituals that mix love, jealousy, and worship.

Whereas the Whale Caller transforms life through rituals connected to church music, dancing, confession, and delayed gratification (77), Saluni appeals to the "civilizing" rituals of conspicuous consumption which she takes from the supermarket, the restaurant, the tavern, the radio, the boudoir, and the sport fishermen. Each conveys a different type of longing for enchantment in a rather disenchanted modern world. The story of their relationship blurs the sublime with the ridiculous to the point that the Whale Caller stages a "civilized" restaurant-eating ritual scene for Sharisha the whale (137) and Saluni sets up a rent-a-fish business for tourists and fishermen to photograph and claim the trophy fish caught by the Whale Caller (167–70). By confronting the Whale Caller with a distorted, parodic mirror of his own values and rituals of nature worship, she challenges him (and Mda challenges his readers) to reconsider his sentimental attachments. The "public eating" scene, in particular, satirizes first-world environmentalist voyeurism facilitated by the whale-watching tourism industry and television nature shows.[17]

Although we don't come to the violent death of Sharisha until the end of the novel, her wounds haunt the story. In the first sentence of the novel, Mda tells readers that "the sea is bleeding from the wounds of Sharisha" (3). Despite this premonition that this whale—and all she represents—is endangered, nothing can prepare us for the violence of her death. In frustration over the quarrel with Saluni and out of balance with himself, the Whale Caller yearns for Sharisha and recklessly blows his kelp horn as he has never blown it before (215–16). The Whale Caller is so focused that with closed eyes he does not realize that it is the whale in front of him and not his imagination conjuring her up. Though he tries to coax her back out of the shallows, his efforts are in vain. The transgression has already occurred; she is already beached on the shore. When "the experts from Cape Town" use explosives to alleviate the whale's suffering (223), the Whale Caller blames himself for luring her selfishly to "such a terrible end" (229) just to heal his own wounds.

When he sees that Sharisha's calf is attracted to his horn playing as he attempts to call Saluni with Saluni's song (229), the Whale Caller gives up his horn playing altogether and plans to wander the shores as "the

Hermanus penitent" (230) for the rest of his days (even before he has heard about Saluni's violent stoning at the hands of the Bored Twins [225–28]). The Whale Caller thus becomes the Ancient Mariner by the end of the novel, haunted by his own albatross, his complicity in the violent death of Sharisha. Mda's readers are left—sadder and wiser—to consider the implications. By pairing Saluni's self-indulgent "worldliness" (76) with the Whale Caller's asceticism and self-mortification, Mda satirizes and unsettles our ideas about love, addiction, sex, confession, eating, and worship. The Whale Caller leaves us with the idea that Sharisha's calf is probably better off on its own than "enslaved" or addicted or in love with his kelp horn: "Go, little one. You do not want to know me" (229), he says. Yet we are left wondering, where will this total renunciation of sentimentalism leave the postcolonial environmentalist?

The renunciation of sentimental attachment to charismatic megafauna is also an issue in Ghosh's *The Hungry Tide*. Although it is through our attachments that we care for the environment, it is naïve and sometimes dangerous to neglect the complexity and diversity of the local ecosystem. Heeding this caution, Ghosh presents an optimistic tribute to idealism in depicting how a cosmopolitan cetologist can work cooperatively and responsibly with the local knowledge and songs of the fisherman who knows this tide country so well. Yet Fokir's song unsettles both cosmopolitan characters and readers into the humbling acknowledgment of the limits of their understanding of local concerns.

Because the main characters of *The Hungry Tide* both end up attempting to understand and convey a local ecopolitical history to the world, the novel has attracted the attention of scholars eager to bridge ecocritical and postcolonial discourses. Most have read the novel as Ghosh's contribution to the debate over whether cosmopolitan elites should be the conveyers of local subaltern experience. Saswat Das contends that by writing in English, Ghosh loses too much in translation (184–85), but Rajender Kaur, Christopher Rollason, Terri Tomsky, Alexa Weik, and Pablo Mukherjee argue that the novel demonstrates the process through which cosmopolitan elites must go in order effectively and responsibly to use their privileges and agency in solidarity with the disenfranchised. Mukherjee points out that Ghosh is not suggesting that such responsibility be taken lightly or that the task of understanding and reporting is perfect. In fact, Mukherjee insists, "much of what Kusum, Fokir, Horen say may be incomprehensible to the elites, much of it mistranslated, misunderstood. But they are seldom dismissed, and it is in the novel's refusal to force transparency on to them, in its deference to silences and gaps, that differences are humanized, contacts made, a different idea of the universal glimpsed" (*Surfing the Second Wave* 151). We can extend Mukherjee's point here to consider the attentiveness to gaps, silences, and the inevitable slippage of translation in relating to animal others—although in the present context we might want to think of dignifying rather than "humanizing" differences.

Insofar as readers identify with one of the cosmopolitan characters who learn to reflect on their own complicity and revise their positions, the novel teaches cosmopolitan readers to temper the ways in which their cosmopolitanism contributes to forms of globalization that do not benefit the disenfranchised human and nonhuman beings. Piya, a dedicated young Indian-born, American-raised cetologist, travels in search of rare river dolphins to the Sundarbans.[18] Along the way she encounters the self-centered, successful urban professional translator Kanai and the refugee fisherman Fokir, who ironically[19] embodies the indigenous knowledge and sacred connection to the local ecosystem, where the ocean tides "intermingle" (364) with the river water, and where local gods combine Hinduism and Islam. With Fokir's help, Piya makes an important discovery that may contribute an explanation of the connection between salt and freshwater varieties of Irrawaddy dolphins (123–27). Her epiphany not only launches her idealistic career but, together with what she learns by attending to the limits and gaps in her understanding of Fokir, of dolphins, of her Bengali heritage, and of the tide country, also sheds light on her search for identity, purpose, and a place she can call "home" (399–400).

Fokir rescues Piya from the manipulative Forest Guard and from the waters of the Sundarbans and ultimately sacrifices himself sheltering her from the winds of a cyclone.[20] He is a man of few words and he and Piya share no common language. Nevertheless, to Piya at least, they share a connection to the dolphins and their habitat, and, at least initially, it seems "more honest [to her] that they could not speak" (159). Piya's worldview and relationship to Fokir is complicated when she first hears Fokir sing what we later learn to be "The Miracles of Bon Bibi or the Narrative of Her Glory" (354–60).[21] She is surprised to hear that "his voice sounded almost hoarse and it seemed to crack and sob as it roamed the notes. There was a suggestion of grief in it that unsettled and disturbed her" (98–99). When he sings, she no longer sees in him the "muscular quality of innocence" (99) but instead Piya is led to wonder "whether it was she who was naïve" (99). Such recognition of her own innocence prepares Piya for the lessons ahead. Since the dolphins are Bon Bibi's messengers (307), the unsettling grief Piya discerns in Fokir's voice works to join the vulnerabilities of companion species—human and nonhuman, local and cosmopolitan.

Kanai composes a translation of Fokir's song and adds a preface acknowledging the limits of his capacity for translation as a parting gift to Piya (353–60). The translation, undertaken after Fokir teases him into recognizing his own cosmopolitan vulnerability (317–31), becomes for Kanai a project of confronting his own self-importance. The gesture provides hope that Kanai will temper his cosmopolitan smugness and learn to respect those whose *gyan* (knowledge) can be found in their *gaan* (song) (212). Ghosh is suggesting that this legend (like the Irrawaddy dolphin, the Hamiltons in Lusibari, Nilima and Nirmal, Fokir and Horen, and the people of Morichjhāpi) has been creatively adapted to its locale and therefore should be respected on these terms not according to some universalizing criteria. Further, translation of such a text should acknowledge its own limitations as a translation. Ghosh implies that this applies to his own writing as well.

Thus Fokir's song is the first hint that Piya's romanticized view of Fokir does not allow her to appreciate fully the depth and complexity, the unsettling mystery of his life. Later, Piya is forced to confront her romanticized image of Fokir as "some kind of grass-roots ecologist" (297). When villagers surround and intend to kill a predatory tiger, she tries to intervene and assumes Fokir will help her. Instead, when she forces her way through the crowd to confront the mob, she finds him joining in the attack (294–95). Through the tiger-killing episode, Piya gains perspective on how conservation policies she supports on behalf of charismatic megafauna most often do not take into consideration the lives and livelihoods of the people who live within these ecosystems (301). Kanai explains to her that the tiger had killed people from the village and yet:

> These killings are never reported, never written about in the papers. And the reason is just that these people are too poor to matter. We all know it, but we choose not to see it. Isn't that a horror too—that we can feel the suffering of an animal, but not of human beings? [. . .] We're complicit in this, Piya[. . . .] [I]t was people like you [. . .] who made a push to protect the wildlife here, without regard for the human costs. And I'm complicit because people like me—Indians of my class, that is—have chosen to hide these costs, basically in order to curry favour with their Western patrons. It's not hard to ignore the people who're dying—after all they are the poorest of the poor. (300–301)

Piya and Kanai are both challenged to rethink their complicity through this incident. Ghosh is encouraging readers to consider what Ramachandra Guha calls "the paradox of global environmentalism": namely, that those who worry the most about the destruction of nature are usually those who are making the problem worse. Ghosh joins Guha and Vandana Shiva in objecting to the primarily American construction of nature as untouched wilderness and to the neglect for the poor human beings who dwell near these refuge nations set aside for protected charismatic megafauna.[22]

In this context Ghosh also calls attention to the case of Morichjhãpi, a Marxist utopian community of displaced people illegally settled on an island set aside as part of a nature preserve. The government harasses and eventually violently attacks the village, claiming that they want to protect the environment.[23] Kusum, who is one of the Morichjhãpi refugees, wonders, "Who are these people [. . .] who love animals so much that they are willing to kill us for them? Do they know what is being done in their names?" She concludes that such conservationists must "have forgotten that this is how humans have always lived—by fishing, by clearing land and by planting the soil" (261–62). Clearly, this voice of the community expresses the local complaint about international conservation policies and their enforcement.[24] If we forget that human animals have always lived and found purpose in relation to earth, ocean, and other animals, we no longer have a home of any kind.

The cetacean turn in postcolonial literature draws our attention not just to whales and dolphins but also to the people who connect with them in related ecosystems and who face similar or analogous threats to their livelihoods. The point is not to reinscribe a myth of a nobler savage by finding the Zulu Dr. Doolittle, but to look closely at the ecosystems in their local arrangements and recognize the limitations of our understanding. These writers show us how, as Ghosh puts it, "[f]iction [. . .] can help people inhabit a place—to inhabit it in the fullness of their minds, to inhabit it with their imaginations, to see the ways in which lives link together, the lives of animals, the lives of trees, the lives of human beings" ("The Author Talks"). When we look closely, we are reminded that the human animal is linked somehow to the lives and to the vulnerability of other animals and living beings. But we do not miraculously gain full access to local knowledge. Rather, in each of these works there is as much acknowledgment of the loss and the violence as there is appreciation for what can be approached or glimpsed or translated effectively. We find that reminder of the vulnerability of our knowledge and relationships to human and nonhuman others in songs and stories that are expressions of a deeper current than reason can articulate or that knowledge can hold: the founding myth of Paikea, the prayers and songs that the people of the whale pass down and rediscover through generations, Sharisha's song on the Whale Caller's kelp horn, and Fokir singing "The Glory of Bon Bibi." We find that reminder also in the survivance humor, laughter, and spyhopping irony of the artists of postcolonial ecology.

As we have seen, these novels provide localized challenges to environmentalist universalism as well as to postcolonialism's tendencies toward its own kind of universalism through their focus on the people of the place who encounter the extra-human world. In an article called "'Greening' Postcolonialism: Ecocritical Perspectives," Huggan argues that ecocritical perspectives on postcolonial writing can draw attention to any unjustified anthropocentric bias, while postcolonial criticism, for its part, challenges the universalizing claims of environmentalism that tend to neglect the specific historical, material, and political contexts of ecological concerns (720). Wherever these works subscribe to the myth of the "ecological Indian," that subscription is largely "strategic exoticism" aimed at subverting that representation and reclaiming some agency that has been misplaced when outsiders have infringed on the local scene. While songs of intermingling with cetaceans as ancestors and companion species may seem to sentimentalize the bond to nature, these novels, on the contrary, offer correctives to the sentimentalizing tendencies of environmentalism, for, in such intermingling relationships, an excess of attachment can be counterproductive. The Whale Rider must leave the whales and return to guide her human community; the Whale Caller learns (albeit too late for

Sharisha) to renounce his desire to enact physically the mystical intimacy he finds through the music he makes with the whales; and the cetologist realizes that to honor the fisherman and the ecosystem within which he dwells, she should work with the local leaders. These novels also offer correctives against sentimental attachments to precolonial cultural authenticity for its own sake. Koro must relax rigid attachment to male leadership in order to recognize Kahu's gifts for leadership. Ruth protests the notion that cultural whaling is the way to revive A'atsika culture especially when so little attention is given to the ecospiritual rites associated with whaling. And the sentimental attachment to the cetaceans themselves is complicated in these novels as well. Despite Kahu's feat of riding the sacred whale out to sea, her success is haunted by the 200 whales who died earlier. It is the Whale Caller's selfish desire that lures Sharisha to her violently inscrutable death. And Piya and Fokir grieve over the carcass of an Irrawaddy dolphin calf struck "by the propeller of a fast-moving boat" (345–46). The senseless deaths of the stranded, hunted, or injured cetaceans haunt these stories as much as the loss of Marco, Saluni, and Fokir. Amidst the outcries against such violence, these four works maintain the uncanny otherness of the cetaceans despite some limited communication and interspecies companionship.

Furthermore, these novels present the caution that a sustainable future must avoid imperialist nostalgia. In many places the nostalgic projects of collecting stories and artifacts provide the resources and points of departure or connection for postcolonial reclamation of culture.[23] Similarly, the whole notion of endangerment provides environmentalists with a sense of urgency that we may lose out on something if we are not careful. Yet postcolonial ecology must be grounded in deeper values as indigenous people claim their agency and celebrate their survivance despite the forces that converge to conquer them through annihilation, cultural genocide, conversion, secularization, self-hatred, forced adoption, colonization of the mind, forced migration from their lands, alienation from their livelihoods, coercion to participate in a cash economy, or assimilation. Survivance works through irony and tricksters to ensure that indigenous people are not locked in an unchanging and fixed precolonial culture; rather, they move with the times and creatively adapt to their changing ecosystems: Kahu teases Koro to loosen up his rigid hold on tradition; Mda's readers are confronted with our own complicity in turning the spectacle of charismatic megafauna into a tourist commodity we consume; and the untranslatable in Fokir's song reminds us of the animal vulnerability we share and, therefore, helps us take that startling step beyond anthropocentrism. Environmentalism also must be more than a nostalgia that anticipates the future loss of forms of life in our ecosystem. Again, listening for the local values of relating to the extra-human world that are expressed in the myths and the songs may be the way. What we may never be able to understand in the songs of the whales and the chatter of the dolphins should remind us that the environment exceeds our grasp and that our own sustainability as well as our animal vulnerability is inextricably bound up in our nonhuman ancestors and companion species.

NOTES

I want to thank the editors of this collection for providing valuable feedback and suggestions on several drafts of this essay.

1. J. R. Wytenbroek follows the fable into fantasy novels by Welwyn Wilton Katz and Madeleine L'Engle. Kim Kindersley's film *Whaledreamers* builds its environmentalist and world peace argument by suggesting that indigenous connections to whales can lead people around the world to heal human divisions of all kinds.

2. See also Vizenor, *Manifest Manners*, and Kroeber 25–26.

3. For Huggan "strategic exoticism" is where "postcolonial writers/thinkers, working from within exoticist codes of representation, either manage to subvert those codes [. . .] or succeed in redeploying them for the purposes of uncovering differential relations of power" (*Postcolonial Exotic* 32). Michael Harkin tracks cases of Native American cultural centers and museums where indigenous groups have represented themselves to visitors with an irony that provides a postmodern and postcultural intervention to disrupt the degrading and dehumanizing imperial representations that have taken on a life of their own through exhibitions, Wild West shows, and Hollywood simulations. Harkin predicts that "increasingly, Indians and other aboriginal groups will attempt to seize control of [the tourist encounter] by playing against type, by explicitly addressing stereotypes, and above all, by introducing irony into the equation" (583).

4. Brenda Peterson, in "Apprenticeship to Animal Play," makes the case that human animals are drawn to other species out of a deep need and unconscious desire for a more playful attitude toward life. The centerpiece of her essay—which begins with her own cat and draws upon research on primate play—is her firsthand description of a group of women dancing with female dolphins in the wild. The mystery of such interspecies play draws us in to consider what the animals are trying to tell us. At the limits of our abilities to communicate and comprehend, we puzzle over and project meanings onto these encounters.

5. Elizabeth DeLoughrey's discussion of Kamau Brathwaite's theory of "tidalectics" is relevant here (*Routes and Roots*, 1–48). The cetacean turn in postcolonial literature includes works linked less by human roots (nation, language) and routes, and more by the migrations of the cetaceans and their visitations upon coasts where human beings dwell.

6. Animal liberationists like Peter Singer have been criticized for merely redrawing the arbitrary human/animal line between fellow animals and expendable organisms (Garrard 136–40), in effect, expanding the humanist and anthropocentric bias rather than questioning it (Calarco 128). The "challenge," Matthew Calarco insists, is to address the question of the animal "altogether without the guardrails of the human-animal distinction" (149). I'm suggesting that, by acknowledging our shared vulnerability and interdependence, we humans find a place within our ecosystems rather than outside of them looking in.

7. J. M. Coetzee's Elizabeth Costello, Jacques Derrida, Cary Wolfe, and Calarco engage similar questions about stepping beyond human exceptionalism in order to develop posthumanist, nonanthropocentric philosophies of animal life.

8. In discussing Ihimaera's *The Whale Rider*, five texts are relevant: the 1972 short story called "The Whale," the 1987 novel *The Whale Rider*, the 2002 Niki Caro film called *Whale Rider*, the revised, "international" movie tie-in version of the novel released in the United States in 2003, and the thirtieth-anniversary revised edition of the short story released in 2003. Crucial differences in these works coincide with the development, growing confidence, and global reach of the Maori Renaissance. See also Allen 134–35 and Prentice.

9. The novel, more effectively than the 2002 Niki Caro film, emphasizes how the separation is the work of the "arrogance" of man (27, 116) in the inhumanity of man to man in the plantation colonialism that the narrator Rawiri witnesses in Papua New Guinea (65–76), in the bloody whaling history that Koro recalls and relates to the "temptations" of "commercialism" (50–52), in the nuclear testing that disorients the whales (57–59), and the "wedge" modernity drives into the world to divide it "into the half [man] could believe in and the half he could not believe in" (116).

10. Such a revaluation corresponds to the Oceanic revival of canoe voyaging (see DeLoughrey, *Routes and Roots*, 96–157) and the reconceptualization of Oceania as a sea of islands (Epeli Hau'ofa). In the film, Porourangi's unfinished waka (canoe) looms over the community as a broken link to an apparently obsolete past until it is launched at the end of the film to mark the shift from survivalism to survivance.

11. The myth of the ecological Indian is a neocolonial reiteration of the myth of the noble savage, which holds that indigenous peoples have an essential and uncomplicated connection to nature. See Shepard Krech III and Greg Garrard (124).

12. Hogan acknowledges the counsel of "the Quillieute Nation and other paddling Nations with beautiful canoes and paddlers who do not kill" (*People of the Whale* 303). In *Sightings: The Gray Whales' Mysterious Journey*, the Quileute feature prominently as neighbors to the Makah who share a similar whaling heritage and who respect Makah treaty rights but who themselves have chosen to refrain from whaling (Peterson and Hogan 190).

13. Hogan indicates here and elsewhere in this and other works that the connection to the environment is not merely a connection to megafauna but to plants as well. See also *The Sweet Breathing of Plants: Women Writing on the Green World*, edited by Hogan and Peterson.

14. For a thoughtful analysis of the Makah whale hunt from the perspective of cross-cultural ecofeminist ethics, see Greta Gaard. See also Hogan's "Silencing Tribal Grandmothers." For detailed account of the events as they unfold, see Robert Sullivan.

15. Similarly, at the height of the popularity of the dolphins as "humans of the sea" media phenomenon, John Lilly proposed that the United Nations recognize the "Cetacean Nation." The idea still has its adherents. See http://www.cetacean-nation.com.

16. Mda's criticism of tourism comes across sharply through Saluni's keen analysis explaining why the restaurant owner shoos away the opera-singing boy from Zwelihle township: "Lunga Tubu's presence here destabilizes the serenity of Hermanus" by reminding the rich tourists "that only a few kilometers away there is another world that is not at peace with itself" (86).

17. Such scenes of visual consumption satirize what Garrard calls "ecoporn" (151–54). In Mda's work it seems that connections made visually lead to destruction while those that are made aurally resonate deeply—albeit with problematic implications for eroticizing the relationship to nature (see Anthony Vital, "Situating Ecology" 310–12).

18. The Sundarbans are a group of islands and archipelagos of mangrove forests that make up the Ganges River Delta south of Kolkata bordering and including parts of Bangladesh. This setting fits Buell's depiction of "watershed aesthetics," a bioregionalist conception of where people dwell within an ecosystem (*Writing for an Endangered World* 243–65). The interpenetration of fresh and salt water, according to Ghosh, creates "hundreds of different ecological niches," "microenvironments" that move as "floating biodomes, filled with endemic fauna and flora" (*The Hungry Tide* 125). The megafauna adapted to this watershed include crocodiles, tigers, and two species of river dolphin. Human beings have also settled here, although they have historically been challenged by the cyclones, the changing tides, tiger attacks, poor planning, the Partition of India and its legacy, and by tiger conservation efforts.

19. As Mukherjee points out, it is important to consider that Kusum and Fokir, as refugees, are also migrants to the Sundarbans.

20. Fokir's heroic self-sacrifice reenacts that of Timothy in protecting Phillip in Theodore Taylor's *The Cay*.

21. Bon Bibi is the goddess of the forest who helps those who call upon her (Ghosh *The Hungry Tide* 103), and the dolphins are her messengers (307). The story has Muslim origins but Hindu features (103, 246–47, Rollason 6–7). Nirmal, the Marxist schoolteacher, dismisses the legend as "false consciousness." Fokir, his mother Kusum, and Horen, their guardian, however, are devout believers.

22. See also Vital, who considers the South African context in relation to an earlier work by Mda and a work by Coetzee ("Situating Ecology").

23. Ross Mallick provides a more thorough explanation of the contexts and significance of the Morichjhāpi massacre. Ghosh acknowledges Mallick's text in his "Author's Note" (402). In an interview about this issue, Ghosh holds up the Morichjhāpi experiment as an alternative model of how poor people of the world deal with their own poverty in contrast to the explanations of how poverty and despair inevitably drive the poor to commit such violent acts as 9/11 terrorism. He also holds up the Morichjhāpi example for the irony that the same government who kicked these poor people out in order to protect the forest and its wildlife recently wanted to let the Sahara group erect in the Sundarbans a world-class tourist resort, complete with a floating hotel, jet skis, and scuba diving. Ghosh wrote against the Sahara project in an Indian magazine and reports that the project now is dead ("The Author Talks").

24. Project Tiger is an instance of what Rob Nixon sees as "erasing the history of colonized peoples through the myth of the empty lands" ("Environmentalism" 235).

25. Interest in indigenous cultures continues to work, in part, from the shadows of such imperialist nostalgia. Rona Tamiko Halualani's ethnography of "touring the native" in Hawaiian cultural tourism history and politics offers a compelling illustration of how imperialist nostalgia is deployed as a colonial gesture of self-congratulation veiled with a measure of honor for the spectacle of the "lost" or dying culture and civilization.

9

Compassion, Commodification, and *The Lives of Animals*

J. M. Coetzee's Recent Fiction

Allison Carruth

> Contemporary criticism seems to be confirming the oft-quoted [Claude] Lévi-Strauss phrase that "animals are good to think with." The question becomes this: What are the methods and parameters of such thought and are the animals invited to the table? If so, are they there as companions with whom we break bread, or are they flesh that is eaten, or do they work within some other modality of, perhaps, wildness? The animal poses for us a range of ontological and epistemological questions that is in part why so much is being written about them.
> —Richard Nash and Ron Broglio

In their introduction to a special issue of the journal *Configurations*, Richard Nash and Ron Broglio observe that the humanities have "arrived at an animal moment" (1). To the extent that a canon exists within this emerging field of critical animal studies, South African writer J. M. Coetzee occupies a central place in it. As part of the prestigious Tanner Lectures, academic audiences gathered at Princeton in 1997 to hear Coetzee address the very questions that Nash and Broglio outline. Coetzee did not deliver a lecture per se but instead read a short novella entitled *The Lives of Animals*, a story in which the aging Australian novelist and vegetarian Elizabeth Costello visits a fictional Boston college to deliver a series of invitational talks entitled "The Philosophers and the Animals" and "The Poets and the Animals."[1] Despite the novella's unconventional form and provocative ethical stakes, critics have given *The Lives of Animals* relatively short shrift.[2] The text merits sustained scrutiny, however, not simply as a prequel to the 2003 novel *Elizabeth Costello* but as a foundational text for postcolonial ecocriticism, on the one hand, and critical animal studies, on the other.

Early on in *The Lives of Animals*, Costello's son John, an assistant professor of physics at the fictional Appleton College, frames his mother's impending lectures on animals as unorthodox and unwelcome. Although his mother has been invited to Appleton "on the basis of her reputation as a novelist," John bemoans that she has elected to speak "not about herself and her fiction, as her sponsors would no doubt like, but about a hobbyhorse of hers" (16). This figure of speech is patently tongue-in-cheek, for Costello's "hobbyhorse" proves to be a critique of animal commodification in postindustrial economies and an attendant call for compassion with the embodied lives of other animals.[3] Much to the chagrin of John and his philosopher wife, Norma, Costello variously exhausts and outrages her audiences while at Appleton, where she delivers a formal lecture on the injustices of animal testing and confined feedlots, leads a seminar on the poetics of panthers and jaguars, and participates in a closing debate on animal rights with Appleton philosophy professor Thomas O'Hearne. Critics suggest that the novella's rhetorical conflicts over animals reflect, primarily, Coetzee's long-standing interests as a postcolonial novelist in human acts of cruelty and sympathy that either foreclose or enable an ethical relation to others.[4] Such readings stress Coetzee's investments in human rights and social ethics, against which Costello's animal discourse takes shape much like her fictional listeners perceive it, as "rambling" and "confused" (*LA* 31, 44, 69). Sam Durrant argues, for example, that *The Lives of Animals* "unequivocally rehearses the failure of Costello's sympathetic imagination" and rejoins that failure by offering "a new kind of ethical and literary relation, a relation grounded precisely [. . .] on the recognition of the other's fundamental alterity" (120).[5] However compelling, this interpretation too quickly recasts *The Lives of Animals* as a meditation on the limits to knowing any other being—collapsing the text's representation of commodified animals into discourses of *human* otherness, exploitation, resistance, community, and sympathy.[6] Other critics certainly attend to Coetzee's concern with animals in his novels *Disgrace* and *Elizabeth Costello* (which included the Tanner Lectures as chapters 3 and 4), contending that the texts advocate against Cartesian dualism and for the continuity of species.[7] These critics figure the discourses of animal rights and human rights (if not always the bodies of humans and animals) as natural allies in postcolonial fictions that foreground environmental problems.

Coetzee's recent fiction offers fruitful conceptual ground, in other words, for the emerging field of postcolonial ecocriticism, which, this collection demonstrates, investigates the confluences of oppressed communities and endangered ecosystems, social movements and environmental crises, as well as human beings and other animals. Engaging with seminal critiques of Western environmentalism, Cara Cilano and Elizabeth DeLoughrey argue that postcolonial literature and theory provide a valuable framework for ecocriticism by emphasizing the necessity as well as the difficulty of representing otherness, "thereby introducing an element of provisionality into any ecocritical reading" (76).[8] Cilano and DeLoughrey further suggest that postcolonial ecocriticism should investigate any text, regardless of its setting, that engages critically with the social *and* environmental ramifications of imperial-capitalist systems (78). Focusing on *The Lives of Animals*, I argue that Coetzee's postapartheid work turns on a persistent but ultimately fragile alliance of ecological and social injustice. The fragility of this alliance hinges in turn on a central premise in his recent fiction that the compassion required to feel with and act on behalf of other animals might come at the expense of one's affinities with other human beings. While decolonial movements have deployed animals as symbols to generate compassion for politically oppressed communities, *The Lives of Animals* dramatizes our resistance to the inverse strategy of deploying human bodies as symbols of animal suffering. At the same time, Coetzee's novels imply that compassion for animals—and, above all, for the globally traded bodies of livestock—depends on our ability not just to think about animals or just to codify their rights but also to imagine our bodies in terms of theirs.

Coetzee's decision to deliver the Tanner Lectures in the guise of a fictional character with whom he shares only a career (novel writing) and a diet (vegetarianism) must have surprised many members of the original audience. To appreciate this reaction, we need only imagine the Nobel Prize–winning novelist standing at a lectern before a silent auditorium of scholars and opening his first of two lectures on animals with the following lines:

> He is waiting at the gate when her flight comes in. Two years have passed since he last saw his mother; despite himself, he is shocked at how she has aged. Her hair, which had had streaks of gray in it, is now entirely white; her shoulders stoop; her flesh has grown flabby. They have never been a demonstrative family. A hug, a few murmured words, and the business of greeting is done. (*LA* 15)

This scene of John and Elizabeth's reunion seems at once unconventional and banal as an opening to a lecture entitled "The Philosopher and the Animals." It proves to be a meaningful beginning, however, in the sense that Elizabeth Costello's character troubles the hierarchies that demarcate other beings from one's next of kin. The airport gate that reunites Elizabeth and John as estranged family members is retrospectively significant in the context of *Elizabeth Costello*. As readers familiar with the 2003 novel will recall, Costello arrives—after seven chapters in which she lectures on literary realism, the African novel, humanism, eros, obscenity, divinity, and, of course, animals—at yet another gate. *That* gate marks the end of both *Elizabeth Costello* the novel and Elizabeth Costello the protagonist. In the novel's final chapter (or "lesson"), Costello finds herself in a purgatorial city where she is summoned to "make a statement" of belief before she may pass through its apparently celestial gateway (*EC* 194).⁹ This purgatorial ending exceeds the bounds of the novel, moreover, when Costello resurfaces as the irksome, ghostly character who takes up residence with the injured middle-age character Paul Rayment in the 2005 novel *Slow Man*.

Elizabeth's purgatory in *Elizabeth Costello* and *Slow Man* proves crucial to understanding the fictional lectures that comprise *The Lives of Animals*. Across these three texts, Costello figures as an outcast who is cast out not so much from a Christian afterlife as from human kinship with the people who are ostensibly closest to her: her son John, her sister Blanche, and her former lover Emmanuel Egudu. Chris Danta reads Costello as isolated from other human beings because of her "staunch" advocacy for a "philosophy of the body" that locates humans on a radical continuum with all other creatures (727–28). In fact, Costello imagines that her isolation stems not from philosophical precepts but from her "special fidelities" as a writer to becoming the other (*EC* 221–22). In her words to the judges who demand a statement of belief, Costello suggests that a writer's most radical fidelity must be to the embodied lives of other animals. Here we might consider the postscript to *Elizabeth Costello*: a seventeenth-century letter to Francis Bacon from Elizabeth, Lady Chandos, that Coetzee offers as a source text for Costello's modern-day lectures and musings. In the fictionalized letter to Bacon, Lady Chandos details her husband's madness, which, she suggests, emanates from a belief that "each creature is key to all other creatures" and thus can be understood through figurative language and, above all, through allegory (*EC* 229). However, Lady Chandos correlates her husband's madness not simply to his excessive use of figurative language ("saying one thing always for another") but also to his obsession with inhabiting an animal body; as she queries Bacon, how "can I live with rats and dogs and beetles crawling through me day and night?" (*EC* 228–29). These entreaties draw into relief Elizabeth Costello's "special fidelities" to other creatures. For in response to Lady Chandos's 1603 letter, Costello would likely argue that poetry and narrative (rather than philosophy or science) are uniquely poised to comprehend "rats and dogs and beetles" by representing them figuratively while embodying them corporeally. Costello thus seems to be a kindred spirit to Lord Chandos rather than to her namesake, Lady Chandos. That said, Costello parts ways with her seventeenth-century compatriot by calling into question the neo-Platonic obligations of literature to transmute the animal body into a vehicle for abstract knowledge or divine creation. In *The Lives of Animals*, Costello maintains that literature should privilege not the divine, nor even the human, but rather what the late ecofeminist Val Plumwood terms "the other-than-human world" (*Environmental Culture* 144). Costello's desire to feel for other animals comes at a price, however. As her son John repeatedly suggests, his mother's "powers" to feel for and think her way into "other existences," which define her novelistic practice, also threaten to rupture her filial ties (*LA* 22).

The purgatorial ending of *Elizabeth Costello* further proves crucial to *The Lives of Animals* by undercutting interpretations of the novella as a mostly metafictional work that is less about the *lives* and more about the *literariness* of animals. In the final scene of *Elizabeth Costello*, an arguably postmortem Costello pokes fun at her initial impulse to interpret symbolically the scarred dog who half-heartedly guards the gate: "His eyes are closed, he is resting, snoozing. Beyond him is nothing but a desert of sand and stone, to infinity. It is her first vision in a long while, and she does not trust it, does not trust in particular the anagram GOD-DOG. *Too literary*, she thinks again. A curse on literature!" (*EC* 224–25, emphasis in original). Coetzee's readers have learned by this point to distrust such proclamations. Despite its obvious ironies, however, Costello's "curse on literature" can be understood as largely earnest. Coetzee repeatedly figures literary language as at once an aid and an obstacle to feeling compassion for other animals. His recent fiction suggests that interspecies kinship may be at odds with human kinship because the latter relies on *making use of* animals not only as material sources of food, labor, companionship, and scientific experiment but also as symbolic resources. Plumwood defines commodification as a form of "instrumentalism" that, in making use of the other as "*no more than* something of use," includes material and semantic practices (159, emphasis in original).[10] Danta suggests that Coetzee "uses the address of the animal (body)" instrumentally, in Plumwood's sense, "to interrupt or suspend the human self's passage toward [. . .] a consecrated state of being" (734). On this view, animals function in Coetzee's fiction as instruments for a mostly human drama (734). However, animals also appear in *Disgrace* and *Elizabeth Costello* as embodied beings who occasion reciprocity alongside instrumentalism. Elizabeth Costello's narrative dramatizes the consequences of such animal embodiment in literature, in that her effort to represent the animal body partly forecloses her kinship with friends and family members and, moreover, seems to make her a *pariah*.[11]

Critical readings of *The Lives of Animals* have fallen into more or less two camps: those that classify the text as a work of metafiction and those that classify it as a jeremiad on animal rights. In his recent assessment of postcolonial ecocriticism, Graham Huggan emphasizes the "aesthetic play" that permeates *The Lives of Animals*, categorizing Costello's talks as "mock-lectures" that draw on the stock tropes of animal fables ("Greening Postcolonialism" 709). Although Huggan views the fable genre as central to postcolonial narratives of the environment, in *The Lives of Animals*, he argues, "ecologism itself becomes a fable of the impossible attempt to escape anthropocentric thought" (713). Questioning Costello's call to feel for nonhuman animals, Huggan supports the view that *The Lives of Animals* is more a metafictional than environmentalist text.[12] By comparison, political theorist Amy Gutmann observes that "Coetzee displays the kind of seriousness that can unite aesthetics and ethics" by offering a literary rejoinder to the philosophical discourse of animal rights (3). Two of the four scholars who delivered formal responses to Coetzee's Tanner Lectures at Princeton—religious studies scholar Wendy Doniger and primate expert Barbara Smuts—echo Gutmann's assessment of *The Lives of Animals* as a sincere if fictionalized discourse on animal justice.[13] Smuts, for example, classifies *The Lives of Animals* as a traditional philosophical dialogue (93), while Doniger responds to what she views as Coetzee's "deeply moving" arguments "for the inevitable, if unfalsifiable, links between communion with animals, compassion for animals, and the refusal to torment, if not necessarily the refusal to kill and/or eat, animals" (107).[14]

In contrast to Huggan, then, these scholars seem to agree on the seriousness of *The Lives of Animals*, an assumption that also underlies the critical reception of Coetzee's apartheid-era novels. In a 2004 essay, postcolonial critic Derek Attridge responds to those South African writers who fault Coetzee for obscuring the historical record of colonialism and apartheid via unreliable narrators and thematic ambiguities.[15] Focusing on early works like *In the Heart of the Country*, Attridge theorizes Coetzee's fiction as an "ethical modernism." Attridge acknowledges that Coetzee's creative project is not that of social realism, which would "provide new and illuminating details of the painful history of Western domination" in Africa ("Ethical Modernism" 670). Rather, his fiction addresses South African history obliquely by employing the multiperspectival and nonchronological techniques of modernist fiction to engage his reader with "figures of otherness," subordination, and, hence, a fundamentally decolonial project (Attridge 655).[16] Rita Barnard likewise asserts Coetzee's investment in postcolonial politics but directs critical attention to the significance of nonhuman others in his work. In her analysis of *Disgrace*, Barnard interprets the relationship between David Lurie and abandoned dogs at the Shaw's animal shelter as a political allegory that asks South African readers to feel beyond the ties of kinship or ancestral land by imagining community with strangers and, in particular, with divested groups ("J.M. Coetzee's *Disgrace*" 222–23). Attridge and Barnard thus position Coetzee as a postcolonial novelist whose literary affinities are with Western modernism as well as African literature, language, and history. In making a case for Coetzee as a postcolonial novelist, however, they construe the animals that populate his novels as no more than allegories for human narratives. Barnard, for example, reasons that the compassion David Lurie comes to feel for dogs in *Disgrace* functions as a metaphor of compassion for "the suffering of many," by which Barnard means the multiethnic and multilinguistic human community of South Africa (222–23).[17] The postcolonial framing of Coetzee tends then to recapitulate the anthropocentrism that his recent novels variously critique, satirize, and parody. This interpretive paradigm centers on the limitations to reading others. In contrast, my intervention in Coetzee criticism invites a more sustained attention to the embodied status of animals in his corpus.

Coetzee's postapartheid texts (*The Lives of Animals, Elizabeth Costello, Slow Man,* and *Diary of a Bad Year*) mark a significant departure within that corpus, although not only for their evident movement away from the racial politics and rural landscapes of South Africa toward the urban and notably institutional spaces of Cape Town, Boston, Adelaide, Sydney, Melbourne, and Amsterdam.[18] These texts also move away from the Kafkaesque morbidity and violence of earlier novels in staging banal and often comical plots.[19] As evidence of this shift, we can compare the political violence that permeates *In the Heart of the Country, Life and Times of Michael K, Waiting for the Barbarians,* and *Age of Iron* to the Adelaide cycling accident that opens *Slow Man* or the academic lecture circuit that structures *Elizabeth Costello.* Such banal plots frequently dovetail with sudden instances of the bizarre and the surreal. *Elizabeth Costello*, for example, narrates Elizabeth's journey from a "gig" lecturing on the African novel aboard a cruise ship to the proverbial gate where she tries to defend her vocation as a novelist. As already noted, Coetzee's subsequent novel *Slow Man* extends this plot when Costello returns from the dead to haunt (or, more aptly, harass) the injured bicyclist Peter Rayment. This melding of the quotidian, the comical, and the surreal situates Coetzee's recent fiction in the traditions of postmodern fiction and, more pertinently, postcolonial magical realism.

In *The Lives of Animals*, moreover, the novella's hybrid form functions as a critique of anthropocentrism that is best understood as postcolonial. Peter Singer—the fourth official respondent to Coetzee's Tanner Lectures—illuminates the surreal banality of *The Lives of Animals*. Unlike his fellow respondents (Doniger, Garber, and Smuts), Singer does not respond to Elizabeth Costello's lectures with an academic argument of his own. Instead, he crafts a self-consciously ordinary short story. The story takes place in a middle-class North American kitchen, where a teenage daughter (Naomi) debates with her father (Peter Singer) the finer points of Elizabeth Costello's call for interspecies compassion. The tone of Singer's story is light, and the family debate takes the form of banter. Echoing the mundane opening of *The Lives of Animals*—the airport arrival of Elizabeth Costello and subsequent "light supper" with John and Norma—Singer's third-person story begins at the breakfast table:

> When Naomi comes down for breakfast, her father is already at the table. Though there is a bowl of muesli in front of him, his attention is on the typescript that is lying on the table beside him. For Naomi the only unusual aspect of this scene is the depth of her father's frown. She fills her own bowl with muesli, covers it with soymilk, flicks a dangling dreadlock out of it, and breaks the silence:
> "Let me guess . . . It's a paper from a graduate student who majored in cultural studies before turning to philosophy?"
> "No. This is worse. Not the paper itself—that's really interesting. But it's a more serious problem for me."
> "Like?"
> "You know how next month I'm going to Princeton to respond to that South African novelist, J. M. Coetzee, who's giving a special lecture

about philosophy and animals? This is his lecture. Except that it isn't a lecture at all. It's a fictional account of a female novelist called Costello giving a lecture at an American university."

"You mean that he's going to stand up there and give a lecture about someone giving a lecture? *Très post-moderne.*"

"What's postmodern about it?" (*LA* 85)

This ironic dialogue between the fictionalized Naomi and Peter Singer initially implies that *The Lives of Animals* is less a "serious problem" for animal ethicists than a "postmodern" spoof of academic discourse. As Naomi quips, Coetzee is partly rearticulating, partly parodying Jean Baudrillard's definition of postmodernism as a Zeitgeist characterized by media simulation and mimicry—in Naomi's words, "all that stuff about [. . .] breaking down the distinction between reality and representation and so on" (85). However, Singer's short story cautions us against dismissing the all-too-real animals that motivate Coetzee's unorthodox lectures. In response to readers who encounter the bodies of animals primarily via postmodern forms of mediated experience such as advertising, animation, pet stores, and supermarkets, *The Lives of Animals* asserts the live and dead animal bodies in which contemporary systems of commerce, consumption, and culture traffic.

In Singer's story, Naomi and Peter debate Elizabeth Costello's case for an egalitarianism that values the lives of animals as utterly equal to those of human beings (*LA* 86–87). Akin to the fictional academics in *The Lives of Animals*, Singer questions Costello's comparison of concentration camps in Nazi Germany to factory farms in the United States (although he acknowledges that "a comparison is not necessarily an equation") (*LA* 86). Singer challenges Costello's implicit argument that a nonhuman life is emotionally and ethically equivalent to a human life: "a more radical egalitarianism about humans and animals [. . .] than [Singer] would be prepared to defend" (*LA* 86, 90). Singer defends the principle that human kinship takes emotional and ethical precedence over "the consideration" of other animals' interests, and he defends philosophical reasoning (against Costello's skepticism about logic) for enabling us to think through the relative interests of different beings (*LA* 87). While father and daughter share a basic commitment both to philosophical inquiry and to vegetarianism, Naomi becomes a foil to Singer when she affirms Costello's argument that all animals have "wants of their own," value their lives, and, thus, are not as dispensable as modern husbandry and animal testing practices might have us believe (*LA* 89).

The debate between Peter and Naomi demonstrates that Elizabeth Costello makes deliberately provocative arguments about the relationship of human and animal rights in a period marked by scientific testing and confined feedlots. Coetzee embeds the very objections to Costello's claims that Singer raises in the voices of other characters—including Costello's daughter-in-law Norma, a non-tenure-track philosopher, and Abraham

Stern, a poet at Appleton who refuses to attend the postlecture dinner after taking offense to Costello's analogy of Nazi concentration camps and animal feedlots. In the fictional frame that introduces Costello's second talk (the seminar entitled "The Poets and the Animals"), Stern sends a letter to Costello explaining his critique: "You took over for your own purposes the familiar comparison between the murdered Jews of Europe and slaughtered cattle. The Jews died like cattle, therefore cattle die like Jews, you say. That is a trick with words which I will not accept" (*LA* 49). Stern lambastes Costello for her use of analogy to convey the suffering of domesticated animals in feedlots and meatpacking factories. Although Stern finds the stock comparison "Jews died like cattle" to be persuasive and ethical, he finds the inverse comparison insensitive at best and inhumane at worst. His objection suggests that the vehicle and tenor within any comparison serve categorically different functions, a position that runs counter to the prominent theory of metaphor advanced by Paul Ricoeur and John Searle.[20] On the latter view, whether we say, "Jews died like cattle" or "cattle die like Jews," each term serves to illuminate the meaning of the other; the vehicle and the tenor are, in other words, semantically equivalent. The conflict between Costello and Stern calls this theory of metaphor into question by suggesting that animal-human metaphors function in practice to represent human experience and to create human-centered narratives. In turning a habitual animal metaphor on its head by making livestock the *tenor* rather than *vehicle* of a comparison, Costello implicitly critiques the anthropocentric ethics of figurative language and, as such, upsets many of her listeners.

Costello challenges the anthropocentric priorities of both ethics and literature more thoroughly than established arguments in philosophy for extending to at least certain animals legal rights and just treatment. In *Animal Liberation*, Singer makes the case that many animals merit respect, care, and legal consideration because fundamental social rights are not contingent on individual, embodied aptitudes but on abstract principles of equality, altruism, and tolerance (section I, paragraphs 1–2). Singer maintains, however ambivalently, that other animals are dependent upon and subordinate to human beings for ethical and legal recognition (section III, paragraph 18).[21] Plumwood critiques this framework for animal rights because of its "neo-Cartesianism" (*Environmental Culture* 143–53, 159). Responding directly to the tracts of Singer and Tom Regan, Plumwood argues that the "attempt to *extend* the privileged category of the human [. . .] rather than to try to break human/nature dualism[s] down" is an "exercise in boundary extension which otherwise retains the basic conceptual framework" of Cartesian humanism (143). In the rhetorical drama of *The Lives of Animals*, Costello's arguments about animals resonate with Plumwood's call for a "counter-centric ethic" that avoids dualism by resituating "humans in ecological terms and non-humans in ethical terms" (124, 8–9). Costello denounces both philosophy and biology for perpetuating the hierarchical segregation of humans from other species

(*LA* 22, 66). Although Costello acknowledges those philosophers who interrogate the categories of human and animal, from Aristotle to Jeremy Bentham, she ultimately rejects Western philosophy because, echoing Plumwood, it privileges the human mind and body and thus categorizes other animals as "thinglike" (*LA* 23). Costello evokes outrage from her audience precisely because she disturbs the priority of the human in ethical discourses of animals by aligning herself with other creatures, ranging from literary figures such as Kafka's Red Peter to the livestock who inhabit confined feedlots (*LA* 18–30, 51–53, 65–66).

Why should we understand this critique of anthropocentrism as postcolonial? However unreliable Costello may be as a protagonist, her arguments for what Singer terms a "radical egalitarianism" between humans and other animals rely on postcolonial principles. As evident in her censure of slaughterhouses, Costello maintains that animals are institutionally oppressed and, therefore, merit compassion as well as legal recognition. *The Lives of Animals* develops its rhetoric of animal oppression, moreover, through an implicit critique of capitalism's systematic commodification of meat and other animal products. In mapping the latent affinities that connect postcolonial theory and ecocriticism, Huggan observes that the two fields share an interest, among others, in "historically situated critiques of capitalist ideology" ("Greening Postcolonialism" 720).[22] *The Lives of Animals* offers a test case for this shared interest—and thus for postcolonial ecocriticism—by demanding that any critique of capitalism must begin by feeling with and considering the interests of other animals.

As we have seen, *The Lives of Animals* performs a contentious dialogue on animals that ranges across issues of meat eating, animal testing, food taboos, Cartesian philosophy, and speciesism. Framing Costello's lectures as performative, Gayatri Spivak aptly characterizes the text as *"staged speculations about animality and the human"* ("Ethics and Politics" 25n10, emphasis mine). Other scholars concur with Spivak's assessment. For example, Gutmann introduces the published version of *The Lives of Animals* by observing that it was not really Coetzee who lectured academic audiences in 1997 on "the way human beings treat animals" but rather a dramatic cast of characters (3). To Gutmann's point, the debates that comprise *The Lives of Animals* occur simultaneously between Elizabeth Costello and the faculty members of Appleton College and between J. M. Coetzee and the four scholars who responded to him at Princeton. We can understand *The Lives of Animals*, then, as a kind of rhetorical theater. Viewed as theater, the text must be read not simply through Elizabeth Costello's monologues but also through the heteroglossic exchanges among other characters that take place during postlecture conversations and meals. Discord erupts in these scenes as others respond to Costello's arguments that the commodified use of animals in feedlots and laboratories is not only analogous to but ethically on par with human oppression.

Put differently, Elizabeth Costello represents only one of several perspectives on animals in *The Lives of Animals*. Readers imagine that the text's animal politics—particularly vis-à-vis meat—inhere solely in Costello's lectures, however ironically framed we acknowledge the lectures to be. I would argue that we pursue the text's politics of animality and the animal other in its banal scenes of eating as well as in the high-minded lectures that surround those scenes. Here, Peter Singer is again on track. Opening his rejoinder to Coetzee with a vegetarian breakfast of muesli and soymilk, Singer invites readers to turn their attention to the numerous meals that precede and follow Costello's lectures at Appleton. Beginning with the "light supper" that Norma prepares for the family upon her mother-in-law's arrival, *The Lives of Animals* makes eating a crucial subtext for Costello's lectures (15). While the many metaphors permeating the novella's dialogue transmute bodies into ideas ("hobbyhorse," "close to the bone," "food for thought," and so on), its scenes of eating in turn transmute the minds of scholars into the fleshy bodies of animals (*LA* 16, 42, 45).

Consider, for example, the description of the Faculty Club dinner that takes place after Costello's first lecture:

> There is still the dinner to get through. [. . .] With grim interest [John] looks forward to seeing how the college will cope with the challenge of the menu. [. . .] Are her distinguished fellow guests going to have to fret through the evening, dreaming of the pastrami sandwich or the cold drumstick they will gobble down when they get home? Or will the wise minds of the college have recourse to the ambiguous fish, which has a backbone but does not breathe air or suckle its young. (*LA* 37–39)

John's third-person reflection, which weaves through several pages of factious dialogue, grounds the scholarly debate over the capacities of animals to reason and feel pain in an image of the commodified bodies within the modern food system. In this internal monologue, John moves from the "pastrami sandwich" and "cold drumstick," which he imagines await the omnivorous diners at home, to the biology of the "ambiguous" red snapper that the faculty club elects to offer the group, alongside a vegetarian entrée. The filleted body of a fish thus draws into relief the processed character of meats like pastrami, whose ecological origins are obscure at best. When John refers to the backbones and gills of fish, his monologue, by inference, invites Coetzee's readers (if not Costello's fellow diners) to conjure up the mammary glands of cattle and pigs. In this same scene, John's mother responds to the question of why she became a vegetarian by quoting Plutarch's visceral condemnation of meat eaters for consuming "the corpse of a dead animal," chewing "hacked flesh," and swallowing "the juices of death-wounds" (*LA* 38). While certainly less graphic, John's musings on the "ambiguous" body of a fish as neither vegetable nor mammal proves just as important to the scene's discourse on animal consumption. With the implicit exchange between mother and son, the text counters Costello's vegetarianism by making the ethical quandary of the scene not whether to eat meat but rather how to embody and make visible the food chain.

The manifestation of animals as food in *The Lives of Animals* reveals a crucial principle for postcolonial ecocriticism: regardless of dietary practices or cultural food taboos, every human body is a consumer of the other-than-human world and, by extension, is implicated in those systems that make use of other beings. This principle comes into focus when, at the same faculty dinner, John employs a metaphor to characterize Norma's criticisms of her mother-in-law's vegetarianism. "Now she is getting really close to the bone," he reflects, "There is a certain amount of shuffling; there is unease in the air" (42). The figure of speech defamiliarizes a habitual metaphor by evoking the hunt and the slaughter, those ancient human acts that gave rise to the now-dead metaphor "close to the bone." As Norma grates on Costello—"getting really close to the bone"—the wider community of faculty eaters morphs into a herd of wild animals, "shuffling" and ill-at-ease. This use of figurative language seems central to rhetorical conflicts over meat eating and animal rights that structure the novella. In contrast to Costello's use of Jewish concentration camp prisoners as vehicles for representing confined livestock, however, John's metaphor would appear to satisfy Abraham Stern in that it subordinates animals (in this case, the herd) as the vehicle of a metaphor whose tenor is human (the uncomfortable scholars). And yet, the figurative specter of the herd does something else here by transforming a table of academic eaters, if only for an instant, into the animal bodies that they are variously thinking about, representing figuratively, and consuming. In this way, the animal others for whom Costello wants her listeners to feel a radical form of compassion enter *The Lives of Animals* as at once alive and dead, visceral and symbolic, ethical subject and edible object. Despite Coetzee's own vegetarianism, the text thus articulates an animal ethic that does not center on dietary restrictions, which could perpetuate hierarchies of plant, animal, and human. Rather, the novella posits a more radical revolution of the food chain in suggesting an ethic of animal compassion and justice that upends our "special fidelities" to next of kin and to kindred beings.

If the price of Costello's compassion for other species is the kinship of family, friends, and colleagues, that loss serves to censure the implicitly colonial taboo on feeling too much for the other—a taboo that we can theorize as a consequence of both imperialism and capitalism. *The Lives of Animals* locates Costello's call for interspecies communion in a particular context: the postindustrial and late capitalist system of husbandry known as the confined feedlot operation. Costello develops her comparison of concentration camps and slaughterhouses as part of a jeremiad on the "production facilities" that feed, house, and sell livestock to slaughterhouses (21). Stern's moral objection to Costello's analogy that cattle die like Jewish prisoners is persuasive. However, the text situates this analogy in a historical context that might alter Stern's response. Confined feedlots emerged in the United States during World War II and became pivotal to the rise of the United States as a global food power.[23] Moreover, postwar factory farms in the United States, in many cases, replicated the environment of concentration camps in Nazi Germany. In this context, Costello's provocative figures of speech are also *more than* figures of speech in that they encode the systematic violence and genocide of World War II as a literal influence on the physical environment in which most livestock animals now live (*LA* 59).

This specter of World War II in *The Lives of Animals* clarifies the significance of its geographical imagination: the narrative of an Australian novelist visiting the United States to address, among other things, North American feedlots. In the context of the postwar meat industry, Costello's controversial analogy is a kind of red herring in the text. While Costello seems to direct her listeners' attention to Nazi Germany—a geographic tug that she extends in citing the fictionalized lectures of Franz Kafka's famous animal character Red Peter—her invective against the "production facilities" that fuel the contemporary food economy obliquely targets the United States, the world's largest producer and exporter of meat. In the informal seminar on the second day of her visit, Costello entreats her listeners to "read the poets who return the living, electric being to language; and if the poets do not move you, I urge you to walk, flank to flank, beside the beast that is prodded down the chute to his executioner" (*LA* 65). With this incantation, Costello invites her immediate audience of aspiring writers and literary critics to enter an actual working slaughterhouse and "walk, flank to flank" with cattle through its disassembly line. By extension, she evokes a much longer food chain of breeders, ranches, feed companies, trade agreements, distribution networks, and marketplaces that demarcate the life—and afterlife—of those animals whose lives are now so thoroughly commodified. That said, Costello's rhetoric does not translate neatly into ethical tenets and political praxis, a problem that one of her listeners highlights at the end of her first lecture:

> "What wasn't clear to me," the man is saying, "is what you are actual targeting. Are you saying we should close down the factory farms? Are you saying we should stop eating meat? Are you saying we should treat animals more humanely, kill them more humanely? Are you saying we should stop experiments on animals? [. . .] Can you clarify? Thank you." (36)

This query conveys the bewildered responses that Elizabeth Costello repeatedly induces during her visit to Appleton. At the same time, the audience member's questions offer a set of concrete ethical choices for readers of *The Lives of Animals*: to close down factory farms, to stop eating meat, to treat animals more humanely, to kill them more humanely. In his analysis of *The Lives of Animals*, Huggan argues that "animals are functionalized in a drama of human mortality and suffering—one in which the attempt to reach out to the animal world [. . .] is counteracted by the ironic awareness of animals as objects of human desires and needs: objects of exploitation and abuse, objects of charity and affection" ("Greening Postcolonialism" 714). In response, I would argue that *The Lives of Animals* counteracts the instrumental status of animals by interrogating how we might relate to other animals not as companions, commodities, or symbols that serve human interests but as embodied subjects.

The Lives of Animals further suggests that critics conceptualize figurative language as an ethical problematic for the field of postcolonial ecocriticism. Subverting the usual role of other animals in literature as symbols within human dramas, Coetzee's approach to figurative language posits an ethics of justice that centers on the nonhuman rather than human world.[24] *The Lives of Animals* thus troubles postcolonial studies by employing human bodies as figurative vehicles that enlist our sympathies less with the history of political colonialism and more with the still-colonial lives of animals. Yet *The Lives of Animals* is not an environmentalist—or even an animal rights—text in any conventional sense. Coetzee's lectures on animals, as delivered by the "fleshy, white-haired" novelist Costello, do not concretize the imperial practices of the global meat industry, nor do they employ social realism to document the confined environs and ecological consequences of feedlots (*LA* 16). Rather, the lectures deploy literary tropes to hazard a decolonial ethics emanating from the view that environmentalism might depend less on legal strictures or ethical obligations than on emotional attachments—on the capacity to feel for and thus to act in the interests of other creatures.

NOTES

1. The fictional college is set in "suburban Waltham," a likely reference to the Boston suburb of the same name where Bentley University is located (*LA* 15). Note that my references to *The Lives of Animals* will be abbreviated as *LA* throughout the essay.

2. See, for example, Barnard "J.M. Coetzee's *Disgrace*," Herron, Lanchester, Lodge, and Hacking.

3. I use the term "other animals" to indicate animals other than humans.

4. See Baker, Durrant, and Head.

5. Dominic Head echoes Durrant: "The justification of an ecological philosophy is called into question where Costello is struck by the irony that the knowledge and appreciation of ecosystems can be comprehended by human beings alone and so cannot lead to a state of at-oneness" ("A Belief in Frogs" 112).

6. In her response to the novella, for example, Marjorie Garber recasts the text as more metafictional than ecological: "In these two lectures we thought John Coetzee was talking about animals. Could it be, however, that all along he was really asking, 'What is the value of literature?'" (84).

7. Judith Shulevitz sees the "main argument" in *The Lives of Animals* as follows: "We must enter into animals' experience, travel with them from the meadow or jungle or pen into the slaughterhouse and laboratory cage" (paragraph 9). In an analysis of *Disgrace*, Tom Herron suggests that Coetzee "register[s] the suffering of animals in South Africa as not more important than but on a continuum with human suffering" (474).

8. Here, Cilano and DeLoughrey draw on Édouard Glissant's *Caribbean Discourse* and Ramachandra Guha's essay "Radical American Environmentalism: A Third World Critique." As Cilano and DeLoughrey argue, such writers and thinkers of the global South call on ecocriticism to engage with issues of cultural difference, globalization, and colonial history alongside environmental issues and injustices.

9. My references to *Elizabeth Costello* will be abbreviated as *EC* throughout the essay.

10. In this section of *Environmental Culture*, Plumwood critiques dogmatic veganism as a misinterpretation of instrumentalism. In Plumwood's words, "we cannot give up using one another (or other creatures) but we can give up use/respect dualism, which means working towards ethical, respectful and highly constrained forms of use" (159).

11. I select the term *pariah* here to evoke the South Asian connotation of a person whose low caste and outcast status stems from his or her agricultural labor and care of livestock.

12. Marjorie Garber, one of Coetzee's respondents, echoes Huggan somewhat by arguing that the novella ultimately is about neither the ethics of eating meat nor the nature of animal sentience but rather the intrinsic "value of literature" vis-à-vis other forms of human discourse (84). Garber writes that that novella's "effect is to insulate the warring 'ideas' (about animal rights, about consciousness, about death, about the family, about academia) against claims of authorship and authority" (79).

13. These responses are reprinted in the Princeton University Press edition of *The Lives of Animals*.

14. One of the book's reviewers, Ian Hacking, also stresses Coetzee's earnest appeal for human sympathy for and moral identification with animals.

15. See also Franssen and Wenzel "The Pastoral Promise and the Political Imperative."

16. Attridge argues that Coetzee deploys experimental syntax to unsettle readers' ethical judgments and to engage them as "ethical participant[s]" in "the complex and freighted responsibility to the other, a responsibility denied for so long in South Africa's history" ("Ethical Modernism" 670).

17. Barnard observes that the rural setting of *Disgrace* in the Eastern Cape is inherently more heteroglossic than the rural setting of Coetzee's apartheid-era novels in the Karoo region ("J. M. Coetzee's *Disgrace* and the South African Pastoral" 210). Connecting *Disgrace* to Franz Kafka's *The Trial* and to the theoretical writings of Deleuze and Guattari, Tom Herron argues, akin to Barnard, that Lurie becomes doglike after the attack on his daughter and him so that his human sympathies might be "expanded" (486).

18. I should note two important appearances of rural South Africa in these novels: the extended narrative in *Disgrace* of Professor David Lurie's exile from Cape Town to his daughter Lucy's small farm on the Eastern Cape and, less noted by critics, Costello's trip in lesson five of *Elizabeth Costello* to "rural Zululand," where she begrudgingly watches her sister Blanche deliver a speech against humanism (*EC* 116).

19. Kafka remains a crucial influence on these texts nonetheless, as seen in Elizabeth Costello's recurring allusions to Red Peter's "Report to an Academy" in her defense of animal sentience. For extended commentary on Kafka's influence on Coetzee see especially, Franssen, Herron, Huggan "Greening Postcolonialism," Lodge, and Maslin.

20. I have in mind the rhetorical—rather than cognitive—definition of metaphor as an economical figure of speech that conceptualizes, or figures, one person, place, idea, or object by comparing it to another. My argument here is that animals have functioned in literary history most often as metaphoric *vehicles*: secondary subjects that illuminate the primary term, or *tenor*, in the metaphor. See especially Ricoeur and Searle.

21. For example, Singer argues as follows: "Animal Liberation will require greater altruism on the part of mankind than any other liberation movement, since animals are incapable of demanding it for themselves, or of protesting against their exploitation by votes, demonstrations, or bombs" (III.18).

22. In his article "Toward an African Ecocriticism: Postcolonialism, Ecology and *Life and Times of Michael K*," Anthony Vital also conceives of postcolonial ecocriticism as a field that foregrounds "materialist" critiques of poverty, capitalism, and modernity. Through such critiques, Vital believes "postcolonialism can best find rapprochement with ecocriticism" (*Research* 100).

23. For historical accounts of industrial agriculture and U.S. economic and military policy after World War II, see Kimbrell, Kroese, and Mander.

24. My conclusion is informed by Martha Nussbaum's "capabilities approach" to jusice, which sees justice as a structure that allows individuals to live with dignity by enabling their fundamental abilities ("Moral Status" B6). Fleshed out in her book *Frontiers of Justice*, Nussbaum identifies three cases—marked by "large asymmetries of power"—which, she argues, neither the Kantian social contract nor utilitarian traditions adequately address: "justice for people with disabilities, justice across national boundaries, and justice for nonhuman animals" ("Moral Status" B6). With respect to nonhuman animals, Nussbaum argues, "the capabilities approach, which begins from an ethically attuned concern for each form of animal life, offers a model that does justice to the complexity of animal lives and their strivings and flourishings" ("Moral Status" B6). Nussbaum tends to analogize nonhuman animals and disenfranchised humans, however. *The Lives of Animals* implicitly rejects this approach by suggesting that such analogies subordinate nonhuman animals to human beings. Moreover, Nussbaum defines justice as a corrective to affective sympathy: "In some ways, our imaginative sympathy with the suffering of nonhuman animals must be our guide as we try to define a just relation between humans and animals. Sympathy, however, is malleable. It can all too easily be corrupted by our interest in protecting the comforts of a way of life that includes the use of other animals as objects of our own gain and pleasure. That is why we typically need philosophy and its theories of justice" ("Moral Status" B6). By comparison, even as *The Lives of Animals* calls Elizabeth Costello's critique of philosophy into question, the text ultimately privileges sympathy over logic as the foundation for animal ethics.

10

"Tomorrow There Will Be More of Us"

Toxic Postcoloniality in *Animal's People*

Pablo Mukherjee

The Bhopal gas tragedy of 1984 is often dubbed the world's worst industrial disaster. The release of a deadly cocktail of toxic gases, mainly composed of methyl isocyanite (MIC), from the pesticide factory owned by the giant multinational company Union Carbide, affected an estimated two hundred thousand people out of the nine hundred thousand who lived in this rapidly expanding central Indian city. Between five and ten thousand people were killed immediately, with a further sixty thousand sustaining injuries and a significant number succumbing to these over the next days, months, and years. The horrific damage to animal and plant lives remains largely uncharted.[1]

The incident offers a grim summary of a number of issues central to the historical and environmental conditions of not just contemporary India, but of the countries of Africa, Asia, and Latin America that constitute what is frequently called the postcolonial world. In that it involved the accidental release of massive amounts of toxic gas from a pesticide factory, it raises questions about the viability and ethics of the use of artificial poison in the process of growing food crops vital to the survival of the inhabitants of the former European colonies. In that the gas was released from a factory built in a populated urban area, it raises the question of the spatial politics of environmental toxicity, about who decides to build or dump what where and how these decisions affect a disproportionate number of human and nonhuman beings who have little say in the matter. Finally, in that the factory was owned by an American multinational company, the tragedy raises questions about the international framework of law, justice, and rights (or lack thereof). The legal wrangle over accountability and compensation seemed to expose the premises that environment, and indeed, the very concept of the human carried radically different values in the global north and south. It underlines the urgent need to rethink and reframe the issue of universal rights, both of humans and nonhumans, as a bulwark against the recurrence of such devastations amongst the most vulnerable beings on earth.

The international recognition given to Indra Sinha's 2007 novel about the Bhopal gas disaster, *Animal's People*, provides us with an opportunity to look at some of these issues within a literary cultural framework, and in turn raises several questions about the general relationship between the environment and culture of the world's postcolonial zones. Did the shortlisting of the novel for the prestigious Man Booker prize have anything to do with the fact that this was a work by a cosmopolitan author (who grew up and lives in England and France) writing in English? Are novels about environmental disasters received better in an era saturated with debates about global warming and impending catastrophe? I want to approach these issues here by taking the Bhopal disaster as an appropriate, if somewhat extreme, synecdoche of the everyday condition of postcolonial existence. The event concentrates into the span of a night the essence of the battle for survival in which the majority of the inhabitants of the postcolonial global South (and hence, that of the world) are locked. Sinha's novel, written nearly twenty-five years after the incident itself, will be taken as an example of a literary negotiation with the tragic aura that Bhopal still radiates—an aura that contains significant information about the state of our contemporary world as well as clues about how to confront, survive, and change it. In order to gauge the success of Sinha's literary intervention, we will first have to acquaint ourselves with the contours of the Bhopal tragedy.

"PLAYING WITH POISON"

At first, the air smells of burned chilies. If you do not get away as fast as possible, soon you find yourself in a thick white mist. Your eyes, throat, and lungs begin to burn and fill up oozing fluid and melting tissues. Then you lose control of your nervous system, vomit uncontrollably, and seize up with cramps. If you are lucky, you lose consciousness and die. If not, your death is a long, drawn out, agonizing affair. If you survive, your lungs and eyes will never work properly again. Muscle pains and ulcers will prevent you from working or leading a normal life. You will give birth to unimaginably deformed, dead babies.

This, on the night of December 4, 1984, and over the subsequent months and years has been the experience of around two hundred thousand citizens who lived within forty square kilometers of the Union Carbide pesticide factory located in Bhopal. In the immediate aftermath, a clear tonal difference emerged between Indian and U.S. coverage of the event. Overall, the Indian newspapers like *Hindustan Times*, *Hindu*, and *Statesman* all reported the dizzying numbers of casualties, and then the structural failures of Union Carbide that had led to the disaster. According to K. Gopalakrishnan of *Hindustan Times*, safety protocols in the cleaning of the MIC storage tank had been broken (1). Archana Kumar wrote in the same paper that none of the residents of the extensive shantytowns that had grown up around the factory had ever been told by the managers what the "long siren" (that had been sounded as the gas escaped) meant, and that when they saw the large plume of gas they had in fact run toward the factory to offer help (1, 5). There was also speculation about the nature of the killer gas—was MIC fatal or were there other gases such as phosgene and even cyanide in the mix? Furthermore, it was reported that the factory had been incurring huge losses and its closure following the disaster would actually benefit Union Carbide. The *Hindu* exposed that MIC had a cyanide base and, contrary to what the company spokesperson was saying, at least an hour, not "a matter of minutes," had passed before the leak had been brought under control ("350 Killed" 1). The *Statesman* also followed the suggestion that other gases such as phosgene may have escaped and in an editorial raised the question of international corporate responsibility ("Playing with Poison" 8).

In contrast to the Indian reportage, the American media by and large quickly fell behind Union Carbide's line of defense. Essentially, this boiled down to two interlinked positions—first, that the accident had nothing to do with any structural deficiency or negligence on the part of its American owners; second, the accident had everything to do with Indian failures of management and human error. Warren Anderson, then the chairman of Union Carbide Corporation, summed these up in two statements—"Our safety standards in the U.S. are identical to those in India . . . same equipment, same design, same everything." He continued, "You can't run a $9 or $10 billion corporation all out of Danbury. . . . Lines of communication were broken at the Bhopal plant. Compliance with these procedures is the responsibility of the plant operators" (Everest 18–19). The American media not only failed to challenge Anderson, but amplified the implications of his message manifold. Both the *Wall Street Journal* and *New York Times* unequivocally blamed the accident on Indian failure to live with advanced technology. Indeed, the *Wall Street Journal* trumpeted the cause of the America-based company and implied that the cost of the Bhopal tragedy was worth paying for the general benefit of India and the world:

> With recriminations flying, it is worthwhile to remember that the Union Carbide Insecticide plant and the people surrounding it were there for compelling reasons. India's agriculture had been thriving, bringing a better life to millions of rural people. . . . Indians need technology. Calcutta-style scenes of human deprivation can be replaced as fast as the country imports the benefits of the West's industrial revolution and market economics. (quoted in Everest 107–108)

At other times it vigorously blamed Indian "nationalism" for the tragedy, alleging that it was the Indian government that prevented the appropriate level of American control over the factory—"when control over an affiliate is diluted . . . fewer resources are typically committed by the parent" (quoted in Everest 120).

It is worth examining for a moment the material strata of this divide between the Indian and American perspectives on Bhopal. By the mid-1970s, when it planned and executed its arrival in Bhopal, Union Carbide Corporation had 130 subsidiaries in forty countries, 120,000 employees, and an annual turnover of $6.5 billion (Lapierre and Moro 32–33). At the time of the Bhopal disaster, it was the thirty-fifth largest U.S. industrial company, with $11 billion in assets and $9.5 billion in sales. Its Indian subsidiary was the fortieth largest industrial business in the country, with a profit of $8.8 million (Everest 20–21). Union Carbide arrived in India with the promise of accelerating the country's drive toward attaining self-sufficiency in the production of food grains and the eradication of poverty and hunger. It routinely claimed that fertilizers and insecticides manufactured in its factories would double or quadruple the grain yields across the country. Such promises, bathed in the aura of so-called first-world technical and commercial efficiency and wrapped in financial sweeteners, helped the company to retain full control of its operations in India. Contrary to the assertions in the American media, Union Carbide was exempt from the usual 1973 Indian Foreign Exchange Regulations rule that limited foreign capital to no more than 40 percent ownership of Indian subsidiaries. Arguing that it employed "advanced technology" and would contribute substantially to foreign-exchange earnings, the corporation retained 51 percent ownership of its Indian operations (Everest 126).

Unfortunately, the "advanced technology" trumpeted by the corporation concealed many false notes. In the United States' Kanawha Valley, where the corporation's main research institute was situated, cancer rates were 21 percent higher than the national average and Union Carbide had been fined for dumping carcinogenic waste into the Kanawha River. Two reports into the MIC production process by the Mellon Institute, in 1963 and 1970, found that when subject to heat, the chemical broke down into potentially lethal gaseous molecules that included hydrocyanide acid. Between 1980 and 1984, the U.S. federal Environmental Protection Agency logged sixty-seven leakages from the MIC units of Union Carbide's research laboratories (Lapierre and Moro 46–56). If it was bad enough at home, when it came to its global subsidiary interests, Union Carbide's sole focus was on making the maximum profit at the cost of minimizing investments in environmental safety. Edward Munoz, a former managing director of Union Carbide's Indian subsidiary, confessed that he had argued for "token storage"—small amounts in individual containers—but had been overruled by the corporation's American engineers who preferred large bulk storage tanks to cut down on the cost of production (Everest 31). When Munoz compared this practice with French and German producers of MIC, he was told "[Y]our engineers are out of their minds. They're putting an atom bomb in the middle of their factory that could explode at any time" (Lapierre and Moro 98). These were not callous oversights, but illuminations of the structural logic of the corporation. By 1984, the profits of the Bhopal unit of Union Carbide were steadily falling. Licensed to produce 5,250 tons of pesticide per year, it was now producing only 1,657 tons. Its losses for the year stood at $4,069,442 (Chouhan 19). The company's response, predictably, was to ruthlessly cut jobs and stop investing in safety measures. Permanent employment was cut from 850 to 642, and the MIC production unit was supervised and maintained by six instead of twelve workers (Everest 46, Lapierre and Moro 205).

The dismal results of these measures were first felt by the workers themselves. A worker at the MIC unit, P. R. Koshe, recalled being regularly exposed to MIC, naphthol dust, and carbon tetrachloride solvent and "experiencing indigestion, choking, giddiness and vomiting" (Chouhan 92). In December 1981, Ashraf Lalla, another worker, died after inhaling phosgene. True to form, Union Carbide blamed the dead worker for removing his gas mask, but his coworkers pointed out that storage of phosgene was prohibited when the plant was not in production and no one had warned Ashraf before he went on cleaning duties there (Chouhan 34). After Ashraf's death, the worker's union put up six thousand posters warning the citizens of Bhopal about the condition of the plant, and as a result, suffered systematic harassment (Everest 50–52). In many ways, these early stories of the Union Carbide workers are chronicles of the deaths of December 4, 1984, foretold.

The legal battle that followed the Bhopal tragedy had most obviously to do with the issues of accountability and compensation, but its progress (or the lack thereof) grimly illustrates the global *realpolitik* about the value of environment and human and nonhuman lives—that these are expendable in the interest of accruing corporate profit, and that this is especially so if the profit accrued is in the interest of the ruling classes of the "core" Euro-American countries. Union Carbide argued that as an American multinational, it could neither be charged nor tried in India nor in U.S. courts since it held that American juries would not be able to comprehend the reality of the daily Indian life:

> Indeed, the practical impossibility for American courts and juries, imbued with U.S. cultural values, living standards and expectations, to determine damages for people living in the slums or "hutments" surrounding the UCIL plant in Bhopal, India, by itself confirms that the Indian forum is overwhelmingly the most appropriate [for the legal trial of the case]. Such abject poverty and the vastly different values, standards and expectations which accompany it are commonplace in India and the third world. They are incomprehensible to Americans living in the United States. (quoted in Everest 155)

In addition to being brutally expressive of the global dispensation, this legal defense is also a philosophical position that assumes an unbridgeable gap between two apparently discontinuous worlds. It suggests that Americans and Indians can never comprehend each other because of the material differences in their everyday lives that instill divergent ways of seeing and understanding reality, to the extent that there can be no common agreement as to what it is to be human.

The spurious logic of this position is not difficult to unpack. But if our brief summary of the Bhopal tragedy has shown the historical and material bases on which such a philosophy of difference and discontinuity is constructed, it should also alert us to the problem of conceiving any ideas of universal *rights*—whether human, nonhuman, or environmental. Given the power behind this vision of separation—essentially an apartheid worldview—as summed up in Union Carbide's legal statements, how is it possible to think of a universality built on the basic blocks of equality and justice? These twinned themes of persistent historical inequalities and the resultant ideologies of difference, and the effort to redress them through a conception of universal rights, form some of the core concerns of Sinha's novel.

"DEFINITELY THE RIGHT ANIMAL"

"I used to be human once"—so begins Sinha's narrator, whose voice reaches us through a series of tapes containing a linguistic mixture of Hindi, English, French, Bhojpuri, and Urdu languages, and transcribed by an unnamed editor. Later he entertains an American doctor by singing a song that begins, "I am an animal fierce and free / in all the world is none like me" (Sinha 1, 172). Animal's proclamation of his nonhuman identity gives voice to a scandal that lurks behind the tragedy of Bhopal—if there are those who, by the dint of their underprivileged location in the hierarchy of the "new world order," cannot access the minimum of the rights and privileges that are said to define humanity, what can they be called? It also lends voice to a further set of questions—what happens when the rights and privileges of humans are achieved explicitly at the expense of the sufferings of the majority of nonhuman beings, and how can we imagine an alternative practice?

These questions, which often appear under the broader terms of the nonhuman or animal rights debate in the works of Peter Singer, Donna Haraway, Susan Armstrong, Ted Benton, and David DeGrazia, have come to assume an important element in environmentalist discussions. Analyses of historical, material, and ideological forces that first draw up, and then patrol, the various boundaries between humans and nonhumans and which subsequently lead to a degradation of their common environments have assumed a central importance for many of these thinkers. Sinha's signature move in the novel is to show the specifically postcolonial forms in of these issues embodied in an apocalyptic Bhopal.

One classic argument for extending human rights to nonhumans and animals has been to point out the central contradiction that lies at the heart of the concept of rights itself. As Paola Cavalieri shows, the idea of rights is negative and institutional, based on a definition of humans as "intentional beings and agents." Only such agents who "fulfil the requisite of intentionality" are characterized by the "capacity to enjoy freedom and welfare" (30). Clearly, if the intention to enjoy freedom and well-being qualifies one to possess rights, then the rights cannot be confined to humanity itself. On the one hand, many nonhumans possess the cognitive-emotive intentionality to enjoy freedom and welfare; on the other hand, many humans, because of congenital or accidental disabilities, do not. This kind of thinking also throws open the question of what it is to be human and how this is properly understood via relations with nonhumans. Peter Singer, who uses a neo-Benthamite position to propose an extension of the principle of equality to all humans and nonhumans, suggests that

> our concern for others ought not to depend on what they are like, or what abilities they possess. . . . [T]he fact that beings are not members of our species does not entitle us to exploit them, and similarly the fact that other animals are less intelligent than we are does not mean that their interests may be disregarded. (33)

For Singer, the core element of the concept of rights is provided by Jeremy Bentham in his treatise on *Principles of Morals and Legislation*. Here, anticipating the day when animals would acquire those rights "which never could have been witholden to them but by the hands of tyranny," Bentham pinpoints the common feature between human and nonhuman beings that overrides all the other apparent differences between them—"The question is not, can they *reason*? Nor can they *talk*? But, can they *suffer*?" ("Practical Ethics" 35). It is on this common capacity to suffer that Singer issues his call for equality and justice for all beings.

Nonhuman and animal rights debates, then, ask us to fundamentally reassess our understanding of being, belonging, and communality. As Paul Shepard reminds us, "Wild animals are not our friends. They are uncompromisingly not us nor mindful of us, just as they differ among themselves. . . . We cannot comprehend the world as it is experienced by a bat, a termite, or a squid" (512). The trick, then, is to imagine a principle of equality based on difference, rather than normative homogeneity or similarity. Quite often, this attention to difference takes the form of imagining distinctive forms of individual identity or personhood and then seeing how these are functions, not of separation or singularity, but of relationality.

The question of a relational personhood is also addressed by Martha Nussbaum's "capabilities approach" to determine the moral status of animals. Nussbaum asks, "What are people actually able to do and to be?" and then develops ten areas that each person should be entitled to in order to attain their capabilities, including life, health, bodily integrity and affiliation ("Moral Status," 31). Nussbaum's idea about "the dignity of forms of life that possesses both deep needs and abilities" makes room for all living creatures who have "innate capacity for some functions that are evaluated as important and good" (33). Developing this line of argument, Sarah Whatmore has called for a reconfiguration of the concept of agency (the capacity to act that is central to our idea of personhood) in order to expand our understanding of personhood. A proponent of actant network theory derived from the thinking of Bruno Latour, Whatmore holds that the normative scanting of the agency of nonhumans is "an effect of particular, and partial, configuration of social practice and discourse." To challenge this state of affairs, Whatmore suggests we view agency as "a relational effect generated by a network of heterogeneous, interacting components." Nonhuman agents are a vital to the functioning of this network, since "they attach us to one another . . . and define our social bond by their very circulation" (340–41).

Along with personhood, these theories of nonhuman personhood and agency then ask us to reconfigure our ideas about communality, relationality, and universality. It is easy to see why these ideas have enabled us to reconceptualize what we understand as environment. Following them, it is no longer possible to see it as something that exists outside the realm of the human or the social. Rather, environment must be seen as a mutually sustaining network where humans and nonhumans are always already linked with each other, and on whose collective action and prosperity the functioning of this network depends. Additionally, this vision radically disputes the narrative of the mutually exclusive global "North" and "South" that we have already seen in the rhetoric of Union Carbide and the American media. The world appears to us not as divided into discrete mutually exclusive units, but as one entity, albeit for historical reasons (capitalism and its concomitants, colonialism and imperialism) stratified and uneven.

Indra Sinha's protagonist Animal may be said to embody the whole range of these issues. His scarred and deformed existence, and his vehement denial of belonging to the human species, at first sight appears to confirm Union Carbide's historical defense—that rights, and indeed, being considered human, are for those who possess sufficient power and wealth. The rest, nonhumans, are not entitled to any rights—not to health, not to life, not to affiliation. If this were so, Animal would be no more than a cry of despair hideously embodied. Yet as Zafar, Animal's friend and activist, says to him as he lies close to death from a hunger strike he has undertaken to protest the Indian court's failure to punish Union Carbide, "Well my brother . . . [you are] definitely the right animal" (Sinha 303). Wherein lies this sense of rightness? Can Animal's declaration also be heard as one of defiant belonging? Can Bhopal mark not merely the nightmare of mutual antagonism but also the beginning of a sense of common belonging and community? We turn to look at Animal in some details next in the light of these questions.

"IN ALL THE WORLD IS NONE LIKE ME"

The historical Bhopal is reincarnated as the city of Khaufpur in Sinha's novel. The gift that the poisoned air brings to Animal, a teenager orphaned by the tragedy, is not merely a deformed back that forces him to crawl on his hands, but also his new identity as a nonhuman being. From the ground level, he casts an eye on the human world with Swiftian disgust—"The world of humans is meant to be viewed from eye level. Your eyes. Lift up my head I'm staring into someone's crotch. . . . I know which one hasn't washed his balls, I can smell pissy gussets and shitty backsides . . . farts smell extra bad" (2). From this perspective, it appears that Animal has developed a sense of absolute difference from those humans who are powerful enough to possess abstractions such as "rights" and "justice." Addressing the Australian journalist who gives him a recorder to tape his story, he says as much: "[M]any books have been written about this place. . . . You will bleat like all the rest. You'll talk of rights, law, justice. Those words sound the same in my mouth as in yours but they don't mean the same" (3). It soon also becomes apparent that Animal's sense of absolute difference from humans has gradations built into it. He senses that his distance from the Australian journalist, for example, is much greater than that from his fellow gas victims and the destitute in Bhopal. When asked to imagine the world's eyes opened by his story, he mocks, "What can I say that they will understand? Have these thousands of eyes slept even one night in a place like this? . . . When was the last time these eyes had nothing to eat? These cuntish eyes, what do they know of our lives?" (7–8). Both distance and proximity are heartfelt here—distance from the global would-be consumers of his story, and the relative closeness felt with the destitutes captured in the "we" of the sentence.

Despite Animal's protestations, he is surrounded by humans who deny his declared identity as a nonhuman and who are keen to point out their common bonds. Zafar asks him to think of himself as "especially able" and says he should consider himself as a human being entitled to dignity and respect. Farouq, the streetwise friend with whom Animal regularly engages in banter, thinks his self-proclaimed identity is just an excuse to evade social responsibility:

> Trouble with you, Animal . . . is you think because you've a crooked back and walk with your arse in the air no one should dare to criticise you. I'm an animal, always you're bleating. . . . I don't have to do like the rest of you, laws of society don't apply to me because I'm such a fucking animal. (87)

If we think in terms of the nonhuman/animal rights debate examined earlier, it is not surprising that the nature of Animal's being is a subject of debate. Sinha freights Animal with exaggerated amounts of both the liabilities and powers that nonhumans share with humans as well as the "human-definitive" features that mark the acts of species boundary-making. Roaming the desperate margins of Khaufpur, Animal's remarkable capacity for survival finds its most memorable expression in his twin drives toward copulation and feeding. A scavenger, there is nothing that Animal will not eat in order to stay alive, including bits of himself:

> Inside of left foot, outer of right, where they scrape the ground the skin's thick and cracked. In gone times I've felt such hunger, I'd break off lumps of the dry skin and chew it. . . . I am reaching down to my heel, feeling for the horny edges, I'm sliding the thumbnail under. There, see this lump of skin, hard as a pebble, how easily it breaks off, mmm, chewy as a nut. Nowadays there's no shortage of food, I eat my feet for pleasure. (13)

It is while scavenging that he forms an unshakable bond with Jara, "a yellow dog, of no fixed abode and no traceable parents." As they fight for bits of banana skin, nubs of meat and flecks of fish in the rubbish dumps, Animal is initially scared of Jara's sharp teeth, orange-brown eyes, and snarling, growling mouth until one day something snaps in him and he charges at her on all fours, "growling louder than she, the warning of a desperate animal that will stick at nothing" (17). The pair remains inseparable for the rest of the narrative.

Animal is also, as Farouq puts it, "made like a donkey." For much of the book, his priapic urges mark his isolation from the world of humans who play by the rules of their erotic conventions. Sensing that he is locked out of this world, Animal takes refuge in frequent masturbation and fantasies about the women who befriend him. This seems to enhance his nonhuman nature in the eyes of his human associates. When they urge him to spy on Elli, the American doctor, naked in her bath, they ask him to climb the mango tree like a baboon or a monkey. Animal, hidden among the branches, observes Elli but instead of relaying the details about her body to his audience below, he thinks about the predicament of his own liminal identity:

> Animals mating with human female, it's unnatural, but I've no choice but to be unnatural. Many times I would dream that she and I were in love, sometimes we were married and naked together like in the movies having sex. . . . This frightened me, I despise hope. (78)

If hunting for food and incessant but lonely sex mark Animal's nonhuman nature, his linguistic prowess and capacity to imagine the minds of other humans endow him with exaggerated "human-definitive" capacities. Animal chatters in a polyglot mixture of Hindi, Urdu, Bhojpuri, English, and French. His clever tongue, he says, "could curl itself into any language." While the poison gas deprived others, such as the French nun Ma Franci, of their linguistic ability, it seems to have made Animal linguistically precocious. He is the translator par excellence in Khaufpur's cosmopolitan world, made up of local activists, visiting Australian journalists, American doctors, and French nuns. It is his linguistic glue, as it were, that holds the threads of the relationships around him. Animal explains that like all good translators, he can sense linguistic meanings even when he is unfamiliar with the words—"When ma shouted, *sallo purqwateu na parlapa lalang yumain?* I had no idea what the sounds meant, but I knew what *she* meant." This, of course, helps him gain the confidence of Elli, who is suspected of working for the Kampani (Union Carbide's name in the novel) and is boycotted when she arrives to open a free medical centre in Khaufpur. This also gives him the upper hand in the bargaining about his story with the Australian journalist—while Animal can understand what he is saying, there is no way for him to understand how Animal mocks him with obscene songs and taunts. Animal succeeds in getting the coveted pair of shorts, a cigarette lighter and a tape recorder from the journalist, in return of a promise to deliver his stories to him, which he does not. It is a small victory against the "world of eyes"—humans who possess the power to destroy his world.

Not only is animal linguistically gifted, but he also possesses that other requirement that Daniel Dannett and others have posited as a condition of personhood—the ability to recognize the "'inner minds' of other persons." In fact, Animal has this in uncanny abundance—"Since I was small I could hear people's thoughts even when their lips were shut, plus I'd get en passant comments from all types of things, animals, birds, trees, rocks giving the time" (Sinha 8). Further, he can visualize the thoughts of others, literally see as they see the world. When Elli expresses her shock at the destitution of the poor of Khaufpur, Animal can temporarily see his own environment as it appears to Elli:

> When Elli says *earthquake* suddenly I am seeing it as she does. Paradise Alley is a wreckage of baked earth mounds and piles of planks on which hang gunny sacks.... Everywhere's covered in shit and plastic. Truly I see how poor and disgusting are our lives. (Sinha 106)

This combined ability of linguistic precocity and intense recognition of the inner life of others enable Animal to adopt what we might call a transpersonality, an ability to experience the objective existence of the entire environment of Khaufpur as a network composed of related subjects, *including himself*. In Sarah Whatmore's terms, he is the "actant" per excellence, and the entire human and nonhuman matrix of Khaufpur—what we call its environment—are "networked" through him. We might say that the very historical inequities that have poisoned the postcolonial environment that Animal inhabits, has also conferred upon him a capacity of visualizing and realizing a merger with the collectivity that such an environment (and indeed, any environment) is composed of. Animal's transpersonality, in other words, is the specific product of a postcolonial condition where the environment has sustained a massive bombardment from the predatory forces of global capitalism.

Animal's ability to literally step out of his skin and see as others see him at the same time as he sees others, can often shape his narrative style. For example, often, his first-person perspective demonstrates qualities more usually associated with a third-person omniscient narrator:

> Bird that I am sees all, white palace of gone rulers on hill, lake looks pale green from up here, eye slides along a road lined with dirty buildings. . . . [F]ar below, an animal is moving slowly along a lane. What kind of creature is this, arse canted steeply into the air? Dromedary? Centaur? Short way behind a smaller, also non-human being strolls, stopping now and again to stretch sleepy jaws. (Sinha 133)

Animal then, embodies exaggerated human and nonhuman qualities. We might say that he is the location where these meet, and, as such, his very existence is an argument for their continuity and their ontological equality. This enables him to mediate between not merely humans of various kinds, but also between nonhumans with humans. For some reviewers and critics, this has made him a less effective character than he might have been. Lucy Beresford has declared "Sinha's flirtation with magical realism, conveying Animal's ability to converse with foetuses, and the musings of several delirious or psychotic characters, might not be to every reader's taste" ("Village of the Damned"). But, as we have seen here, Sinha's understanding of the Bhopal tragedy as a site that releases a debate about fundamental essence or being of humans requires a figure such as Animal, hovering between the worlds of the human and nonhuman and making apparent the umbilical bonds that bind both. Animal's conversations with the deformed, aborted fetuses, for example, are perfectly consistent with the logic of Sinha's vision. This is hardly "magic realism" in the gimmicky, often misunderstood sense of the term, but realism fitted to express the horrors of a reality that threatens to escape the ordinary normative boundaries of style.

Animal first meets Kha-in-the-jar, as he calls the fetus with two heads, when he is in the chambers of a doctor where Ma Franci has taken him to see if his own deformity can be cured. Busy translating Ma's French for the Doctor, and his Hindi for Ma, Animal quickly realizes that the two-headed fetus floating in the preservatives is asking to be freed from his confinement. Animal and Kha mirror each other in that they have both been placed beyond the pale of normative humanity by the Kampani's poison gas. But Kha says, Animal is at least alive while he is "fucking waiting to be born" (Sinha 58). Kha holds that while all beings on earth have imbibed some of the poison, he and his fellow fetuses, being the youngest of the Kampani's victims, have decided to "undo everything that the company does. Instead of breaking ground for new factories to grow grass and trees over old ones, instead of making new poisons, to make medicines" (237). The release of Kha from the jar will be a part of the Animal's defiance against those that seek to destroy him and his world. Between them, Animal and Kha articulate a peculiarly postcolonial form of resistance, peculiar since it derives its strength from the very poison with which the Kampani seek to disable them. The poison kills and maims, but it paradoxically enables its victims to leave behind their monadic selves and reach for a collective consciousness. This consciousness is far from monolithic but, as the constant arguments between Animal and everyone else shows, is scored by debates and dissent. And it is all the stronger for this. What Sinha models for us, in effect, through Animal and his friends, is the emergence of a *politics* of transpersonality and collectivity in response to the toxic degradation of a postcolonial environment.

Animal's final wandering in the jungles after a suicide attempt, and his hallucinatory communication with trees, the moon, and the animals, have attracted criticism for its alleged heavy-handed Christian allegory of resurrection. Yet, in the novel's schema, this episode is crucial for establishing the principle of "different-yet-equal" that we have seen is the philosophical cornerstone of both the human/nonhuman rights debate and the postcolonial consciousness of resistance to the oppressive toxicity of multinational capitalism. After repeatedly asserting his separation from humans, Animal must also come to terms with the specific kind of relationship with other nonhumans—that he is simultaneously distinct from them and related to them. The trees cannot feel his pain and as he screams abuse at them; he hears them say that he doesn't scare them. When he captures a lizard for food, it pleads to be spared. When released, it says, "You are human, if you were an animal you would have eaten me" (346). This sensation of being distinct from both humans and nonhumans gives rise, at first, to a defiant assertion of isolation in Animal: "If this self of mine doesn't belong in this world, I'll be mine own world. . . . I, the universe that was once called Animal, sit in the tree and survey the moonlit jungles of my kingdom" (350). But his acceptance of him as he is, and his realization that others—both humans and nonhumans, local Khaufpuris and cosmopolitan Americans—do the same, soon gives rise in Animal to a sense of distinctive belonging. Zafar, Farouq, Jara the dog, and others find him after days of searching the forest. As they leave, "The animals that were absent before now choose to show themselves. . . . Birds we see, deer in the distance. . . . [B]y a place where water is running's laid a long white snake skin, perfect from nostril to tip of tail" (357). This vision of collectivity, one where personhood remains distinctive yet always relational, is a site from where the struggle for recognition and justice can begin. The novel closes with Animal deciding not to go the United States for an operation that would straighten his spine, since he does not need to do this now in order to belong. He senses that his "people" are composed precisely of the humans and nonhumans who unite in celebration of his rescue from the forest. He leaves us with his defiant reminder: "[T]omorrow there will be more of us."

However, this realization of an ontological sense of collectivity and equality does not, in Sinha's novel, automatically or easily replace the actually existing historical reality that conspires to prevent the proper achievement of these ideals. Sinha is not naïve. Rather, he shows, following the historical lessons of the Bhopal tragedy, that only a modicum of these ideals can be attained over and against the prevailing condition of the world. Sinha is not hesitant about naming the power that maintains this lamentable present state of the world—the corrosive short-term greed and drive for profit that is embodied in the contemporary multinational corporations. The global reach of these institutions means the receding of local or national interests, and the firm entangling of the interests of cosmopolitan ruling classes against that of the overwhelming majority of the world's inhabitants. The postcolonial consciousness of resistance that Animal, Kha, Zaffar, and other people of Khaufpur demonstrate, is only ever realised against the material and ideological forces exuded by this powerful clique—forces that are determined to enforce mutual incomprehension and hostility in order to maintain its own interests.

Characters located at the various points of the global divide certainly express their mutual incomprehension of one another's lives. After watching the terrorist attacks in the United States on September 11, 2001, on television, Zafar intervenes in the debate about its authenticity by pointing out, "We know zilch about their lives, they know nothing of ours, that's the problem" (66). Similarly, Elli, when confronted with the boycott of her free clinic by the Khaufpuris, is mystified:

> I swear I don't understand Khaufpur. . . . This is the strangest thing about Khaufpur, that people put up with so much. . . . But wait, let someone come along with an open hearted offer of help, these same citizens can't tolerate it, in fact find it so intolerable they must mount a boycott. (151)

But this is not just a matter of incomprehension between a gleaming United States and impoverished Khaufpur. In Khaufpur itself, there is no shortage of people on the right side of corporate capital who argue, like Elli's doctor friend, that the victims of gas were expendable because their poverty would have doomed them to an early death anyway. If anything, like the historical victims of the Bhopal tragedy, it is such members of the local or national ruling classes who provoke Animal and his people most. When he hears an Indian lawyer defend the Kampani in court, Animal wonders, "Holy cunt, what a twisted nain rabougri is this from our own city to take the side of the Kampani?" (Sinha 53). When the local police, led by a much-hated officer, beat up Nisha—Zaffar's lover and also the woman Animal covets—and her father during a protest against the compensation deal between the Kampani and the government, Animal leads the visceral revolt (Sinha 313). The bonds that bind these local elites to the Kampani are well understood by the protestors. "Go lick the arse of your Chief Minister, who licks the hole of Peterson," they shout to the police. The Kampani's American lawyers, among them Elli's ex-husband, arrive to negotiate the deal. The gulf between their interests and the victims is illustrated when one of them complains of missing his two Italian greyhounds that sleep with him in his palatial house. Sinha does not offer any magic bullet to slay these powerful forces of separation and hostility. The resistance embodied by Animal and his people cannot yet be a victory march, but it can name the beginnings of an uprising.

It is in the sparking of this uprising that Animal's role as translator assumes paramount importance. As we have seen, the liminality accorded by the combination of his human- and nonhuman-definitive powers paradoxically makes him the ideal mediator between fractured communities. His greatest achievement is helping forge a bond of solidarity between Elli and the Khaufpuris. When she arrives within days of a legal decision compelling the Kampani's appearance in an Indian court, she is suspected of being a spy engaged to fabricate medical data that would help the Kampani in its legal defense. Zafar organizes a boycott of her clinic, and it is only Animal, with his nonhuman instinct, and Somraj, Nisha's father, who suggest that she may be a friend despite her nationality. The ensuing romance between Elli and Somraj, united by their passion for music and sense of justice, can feel contrived. But what livens this plotline is Animal's struggle to trust Elli. He has been asked by Zafar to spy on her activities, but she is his only hope of being cured. His instincts tell him that she is on their side, but he sees her talking to her ex-husband, the Kampani's lawyer. Ultimately, Elli embodies a wager of faith in the novel—are beings framed by vastly disparate conditions capable of solidarity? As he ferries stories of Elli's medical and musical skills and her fierce commitment to the victims of Khaufpur to his people, Animal's struggle to trust Elli is a proof of Zafar's dictum that a struggle based on love is stronger than one based on hope. His stories erase the Khaufpuri's mistrust of Elli, and her saving of Somraj and their eventual marriage, makes her one of them.

"TOMORROW THERE WILL BE MORE OF US"

To conclude, Sinha's novel attempts a recreation of the historical environment of Union Carbide's poisoning of Bhopal and its aftermath. His narrator, one of the thousands of the disabled victims, begins by declaring he is not human, thereby exposing the horrendous logic of global corporatism that recognizes only the powerful and the privileged as capable of bearing signs of humanity—including practices such as rights and justice. Animal's journey toward a transpersonal commonality forms a politics of belonging that defies this logic and the material forces that sustain it. His final insurrectionary promise of the spread of this collective is a warning to those who wish to continue to deny personhood to other humans and nonhumans around them. This vision of transpersonality and collectivity, where environment appears as a network composed of agents who must share labor and information in order to survive, offers a glimpse of redemption against the material forces of transnational capital and the apartheid philosophy of anthropocentrism it spawns. As the boundaries between humans and nonhumans are dissolved in the manic existence of Animal, we begin to hear the drums of an uprising.

Seen in this light, the blasted and ravaged *postcolonial* grounds of Khaufpur/Bhopal provide an ideal base for the story, since the toxic logical outcome of the contemporary mantra of globalization and development find their fullest expression here. The disenfranchised beings bear the cost of the poisoning of the air and soil of the city, while the elites spout neo-Malthusian theories about the inevitability (and desirability) of their demise from a safe distance. But paradoxically (and inevitably), it is the same poisoned air and ground that first produces, and then spreads, the possibility of resisting the forces of these elites and their toxic weapons. In doing so, the novel holds out the possibility of the defiance of the forces of the few by that of the many who struggle without hope, but with suffering and love. Suffering and love here is understood as the realization of an identity that recognizes the singularity, plurality, and unity of beings and a mode of nondestructive inhabitation. And the novel imagines an ethics from which the resistance to the lethal environment of postcolonialism may be mounted.

NOTE

1. There is a large volume of literature on Bhopal. For a good summary of estimates of victims, composition of the toxic gas, and details of the factory operations, see Larry Everest, 16–18.

PART IV

MILITOURISM

11

Heliotropes

Solar Ecologies and Pacific Radiations

Elizabeth DeLoughrey

> The Age of Ecology began on the desert outside Alamogordo, New Mexico on July 16, 1945, with a dazzling fireball of light and a swelling mushroom cloud of radioactive gases.
> —Donald Worster, *Nature's Economy*

> Nothing "is more friendly to man, or more necessary to his well-being than the sun. From the sun you and I get . . . the energy that gives life and sustains life, the energy that builds skyscrapers and churches, that writes poems and symphonies."
> —David E. Lilienthal, Chair of the Atomic Energy Commission

Like heliotropes, we turn to the sun and its emissary rays to locate the cause and solution for ecological crisis. The solar radiation that determines life on earth has become part of our conversation about a planetary greenhouse whose temperatures are rising. To address the energy crisis and increasing planetary irradiation, we turn to solar solutions. To trope is to turn, and human technology is heliotropic as it turns to the sun to harness its solar energy and to protect the climate from excessive radiation. Solar panels follow the path of the sun, wind farms harness the sun's energy, hydrogen fuel is derived from the sun's constitutive elements, and we replicate solar energy (fusion) on earth through the global expansion of nuclear power "plants."

Physicist David Whitehouse has observed that the sun "is everywhere; in our past, present, and future" (5). Yet for a figure so ubiquitous and determinative, the solar is rarely considered when discussing concepts of the globe, which understandably take on an earthly tenor. The increased consciousness of the globe as an interconnected whole has been tied to radical social, environmental, and economic changes since the 1960s. This rise in global thinking has been associated with the increased ecological awareness inspired by the image of the planet as a fragile island dating from the *Apollo* space mission photographs of 1968–69,[1] which were widely utilized to promote the first Earth Day (1970). This ecological turn catalyzed the organization of the United Nations Conference on the Human Environment in Stockholm (1972), which sought to establish a territorial mandate for global environmental sovereignty, and later the World Charter for Nature (1982), which critiqued nuclear militarism and its devastating environmental impact. While these movements all contributed to a radical shift in bringing together globalism and ecology, I want to trace their precursors farther back in time. I argue that the modern concept of global ecology derives from the literal fallout of the Cold War, and position solar and military forms of radiation as key traces of globalization.

The Age of Ecology, as Donald Worster suggests in the epigraph, is simultaneous with the Atomic Age, registered as a dual threat to the planet in terms of nuclear annihilation (the explosive event) as well as radioactive fallout (the aftermath). In American Cold War propaganda, these weapons of mass destruction were naturalized by likening them to harnessing the power of the sun, and their radioactive by-products were depicted as no less dangerous than our daily sunshine. The militarization of the environment became so naturalized that the American public casually blamed any inclement weather on the atomic bomb.[2] Reporters suggested that the military change the globe by setting off nuclear weapons in the Arctic to melt the ice caps and thereby "give the entire world a moister, warmer climate" (quoted in Boyer 111).[3] This request went unheeded, but the two thousand and more nuclear weapons detonated on earth have changed our environment by radically increasing our levels of militarized radiation. The modern understanding of our planet as an ecosystem writ large is attributable to our consciousness of at least two forms of radiation: the solar rays that warm our global climate, and the radioactive fallout that has permeated the earth since the first detonation of the hydrogen bomb in 1952. In invisible ways, the history of worldwide military irradiation has been an important material and symbolic precursor of our current articulations of global warming.

Well before the development of the hydrogen bomb, the Manhattan Project reporter William Laurence described atomic energy in 1946 as a "promise" to "bring the sun down to earth as its gift to man" ("Atomic Energy" 90), a promethean metaphor that echoed President Truman's announcement of the atomic bombing of Hiroshima as a mere harnessing of solar power.[4] When nuclear radiation became a global concern, the Atomic Energy Commission (AEC) and its allies utilized solar analogies to conflate man-made weapons with natural energy from the sun. In 1947 AEC Chair David E. Lilienthal likened atomic energy to solar energy, arguing that nothing "was more friendly to man or more necessary to his being than the sun ... In its rays is the magic stuff of life itself" (335). These metaphors invoked the sun's power in a way that deliberately "confused" the public, as President Eisenhower demanded, about different types of radiation and their risks.[5]

The solar analogies and ecologies I explore in this essay are fraught with erasures, understandably so when we consider that the sun's affects, light and radiation, are invisible. Accordingly, Jacques Derrida has called the heliotrope "the father of all figures of speech," which is "the most natural" and simultaneously the most unrepresentable ("White" 44). The sun is the "essence of that which is," and yet we cannot look at it (43). He bases this on Aristotle's failure to find a word to describe the sun's casting forth rays of light as sowing is to the casting forth of seed. In this failure of language Derrida locates the sun's radical alterity. While I make no claims to fill this semantic gap, I suggest that the closest modern signifier of this alterity is radioactive fallout, and that the persistent use of solar metaphors for understanding nuclear weaponry have been vital to naturalizing global militarization.

In pursuing this complex relationship between Cold War ecology and radiation, I examine the solar metaphor—the heliotrope—and its by-product, radiation, as traces of modernity, figures for alterity, and the material legacy of the militarization of the Pacific Islands. Foregrounding the solar turn or heliotrope has important consequences for rethinking the material boundaries of ecocriticism as well as implications for understanding how postcolonial writers have reconfigured an alternative vision of solar ecopoetics. A number of indigenous Pacific writers including Witi Ihimaera, Albert Wendt, and Chantal Spitz have inscribed what Paul Virilio calls the "wars of light" as the most recent phase in the military globalization of the region. This concern might be traced back to the work of Maori poet Hone Tuwhare, whose earliest poems sought to denaturalize the heliocentrism of military "nukespeak." In exploring how the history of nuclear radiation has contributed to consciousness of a global ecosystem, this essay foregrounds the grammar of solar ecologies, placing indigenous writers of the Pacific at the forefront in questioning the military logic of heliocentric metaphors.

I. TRACING RADIATION ECOLOGIES

The Atomic Energy Commission was not only largely responsible for the radioactive militarization of the planet but also informed the ecological discourse that we use to inscribe it. In popularizing the new term "ecosystem" in 1935, the botanist Alfred George Tansley drew from the field of physics to describe the relationship between organisms and their habitat, arguing that one might employ the ecosystem as a model to study "the universe as a whole down to the atom" (64). Tansley's invocation of atomic physics was prescient: within twenty years the American militarization of science would usher in a new era of ecology modeled on nuclear radiation. Few scholars have traced the close relationship between the rise of the Age of Ecology and the Atomic Age, the mutually constitutive relationship between radioactive militarism and the study of the environment. Worster's foundational book *Nature's Economy* suggests that nuclearism catalyzed public consciousness about the invisible pollution of the global environment, a new understanding of interconnected space that helped Rachel Carson in 1962 redirect widespread fears of radioactive fallout toward contamination by pesticides (Worster 340).[6] While he rightly points to science's paradoxical role in the destruction and conservation of the environment, Worster overlooks how ecosystem ecology was catalyzed by the AEC in its surveys of the radioactive aftermath of its Pacific Island nuclear tests.

Ecology is modeled on the concept of a closed system, so it's not a coincidence that island colonies were chosen for both the nuclear tests and their radioactive surveys. While often deemed peripheral to modernity, we know that islands have in fact been at the center of the development of modern ecological thought. Richard Grove has demonstrated how tropical island colonies all over the globe served as vital laboratories and spaces of social and scientific experiment in ways that deeply informed seventeenth- and eighteenth-century conservation policy and modernity. I would like to propose a similar relationship between the American island colonies of Micronesia and how they helped constitute atomic modernity as well as the new field of ecosystem ecology.[7] Joel Bartholemew Hagen provides a compelling history of the "symbiosis . . . between atomic energy and ecosystem ecology," particularly as it was organized by Eugene Odum, the field's "founding father" and his brother Howard T. Odum (101). With the rapid expansion of nuclear testing in the Cold War and the subsequent radiological contamination of the planet, the AEC contracted the Odums to study the radioactive fallout in the Marshall Islands (Micronesia). Thus the field of "radiation ecology" began in the Pacific with the Odums' study of the militarized Enewetak Atoll, a chain of islands that functioned as an AEC laboratory for over forty nuclear weapons tests between 1948 and 1958. As islands were already associated with the contained space of a laboratory, this nuclear testing provided the first opportunity for ecologists to study a complete ecosystem through the trace of radiation. Understood as a "landmark in ecological research" (Hagen 105), Odum and his brother's work on the irradiation of the coral reefs provided ecologists with a model of a structured, self-regulating ecosystem (105) and the first theorization of shared resource relationships in nature which they termed "mutualism" (104). In turn, AEC-funded research laboratories and programs in radioecology were organized at universities and at nuclear power sites all over the United States, creating an "invisible college" (Golley 74) and catalyzing the institutional development of ecosystem ecology (Hagen 112).

This entanglement between ecology, radiation, and militarization is visible in Eugene Odum's 1957 article, "Ecology and the Atomic Age," which argued that "science advances on a broad *front*. . . . It is analogous to the *advance of an army*; a breakthrough may occur anywhere, and when one does it will not penetrate far until *the whole front* moves up. Thus, ecologists need not feel bashful about *attacking ecosystems* so long as they observe the rules of good science" (my emphasis 28). Although Odum is considered a key inspiration to the environmentalist movement because his theories shifted scientific thought away from a mechanistic approach and toward the interdependence of systems (Craige xix), his Cold War writing demonstrates the militarization of scientific grammar. In bracketing off ethics in this war for knowledge, he encourages the scientist to "attack" ecosystems already devastated by nuclearization.

Odum and his Cold War contemporaries were not merely studying nuclear fallout but also introducing radioactive tracers into the environment to determine how energy was transformed in a contained system. When we consider these events in light of Theodor Adorno and Max Horkheimer's critique of instrumental rationality, published just before the world's first atomic explosion, their articulation of modernity seems prophetic. Arguing in 1944 that the instrumental rationality of the Enlightenment perpetuates its self-destruction, they explained, "the fully enlightened earth radiates disaster triumphant" (3). Although their use of the term "radiates" was metaphoric, their work helps us understand the logic that permitted radiation to become a tool for ecological science without regard to environmental preservation. The invisible Cold War legacy of the irradiated earth demonstrates all too poignantly that "what men want to learn from nature is how to use it, in order wholly to dominate it and other men" (Adorno and Horkheimer 3).

II. "THE FULLY ENLIGHTENED EARTH"

The "fully enlightened earth" has been a primary concern in the Pacific Islands, a region often deemed peripheral to modernity and yet the site of nearly continuous nuclear weapons testing in the fifty-year period from 1946 to 1996. Since their initial contact with Enlightenment-era cartographers, painters, and naturalists, the Pacific Islands have been incorporated into an especially visual economy of colonialism in which the ethnicity of the region's peoples, the exoticism of tropical light, and flora and fauna were studiously mapped, painted, and inscribed for European display and distribution.[8] By the mid-twentieth century, the region entered an entirely different economy of light when hundreds of nuclear detonations conducted by the United States, France, and the United Kingdom produced a new atomic cartography and a militarized grammar of "radiation atolls" and "nuclear nomads."[9]

Paul Virilio's argument that light and visual media, from the spotlight to the camera lens, illuminate and perpetuate the modern landscape of

THE DAWN OF THE NUCLEAR AGE

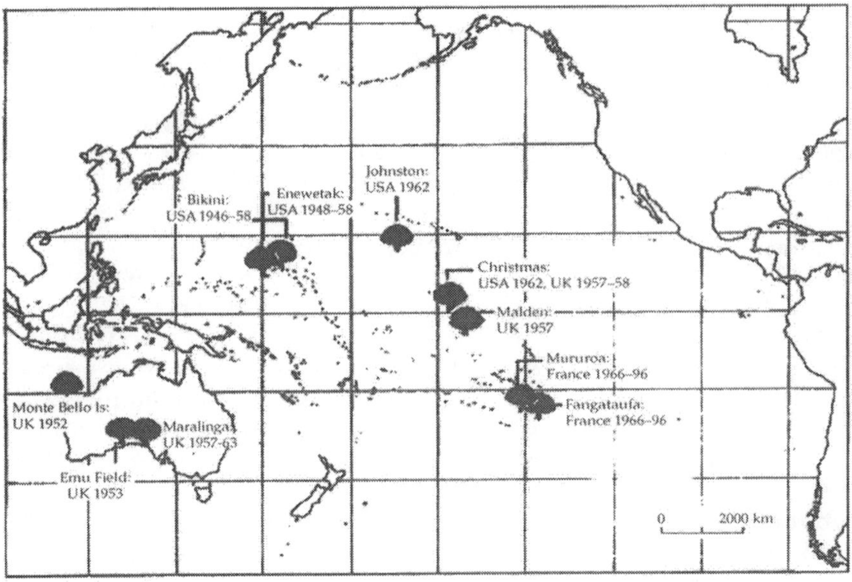

Fig 11.1 Nuclear Map, courtesy of Stewart Firth.

war is especially relevant to the hyper-visuality of the nuclear tests in the Pacific Islands. This excess illumination was a vital tactic of the Cold War, in which hundreds of Hollywood photographers and film makers were hired by the U.S. military to produce the spectral aesthetics of violence. This photographic and cinematic archive of the wars of light was distributed worldwide and is now ubiquitous on the Internet.[10] The U.S. military produced postcards of nuclear explosions at Bikini and Enewetak as keepsakes for their soldiers (Weisgall 150), many of whom, like the Marshall Islanders, were already carrying mementos of light in the form of radioactive cesium, iodone, and strontium.[11] In keeping with the depiction of the weapons as natural as the sun, AEC news reels about the nuclear tests at Bikini Atoll featured the islanders singing "You are my Sunshine" (Weisgall 176, *Radio Bikini*). So irradiated was the marine life at Bikini, as the Odum brothers discovered, that the fish produced autoradiographs, impressing their own images onto photographic plates and film (Boyer 92).

The discourse of what Teresia Teaiwa terms "militourism" ("Reading" 249),[12] the mutual constitution of the military and tourist industries, renders one tropical island as a substitute for any other, suppressing the historical depth and geographic breadth of the militarization of the Pacific. Yet nuclearization has long been a concern for the region's writers, who have engaged in regional, ecological, and global terms with the heliocentrism of the "fully enlightened earth." As theorists have demonstrated, forms of resistance to the violent reach of globalization have included a revitalization of local and indigenous epistemologies, evident in Pacific sovereignty movements that challenge what Virilio refers to as modern "light wars," which begin with the use of the searchlight and extend to the camera and to nuclear weapons (*War and Cinema* 68). Regional activism, including lawsuits against the United States and petitions to the United Nations, demonstrate the mutually constitutive relationship between decolonization and denuclearization.

Although the dominant forms of American environmentalism have tended to minimize postcolonial contributions to ecological thought, the Pacific was a vital space of antinuclear activism and legislation. Initially annexed as an American Trust Territory, the Republic of Palau drafted the world's first antinuclear constitution in 1979. Since the advent of the Cold War, the Nuclear Free and Independent Pacific Movement, largely coordinated by women, has actively sought to ban nuclear waste dumping, nuclear testing, and the transit of nuclear-powered submarines.[13] Although not always successful, these movements make the region distinctive from other postcolonial liberation histories. The profoundly regional basis to Pacific Island decolonization, its largely Christian coalition of support, its long engagement with U.S. militarization, and its early inculcation into the modern wars of light suggest the ecological importance of decolonization and the region's vital critique of nuclear heliocentrism.

III. PACIFIC LITERATURES OF LIGHT

Since World War II, Pacific writers have engaged with the legacies of the wars of light, critiquing the militarization and destruction of regional ecologies.[14] For instance, in his 1987 novel *The Whale Rider*, Maori author Witi Ihimaera inscribed an ancient pod of ancestor whales, disoriented and beaching themselves after the French detonate hundreds of nuclear weapons in the Tuamotu Archipelago of Tahiti. In Ihimaera's novel, the whales are the first to notice the marine "contamination seeping from Moruroa," the increasing "radiation" which brings fearful "genetic effects" on their pod. This is rendered visible as an underwater "lightswarm of luminescence" that is "sparkling like a galaxy." The whales perceive a "net of radioactive death" and alter their course, ultimately beaching themselves. Although the ancients followed the pathway of the sun to settle Aotearoa (30), the generative movement into Te Ao Marama, the world of light, has been appropriated by the militarization of light. This ecological crisis ultimately facilitates a new generation of female leadership in the community (58). The next generation is thus encouraged to continue the decolonization process by turning to ancestral models of ecological "interlock" (Ihimaera 40).

Samoan writer Albert Wendt has inscribed the legacy of the wars of light in his dystopian novel *Black Rainbow* (1992), which depicts a nuclear doomsday clock that is a continual touchstone to the protagonist and determines the apocalyptic temporality of the text, and, by extension, the Pacific as a region. The novel's title is adapted from Maori artist Ralph Hotere's paintings about French nuclear testing in Moruroa, artworks that the protagonist transports with him in his flight from agents of the homogenizing corporate state.[15] The concept of the "black rainbow" in both Hotere's and Wendt's work nicely demonstrates the paradox of representing nuclear radiation and the annihilation of the normative visual spectrum of light. This connection between artistic production and the history of light is evoked in Wendt's subsequent publication, a Pacific Island anthology described as a "rainbow of poetry and prose" (1) and entitled *Nuanua* (1995), the term in many Oceanic languages for the rainbow. While Wendt emphasizes the rainbow's definition as a symbol of Pacific diversity, one could also foreground its role as a figure for the mediation between the earthly and the divine. This relationship between the material and supernatural has been explored by other Pacific writers and functions as an important historic component of American nuclear discourse, beginning with naming the first atomic detonation "Trinity."

Pacific writers have configured the regional shift to atomic modernity in terms of the desacralization of light and land, what Adorno and Horkheimer had termed the "disenchantment" produced by instrumental rationality. In her depiction of the French wars of light in the Pacific, Tahitian writer Chantal Spitz opens her novel *Island of Shattered Dreams* (1991) with two heliotropic cosmologies. The first, written in Tahitian, inscribes the separation of the earth and sky to create Te Ao Marama, the world of light, a genealogy linking humans with the divine common to many traditions of the Polynesian Pacific. This is followed by a passage from Christian genesis of the divine creation of light and its separation from darkness, including man's decree of dominion "over all the earth" (10). Like Polynesian accounts, the Biblical genesis replicates the movement of formlessness to form, the construction of earthly temporality, and the association of light as a legacy of knowledge of the divine. In juxtaposing these two cosmologies, Spitz highlights the remarkable difference in how this shift of form produces different ecological results: the Tahitian positions the human as a genealogical product of divine nature, while the Christian narrative positions the natural world in terms of its distinction from the human and therefore authorizes dominion. This rupture between divine cosmology and disenchantment is visible in the novel's narrative trajectory, which moves from an epic language of cosmogony, the world of Ra, "the majestic lord of light" (80), toward the temporal discourse of progress and nuclear colonialism. Narratively the novel shifts from allegory to realism once French missiles are housed in the "sacred belly" of Tahitian land. A novel that begins with lyrical inscriptions of its characters as "children of light" shifts to inscribe light in terms of fears that Tahitians will be "burned to a crisp" (85) by nuclear missiles. French physicists introduce the Enlightenment discourse of instrumental rationality, what

Spitz refers to as "the logic of men" (145), changing narrative and history as Tahitians are displaced from a sacred discourse of genealogy into the consumerist and neocolonial "light-filled city" (148) that produces cancer, alienation from ancestral language, and an economic legacy of nuclear dependents.

More recent Pacific texts have emphasized the destructive heliocentrism of the nuclear age. James George's novel *Ocean Roads* (2006) depicts the flight of nuclear physicist Isaac Simeon to New Zealand after his work for the Manhattan Project. In coming to understand his responsibility for the irradiation of Nagasaki, Hiroshima, and the Bikini Atoll, he describes himself as a "disciple . . . of light" (61), a creator of the scorched earth, an unconscious participant in the modernity of excessive illumination where, as Virilio protests, "nothing is sacred . . . because nothing is . . . meant to be inviolable. This is the tracking down of darkness, the tragedy brought about by an exaggerated love of light" (*Vision Machine* 35). Isaac disobeys his father's orders not "to look into the sun" (73) and recognizes himself as "more a child of the sun than the earth" (340). The novel, structured in series of flashes and flashpoints of violence, inscribes how diverse figures of light such as nuclear radiation, cinema, radiation therapy, and war photography have all helped to constitute the bodies of history in the Cold War Pacific.[16]

Like Spitz, George inscribes the nuclear desacralization of space and how it produces a shift in narrative temporality. He frames his complex novel with a description of the Trinity site, a space of memory for the characters that also signifies the commencement of the Atomic Age and a new way of reckoning time. The AEC's decision to name a weapon of mass destruction "Trinity" suggests the desacralization of space and time: the apocalyptic powers of militarized light are mystified by reference to Christian frameworks for the mediation between the human and the divine (Rhodes 571-72, Weart 101). As I will explain, this thematic concern can be traced back to Hone Tuwhare's poetry, which reflects some of the earliest Pacific writing about the heliocentrism of the Atomic Age. Pacific texts have turned to light, radiation and the sun as constitutive elements of a new ecology of modernity, one that reflects the disenchantment when the complexity of cosmological narratives are reduced to the secular wars of light.

I interpret the figure of light as an emissary of the sun as well as the sign of nuclearization and radiation. It is by turning to the figure of the sun and its by-product, radiation, that I register a shift from our material reckonings of globalization to Gayatri Spivak's concept of planetarity. If globalization is characterized by visuality and illumination, planetarity provides a means to think through—but not necessarily to represent—that which is rendered invisible, that which is thrown into shadow. Planetarity, in Spivak's definition, is the figure for alterity, generally read in terms such as "mother, nation, God, nature" (*Death of a Discipline* 73). While agencies such as the AEC argued that nuclear radiation "was a familiar part of the everyday environment" (Boyer 314) and "just one more of the hazards of contemporary living" (Lap 111), the concept of planetarity denaturalizes that familiarity. In contrast to instrumental rationality, it is the process by which the familiar is rendered uncanny, unhomely. It is the "defamiliarization of familiar space" (Spivak 77).

Spivak asks that literary study "take the 'figure' as its guide," to "disfigure it, read the logic of the metaphor," to foreground the ethics of reading. Tracing the figure of light helps us see how "nukespeak" naturalized military radiation across the planet. This was done by associating man-made radiation with its solar counterpart, and by likening atomic detonations on earth as harnessing the power of the sun. The repeated connection between a military lab product (a nuclear weapon) and its cosmic figure (the sun) thus naturalized atomic weapon production and helped to eclipse hundreds of nuclear detonations set off in the Pacific Islands until 1996, radioactive traces that we carry in our bodies today. Our lack of recognition about our own irradiation is tied to the ways in which the master metaphor, the heliotrope, has been configured as both a natural and unrepresentable figure for global nuclear fallout.

The detonation of the fifteen-megaton thermonuclear (hydrogen) bomb *Bravo* at Bikini Atoll (1954) catalyzed global consciousness about the dangers of military heliocentrism. *Bravo* covered the surrounding islands and eventually the planet's atmosphere with radioactive strontium, cesium, and iodine. It was an ecological and political relations disaster because it exposed thousands of Marshall Islanders to nuclear fallout, contributing to countless miscarriages, leukemia deaths, thyroid cancers, and the kind of chromosome damage that knows no temporal or genealogical limit. Estimated at 1,000 times the force of the bombs dropped on Hiroshima and Nagasaki, *Bravo* has been called the worst radiological disaster in history: fallout was detected in rain over Japan, in lubricating oil of Indian aircraft, in winds over Australia, and in the sky over the United States and Europe (Jungk 310). While the "One World or None" antinuclear movement in 1945 generated some of the earliest global environmentalism (Boyer 76), by the 1960s every person on the planet was in fact globally connected thanks to the absorption of the radioactive fallout from hydrogen weapons detonated in the Pacific.

Bravo and the subsequent two thousand or so nuclear tests on this planet, Eileen Welsome observes, "split the world into 'preatomic' and 'postatomic' species" (299). Radioactive elements produced by these weapons were spread through the atmosphere, deposited into water supplies and soils, absorbed by plants and thus into the bone tissue of humans all over the globe. The body of every human on the planet now contains strontium-90, a man-made by-product of nuclear detonations (Caufield 132), and forensic scientists use the traces of militarized radioactive carbon in our teeth to date human remains.[17] This invokes an invisible and ephemeral trace of what Rob Nixon has called "slow violence": the nonapocalyptic threats to our survival such as depleted uranium weapons, desertification, and the toxic ecologies that Rachel Carson brought to public consciousness. Radioactive fallout presents us with the most invisible yet pernicious form of the wars of light, one directly tied to the transformation of the human body, and a disturbing sign of our true merger with the environment.

IV. NO ORDINARY SUN

The radiation we carry in our bodies is a form of memory, but why is it so invisible to narrative and to history? I want to suggest that its narrative erasure occurs through dual processes of language—first, the naturalization of nuclear radiation as solar energy by AEC propaganda, and second, the process of transference, diversion, and/or substitution made possible by metaphor itself. Metaphor has been articulated as a form of displacement, a move from one object to another that foregrounds resemblance and renders the invisible visible (Ricoeur 34), just as much as it "eclipses" or subsumes other possible modes of relation (110). Metaphor is also deeply connected to the process by which nonhuman nature is rendered accessible and, following Girard Genette, the way that "language spatializes itself" so that space becomes language and thus articulates itself to us (in Ricoeur 147). Turning to the work of Maori poet Hone Tuwhare, we can see how these functions of metaphor have sought to naturalize nuclearization as the presence of the sun on earth, yet following Spivak,"de-figure" this association so that we can begin to grasp the extent of its erasures.

Tuwhare's "No Ordinary Sun," a five-stanza poem written in the late 1950s on the heels of British and American atomic tests in the Pacific, repeatedly negates the solar metaphors accorded to the nuclear bomb that so successfully naturalized the violence of the expanding nation state. While we generally associate natural metaphors with terrestrial matter, such as the trees and soil that are thought to root human relationships to the land, the discourse of military nuclearization has drawn from solar metaphors to naturalize state violence. Before turning to Tuwhare's poem, allow me to briefly summarize the military context in which he was writing.

Famously, Robert Oppenheimer, director of the Manhattan Project and so-called father of the atomic bomb, borrowed from the *Bhagavad-Gita* to describe the Trinity explosion (1945) as "the radiance of a thousand suns" (quoted in Jungk 201). Nuclear weapons are often described as harnessing the power of the sun, or of releasing the universal power of the Big Bang and therefore replicating the origin of our universe. These analogies provide a neat semantic parallel between an explosive event that generates planetary life, and the violent force of nuclear weaponry which is depicted as a destructive force that ultimately generates its opposite, world peace. To assimilate the supposed peacekeeping nature of the nuclear bomb is to suppress its violence at detonation and to place it unquestionably in a part-for-whole relationship that fabricates a future of world peace. The use of this supernatural and often religious discourse, including the use of names such as "Trinity" for a weapon of mass destruction, Jeff Smith argues, "obscures the continuities between atomic weapons" and the instrumental rationality of science (Smith *Unthinking the Unthinkable* 2).[18]

The atom has long been imagined in Western philosophy as a synecdoche for the solar system in which electrons or planets orbit a stabilizing nucleus or sun.[19] The pedagogical analogy between the atomic "miniverse" and the solar system was a part of the modern discourse of ecology, as we've seen in the new grammar of the ecosystem, and was vital to the public discourse of the nuclear era. For example, nuclear primers produced by the Los Alamos Atomic Bomb Laboratory would begin with the nucleus/ sun analogy, and then immediately liken man-made nuclear energy to "the energy which keeps the stars shining" (Marshak, Nelson, and Schiff 12). This "sunny side of the atom," as Paul Boyer has shown (299–301), was a vital metaphor in garnering public support for atomic weaponry and in minimizing the recognition of the damage caused by the global spread of nuclear radiation (314). Thus AEC physicists could quell public fears of increasing militarized radioactivity by asserting that "radiation is just as much a natural phenomenon as anything else" (Lilienthal in Boyer 308).

Much of the language that connected the nuclear bomb with the power of the sun can be attributed to the *New York Times* journalist William Laurence, whose consistent cosmic hyperbole about the power of atomic explosions was copied, often verbatim, by countless other reporters and politicians (Weart 104).[20] Laurence wrote President Truman's speech which likened the bombing of Hiroshima to "harnessing . . . the basic power of the universe" and the "force from which the sun draws its power" (quoted in Weart 103). In his popular book *Dawn over Zero*, Laurence described one atomic bomb at Bikini as "a gigantic white sun" (280), which harnessed the "awe of a new cosmic force" (284). While successfully conflating political with universal (and therefore natural) power, these direct analogies between the atomic bomb (a fission device) and the power of the sun (primarily fusion) were inaccurate. Moreover, this begs the question as to how natural it was to unleash a militarized and lab-created miniature of the sun's fusion power on a planet that sustains life through its protective *distance* from the sun. This discourse, Robert Jungk explains, created a public "helplessness in the face of natural forces" (247). So successful were these solar metaphors that the government named their top secret "body snatching" investigation, which collected body parts and cadavers to measure global radiation levels, "Operation Sunshine."[21] The name of the study suggested a heliotropic ecology; it was derived from the analogy between the sun and nuclear radioactivity because after these tests: "fallout, like sunshine, covered the globe" (Welsome 299).

Atomic Age discourse consistently aligned the bomb with the trope of a new dawn, a rising sun, and the birth of a new world.[22] In keeping with the supernatural tropes that inscribed the bomb as the product of a new kind of divinity arose the image of the nuclear cloud as a tree of knowledge.

Observing Test Baker, Laurence famously described the cloud as "a giant tree, spreading out in all directions, bearing many invisible fruits deadly to man—alpha particles, electrons . . . gamma rays . . . fruits of the tree of knowledge, which man must eat only at his peril" (*Dawn* 280). As with the analogy to the Big Bang, American nuclearization of the globe seems predestined: ordained by nature, the cosmos, and divinity.

This association of the sun with cosmic metaphors of radiance and (nuclear) radiation is vital to understanding Tuwhare's poem, which pairs it with the tree, a natural metaphor of human presence on the planet.

"No Ordinary Sun"

Tree let your arms fall:
raise them not sharply in supplication
to the bright enhaloed cloud.
Let your arms lack toughness and
resilience for this is no mere axe
to blunt nor fire to smother.

Your sap shall not rise again
to the moon's pull.
No more incline a deferential head
to the wind's talk, or stir
to the tickle of coursing rain.

Your former shagginess shall not be
wreathed with the delightful flight
of birds nor shield
nor cool the ardour of unheeding
lovers from the monstrous sun.

Tree let your naked arms fall
nor extend vain entreaties to the radiant ball.
This is no gallant monsoon's flash,
no dashing trade wind's blast.
The fading green of your magic
emanations shall not make pure again
these polluted skies . . . for this
is no ordinary sun.

O tree
in the shadowless mountains
the white plains and
the drab sea floor
your end at last is written. (23)[23]

The title, "No Ordinary Sun," frames the poem with a simultaneous creation and destruction of metaphor. On the one hand, the sun can never be "ordinary" because it is our source of life on the planet. There is no such thing as an "ordinary sun," the poem seems to say, and it negates the rendering of any discourse that would normalize it. To make the life-generating center of our heliotropic system an *"ordinary* sun" demands a comparison—it can never function as a singularity; it exists only in relation and in a hierarchy of value. The process of comparison demands two discursive moves which are rendered spatially. First, a sun can become "ordinary" by comparing with other stars and galaxies—this presses the limits of our own earth-bound knowledge. The second way to create a solar comparison is from within our planet, turning to that figure so often depicted as the sun on earth: the nuclear bomb. The opening "no," the negation of the ordinariness that naturalizes the bomb, is rejected even as the poet relies on the metaphorization of the bomb to establish an allegory about the sun and tree.

The unnamed speaker begins with an imperative: "tree let your arms fall." The personification of the tree's limbs doubles the man-made military "arms" that make this metaphor possible (23). The rest of the opening stanza develops the anthropocentrism of the tree and the supernaturalism of the sun, placing the two in unequal relation. The speaker presumes intimacy with the tree and warns it not to raise its arms "in supplication / to the bright enhaloed cloud," foregrounding a spatial hierarchy between earth and sky and the discursive process of mediation that facilitates this connection, even as language supplants the mediating "arms" of the tree. While some have suggested the allegorical mode is overdetermined by the weight of tradition, Tuwhare's emphasis that this is *not* the well-known violence of the "axe" or "fire" suggests a lack of continuity in the narrative of nature. These opening lines inscribe reverence for the supernatural (the sun) in spatial terms, but insist this traditional reverence between the earth and the cosmic should be resisted—this new form of violence is outside of nature. The poem identifies an interpretive gap between the natural earth and the cosmic sun and reveals a rupture in history and nature, even as this gap is mediated by metaphor, the poet, and language.

The second and third stanzas again signal a break in the meditative function between the natural and the supernatural, between the microcosm and the macrocosm. The tree's "sap shall not rise again/to the moon's pull," marking the end of the gravitational relation between the earth and the cosmos. Gravity reflects an invisible and yet determinative curvature of space-time, a nonnarrative marker of cosmic history. Yet the heliocentrism signaled by gravity is arrested by the poet's voice. Developing the analogy of the tree as human body, the speaker advises against our heliotropism: we should let our "arms fall." Moreover, the figures that mediate between the strata such as gravity, the wind, and birds, which are generative to the action of this stanza (the rising sap, inclining head, the tree's stirring), are "no more," called to a halt by discursive mediation.

In this third stanza, the life-ending cause, "the monstrous sun," is finally named. This key figure of alterity is placed in the center of the poem, deemed "monstrous," a word closely associated with irregularity of form, with the unnatural, and often with the unacceptable product of the merger between humans and nature. This introduction of the sun generates a new role for the tree, which now shifts from the anthropomorphic to the arboreal, a (failed) but protective intermediary between the sun and the "unheeding" human "lovers" below whose "ardour," literally, a term for burning, needs cooling. The poet makes an interesting choice here, and perhaps a critique, of the failure of these "unheeding" humans to apprehend their own demise. In this failure of communication between poet and human lovers, it may be that the tree is no longer a trope for the human, but, simply, a tree. To trope is to turn, and these unheeding human figures are heliotropic, oblivious to their burning under the monstrous sun.

The introduction of these unheeding lovers marks a shift in the following (and longest) stanza. While the speaker continues to address the tree in the imperative, the diction becomes self-conscious and even archaic—and increasing in the use of assonance, alliteration, and introducing the first and only full rhyme (fall / ball). In switching narrative codes, this stanza undermines the kind of Romantic nature poetry that draws upon natural tropes for representing the organic development of human illumination. Tuwhare's use of adjectives such as "gallant" and "dashing" to personify nature calls attention to their artifice. Thus a "gallant monsoon" is as incongruous as the nuclear metaphor it is made to bear, its "flash." Similarly, the antiquated language of the "dashing trade wind" jars against the modern warfare "blast." This calls attention to the *unnaturalness* of the nuclear as well as the failure of language to represent natural phenomena. The "magic emanations" of the tree will no longer "make pure again / these polluted skies," a figural juxtaposition of utopian metaphors of nature alongside a dystopian modernity that calls attention to the uneven process by which metaphor transmutes meaning. The ellipses after "polluted skies..." reiterate this gap between knowledge and representation, between metaphor's propensity for resemblance and diversion. The repeated negations of this stanza—"*nor* extend entreaties," "*no* dashing trade wind," "*not* make pure again" (my emphases 23)—suggest the metaphor-negating title of the poem and indeed this particular stanza ends, "this / is no ordinary sun."

The fifth and final stanza of the poem literally destroys its own metaphors and leaves the poet with no earthly landscape to transform beyond language. The stanza begins with a Romantic call, "O tree," turning to the geography of the earth that refuses to yield the metaphors so desperately needed by the poet. As such, the very process by which human language gains its meaning—through its rootedness in natural, earthly metaphor—is eradicated. The speaker turns to the mountains, usually a space of contrast and spatial depth, but finds they are now "shadowless" (23). Similarly, the "plains" are now "white" and the sea floor is "drab." Here nuclearization leads not to a planet determined by darkness, a lack of light, but total light. To return to Adorno and Horkheimer, this "fully enlightened earth radiates disaster triumphant." The sea floor, representing the farthest depths of earthly existence yet also space that is completely unfathomable to human knowledge, is not "revealed" or "illuminated" by the atomic sun, it is simply "drab." These last five lines of the poem also lack color, contrast, and personification of nature, the vehicles that kept this poem in narrative tension.

Lawrence Buell has argued that "apocalypse is the single most powerful master metaphor that the contemporary environmental imagination has at its disposal" (*Environmental Imagination* 285). Given its nuclear topic, the structure of Tuwhare's poem is oddly antiapocalyptic, if by apocalypse we mean inscribing the catastrophic event itself. Unlike almost every other visual and narrative account of nuclear detonations, which capitalize on the stunning visual effects of nuclear explosions and produce an aesthetic of violence, Tuwhare recounts a nuclear apocalypse in which the actual detonation and blast are not inscribed. This is a poem of witness that does not inscribe the act of violence itself. The poem uses the very figures most associated with apocalypse, yet this is not a narrative of sacrifice or renewal, as accounts of destruction often suggest in Maori and Christian traditions. This is a world of total light, but illumination does not follow—this world is "shadowless" and "drab" (23). Tuwhare has chosen to avoid what Fernand Braudel calls the "eventist" model of history, the visual aesthetics of violence that mark the kind of apocalyptic thinking that detracts from our recognition of the *longue durée* of radiation.[24] Thus Tuwhare ends his poem with total radiation, an unrecognizable landscape that resists our domesticating metaphors, one utterly suffused by the violence of the heliotrope, our total illumination.

V. PACIFIC HELIOTROPES

As I suggested at the start of this essay, the literature of Pacific solar ecologies has drawn from European and indigenous traditions. As is evident from this poem, there are at least two cultural traditions that inflect Tuwhare's poetry: first, he grew up speaking Maori and was exposed to a formal oratory in which one addresses so-called inanimate beings such as trees, animals, and features of the landscape, utilizing language to establish humanity's genealogical connections to the earth; and second, Tuwhare's father read the Bible to him as a child to help develop his English. In its first book printing (1964), "No Ordinary Sun" was juxtaposed to a poem entitled "A Disciple Dreams," which questioned the leadership of the church in an era of perpetual war. Given Tuwhare's concern with the meditative function of language and light, we might read this poem as an allegory of Christ and his failures to protect humanity from the hubris of instrumental rationality. Or the tree and its unheeding lovers may reflect the Tree of Knowledge in which light, a cipher for Lucifer, becomes the awful illumination of atomic power in ways that resonate with Laurence's declaration "that alpha particles . . .

and gamma rays (represent) . . . fruits of the tree of knowledge" in the nuclear age.

To position this work in a Maori cosmology, we might consider this poem in relation to the genealogies of light that inform much of Tuwhare's poetry. Tane-Mahuta, the deity of the forest represented by the tree, creates Te Ao Marama, the world of light, by separating the sky deity and the earth mother, bringing light (and life) to the earth. Tane, like the figures of rain, wind, and birds of this poem, is an emissary between earth and sky. The poet's call to cease this intermediary function thus focuses on the failure of mediation itself. The "wa"—the space between—in Maori epistemology represents the potent space of becoming, the space of language, the mediating function of metaphor.[25] As such, the poet inscribes a rupture in the mediating role of light in both indigenous and Christian cosmologies. This rupture in the function of metaphor has great implications for our ability to apprehend and articulate the crisis of planetary irradiation.

Tuwhare's poem anticipates Derrida's observation that we are unwillingly drawn "by the movement which turns the sun into metaphor or attracted by that which turns philosophical metaphor towards the sun" ("White" 51). The power of Tuwhare's poem lies in its resistance to figurative and cosmological readings that would naturalize nuclearization as the sun, would link it to life-generating events such as the Big Bang, or would transmute the atomic era into a cosmological origin narrative. The sun, which is "always turning, thus appearing and hiding itself," is, in Derrida's words, a "bad metaphor which gives only improper knowledge" (52). As such, Tuwhare calls attention to this eclipse in knowledge, and by de-figuring the naturalization of the nuclear, anticipates the dis-figuring of metaphor that Spivak locates as central to shifting from instrumental rationality to ethical responsibility. And this ethical prerogative to disfigure the naturalizing metaphors of militarization has vital implications for both ecocriticism as a field of study and in illuminating our own human history of global irradiation, the most recent of which is reflected in our discourse about climate change.

The tree's "magic / emanations shall not make pure again/these polluted skies"; the power of transmutation that lies in the natural and figurative use of the tree has failed, just as the poet's ability to illuminate the earth after nuclear devastation results in merely a "drab" and "shadowless" landscape. The last words of the poem, the staccato, "your end at last is written," represents one of the few lines that do not assert a negation; this is a positive assertion as well as epitaph. The doubling of the "end at last" underlines the circumscribed powers of the poet and the process of inscription itself. In other words, the demise of the tree is simultaneous with the emergence of writing. The poet's elegiac powers emerge, only through the loss of the landscape from which language gains meaning. This is a small triumph of metaphor in the wake of our planetary irradiation.

NOTES

1. See Cosgrove 257-262.
2. See Smith, H. Alley 89–90.
3. Others argued that atomic weapons could be used to "tidy up the awkward parts of the world" (quoted in Boyer 113).
4. Truman announced the bombing of Hiroshima "as a harnessing of the basic power of the universe. The force from which the sun draws its power has been loosed against those who brought war to the Far East" (quoted in Weart 103).
5. See Boyer 188.
6. See also Lutts.
7. Overtly using the islands as laboratories of radiological experiment, AEC films such as *Operation Greenhouse* (1951) surveyed the Marshall Islands from an airplane, remarking on these "individual test islands [like] . . . a giant lab in the middle of an ocean."
8. See Bernard Smith and Paul Lyons.
9. See Firth, *Nuclear Playground*; Firth and Von Strokirk, "A Nuclear Pacific."
10. See *Hollywood's Top Secret Film Studio*; the films *Radio Bikini* and *Half-Life* document these events. Photos and films of the tests are available widely; see sites such as at http://www.vce.com/ and http://nuclearweaponarchive.org.
11. For more on the nuclearization of the Pacific see Boyer, Firth, and Weisgall.
12. She adopts the term from Louis Owens ("Reading" 91).
13. See Firth, *Nuclear Playground*; Teaiwa, "Microwomen."
14. Important war narratives that predate the nuclear tests include the autobiography of Cook Island author Florence Johnny Frisbie, who inscribed the American militarization of the Pacific in *Miss Ulysses from Puka Puka*, and Vincent Eri, who depicted radical changes to Papua New Guinean village life with the arrival of Australian and American troops and forced labor recruitment.
15. See also the Pacific collection edited by Hall, *Below the Surface: Words and Images in Protest at French Nuclear Testing on Moruroa*. Robert Barclay's *Melal: A Novel of the Pacific* (2002) depicts the American militarization of Kwajalein in particular.
16. George's novel and the alterity of light are explored in my article "Radiation Ecologies."
17. See "Forensics: Age Written in Teeth by Nuclear Tests."
18. See Rhodes for Oppenheimer's naming of Trinity, which he explained derived from a Donne poem that articulates the vexed relation between humanity and the divine (571-2).
19. Scientific uses of metaphor, as scholars have demonstrated, not only connect two disparate entities but validate and naturalize this new relationship and thus are crucial to constructing new paradigms of knowledge. See Boyd, "Metaphor and Theory Change," and Kuhn, "Metaphor in Science."
20. Later that year Philip Morrison, a Manhattan Project scientist, described the Hiroshima bomb to the 1945 U.S. Committee on Atomic Energy as "a small piece of the sun. . . . If you are near the sun, you must expect to get burned" (quoted in Welsome 107).
21. Children who drank milk between the years 1955–65 demonstrate much higher levels of strontium 90 in their bones due to the atmospheric nuclear tests of that era (Stephenson and Weal 131).
22. Weart describes radiation's association with the rays of life associated with life force, the growth of crops, sexuality, and divine illumination (41). See also Chernus, Rosenthal, and Teaiwa "bikinis".

23. My thanks to Rob Tuwhare for allowing me to reproduce his father's poem in its entirety. This analysis of Tuwhare appeared in my article "Solar Metaphors: 'No Ordinary Sun.'"

24. See also Masco, who makes this important point, and who draws upon Adorno and Horkheimer for different ends.

25. See Heim's "Breath as Metaphor of Sovereignty and Connectedness in Pacific Island Poetry," forthcoming from *New Literatures Review*.

12

Activating Voice, Body, and Place

Kanaka Maoli and Ma'ohi Writings for Kaho'olawe and Moruroa

Dina El Dessouky

> Fundamentally, sovereignty is aloha 'āina.
> —Editors, "Mana'o Aloha 'Āina," *Aloha 'Āina*, 1988–89 (PKO 2)

The Protect Kaho'olawe 'Ohana (PKO) editorial statement that opens this essay succinctly exemplifies the emergent and promising conceptual frame of "postcolonial ecologies" that this volume proposes. The PKO is a predominantly—but not exclusively—Kanaka Maoli (Native Hawaiian) grassroots organization whose 1976-93 activist efforts successfully ended over fifty years of U.S. military training and weapons testing on the sacred Hawaiian island of Kaho'olawe. Aloha 'āina is an active cultural and ecological philosophy most commonly translated word for word in English as "love for the land," but Samuel Elbert explains that it has further proverbial connotations, "including love for the land *and the people of the land*" (my emphasis added) (quoted in G. Kanahele 184). Elbert's interpretation reveals how aloha 'āina is a Kanaka Maoli epistemology of active love and responsibility for both human and nonhuman life, one that posits cultural health and ecological sustainability as equal priorities.

The editors of the PKO's *Aloha 'Āina* newsletter emphasize that aloha 'āina is itself an action plan; sovereignty cannot and does not exist without it (2). It is an explicit testament to the concurrent emergence of anticolonial and ecologically mindful indigenous approaches in decolonizing territories such as Hawai'i and Te Ao Ma'ohi (the territory known as "French" Polynesia). Aloha 'āina also critically acknowledges the symbiotic and interdependent relationships existing in the biological world, a world that includes human societies. It asserts that by loving and caring for the land and sea, you not only give back to what physically sustains you, but you also serve as a steward of your own culture, promoting a strong and healthy foundation for its growth and perpetuation. Kahoʻolawe and the PKO reminded Kanaka Maoli that aloha ʻāina could not only restore the integrity of militarily abused Hawaiian land, but could be the basis of a new Kanaka Maoli lāhui (nation). With aloha ʻāina as its organizing concept, this lāhui would offer an ecologically mindful alternative to the boundary-oriented concept of the nation, because "where nationalism and patriotism tend to exalt the virtues of a people or a race, aloha ʻāina exalts the land" (Silva 11). In conceiving a new sovereign construction, Tavini Huiraatira—a leading Maʻohi independence group—proposed "Te Ao Maʻohi" (the Maʻohi world or universe) as an indigenous replacement for the colonially possessive term "La Polynésie Française" (French Polynesia) in 1990. Similar to the Kanaka Maoli lāhui, which is based in the ecocultural philosophy of aloha ʻāina, "Te Ao Maʻohi" is based in thinking that situates Maʻohi people in a broader ao (world or universe). Te Ao Maʻohi conceptually accounts for Maʻohi sovereign subjectivity, but challenges the notion that the islands are defined by an anthropocentric and geopolitically bounded nation.

The island of Kahoʻolawe is a significant starting place for a comparative essay on Kanaka Maoli and Maʻohi postcolonial literatures of the environment.[1] Conventional histories reduce Kahoʻolawe and Moruroa to two tiny, isolated, uninhabitable desert island target zones. However, as Kanaka Maoli moʻolelo (oral histories) suggest, Kahoʻolawe and the islands of Te Ao Maʻohi are neither tiny nor isolated. Tongan scholar Epeli Hauʻofa notes that the limiting "smallness" that Western cultures often associate with Pacific Islands "is a state of mind" ("Our Sea" 91) that imprisons Oceania within false land/sea borders and ignores the ocean environment and the rich cultural history it has sustained for thousands of years. Hauʻofa states that careful attention to Oceanic oral traditions and cosmologies reveals that Oceanic peoples "did not conceive of their world in such microscopic proportions" (90). Kahoʻolawe is an example of this. Though Western assumptions have reduced Kahoʻolawe to a small strip of dry land stranded in the ocean, the island's original place name, Kanaloa, identifies it as a wahi pana (sacred place) by associating it with the great, creative force of the Kanaka Maoli god of the ocean (Kanaloa) (McGregor 255). In Te Ao Maʻohi, Kanaloa is known as Taʻaroa, and in Aotearoa/New Zealand, he is Tangaroa; Kanaloa thus attests to shared Polynesian histories of transoceanic voyaging, and to spiritual and genealogical connections that endure between Oceanic peoples despite their alleged isolation. At the top of Kahoʻolawe's central point, Moaʻulaiki, one can see why Kahoʻolawe is home to the traditional training school for Kanaka Maoli navigators; among the many navigating elements (winds, stars, waves, etc.) that the view from the navigator's chair at Moaʻulaiki reveals, one of the most significant is the channel of Kealaikahiki (the Pathway to Tahiti), an important navigational start and end point for Hawaiians voyaging to and from Te Ao Ma'ohi (McGregor 257–58). By reconnecting distant Kanaka Maoli and Ma'ohi kin and affirming their shared voyaging traditions, Kaho'olawe is a testament to what Hau'ofa calls Oceania's "sea of islands" ("Our Sea" 91).

Kaho'olawe and Moruroa have proven to be powerful, creative forces in their own right. Kobena Mercer's idea that one is only conscious of identity when its assumed foundations are shaken informs my analysis of the great impact of Kaho'olawe and Moruroa, two land and sea places that served as cores of indigenous identity. Kanaka Maoli and Ma'ohi perceived the bombardments of these islands as simultaneously targeting their cultural identities and their territories. Land/sea places are sites of life processes (birth, placenta and body burial, and ancestral return) that mark specific Kanaka Maoli and Ma'ohi genealogies, and that provide knowledge linked to these experiences. Kanaka Maoli scholar Manulani Aluli Meyer explains:

> Indigenous people are all about place. Land/*aina*, defined as "that which feeds," is the everything to our sense of love, joy, and nourishment. *This is not a metaphor* . . . You came from a place. You grew in a place and you had a relationship with that place. *This is an epistemological idea* . . . Land/ocean shapes my thinking, my way of being, and my priorities of what is of value. (219)

Meyer's affirmation that place nourishes and shapes her knowledge and her existence as an indigenous woman further illustrates why place is foundational to Kanaka Maoli and Ma'ohi identities. As places, Kaho'olawe and Moruroa engage indigenous epistemologies that can be thought of as forms of "ecological thinking" (Code 24): modes of thinking and being that privilege subjective continuity, cooperation, and connection between time, places, species, and peoples (24). Thus, the struggles for Kaho'olawe and Moruroa catalyzed the late twentieth-century indigenous cultural, national, and regional sovereignty movements of Hawai'i and Te Ao Ma'ohi.

The critical conjuncture of postcolonial ecologies—a theoretical approach that recognizes indigenous discourses of place and ecology (like aloha 'āina and ao) as central to self-determined postcolonial narratives—provides a basis for my argument that the Kanaka Maoli and Ma'ohi activists and authors I discuss here coarticulate indigenous bodies and island places, advocating the fundamental, interrelated, and equal rights of both human and nonhuman ecological communities. Nine PKO activists demonstrated their commitment to aloha 'āina when they literally put themselves in the line of military fire during five unauthorized island landings on Kaho'olawe between 1976 and 1977; these landings called widespread attention to the bombings and showed that there were Hawaiians willing to risk their lives for the 'āina. In 1995, Ma'ohi rioted in Papeete and burned parts of the Faa'a airport to show their dissatisfaction with the resumption of the French nuclear regime and the culturally imperialist métropolitain (urban/French) administration that accompanied it.[2] Indigenous writers launched an interventionist countercanon of mixed-genre newsletters, testimonies, and novels that contested U.S. and French canonical views of Polynesian bodies and landscapes as part of a Pacific "noble savage" paradise. In designating Pacific Islands as virgin, romanticized nature, Euro-American cultural canons define them as "passive, as non-agent and non-subject," (Plumwood, *Feminism* 4) and thus as "*terra nullius*, a resource empty of its own purposes or meanings, and hence available to be annexed for the purposes of those supposedly identified with reason or intellect" (ibid). Euro-American texts have long represented tropical islands as sparsely populated, as beyond civilization, and as feminized—and thus, receptive—spaces. This discourse has justified U.S. and French practices of what Teresia Teaiwa terms ("Militarism"): the interdependence of neocolonial military and tourist economies. Kanaka Maoli scholar Haunani-Kay Trask links corporate tourism in Hawai'i to continuing U.S. military interests, stating that "fictional Hawai'i . . . demands a dark, sin-free Native for instant gratification between imperialist wars" (137). The Kanaka Maoli and Ma'ohi countercanon that narratives featured in this essay help craft is critical to subverting U.S. and French neocolonial attempts to justify military and tourist complexes as guarantors of "national security."

The indigenous authors I discuss turn to place-based epistemologies such as aloha 'āina and the idea of a more widely integrative Ma'ohi ao as alternate, anticolonial conceptions of national security. Reading these epistemologies as anticolonial demands an acknowledgment of their precolonial and precapitalist origins, and an understanding of their ability to adapt around colonialism rather than simply expire. For example, aloha 'āina has a long history of integration in Kanaka Maoli governing structures. Kanaka Maoli scholar Noenoe Silva's analysis of the 1890s Hawaiian language newspaper entitled *Ke Aloha 'Āina* highlights the centrality of aloha 'āina as both a governing principle and a method of anticolonial resistance in Queen Lili'uokalani's pre-annexation monarchy and lāhui of Hawai'i (Silva). By naming their newsletter *Aloha 'Āina*, the PKO expressed their goals of perpetuating an active ethic of "love for the land and the people of the land" and of honoring the Kanaka Maoli legacy of self-determined cultural, political, and ecological mobilization evident in reading the nineteenth-century Hawaiian language newspaper *Ke Aloha 'Āina*. Aloha 'Āina and Te Ao Maohi are thus both rooted and routed (Clifford *Routes*) epistemological concepts that put indigenous cultures in a strategic position; they recognize the importance of continuity between past and present traditions while being flexible enough to adapt to a changing, new world.

The concepts of aloha 'āina and ao encourage cooperation between Kanaka Maoli and Ma'ohi cultures and ecologies, providing security for the Kanaka Maoli lāhui and for Te Ao Ma'ohi. In constantly thinking about human and nonhuman subjectivities together and in a nonhierarchical relationship, Kanaka Maoli and Ma'ohi literatures innovatively bridge postcolonial and ecocritical thinking, moving beyond divisive limitations present in some theories of deep ecology and social ecology (Plumwood, *Feminism*), and propose conscious actions that respect and perpetuate indigenous cultural growth and concepts of environmental stewardship.

We are all threatened by intensifying ecological and humanitarian crises, though some human and nonhuman communities have been subject to more prolonged and profound devastation from these crises than others. In the closing words of their landmark essay "Green Postcolonialism," Graham Huggan and Helen Tiffin acknowledge our shared burdens by proposing one "truism" of "green postcolonialism" (10), a hopeful framework for those who acknowledge the interconnectedness of the social and the environmental. They write that there is "no social justice without environmental justice; and without social justice—for *all* ecological beings—no justice at all" (ibid). Val Plumwood warns that during such intense crises "time taken for the development of theory seems a luxury indeed" (*Feminism* 6), but still proceeds to flesh out a theory of "critical ecological feminism" (1) that works to "understand the development and the defects in the western story of reason and nature" (6). Plumwood does so not out of some cynical academic indulgence, but with the practical intent of "changing the master story" (190) by turning to "other" narratives—finely tuned bodies of knowledge that have long been ignored in dominant attempts to impose a monolithic capitalist culture—that recover the master story's glaring insufficiencies. Place-specific postcolonial ecological literatures are key to the process of releasing the world from the chokehold of standardizing complexes responsible for so many of the intertwined ecological and humanitarian crises we face today. Turning to Kanaka Maoli and Ma'ohi narratives that equally prioritize the integrity of their peoples and each agent of their land/sea places, this essay builds on the work of Huggan and Tiffin, Plumwood, and other academic, artistic, and activist efforts to reconfigure the dominant master story through a myriad constellation of narratives, each built around the irreplaceable, symbiotic elements of a particular place's cultural, spiritual, and ecological histories.

ALOHA 'ĀINA AND AO AS "POSTCOLONIAL ECOLOGIES"

During early revisions of this essay, I ran into Maori poet and scholar Robert Sullivan. When I mentioned my participation in a volume entitled *Postcolonial Ecologies*, he initially expressed concern that the concept sounded problematic. As we further discussed the framework, he remarked that he supposed such a theory made sense from a nonindigenous perspective. Our exchange made me realize how presumptuous and alienating Western research and its theoretical traditions can be for many indigenous peoples, and why Maori scholar Linda Tuhiwai Smith claims that research "is probably one of the dirtiest words in the indigenous world's vocabulary" (1). The problem seems based in the assumption that cultures and ecologies could be divided and thought separately, a mode of thinking Sullivan ties to typical "nonindigenous" (metropolitan Western) intellectual discourses of "nature and culture." Ma'ohi traditional knowledge, for example, would find this split very uncomfortable; reo maohi (Tahitian) did not have a word separating human culture from "nature" prior to the word "natura," a neologism introduced by the British (Saura 131). Sullivan's concerns made me wonder if postcolonial ecologies might also seem like a forced and artificial construct for other indigenous groups.

Indigenous concerns about research affirm both the limits and necessities of a theory of "postcolonial ecologies" within current Western academic institutions—structures that have undeniable influence over the futures of both indigenous and nonindigenous peoples. Western discourse's dominant treatment of "the human/nature relation as a dualism" (Plumwood, *Feminism* 2) has produced deep ecology and social ecology, polarized efforts that reify the dualism in attempting to rectify it. For example, deep ecology stresses a universal connection of beings that denies all difference, reiterating a penetrative "master consciousness" that does not respect the boundaries of individual subjectivities, thus subsuming and subordinating them altogether (Plumwood, *Feminism* 178). As a product of so-called reason, the human/nature dualism attempts to justify ugly and persistent acts of environmental racism: the choice by powerful actors to impose dangerous and unhealthy activities on places and peoples deemed expendable precisely because these actors reason them away to the realm of the "nonhuman," and thus exploitable. The reliance of environmental racism on Western intellectual notions of a human/nature split and the calculated targeting of marginal (often rural, of color, poor, or indigenous) communities urges new, responsible Western theoretical approaches such as postcolonial ecologies that, although problematic in their construction, acknowledge Western epistemological history's undeniable tendencies to divide human and natural, to exclude some people from the "human" category, and to conveniently use this dualism to colonize or exploit selected peoples and places.

Because my current profession is predominantly informed by Western epistemologies and intellectual traditions, and because I am not Ma'ohi or Kanaka Maoli, postcolonial ecology provides me with a respectful angle from which to interpret Ma'ohi and Kanaka Maoli literary coarticulations of the indigenous body and place during the environmentally racist acts of French nuclearization and U.S. bombing "tests." Both Sullivan's comments and Meyer's work urge me to consider my position, purpose, responsibilities, and choices in writing this essay and in promoting a theory/practice of "postcolonial ecologies": "How will you respond to the 'exotic other'? Will you see the role of its vitality in your own capacity to see and hear? How will it inform your *own* ideas of research, knowing, and being of service to a worldwide awakening? Be open. Be ready. We have work to do" (Meyer 218). While I have no known genealogical connections to Oceania and realize my responsibility to avoid speaking for indigenous voices in my analysis, I share Meyer's goals of enacting a "worldwide awakening" that restores a comprehensive ecological integrity of all places and peoples.[3] This integrity relies heavily on us all opening ourselves—as Meyer encourages—to new ways of knowing and being. Postcolonial ecologies, as a form of ecological thinking, is a "revisioned mode of engagement with knowledge, subjectivity, politics, ethics, science, citizenship, and agency that pervades and reconfigures theory and practice" (Code 5). As a work in ecological thinking, this essay attempts to foreground Kanaka Maoli and Ma'ohi knowledges, subjectivities, ethics, and agency through a close analysis of each place's literary and activist articulations, as well as through the broader indigenous Oceanic regional concepts that contextualize them. It is my duty to use this essay and its framework of postcolonial ecology—in all its discursive limitations—as a conversational space with indigenous Oceanic ways of knowing.

Teresia Teaiwa states that "what articulations demands is a rethinking of difference through connection" ("Militarism" 34). Thus, to better understand why Kanaka Maoli and Ma'ohi narratives of aloha 'āina and ao can be thought of as postcolonial ecological articulations or practices of ecological thinking, it is necessary to discuss the structures of colonization that these indigenous epistemologies can help dismantle. The U.S. and French nuclear/military regimes on Kaho'olawe and Moruroa directed psychological, material, and political layers of violence toward each island and its indigenous peoples. The indigenous languages of 'ōlelo hawai'i (Hawaiian) and reo maohi (Tahitian) were made illegal by the U.S. and French governments in 1896 and 1963, respectively, making way for English and French linguistic and cultural dominance. Each date connects to U.S. and French military legacies and military/nuclear weapons testing regimes in their respective territories. Kaho'olawe was seized in 1941 as a weapons testing site in the name of U.S. national security immediately after Japan's attack on the U.S. naval base in O'ahu's Pearl Harbor; the U.S. military had acquired Pearl Harbor in 1887. Similarly, France's subsequent 1960 and 1962 installations of the Faa'a international airport and the Centre d'Expérimentation du Pacifique (CEP)—both parts of an infrastructure required for the logistics of their nuclear testing—directly preceded France's administrative ban on reo maohi (1963). In addition to helping the United States and France accomplish their geopolitical goals, the U.S. and French bans on 'ōlelo hawai'i and reo maohi were critical to assimilative colonial projects, branding indigenous culture as unacceptable while promoting their own American and French cultures as the social norm. Martinican scholar Frantz Fanon's statement that "to speak a language is to assume a world and a culture"/("Parler une langue, c'est assumer un monde, une culture") (*Peau* 30), is pertinent here.[4] Banning 'ōlelo hawai'i and reo maohi in everyday public life aimed to encourage Kanaka Maoli to distance themselves from living by indigenous ethics such as aloha 'āina, and threatened to dispossess Ma'ohi from their own ao (Ma'ohi world/universe/present life).

The United States' and France's organized displacements of 'ōlelo hawai'i and reo maohi were accompanied by the targeting of indigenous islanders with an amnesia-inducing attitude that belittled islanders and their islands as "too small, too poor, and too isolated to develop any meaningful degree of autonomy" (Hau'ofa, "Our Sea" 89). As Hau'ofa states, this belittlement, "if internalized too long, and transmitted across generations, could lead to moral paralysis and hence to apathy" (90). The mental colonization implicit in U.S. and French regimes aimed to alienate Kanaka Maoli and Ma'ohi from Oceanic epistemologies that envisioned islands as part of a vast, layered, and interconnected oceanic "world" that was "anything but tiny," reducing it to a forlorn set of "islands in a far sea" in an effort to erode the empowering "sea of islands" (91) concept inherent to Oceanic cosmologies. Euro-American views of islands as part of a sparsely populated, insignificant and asocial ocean "space" provided a convenient rationale for the U.S. and France to legitimize their testing programs. As Huggan and Tiffin point out:

> The very definition of "humanity," indeed, depended—and still depends—on the presence of the *non*-human, the uncivilized, the savage, the animal. . . . Western justification for colonization proceeded from this basis, and, as Val Plumwood has argued, understood non-European territories and the peoples that inhabited them as "space": places "unused or empty areas of rational deficit" ("Green" 6).

Huggan and Tiffin, expanding on the work of Derrida and Plumwood, analyze the Western colonial processes of categorizing select peoples, species, and places as nonhuman, female, other, irrational, and thus exploitable. The United States' and France's claims that Kaho'olawe and Moruroa were barren or uninhabited served as their excuses to abuse them. One 1991 U.S. military testimony claimed that Kaho'olawe permitted "our citizen soldiers to use her beaches to train" (A. Lloyd quoted in Aiu 104), signifying Kaho'olawe as a void female space to be filled by male, human subjects on behalf of the United States. This reveals the boundary line of "obdurate species" (and race and gender) (Huggan and Tiffin, "Green" 6) that rationalized the United States' fifty-year tests. Similarly, the French military's assignment of female code names such as "Brigitte" and "Hortensia" to the islands comprising Moruroa suggests France's vision of the atoll as a series of barren, female striking zones at the disposal of French nuclear violence.[5] That the names are also European suggests France's desire to erase records of any indigenous language, history, or presence, and to induce the paralyzing colonial amnesia that Hau'ofa warns about.

THE PIKO AND PŪFENUA: FORTIFYING INDIGENOUS PLACE CLAIMS

The risky actions of Kanaka Maoli and Ma'ohi activists putting their bodies on the line for Kaho'olawe and Moruroa in 1976–77 and in 1995 represent a level of commitment and care usually reserved for one's own family. The Polynesian tradition of burying a newborn baby's umbilical cord and placenta ("piko" for Kanaka Maoli, and "pūfenua" for Ma'ohi) in her ancestral territory after birth reaffirms the baby's familial ties to her lineage and to that particular place.[6] The burial inscribes the child as part of that place's genealogy, and acts as a valid record for identifying ancestral lands. Both Kanaka Maoli and Ma'ohi communities express their familial bonds with the land through their languages and oral histories; Kanaka Maoli mo'olelo of Hāloa trace the first Maoli person to the kalo plant (Handy, Handy, and Pukui 64), and the word "fenua" in the reo ma'ohi concept of pūfenua also means land (Saura 37). In addition to these cultural nuances that reiterate strong beliefs positing the land and body as family members, the Polynesian notion of family is expansive and not limited to immediate genetic links. For example, many Hawaiians think of 'ohana as "large extended-family networks" (McGregor 15) that are multigenerational, and that can include relatives from marriage and adoption, in addition to blood relatives (G. Kanahele 320). In that sense, if we consider the Hawaiian concept of 'ohana, the land is a family member and thus participates within the set of values that traditional epistemologies help guide the 'ohana to live by: "generosity, reciprocity, kōkua (social services, help, aid, support), laulima (labor, cooperation, joint action, working together), industry, loyalty, and giving" (G. Kanahele 393). We can interpret both Kanaka Maoli and Ma'ohi actions to protect the rights of the land and its people as motivated by the loyalty, support, labor, and love that many Polynesians feel are necessary in a healthy family.

'Ohana and aloha 'āina, two concepts that center around loyalty and love, should not be dismissed as essentialist or romanticized. The English word "love" has a tendency to be associated with the emotional, and thus, is too often easily written off as naïve, weak, and not to be taken seriously (Fromm; hooks). However, it is important to remember that loyalty and love—particularly when moving beyond feeling and into focused action for one's family—both require genuine willpower and labor. Laulima, the Kanaka Maoli concept of labor that Native epistemologies consider a necessary value for a successful 'ohana, is also a critical value that the PKO demonstrates in its actions, because it implies the dedication, toil, tenacity, and heart necessary for taking care of one's 'ohana and 'āina. In order to love and serve the 'āina and those whom it nourishes, somebody has to serve as a flesh-and-blood buffer between the land and anyone who seeks to harm it, and somebody has to be willing to put in the strenuous and gritty labor of working the land and tending to it. These are two priorities that the PKO demonstrated early on through occupying

Kahoʻolawe to disrupt the Navy's harmful bombings. Once the PKO convinced the United States to commit to a cease-fire and reclaimed its legal rights to access and care for Kahoʻolawe, the PKO began its monthly huakaʻi (landing/access). During these huakaʻi, members volunteer their time and energy to help restore the island's watershed and vegetation, helping it recover from years of harmful munitions and livestock erosion, and thus helping Kahoʻolawe thrive as a "cultural kīpuka" (oasis), a community "from which Native Hawaiian culture can be regenerated and revitalized" (McGregor 8). Protecting and cultivating Kahoʻolawe and its human family members takes hard work, discipline, determination, and sacrifice, and more than twenty years after the cease-fire (of 1990), the PKO continues its laulima to heal the ʻāina and replenish it.[7]

Kumu hula (hula master) and kupuna (elder) Pualani Kanahele's 1992 mele (chant/poetic song), "He Koʻihonua no Kanaloa, he Moku" ("A History for Kanaloa, an Island"), recognizes the fruits of this continuing laulima, proclaiming the wahi pana of Kanaloa/Kahoʻolawe as the sacred core of Kanaka Maoli culture, and the foundation for reinstating sovereignty. Toward the end, her mele states:

> The day for sovereignty is at hand
> The day to return the island
> The day to return the ancestral influence
> It is at the Mua Haʻi Kūpuna where it is born
> To be established in the navel of the islands
> A steadfast land for the Hawaiians. (P. Kanahele 109)[8]

The title of this mele "A History *for Kanaloa*, an Island" (my emphasis added) implies that, as with most forms of Kanaka Maoli moʻolelo, mele are often based around a specific place. Christina Bacchilega notes:

> In most, if not all moʻolelo, "place" situates events, heroes, tellers and listeners, memories and emotions in ways that connect the creation and transformation of landmarks with familial or genealogical relations. Indeed, animated, specific, and emotionally charged localization is the backbone (not the descriptive ornamentation) of Native Hawaiian narrative traditions. Furthermore, place continues to be at the heart of twentieth- and twenty-first century mele (poetic song) and hula compositions. (8)

It is worth noting that Kanahele's mele first establishes Kahoʻolawe as a wahi pana through tracing the island's own genealogical connections to its divine predecessors, then proceeds to connect it to present-day Kanaka Maoli. The mele thus contextualizes Kahoʻolawe in a continuum of supernatural, natural, and human histories.

This mele speaks of Kanaloa/Kahoʻolawe directly in terms of human anatomy and life processes; it also illustrates why the body is such a convincing cultural and political force when it is coarticulated with land issues. Kanahele's framing of Kanaloa as both a body with a piko (translated as "navel") and as the piko of the Hawaiian island group itself recognizes it as a life form, and more particularly, as one that inherently connects all Hawaiians back to their collective islands through "the return of ancestral sovereignty" (P. Kanahele 109). In addition to "umbilical cord" and "navel," Hawaiian kaona (hidden messages/multiple meanings) extend piko to mean "blood relative." Associating Kanaloa with the piko—as umbilical cord, navel, and blood relative—implies that Kanaloa connects to the other Hawaiian Islands and to the Hawaiian people in a direct familial relationship. Therefore, as Bacchilega's discussion of mo'olelo also helps assert, Kanahele's personification of Kanaloa in mele form is thus more than a poetic gesture or "descriptive ornamentation"—it intentionally reaffirms the genealogical relationships of Hawaiians to Kaho'olawe/Kanaloa, and fortifies Kanaka Maoli sovereignty claims.

In her 1991 novel, *L'île des reves écrasés/The island of crushed dreams*, Chantal Spitz turns to the figure of the pūfenua and integrates Ma'ohi chant and prayer to narrate the shared subjectivities of the Ma'ohi body and place in indigenous terms. Part of the novel tells the troubled love story of a Ma'ohi man, Terii, and his lover Laura Lebrun, a French métropolitaine (urban/French) woman who comes to work in the region as a technician at the Centre d'Expérimentation du Pacifique (CEP). In a chapter called "The Tearing"/("La Déchirure") Spitz describes how Terii's love affair with Laura plagues him with inescapable feelings of guilt:

> Throughout all these years, he refused to know what was happening on the motu (small sand island), wanting to ignore that the program was being carried through day after day, pushing back to the deepest part of his memory the image of missiles erupting in the stomach of his Land, of their Stomach, forever linked to the image of the woman that he loves. (*L'île* 169)[9]

Terii's feelings of complicity with the violent assault of nuclear weapons on his Ma'ohi world is clear here. The thought that Laura, a woman with whom he shares an intimate connection, is instrumental in the tearing apart of his native land—a being with whom he shares his own stomach, the very core of his identity—is too painful for him to confront. Perhaps even more excruciating to him is his paralytic acceptance of the ongoing military aggression rupturing his identity and his islands by "erupting" in their common stomach. Both his relationship with Laura and his own amnesia become nuclear missiles that rip out his pūfenua—and thus his identity—from the motu in which it was buried.

The third-person prose passage follows with Terii's own exasperated, desperate voice praying to "God of the sky/heaven"/("Dieu du ciel") (*L'île* 170), a divinity whose religious categorization Spitz deliberately confounds. Terii reconnects himself to the Ma'ohi world that nuclear testing has dispossessed him from through the following verses:

> All these burned lands
> All these raped seas

> All these scorned men
> All these crushed women
> All these fragmented children. (Spitz, *L'île* 171)[10]

Here, as in the rest of the prayer, there is no "I"/("je"). For once, Terii steps outside the boundaries of human dialogue and tries to communicate with other agents in the larger Ma'ohi universe. In each of these oral verses, Terii acknowledges the distinct subjectivities of that ao, and that each suffers from the collective destruction of nuclear testing. In leaving his subjectivity out of the prayer, he forces himself to reconsider his experience through those of scorched earth and raped sea, scorned man, shattered woman, and fragmented child. As a moment of spiritual awakening, the prayer marks Terii's first steps toward reengaging Te Ao Ma'ohi.

KANAKA MAOLI AND MA'OHI (NON)/HUMAN SUBJECTIVITIES

Silva's example of Kanaka Maoli strategically adapting their lāhui to be "a nation in a form familiar to Europe and the United States" (9) so that foreign leaders would not mistake Hawaii's sovereignty is useful for understanding Spitz and the PKO's genre choice. Although Spitz and the PKO borrow Western genres—the novel and newsletter, respectively—to communicate self-determination to broad audiences, their use of verse and visual forms within these genres, along with their attention to (non)/human subjectivities, engages Oceanic narrative modes.

A comic in the *Aloha 'Āina* 1989–90 Makahiki edition by S. Fetta poignantly honors the land's voice and subjectivity, recognizes its creative and destructive capacities, and acknowledges it as a teacher (PKO 2). Like many of the features in the PKO's newsletter, the comic and its accompanying article does not specifically address Kaho'olawe but, rather, calls attention to circumstances where militouristic structures violate sovereign indigenous land and people throughout the archipelago. The comic deals with the island of Hawai'i. As Maui resident Mary Groode explains in the article, twelve proposed geothermal plants for Puna, Hawai'i, were "part of the state's plan to create electricity for O'ahu" (PKO 2). Since O'ahu accounts for most of the tourist population, which outnumbers state residents six to one (Trask 138–40), O'ahu tourists are the primary consumers of Hawai'i's energy supply. The plants would impact archaeological sites, put nearby residents in danger, threaten Wao Kele o Puna's unique rainforest, and desecrate the island's creative deity, Pele (PKO 2). But rather than privilege a bounded gender ideology that promotes a "conjunction of passivity with non-violence and the feminine" (Shiva, *Staying Alive* 52) and thus victimizes Hawai'i or Pele, the comic suggests that Pele is aware and watching what goes on around her, and can explode with massive force at a moment's notice. By addressing Hawai'i/Pele's subjectivity, the cartoon recovers "the feminine principle" (Shiva, *Staying Alive* 53), by "seeing nature as a live organism" (ibid) and by "seeing woman as productive and active" (ibid). With the heading, "Famous last words of . . . a geothermal driller," Fetta's cartoon also includes a small stick figure standing on top of the reclining, mountainous Pele saying, "Hey! Trust me! What could go wrong?!" (PKO 2). The stick figure's statement appears ignorant next to Pele, who, although seemingly "passive" in her dormant volcanism, rests with one eye open, as if to warn those who seek to exploit her through intrusive geothermal drilling of her imminent activity. Since the action of drilling has a phallic connotation, Fetta's cartoon can also be read also as a cautionary tale that subversively recovers the feminine principle in men as well, and, by doing so, urges "action and activity to create life-enhancing, not life-reducing and life-threatening societies" (Shiva, *Staying Alive* 53).[11]

Ma'ohi writer Rai Chaze (formerly published under the names Michou Chaze and Rai a Mai) focuses on (non)/human subjectivities in her 1990 text, *Vai: La rivière au ciel sans nuages/Vai: River in a Cloudless Sky*. The editorial preface warns that *Vai* should be categorized neither as novel nor short story collection, but thought of as a fragmentary "book of memories" (Chaze 4). Chaze's complication of Western generic boundaries leaves her space to assemble the mosaic of narrative modes and (non)/human subjectivities that contribute to her own experiences and memories. In "Césure," her cast of Ma'ohi characters includes a female narrator, a young, still green coconut, and the earth; indigenous beings do not reside in tangible human bodies here, but live the same experiences as nonhuman ecological beings and elements, putting them in notable contrast with France's anthropocentric world of "intelligent men"/("hommes intelligents") (Chaze 68). Chaze's writing acknowledges the disconnect between French and Ma'ohi worldviews, foregrounding France's inability to recognize Ma'ohi ways of knowing/being, and demanding French and Ma'ohi accountability for this newly created epistemological void.

In "Césure," a female narrator retraces her memory of the ecological, physical, and psychological chain reactions set off by one of the French military's nuclear tests on a small island. The narrator's account begins with her drawing a coconut tree that she describes as "all silly and green"/("tout bête, tout vert")(67) in the foreboding encroachment of a premature nightfall, which she likens to "an enormous weapon without end"/("une arme énorme sans fin") (67). The apocalyptic tone of nuclear testing enters early and casts a disturbing shadow over the island's innocent nightscape of resting coconut trees and tiare flowers, and the calm flow of ocean waves over coral reef. As the title "Césure"—which carries connotations of a physical cut or verbal hyphenation—indicates, the island's environmental rhythms will be brusquely interrupted by foreign military violence, identified as, "the light of the intelligent men"/("la lumière des hommes intelligents") (Chaze 68), and as a floating mushroom followed by an abrupt "Boum!" (ibid) that signifies the clear arrival of the nuclear bomb. What ensues is a vivid description of the physical and emotional trauma that the narrator experiences from the island's perspective, and the slow aging and "gray"/("gris") (Chaze 69) decay of a once vibrant and healthy environment in the bombing fallout.

When the bomb arrives, the Ma'ohi subject's emotions clearly mirror those that the earth feels. She writes, "And the ground trembled. I clung to the wall covering the reef. And the earth continued to tremble. I trembled with her from fear, from cold, from terror, from anxiety, and from within myself. Boum! The coconut tree all silly and green, folded over" (68).[12] Both narrator and earth "tremble" here, bending over and bracing for their lives. Human and nonhuman share the same immense, encompassing psychological trauma specific to the nuclear test. In creating this deeply impressionable image, Chaze imbues island place with the same living, breathing, cognitive, and emotional qualities of a human subject, giving both her Ma'ohi narrator and the elements of the place around her a clear voice and a strong identity.

TE AO MA'OHI AND ALOHA 'ĀINA: TOWARD INDIGENOUS MODES OF "NATIONAL" SECURITY

Chaze ends "Césure" with a sharp criticism of those Ma'ohi who accept—in dumbfounded awe and with no resistance—France's grandiose nuclear proposals. The opening image of the coconut that her narrator draws returns, and she states, "the coconut tree still silly, still green, wants to see the aurora"/("Le cocotier encore bête, encore vert, veut voire l'aurore") (70). This implies that the naïve tree, despite having doubled over under the force of nuclear bombs, still desires to witness the grand spectacle of French national defense technologies. The coconut tree can be read as a symbol for those Ma'ohi people who flocked unquestioningly toward a system of French capitalist job "security" by accepting posts as CEP personnel or as administrative workers in the capital of Papeete during testing. In their 1997 published collection of former Ma'ohi CEP workers' testimonies, Pieter de Vries and Han Seur summarize similar sentiments expressed by the workers: "In the beginning many Polynesians thought they were part of a larger enterprise, and looked at the atmospheric tests with awe" (15). Chaze describes shortsighted Ma'ohi giving up sacred, culturally significant places that are "abandoned by men who are ashamed, ashamed of what, they don't know"/("délaissés par les hommes honteux, honteux de quoi, ils ne le savent") (67). Her word choice suggests that it is ludicrous to swap thousands of years of cultural knowledge, ecological sustainability, and sovereign history in exchange for a false and colonizing sense of French national security.

Chaze's "Césure" shares Hau'ofa's attitude that "smallness is a state of mind" (Hau'ofa, "Our Sea" 91) and that the concept of smallness is new and foreign to Oceania, and contradicts the "epic proportions" embraced by Oceania's "*kakai mei tahi* . . . 'people from the sea'" (ibid). Chaze and Hau'ofa urge a move away from such degrading Eurocentric and continental philosophies that encourage Pacific Islanders to replace indigenous systems of self-sufficiency with the unsustainable practices of neocolonial dependency that U.S. and French militourism perpetuates. Hau'ofa suggests that the main goal behind neocolonialism is to "make people believe that they have no choice but to depend" (89). As the following, blatantly militouristic statement by the French agency Pacific Promotion Tahiti, suggests, militourism emphasizes Islander reliance on larger national models:

> The nuclear test center assured comfortable public and private revenues for this territory until 1991 . . . a near unanimity is taking shape in French Polynesia over the fact that tourism constitutes the only hope for her (French Polynesia's) residents to preserve a standard of living comparable to the one they've known for the last quarter century. (Bresson 1)[13]

This passage associates French nuclearization with stability and wealth, and posits tourism as the sole replacement for the declining nuclear economy. As the "petrol of French Polynesia"/("le pétrole de la Polynésie Française") (Bresson 1), tourism is deemed the new saving grace for French Polynesia, a solution that will maintain the supposed economic security that nuclear testing put in place. But as Teresia Teaiwa notes, "While military forces and tourism provide employment and social mobility for many of these islanders, they also drain or pollute natural resources and endanger historical sites" ("Militarism" 22). Teaiwa's statement demonstrates how a militourist model inevitably fails to provide economic and national security for Oceania.

Teaiwa's comments here on militourism illustrate the timeliness of postcolonial ecologies such as aloha 'āina and ao in Hawai'i and French Polynesia, two states that she notes "are still negotiating colonial relationships" (22). These epistemologies are the foundations for the empowering indigenous national models of lāhui and Te Ao Ma'ohi for a reason: they foresee security for their unbounded island worlds in balanced, coalitional, and anticolonial relationships between peoples, life forms, and places.

In his January 1977 personal statement, "Reasons for Fourth Occupation of Kaho'olawe," PKO activist George Helm articulates the applicability of aloha 'āina as a nonviolent, constructive indigenous "national defense" plan. Helm was mysteriously lost at sea during the PKO's final attempt at an unauthorized landing on Kaho'olawe, just two months after stating the following:

> The truth is, there is man and there is environment. One does not supercede the other. The breath in man is the breath of Papa (the earth). Man is merely the caretaker of the land that maintains his life and nourishes his soul. Therefore, 'aina is sacred. The church of life is not in a building, it is the open sky, the surrounding ocean, the beautiful soil. My duty is to protect Mother Earth, who gives me life. And to give thanks with humility as well as ask forgiveness for the arrogance and insensitivity of man. . . . What is national defense when what is being destroyed is

the very thing the military is entrusted to defend, the sacred land of (Hawai'i) America? . . . This continued disregard of our seriousness, this refusal to give credibility to the Hawaiian culture based on Aloha 'Aina, forces me to protest. (Helm quoted in Morales 55)

This statement asks all those who question Helm's right to occupy the island to reconsider their doubts, and instead, to acknowledge his occupation as a responsibility that he feels he must fulfill as a Hawaiian who recognizes his reliance on the 'āina as the backbone of his life and his lāhui. His interrogation of the term "national defense" asks all U.S. citizens to reconsider what they are defending and how they do so, claiming that it is both counterintuitive and imprudent to desecrate national lands, such as Kaho'olawe, which the U.S. claims as its own, through military violence that is masked as "national defense." His simultaneous acknowledgment of Hawai'i as sacred, culturally sovereign land that is also official U.S. territory reminds Hawaiians—indigenous people entitled to cultural sovereignty in addition to the same rights as nonindigenous U.S. citizens—and other U.S. citizens of their collective civil duties to defend their nation(s) by enacting the stewardship principles of aloha 'āina. Helm suggests that stopping the bombing of Kaho'olawe is the first step in allowing the island to again sustain Hawaiian bodies, spirits, and culture, all integral elements of a Hawaiian "national security" model. The PKO's work to restore Kaho'olawe's once life-giving watersheds and honor its sacredness shares in the same sense of reciprocal commitment implicit in Shiva's affirmation that "Nothing is more secure than being able to sit in our organic farm and watch the pollinators flourish or the ladybirds come back to the wheat plants."[14] Helm thus speaks and acts as an equal partner of the 'āina, insisting that his human body should not exist in hierarchical superiority to the 'āina's body.

The final words of Helm's statement attest to the need for indigenous ways of knowing to be taken seriously by the state. Helm sees the legitimate advantages of aloha 'āina—an ethic that treats human and nonhuman bodies with mutual respect—for the overall well-being of Hawai'i. Similarly, Chaze's 1990 piece, "Généalogie," proposes the lessons of place as the basis for young Ma'ohi needing the security of a reconnection with their empowering Ma'ohi universe. The story describes a young girl searching for her genealogy, a resource that will protect her once she has found it. She turns to buildings and the pages of French literature, but comes up empty-handed. When she finally follows her intuition, she finds her genealogy in the branches of a tree: "On the tree that nothing can uproot, not north wind, not cyclone, not progress, not nuclear bombs, not the army, not laws, not the tidal wave, not death. . . . On the tree you have found your ancestors. On the tree, your tupuna (ancestors) watch over you" (Chaze 13).[15] The base of a fruit tree on ancestral land, as Bruno Saura mentions, is often the place that Ma'ohi families chose to bury the pūfenua of each newborn baby (36). Thus, by returning to the burial place of her pūfenua, the girl in Chaze's story also reconnects with her birth, her mother, and the long line of those who gave her life. There, her tupuna continue to animate the tree, helping it grow into the sky and anchoring her genealogy to the land in sturdy roots. Chaze makes it clear that if her will returns her to that tree, nothing—including nuclear tests, new laws, modernization, or the military—can deprive the girl of the Ma'ohi identity that her tupuna have secured for her at its base: her pū fenua. As the heart or "core of land" (Saura 37), this connective tissue provides the very basis for her culture, for her identity, and for her entire Ma'ohi ao.

The Kanaka Maoli and Ma'ohi agents in this essay distrust neocolonialist forces like militourism, and instead seek security for their indigenous nations in postcolonial ecologies such as aloha 'āina and Te Ao Ma'ohi that honor their cultural histories and help guide them through dynamic futures. Their works contribute to an emerging indigenous Oceanic countercanon that itself is aloha 'āina in action; it perpetuates indigenous cultural growth and reintroduces engaged modes of Oceanic ecological thinking.

NOTES

1. This comparative essay builds on ideas from the first two chapters of my forthcoming dissertation, tentatively titled, "Indigenous Articulations of Identity and Island Place in Kanaka Maoli and Ma'ohi Literature of the Nuclear Free and Independent Pacific Era."

2. Ma'ohi writer Titaua Peu's memoir provides a vivid account of Ma'ohi female subjectivity around the time of the riots. See Titaua Peu, *Mutismes* (Papeete: Editions Haere Po, 2002).

3. I owe the 'āina, and what has emerged from my lived experiences with aloha 'āina, for the very existence of this essay. Mahalo nui loa to Davianna Pomaika'i McGregor and to the PKO for inviting me to participate in the August 2008 huaka'i (access) of Kaho'olawe. The 'Ohana's openness and knowledge lend important insights to my own representation of their history and to the endurance of their movement. I give my most profound thanks to Kaho'olawe/Kanaloa for blessing us with a safe and fulfilling huaka'i, and for motivating me to work on this essay. My thanks also to the editors of this collection for their diligence and helpful scrutiny.

4. For texts originally written in French, all translations here, unless otherwise noted, are my own.

5. See French military map of Moruroa Atoll (Firth 99).

6. The English interpretations of Hawaiian words that I use here are courtesy of http://www.wehewehe.org, and those of reo maohi words come from http://www.farevanaa.pf/dictionnaire.php. Both sites are useful online dictionary resources for their respective languages.

7. The PKO is a grassroots community organization whose work is complemented by the Kaho'olawe Island Reserve Commission (KIRC). Both organizations share the vision of "kua'āina stewardship" that will restore the island for future cultural purposes (McGregor 281) but differ in their levels of funding and representation. The State of Hawai'i Department of Land and Natural Resources states that "the Legislature created . . . (KIRC) to manage the Kaho'olawe Island Reserve while it is held in trust for a future Native Hawaiian sovereign entity. The KIRC uses the federal funds designated for State responsibilities in the restoration effort. The KIRC

is administratively attached to the Department of Land and Natural Resources" (see http://hawaii.gov/dlnr/boards/kahoolawe-island-reserve-commission).

8. Ua hōʻea ka lā hoʻihoʻi ea / Ka lā hoʻihoʻi moku/ Ka lā hoʻihoʻi mana kupuna / Aia i ka Mua Haʻi Kūpuna e hānau nei / E kanaloa ʻia ana i ka piko o ka pae ʻāina / He ʻāina kūpaʻa no nā Hawaiʻi (P. Kanahele 109).

9. Tout au long de ces années, il a refusé de savoir ce qui se passait au motu, voulant ignorer que le programme se réalisait jour après jour, repoussant au plus profond de sa mémoire l'image des missiles fusant du ventre de sa Terre, de leur Ventre, à jamais liée à l'image de la femme qu'il aime (Spitz, *L'île* 169).

10. Toutes ces terres brûlées / Toutes ces mers violées / Tous ces hommes méprisés / Toutes ces femmes écrasées / Tous ces enfants éclatés (Spitz, *L'île* 171).

11. S. Fetta, "Famous Last Words . . . of a Geothermal Driller" in Protect Kahoʻolawe Fund, *Aloha ʻĀina* (Kaunakakai, Hawaiʻi: newsletter published by Protect Kahoʻolawe Fund, 1989–90). Image below:

12. Et le sol a tremblé. Je me suis accrochée au mur qui couvre le récif. Et la terre a continué de trembler. J'ai tremblé avec elle de peur, de froid, d'effroi, d'émoi et de moi. Boum! Le cocotier tout bête, tout vert, s'est plié (68).

13. Le centre d'essais nucléaires assurait des revenues publiques et privées confortables à ce territoire jusqu'en 1991. . . . Une quasi unanimité se dessine en Polynésie Française sur le fait que le tourisme constitue le seul espoir pour ses habitants de conserver un niveau de vie comparable avec ce qu'ils ont connu depuis un quart de siècle (Bresson 1).

14. See Vandana Shiva, April 7, 2005, Lecture at Michigan State University (http://www.mediamouse.org/video/2005/04/vandana-shiva-lecture-at-msu.php).

15. Sur l'arbre que rien ne peut déraciner, ni le to'erau, ni le cyclone, ni le progrès, ni le nucléaire, ni l'armée, ni les lois, ni le raz-de-marée, ni la mort. . . . Sur l'arbre, tu as trouvé tes tupuna. Sur l'arbre, tes tupunas te regardent (13).

13

"Out of This Great Tragedy Will Come a World Class Tourism Destination":

Disaster, Ecology, and Post-Tsunami Tourism Development in Sri Lanka

Anthony Carrigan

In *The Shock Doctrine: The Rise of Disaster Capitalism* (2007), Naomi Klein argues that the global spread of neoliberal, "free market" ideology is based on the systematic exploitation of crisis-shocked populations, primarily for the purpose of land acquisition (8). According to Klein, agents of this process—consisting largely of Western governments, multinational corporations, and the governing elite of economically underprivileged states—pursue a doctrine of profit maximization by exploiting vulnerabilities caused by disasters. This helps them gain footholds in new markets, regardless of local sustainability concerns.[1] One example Klein gives is Sri Lanka. This was among the states most severely affected by the South Asian tsunami of December 2004, which "destroyed three-quarters of [the island's] coastline, killed about 35,000 people ... and displaced a further two and a half million" (Salgado 1). The tsunami engendered a nationwide process of reconstruction whose main aims included caring for the injured, rehousing the dispossessed, and restoring the many coastal environments that were flattened by the wave. However, as Klein shows, long-term social and environmental sustainability has been compromised in the recovery process partly as a result of disaster capitalist intervention. This is changing the balance of beach ecologies in favor of economic investors, primarily tourism developers.

One of the most alarming aspects of post-tsunami tourism development in coastal Sri Lanka is the way in which the complexity of human–environmental relations has literally been swept away as homeless communities are displaced to make space for hotels. Alison Rice points out in a 2005 report published by U.K.-based NGO Tourism Concern:

> Ten months after the disaster, thousands of survivors are still . . . in temporary camps. Many of them are being refused permission to return home. Governments and big businesses have plans for the beaches—and the plans don't include the people who used to live and work there. Tourism is the new occupying force. (5)

This created a situation in which, for many doubly disenfranchised locals, reconstruction came to be viewed as "the second tsunami" (16). The link between disaster, tourism development, and recovery in Sri Lanka holds urgent implications regarding how economically underprivileged states negotiate experiences of crisis. This is not least because, as one researcher from the NGO Focus on the Global South wryly observes, post-tsunami development in Sri Lanka has some distinctly neocolonial dimensions: "We used to have vulgar colonialism. Now we have sophisticated colonialism, and they call it 'reconstruction'" (Shalmali Guttal quoted in Klein "The Rise of Disaster Capitalism"). The related power dynamics not only augur long-term dispossession and even annihilation of coastal communities, but also threaten to exacerbate the kind of ecological destruction that has seen numerous signature species—from elephants to sea turtles—become increasingly endangered, along with their natural environments. Whereas Klein's book reveals the ideological workings of disaster capitalism from an antiglobalization perspective, my approach here acknowledges tourism's economic importance to contemporary Sri Lanka. Focusing on Chandani Lokugé's *Turtle Nest* (2003), a novel set on Sri Lanka's southwest coastline immediately before the tsunami, I consider how postcolonial aesthetics can provoke reading strategies that critique dominant modes of disaster capitalism from an ethical standpoint. I explore specifically how Lokugé's representation of child sex tourism and animal abuse exposes connections between post-tsunami sustainability concerns and the state's ongoing reckonings with "compound disaster" (Quarantelli 263).[2] Questioning the logic of capitalist tourism developments from moral and economic standpoints, I outline some of the ways in which ecologically attentive forms of postcolonial critique can help orient broader questions of social and environmental justice (Huggan and Tiffin "Green Postcolonialism" 9). This contributes to two linked aspects of postcolonial ecology explored in this volume: the need to posit different temporal narratives from the linear models associated with Western colonialism and disaster capitalism, and the importance of addressing how culturally localized representations of the nonhuman world can help in confronting human–environmental inequities.

TOURISM AND DISASTER

Despite their seeming opposition, there are many ties between tourism and disaster. One example of this can be seen in relation to war, which is relevant to the protracted crisis of civil conflict in Sri Lanka. Elizabeth Diller and Ricardo Scofidio state that:

> Tourism and war appear to be polar extremes of cultural activity—the paradigm of international accord at one end and discord at the other. The two practices, however, often intersect: tourism of war, war on tourism, tourism as war, war targeting tourism, tourism under war, war as tourism. (quoted in Sönmez "Tourism, Terrorism, and Political Instability" 436)

Such interdependencies highlight the extent to which crisis situations not only contribute to warping more conventional tourism forms but can also become constitutive of them. Links between tourism and disaster expose an array of negative concerns, ranging from the voyeuristic consumption of catastrophes to disenfranchisement of impoverished communities. Yet they also provide perspectives on how more equitable futures might be attained through improving economic and cultural resources in afflicted regions, and asserting sustainable human–environmental relations. Building on the positives that emerge from analyzing such connections is especially important in Sri Lanka because it represents a preeminent site of tourism under the sign of disaster.

The forms of disaster currently affecting the island include almost three decades of civil war. Stoked by conflicting sovereignty claims between the majority Sinhalese and minority Tamil populations, this claimed over 75,000 lives between 1983 and 2009 ("Sri Lanka [LTTE]"). The state is also undergoing a long-term economic crisis, partly precipitated by entry into structural adjustment programs with the World Bank and IMF in the late 1970s, and further exacerbated by civil conflict.[3] Structural adjustment involved the promise of favorable loans for impoverished countries on the condition that they adopted neoliberal economic policies. While these programs initially stimulated economic growth, they also led to rising unemployment, cutbacks in education and public services, decreased provisions for the poor, and currency devaluation. As economic globalization decreased opportunities for communities to pursue traditional livelihoods, rising numbers of people have become dependent on the tourist trade, despite its relative volatility.[4] Rather than creating stable opportunities for locals to take control of tourism enterprises, the circumscriptions associated with ongoing experiences of war and systemic poverty have permitted niches for such morally disturbing activities as war tourism, disaster tourism, and sex tourism. The last has come to represent a further variety of disaster due to the large numbers of children involved. As tourism ethnographer Malcolm Crick observes, Sri Lanka is often viewed in the "international press" at least "as a 'haven for perverts'" (199), with thousands of children now engaging in sexual exchanges on a daily basis. The situation has been enhanced by the government's long-standing refusal to recognize this phenomenon, partly as resulting sanctions would undermine one of the few steady (if reprehensible) sources of tourist currency.[5]

The devastating toll taken by the tsunami was partly due to the ways in which Sri Lankan beach communities were already rendered vulnerable by these ongoing experiences of compound crisis. Such complex interweaving of disasters highlights the importance of considering them as long-term processes that pervade numerous aspects of social life. These observations also hold resonance from an ecological perspective. Ecocritics customarily interpret one of their primary tasks as being "to evaluate texts in terms of their coherence and usefulness as responses to *environmental crisis*" (Kerridge 5–6; my emphasis; see also L. Buell *The Future of Environmental Criticism*). Yet environmental crises are never wholly *natural* but socially and historically conditioned. Moreover, they have disproportionately negative effects on the poorest members of communities in states that are still grappling with the legacies of Western colonialism. This makes them of central concern to postcolonial researchers whose field, like ecocriticism, has emerged over the last three decades in the context of global problems such as climate change, accelerating economic disparities, resource scarcity, and U.S.-led wars. According to Pablo Mukherjee, such conditions have strongly influenced efforts by both postcolonialists and ecocritics to "understand, interpret and offer resolutions for this vast range of crises" (147). The following analysis of Lokugé's novel, *Turtle Nest*, highlights the importance of bringing the conceptual resources of both postcolonialism and ecocriticism together, as its portrayal of unsustainable social and environmental practices is entwined with wider experiences of state crisis. It shows how the text's gendered depictions of abuse—linked strongly with sex tourism—create bridging points between human and nonhuman sustainability concerns, refuting any "unproblematized division between people (on the postcolonial side) and nature (on the ecocritical one)" (Cilano and DeLoughrey 75). This has important ramifications both for how postcolonial Sri Lankan beach ecology is conceptualized and for the management of post-tsunami tourism development in the context of ongoing crisis.

SEX, TOURISM, AND HUMAN–ENVIRONMENTAL INTERRELATIONS

Turtle Nest presents a damning indictment of globalization's effects on local cultures and environments in Sri Lanka. It centers on a beachside fishing village whose trade has been undermined by deepwater Japanese trawlers (Lokugé 88) and curtailed by war, forcing the community to become dependent on a nefarious tourist trade. In the novel's present (roughly contemporaneous with its publication), gangs of local beach boys represent the dominant community faction. Highly disempowered, they survive by manipulating tourism-driven economies of consumption, selling their bodies and exploiting those of the titular sea turtles that breed on the coast, making them spectacles for interested tourists. Lokugé has stated that she meant *Turtle Nest* to portray the "tragic . . . long-term effects of . . . exploitation of children and what it has led to, like the beach boys who grow up in that culture" (quoted in Athique 352). However, such "tragic . . . effects" are by no means confined to the beach boys; they also directly pertain to the novel's two female protagonists: eighteen-year-old Aruni, a migrant returnee in search of stories about her family, and her estranged mother, Mala, who is presumed dead. Switching between Aruni's present-day perspective and Mala's formative years, the novel parallels both their fates with turtle abuse. Using this highly endangered and conspicuously feminized species as a point of human–environmental mediation, the narrative foregrounds how the beach boys assert masculinity in a disaster-afflicted milieu by manipulating ecologically interwoven power dynamics.

Mala is introduced into the text as a little girl who watches as "a baby turtle dropped off [sic] the sky with the rain" and lies squirming on the beach (Lokugé 17). She attempts to nurse the injured creature, but after leaving it to find food she returns to see that "the beach boys had got it. She screamed as they threw it like a ball from one to the other over her head . . . until her mother [Asilin] came out to scold her" (17–18). Asilin's consolation is pragmatically gloomy: "Child, that miserable creature is better dead . . . or else when it grows as big as a house, it will be cut up for raw meat" (18). As the connection between abused turtles and sexually exploited children becomes increasingly manifest, Asilin's commentary raises the question of whether people who experience severely circumscribed or impoverished lives, ending in intense pain and tragedy, are also "better off dead." When not at the mercy of the beach boys, the turtles are mostly seen as meat for eagles—a point that is emphasized in the novel's epigraph. This describes how newly hatched turtles are caught as they scramble "blindly" toward the sea. The sexualized manner in which each captured "infant splays its limbs" in midair "and reaches trustingly into the shell-crushing talons" (v) establishes a metaphorical link with the sex tourism industry, portrayed as involving equally predatory patterns.[6]

Like turtles caught perennially in eagles' talons, impoverished families such as Mala's appear to have little choice but to submit to fates that are beyond their control. This invites a correlative reading that extends to the level of national allegory as the turtles' *dismemberment* bears strong political parallels. Meaning both "to divide and partition (a country or empire)" (*OED* 2) and "to cut off, separate, sever, from the main body: chiefly in reference to a country or region" (*OED* 3.b), the dismemberment of baby turtles is redolent of ethnic divisions within Sri Lanka (a divided or "dismembered" state). The analogy situates the postcolonial island as subject to larger forces, manipulated by global power interests and scarred by internal brutalities. However, I want to suggest that this not only reflects more localized involvement in sex tourism but that the novel's representation of beach ecology shows how these processes of cultural and natural dismemberment are mutually enfolded. This involves seeing the text's human–animal metaphors as operating in ways that situate animals less as "symbols" that protect "culture from awareness of its hostility towards real animals" (Scholtmeijer 295) than as participants in a complex ecological system for which human actions are as much a metaphor as vice versa.

From an anthropocentric perspective, the novel represents the local sex industry's power dynamics as largely harmful, restricting the possibility of attaining sustainable subject positions. For instance, although Mala is skilled at negotiating the economic benefits of sex tourism, her ostracization from the beach community is precipitated by the birth of her "half-white-half-brown baby" (107) who is fathered by a tourist and swiftly sold to a beggar colony (115). Meanwhile, her younger brother Priya's initiation into the beach's abusive economies occurs when, as an eleven-year-old, he is effectively raped by an elderly male tourist. In the present time of the novel, Priya is a forlorn and virtually silent figure, traumatized by years of sexual exploitation and the destruction of his family. Both siblings are shown to instigate sexual encounters in ways that add weight to Julia O'Connell Davidson's refutation of NGO campaigns that target child sex tourism's eradication on the basis that "there can be no 'voluntary' child prostitution . . . because children are incapable of making a free and informed choice to enter prostitution" (30). Seeing Mala and Priya *only* as involuntary "victims" of forces beyond their control denies levels of individual agency, categorically objectifies "the child," and fails to address child sex tourism's root causes or its intersections, in the case of Sri Lanka, with other forms of disaster. However, the overwhelmingly negative outcomes of these characters' involvement in the industry could still appear to symbolize little more than self-expedited exploitation, as they embrace the "talons" of those same economic forces that position Sri Lanka as a baby turtle at the whim of eagles' appetites.

One way in which this point is simultaneously underwritten and undermined relates to how agency among the beach community is differentiated, allowing for degrees of counterexploitation that upset direct correlations between locals and turtles, tourists and eagles. The human–turtle conjunction blurs gendered distinctions of sexual abuse on one hand because, while the beach boys are successful in manipulating the turtles, they are also almost unavoidably "apprenticed," as one character puts it, into a world of "drugs, prostitution, pimping and God knows what else" (88). These economies are part of what Chris Ryan and C. Michael Hall term the "cycle of abuse," fueled by the large numbers of "abused children [who] go on to act as pimps themselves" (127). On the other hand, the beach boys negotiate such disempowerment by establishing some control over the local sex industry. Constrained like Mala and Priya by economic factors, the boys assert agency from within the dominant predator–prey paradigm, pursuing sexual contact with visitors as they glance "surreptitiously at the hotel windows for a lonely tourist" (174) with "predatory eyes" (120). This movement between subject positions highlights the limitation of seeing the relationship between turtles and eagles as simply allegorical of cultural events.

Numerous sociological sex tourism studies suggest that, while it can involve extreme forms of exploitation, sex work provides a means to "create and pursue opportunities for survival, socioeconomic mobility, and migration" among socially and economically disempowered communities (Cabezas 122). Commenting specifically on male beach hustlers in Barbados, Joan Phillips states that "successful negotiations of gender" between the men and female tourists often allow them "to achieve status, material goods, and independence" (199). By contrast, Lokugé's text shows how the negative effects of compound disaster in Sri Lanka, which are arguably amplified by insular topography, contribute to making the beach "a theatre for violence . . . as well as for commerce and escape" (Hulme 59). The various brutalities this engenders raise the question of whether the debilitating effects of tourism's intersection with multiple disasters *foreclose* the possibility of sustainable practices from emerging in this environment. And, if so, what should be made of the human–environmental relations portrayed in the text?

One key problem that accompanies this speaks to an increasing truism within both postcolonial ecocriticism and those branches of tourism studies that deal with postcolonial concerns. It is generally agreed that for less exploitative futures to emerge, local community participation and opinion must be central to sustainable development strategies (Huggan and Tiffin "Green Postcolonialism" 5; Dodman and Dodman 102). However, the beach boys in the text are at times problematically *dehumanized*. In the present time of the novel, the Australian tourist Paul (Aruni's eventual lover) disapproves of the way Aruni allows the beach boys to "cluster around" (51) her, accepting their presents and "behaving with such familiarity with these boys who seemed so feral to him" (51–52). Paul's description of the beach boys as "feral" betrays a tendency to objectify and animalize them, which bears obvious debts to colonialist descriptions of natives as brutal, savage, uncultivated animals (*OED* 2.a). Yet it also registers another sense of the term given by *The Oxford English Dictionary*: "of deadly nature" (*OED* 1.a). The latent threat Paul recognizes in the boys' behavior is fundamental to their gendered negotiations of the beach's power dynamics, working to compromise and even endanger viable female subject positions. This is reinforced as the beach boys gain entrance into a culturally localized and environmentally conditioned mode of masculinity that depends partly on dominance over women who are objectified in similar ways to the turtles.

This is not to suggest a simplistic parallel between women and feminized constructions of nature. For instance, in the opening pages the narrator describes how, even though "she knows nothing of this place," Aruni "wants to zoom in at once, to the very core of it" (3). The invasive pursuit of others' life stories, from which she feels the locals are "barring her" even though "it is *her* story . . . more than anyone else's" (3; original emphasis), aligns her with the dismembering eagles. One beach resident observes how "she wants to gut them out . . . without a care for the blood and pain that would spill" (5). Yet he also sees her as "[d]esolate and confused," with "the eyes of [a] broken-winged bird" (3). This ambivalent subject position, located in the shifting space between exploiter and victim, underpins her vulnerability to exploitation as she is ultimately attacked by the beach boys.

Refusing to heed warnings that "you must be a bit careful on this beach" (25), as it "is not always safe" (50), Aruni follows the beach boys when they tell her the turtles are laying eggs on the sand. Despite noting that "there was hardly any moon," and recalling that "turtles by habit laid eggs on full-moon nights" (236), she allows herself to be hurried across the deserted beach toward the sea. Once isolated from the hotel, the beach boys "held her by the arms . . . clamped shut her mouth, stifling her screams" (238) and take turns raping her. In the process, Aruni is framed as a substitute for the turtles; the boys tell her that, unlike the absent creatures, she will "lay" (237). The narrator describes how "the wind flung her cloth out and away from her like violent flapping wings," as she "struggled for release" (237). Although it also recalls the predatory eagles, the term "flapping" establishes a direct connection with an earlier scene, in which Aruni takes Paul to see a "massive" turtle that has been "forced upside down" by the beach boys and is "flapping its short stumps against its inner sides" (128). While Aruni's environmentalist sympathies prompt her to persuade Paul to pay for its release, he considers the gesture futile as he "is quite sure they will not free the turtle. They will force it away to another hotel, and then when it is exhausted and starved, they'll dismember it for the meat" (129). This earlier scene suggests a disjuncture between Aruni's touristic sympathy for the turtle (an example of the charismatic megafauna around which Western environmentalist concerns often coalesce) and her failure to extend this to the beach boys' negotiations of poverty and exploitation. This becomes hazardous in the novel's denouement, which contrasts Aruni's burgeoning local ecological knowledge with her romanticized conception of her relationship with the boys. Aruni's understanding of natural cycles (the fact that turtles tend not to breed on moonless nights) is compromised by a misreading of human deceit that stems from an uneven appreciation of local culture and nature. Rather than seeing nature as a straightforward allegory of culture, this highlights the need to address how child sex tourism's destructively unsustainable energies affect all aspects of human–environmental relations simultaneously.

In one sense, the ending could be read as emblematizing negative cycles of exploitation in beach space, with turtles representing no more than profoundly negative mediations with the natural world, local culture turning "feral," and all ecological actors involved in a pseudo-Darwinian "survival of the fittest."[7] The brutal gang rape represents a consummation of this process, heightened by wider ongoing experiences of compound disaster. This bears out two points made by Dennis Altman in relation to poverty, masculinity, and civil conflict. Drawing on work by Graeme Simpson and Gerald Kraak, he notes that "many young men who feel powerless and marginalized in a world of rapid change will turn to violence, and rape 'becomes a way of symbolically reasserting their masculine identity'" (8). Altman also states that "under conditions of civil war," sex can become a "realm of torture . . . as shown by widespread rape in Rwanda, former Yugoslavia, or Sierra Leone" (7). Aruni's rape could therefore be seen as an assertion of the beach boys' own diminished autonomy, inflected by deeply uneven experiences of transactional sex and accentuated by the circumscriptions associated with living in a time of civil conflict. This is, however, never fully disentangled from self-consumptive subject positions, as the boys are also ambiguously aligned at points throughout the novel with the women and turtles they exploit. The rape is also allegorical of wider political events. As a minority outsider with a tenuous claim to indigeneity, Aruni's brutalization by the local gang reflects the violent tensions between supposedly nonnative Tamils and the Sinhalese majority. Her victimization is partly predicated on the way she is distinguished from the majority of tourists on account of her diasporic subject position, which also recalls the migratory patterns of sea turtles. The fact that masculine abuse is directed at women and feminized nature implies a fracturing of community that becomes defined by ecological violence rather than custodianship or care. Yet I want to suggest that the novel's narrative structure and generic manipulations problematize negative cycle interpretations of beach ecology in ways that offer productive perspectives on local sustainability. By exploring these, I will highlight how postcolonial aesthetics can help orientate post-tsunami tourism development in coastal Sri Lanka.

RECONFIGURING TRAGEDY: CLOSURE, COMMUNITY, AND ENVIRONMENT

Characterized by elegiac silences and ellipses that emerge from intertwined narratives of death, loss, exploitation, and disaster, *Turtle Nest* is distinguished generically by a strong tragic seam. This is particularly relevant to collective experience in Sri Lanka, given tragedy's link with catastrophe. Derived from the Greek term, meaning "sudden turn, conclusion," catastrophe can be used generally to refer to the "change or revolution which produces the conclusion" or denouement of a dramatic piece (*OED* 1), and more specifically to signify "a conclusion generally unhappy," "a disastrous end," or a "calamitous fate" (*OED* 2). However, the novel's lack of closure regarding the natural environment and the fates of the main characters unsettles the possibility of interpreting it directly in these terms. This is intriguing for conceptualizations of postcolonial ecology, as it speaks both to the operations of ecological time (continuous, cyclical rather than linear, apocalyptic) and to ongoing negotiations of globalization (especially in terms of cultural responses to economic cycles). It also aligns the novel with Frederick Buell's interpretation of changes in environmental representation in American literature since the 1970s, which he sees as having moved from offering "apocalyptic" visions of ecological futures to presenting a "postapocalyptic" view of time and environmental transformation. Rather than suggesting a postcatastrophe perspective on ecological change, the "post" in "postapocalyptic" refers to the previous aesthetic movement (environmental apocalypticism). For Buell, postapocalyptic representation presents daily life as being "closer to experiencing a very *slow* apocalypse" (105; original emphasis) and tends to reveal "no clear path out of crisis" (322). This reflects *Turtle Nest*'s negotiation of tragedy, which responds to ongoing experiences of compound disaster in Sri Lanka by "pull[ing] back the curtain on a portrait of deformation" (F. Buell 322) without offering solutions to the problems posed by unsustainable practices.

Despite the fact that tragedy is conspicuously protean, changing over time and adopting numerous culturally specific guises, its capacity for environmental representation has been significantly challenged, along with more predictably Eurocentric sentiments regarding its genesis and application.[8] The notion that tragedy bears fundamentally inimical relations to balanced or sustainable ecosystems is the central claim of one of ecocriticism's more quixotic founding works, Joseph Meeker's *The Comedy of Survival* (originally published in 1974).[9] Trained as an ecologist and a literary critic, Meeker claims that "literary tragedy and environmental exploitation in Western culture share many of the same philosophical presuppositions." He gives three points of evidence: "the assumption that nature exists for the benefit of humanity, the belief that human morality transcends natural limitations, and humanism's insistence upon the supreme importance of the individual personality" ([1997] 24). In *Turtle Nest*, Meeker's arguments come into conflict. On one hand, the novel appropriates tragic tropes such as trying to "accomplish the impossible" (Meeker [1980] 44), which applies, in different ways, to Mala's and Aruni's attempts to manipulate dominant social structures. On the other hand, it emerges in relation to non-Western cultural reference points and its tragic protagonists (particularly Mala and Aruni) are highly sensitive to the local environment's noninstrumental functions.

This tension highlights *Turtle Nest*'s ambiguous generic status as the novel consistently engages but ultimately deflects from tragic conventions. As discussed earlier, dismemberment—a key feature in tragic texts—features prominently throughout the narrative, connecting the physical dismemberment of turtles by humans and eagles, the severing of Mala and Priya's family, and the tragic dimensions of national division in relation to the war. Yet no actual human dismemberment is portrayed within beach space. This is conspicuous as Mala and Priya's parents are literally dismembered when they move *beyond* the island-within-an-island represented by beach space—pointedly killed in a "suicide bombing at Kochichikade" that left their bodies so mangled they could only be "identified ... by the silver cross still hanging from Asilin's neck" (Lokugé 117–18). Similarly, while death haunts the narrative, none of Lokugé's main characters actually die. Although Mala's death is implied, it occurs only after she leaves the beach for good and she even returns ethereally to Aruni during the rape scene, reversing the typical revenge tragedy formula of evoking ghosts in narrative openings. In the present time of the novel, Aruni's narrative also concludes by evading closure regarding the implications of her rape (especially in terms of legal and criminal issues), how it affects her future plans, and her relationship with Paul. Such generic subversions contribute to a denial of tragic catharsis. One possible interpretation of this is that, despite the severe forms of exploitation that occur within the novel's beach environment, straightforward classifications of these as tragic are destabilized by the wider context of ethnic conflict and bloodshed on the island. Given the genocide that characterizes Sri Lanka's recent history, considering tragedy in individualistic terms appears less meaningful than understanding it as *collective* experience. This generic reconfiguration positions individual tragedy—associated by Meeker with Western anthropocentrism—as inextricable from communal concerns and suggests that tragic endpoints are inappropriate to the ongoing experiences of crisis in Sri Lanka. Rather than seeing the beach just as a synecdoche of the state, this foregrounds how national and global concerns are imbricated in local narratives.

Turtle Nest also highlights how tragic closure is unsuitable for representing environmental issues. While the fate of the turtles—already endangered and subject to further extreme pressure and possible extinction—could be considered tragic, it must still be placed in the context of wider ecological processes in order to avoid romanticizing their condition. As Marian Scholtmeijer observes, animals "impress their reality upon narrative, not by the stability but by the instability of their presence. They refuse to be incorporated neatly into the cultural field" (8). Such "refusals" extend to attempts at interpolating animals and their natural habitats into generic templates without formally reworking these to account for such "unstable" subject positions. Lokugé's postcolonial revision of tragic conventions operates in a manner that helps negotiate the opposition Meeker constructs between tragedy and comedy in terms of their relationships with sustainable ecologies. He argues that "structures in nature ... resemble the patterns found in comedy. Productive and stable ecosystems are those which minimize destructive aggression, encourage maximum diversity, and seek to establish equilibrium among their participants—which is essentially what happens in literary comedy" ([1980] 41). Whereas Meeker sees tragedy and comedy as *metaphorically* emblematizing the contrast between anthropocentric and ecocentric worldviews, Lokugé's text uses the interplay between culture and nature to resituate tropes that might otherwise condemn beach ecology to viciously dystopian cycles of self-consumption. One compelling consequence of this refusal of tragic inevitability (associated with narrative closure and catharsis) is that it demands ethical judgment in relation to the unsustainable energies contained within beach space. Analyzing the transgressive yet environmentally attentive role Mala plays in relation to sex tourism highlights how her personal narrative's tragic outcome is conditioned by the negative actions of a community affected by experiences of compound disaster. Yet it also offers perspectives on how these might be negotiated in ways that curtail tragedy in similarly oppressive milieus.

As one of the novel's protagonists, Mala could be seen to fulfill generic expectations by bringing about her own downfall through her engagement in sexual economies that lead to her ostracization from the beach. However, given Meeker's identification of tragedy's epistemological dependence on "the assumption that nature exists for the benefit of humanity" ([1997] 24), it is intriguing that Mala is portrayed as environmentally sensitive and suffers abuse from members of the deteriorating fishing community, aligning her once more with animals in the text. Rather than constituting the kind of harmonious unit fetishized in paradisal island tourism marketing, the fishing village functions in the text's flashback scenes as a cauldron of interpersonal and gendered conflict. Whereas Aruni's contravention of identity boundaries partly underwrites her objectification by the beach boys in the present time of the novel, Mala is stigmatized by local community members due to her "bold and knowing" behavior toward both tourists and locals (Lokugé 89). As the narrator observes, "the village gossiped about Mala all the time. . . . They said everybody knew Mala was a free-for-all—a basketball that could be shoved from hand to hand" (90). This is further amplified by men who "stream[ed] . . . insults" at her and "flashed their torches at parts of her body" (98–99), and by neighbors who "slung buckets of excrement on the front door of [her] house" (100). Such smearing seems to be communally self-protective, a way of guarding against the morally destructive aspects of sex tourism involvement. However, this idea is compromised first when such codes appear not to apply to the beach boys and second when the community objectifies Mala in similar terms to abused animals.

The description of Mala as "a basketball" is metaphorically preempted by the way in which the beached turtle she tries to resuscitate as a small child is thrown by the beach boys "like a ball from one to the other" (17). Her desire to return captured beach fauna to their natural habitats is therefore connected to the sexual economies in which she participates. Worryingly, local community ethics seem to have become partly entwined with the more abusive economies of sex tourism. Not only in her characterization as a "basketball" but also through the illumination of "parts of her body," Mala becomes a site of commoditization, diminishing her subjectivity. The textual correlation between Mala and the animals she tries to protect implies that a reduction in environmental exploitation is at some level bound to the capacity of Mala (and others like her) to assert autonomy over the beach's dehumanizing economies of consumption, sexual and otherwise. Lokugé's novel does not align women with feminized nature in ways that, as Val Plumwood observes from an ecofeminist position, exclude women and the natural environment "from the world of culture"

(*Feminism* 8). Instead, it suggests that positive integration of characters with local environmental knowledge is essential to the mutual sustainability of culture and ecology. Articulating alternative subject positions for those who might otherwise become trapped in negative cycles of abuse would help counterpoint rather than conspire with sex tourism's commoditizing operations. It could also attenuate the dominance of oppressive constructions of masculinity in disaster-afflicted environments.

At present, many of the strategies for eliminating child sex tourism involve either demonizing sex tourists and encouraging more responsible travelers (which tacitly casts local communities as helpless) or instigating attempts to "revive feelings of social responsibilities of the community, so that the community would be vigilant about those practicing commercial sex" (Amarasinghe xviii). This seems flawed as it conceives "social responsibilities" as a "lapsed," homogeneous category, while its emphasis on vigilance is not only patronizing but also sponsors the kind of stigmatization that Lokugé's novel suggests works against sustainability in the long term. By contrast, the text stresses the need for these considerations to be worked through in ways that confront external management impulses both to segregate social and environmental sustainability planning and to "eradicate" child sex tourism without (a) addressing the deep structures of inequality that provoke it or (b) giving voice to those actors (currently grappling with various forms of abuse, stigmatization, STIs, and difficulties raising children) whose insights might propel future strategy. This includes the muddy but critical admission that the specific disaster represented by child sex tourism is implicated in the wider social, economic, and ecological pressures that emerge from this localized environment's interaction with broader experiences of compound crisis. It is through reconsidering these processes together—and not by isolating and hierarchizing one form of disaster over another—that sustainability might begin to come into view. As I discussed earlier, the catastrophic effects of the 2004 tsunami on Sri Lankan coastlines created a situation in which such insights could help conceptualize more balanced social and environmental operations *in relation to* global tourism demands. I want now to conclude by examining how exploitative developments are threatening the emergence of more sustainable post-tsunami tourism futures on coastal land.

INTERVENTION AND POST-TSUNAMI CONCERNS

Arguing in the *Sydney Morning Herald* in January 2005 that the tsunami-ravaged regions of South Asia have been "neglected" by "'big-name' Australian writers" prior to the disaster, Susan Wyndham cites *Turtle Nest* as an example of lesser-known literature that is "starting to emerge from Asian immigrants to Australia and their children." She notes that the novel is "set on the stretch of beach washed away by the tsunami, and [Lokugé] was there with the turtle farmers last month. Her book is already a historical account 'of the peaceful times of one year before.'" Apart from the puzzling description of the novel's violent ecology as "peaceful," the suggestion that the tsunami's devastating effects render the novel "a historical account" of beach space is potentially troubling. The way in which disasters are contingent on long-term social processes suggests that the issues explored by the novel retain distinct urgency in relation to real-life recovery conditions. Understanding this requires a view of "history" that is not merely backward-looking but that works to unveil the striations of contemporary experience. Disasters are in this sense aligned with ecological rather than apocalyptic time frames; while their outcomes are often deeply tragic, their effects relate more closely to Lokugé's noncathartic representation of tragedy than to forms that privilege closure.[10]

This point is brought into sharp relief when considered alongside the Sri Lanka Tourist Board's post-tsunami assertion that "in a cruel twist of fate, nature has presented Sri Lanka with a unique opportunity, and out of this great tragedy will come a world class tourism destination" (quoted in Shanmugaratnam 2). Here, "nature" is presented as conveniently washing away social problems while presenting glorious new tourism opportunities—a "tragedy" with a convenient end-stop. As Nadarajah Shanmugaratnam recognizes, "the cruelty of the human disaster is explained away entirely as a work of nature"; the failures of human policy with respect to disaster preparation and management—especially in terms of the capacity "to act effectively and impartially"—are "blacked out"; and "nature" is "credited for offering an opportunity to transform the [Sri] Lankan coastal areas . . . as if nature has swept away the pre-existing socially embedded institutions . . . and left the beaches ready to be taken over by the 'hospitality industry'" (2). The way tourism capitalizes on a depoliticized concept of nature here recalls the environmental feminizations in *Turtle Nest* that displace human agency and structures of dominance. Conceptualizing the tsunami as a "great tragedy" in a less glib manner than the Sri Lanka Tourist Board requires consideration of how the event's tragic dimensions are embedded, as Lokugé's novel implies, in the actions of *people* and not just destructive nature.

Testimonies regarding post-tsunami tourism management suggest that the processes of community disenfranchisement Lokugé depicts are being exacerbated. Such displacement augurs not the "erasure" of undesirable elements from swanky new developments—the aim of "blank is beautiful" ideologies that reflect the colonial *terra nullius* principle (Klein *The Shock Doctrine* 3)—but increased instances of sex tourism and environmental abuse as communities fragment. These may be even less visible, even more unregulated than the practices portrayed in *Turtle Nest*, as local people become dispossessed of the limited foothold provided by tenancy of coastal land. Hence, Jeremy Seabrook observes the "savage irony that sex tourism should be one symptom of globalization, the 'integration' of the whole world into a single economy, when both the workers in the industry and the clients from abroad are themselves the products of disintegration of local communities" and "the dissolution of rootedness and belonging" (169–70).

There is, however, a tension between the emphasis I have placed on the ecological reconfiguration of tragedy as processual in *Turtle Nest* and the devastating, "out of the blue" change exacted by the tsunami. Certainly in hard-hit areas, where up to 98 percent of the dead were "small-boat fishing people" (Klein *The Shock Doctrine* 388), it is difficult to see natural disaster as part of a long-term process. Nevertheless, overly apocalyptic assertions of depopulation also play into the hands of disaster capitalists, augmenting linked procedures of tourism-related dispossession that, as Klein points out, were initiated two years *before* the wave struck (391). The "disaster" of reconstruction was grounded in plans to capitalize on the 2002 civil war ceasefire (signaling the temporary cessation of a different disaster), which demanded that "millions of people" sacrifice their homes and traditional livelihoods "to free the beaches for tourists and the land for resorts" (393). In this context, the degree to which the potentially disastrous medium- and long-term effects of the tsunami, both socially and environmentally, can be considered nonprocessual or "out of the blue" is distinctly limited.

One imperative for crisis alleviation that can be derived from *Turtle Nest*'s nuanced portrayal of these procedures regards the need for such insights to be presented as economically and ethically meaningful to tourism corporations and governments. This is all the more challenging as both stand to benefit, in the short term at least, from perpetuating a "divide and rule" tactic with respect to local community opinion and potential resistance, fostering conflict rather than consensus. Such strategies allow neoliberal rationale to drown objections to the exploitative aspects of "world class," "luxury tourism" development. Considering the problem of sustainability in disaster-stricken islands, Sevil Sönmez argues as follows:

> It is unrealistic to believe that islands suffering from ongoing political problems, poverty and the inevitable violent crime that it spawns, can develop strategies for sustainable tourist industries until their major problems are resolved. Ironically, moving towards sustainable development would solve much of the internal strife that riddles some islands. ("Sustaining Tourism in Islands under Sociopolitical Adversity" 165–66)

This double-bind underwrites the tendency to position impoverished communities and states as "helpless" in the face of conflict and disastrous experiences, and therefore subject to external management. Yet *Turtle Nest*'s depiction of tourism and compound disaster suggests another double-bind that works contrapuntally to unsettle doomful assessments of local community exploitation.

Although some villagers in *Turtle Nest*'s coastal community blame the war for the fact that "the rich tourists stopped coming over [. . .] [and]

the hotels are almost empty" (Lokugé 47), the novel's emphasis on how the profitability of beach tourism enterprises is implicated in the negative cycles of local ecologies suggests that such declines are only partly political. In this context, lack of local consultation—and attendant complicity with the objectification, stigmatization, and abuse of vulnerable people and animals—seems almost to render governments and tourism corporations "helpless" in preventing disruption to their enterprises, rather than local people. External intervention of this sort is shown to perpetuate the social and environmental imbalances that render tourism markets unpredictable, threatening long-term investment and industry diversification, which most developers consider economically desirable. Importantly, *Turtle Nest*'s own intervention into these processes projects the possibility of seeing the beach as a creative space from which new practices can emerge.

As Greg Dening has shown, while it is often threatening, traversing the beach can also bring productive change and renewal. The mediating function played by the titular turtles with respect to both humans and the natural environment recalls the fact that, even though such boundary crossing "is always dramatic," it carries with it the potential to "adjust" the "balance" of continually changing island ecologies (Dening 31–32). By subtly illuminating marginalized perspectives on future social and environmental sustainability with respect to tourism, Lokugé's text suggests that, just as the reproductive energies that underpin the beach's representation (and are emphasized by the novel's title) can be manipulated in disastrous ways, this ecology can also be a breeding ground for more positive ideas if sensitively approached. In this sense, one of the "undesirable" social phenomena that the corporate tourism industry's expropriating tactics attempt to "erase"—what its agents might term sex worker "infestation"—could ironically help solve some of the challenges posed by luxury resorts. If cycles of abuse can be effectively linked to perpetually declining cycles of profitability—and Lokugé's imaginative representation suggests a powerful correlation—the economic impetus behind further unsustainable tourism development might be threatened in ways that are redemptive from short-, medium-, and long-term perspectives simultaneously. This enhances the rationale for placing intensely marginalized actors (such as child sex workers) at the center of sustainability planning, emphasizing the significance of linking postcolonial ecocriticism to fiscal discourse. Rather than offering uncomplicated solutions, *Turtle Nest*'s representation of Sri Lankan beach ecology inspires reorientation of urgent debates, drawing attention to the power dynamics that must be negotiated in the process of increasing local consultation and developing more sustainable human–environmental relations. Without such debates informing actions, the potential for less destructive futures to emerge may be lost; the unregulated sex trade will continue to flourish; and Sri Lanka's coastal environments will be subject to further avoidable degradations.

NOTES

1. Although there is much debate over their definition, sustainable practices are generally seen as ecologically sensitive forms of development that maintain intergenerational equity, meeting present needs without compromising those of future populations (Sofield 5). For a fuller discussion of sustainability in the context of postcolonial tourism, see the introduction to Carrigan.

2. Enrico Quarantelli observes that "*complex emergencies* (or sometimes *compound disasters*)" might include "mixtures of civil strife, famines, genocidal activities, epidemics, and large-scale displacement and movement of refugees" (263; original emphasis). Although researchers remain divided on what precisely constitutes a disaster (Kreps 33), I use the term here to embrace both social crises and natural catastrophes, which are almost always interwoven.

3. The reverse could also be true as Bruce Kapferer observes how the "opening of the economy profoundly affected the social fabric of the island," contributing to "a sharp increase in ethnic strife" (37).

4. Arrival figures since 1983 have consistently fluctuated according to the latest bout of violence. For a summary of the links between recent hostilities and tourism, see Gunasekera and Momsen (90).

5. Although the phenomenon of child sex tourism was observed in several government reports before the outbreak of war, few measures were taken to combat the practice; indeed, "a move to adopt harsh measures to deal with the problem was stopped by the Minister of State himself in 1983 when he withdrew draft legislation because the tourism downturn caused by mounting civil unrest seemed to solve much of the difficulty" (Crick 60). This reasoning swiftly proved specious as the problem continued to escalate. Indeed, Crick states that "given the way in which the violence tended to divert other tourists elsewhere," the "very downturn may have led to the percentage of paedophile tourists going to the island greatly increasing over the past decade" (199).

6. The human–turtle link is provocative given Marian Scholtmeijer's comments regarding representations of animal victims in locations like the beach in *Turtle Nest*, which are "situated between the wilderness, with its defiance of human control, and the city, with its obsessive celebration of civilization." She argues that these are often sexually charged domains, as they invoke "that similarly troubled region of the human psyche, that sexual wilderness which human culture seeks most fervently to prune and transform" (180).

7. This phrase was originally coined by Herbert Spencer and was incorporated by Charles Darwin into the fifth edition of *On the Origin of Species* (published 1869) as cognate to "natural selection." I allude here to misapplications of the theory (as in social Darwinism) that assume that only the strongest or "fittest" *individuals* will prevail in the struggle for "survival," rather than the best-equipped *species*.

8. "Europe alone provided tragedy as we know it," asserts Clifford Leech, for instance (12). Although this statement was written decades ago, it continues to be reprinted in volumes such as the New Critical Idiom series' current introduction to literary tragedy.

9. Meeker's book has gone through three editions, each with a different subtitle indicating the ongoing revision of its central thesis. My examples are taken from the second and third editions.

10. The movement described here, between literary form and tragic events in reality, has also been addressed by Ato Quayson in his work on the execution of

Nigerian writer and activist Ken Saro-Wiwa (which itself resulted in part from Saro-Wiwa's opposition to the social and environmental damage caused in Nigeria by the Shell Oil Company; see Quayson chapter 3 and Young "'Dangerous and Wrong'"). For Quayson, literary paradigms like tragedy can "provide tools by which to analyze political actions at the dual levels of structure and agency," helping to "further our understanding of process, change, and contradiction" in relation to "postcolonial history" (58).

14

In Place

Tourism, Cosmopolitan Bioregionalism, and Zakes Mda's *The Heart of Redness*

Byron Caminero-Santangelo

In his highly acclaimed novel *The Heart of Redness*, South African author Zakes Mda depicts the struggles of a local, marginalized community to avert the threat of environmental apocalypse posed by a tourist development scheme. The scheme involves a casino resort to be built near the Xhosa seaside village of Qolorha in the Eastern Cape by "a big company that owns hotels throughout southern Africa" (66). From the perspective of those who support the scheme, it will bring "jobs, streetlights, and other forms of modernization to this village" (67). The novel suggests that this dream of modernization is a relatively worthless commodity being sold to enrich national elites at the expense of the local people and environment. The casino will bring few jobs for the local people, even as it takes away their access to land and resources. The novel focuses especially on the ways that this particular form of tourist-centered development will obliterate the environment: "a project of this magnitude cannot be built without cutting down the forest of indigenous trees, without disturbing the bird life, and without polluting the rivers, the sea, and its great lagoon" (119). The ultimate threat represented by the casino scheme is revealed when the developers come to talk to the people of the village. By the end of the "discussion," the two men are ignoring their audience and debating the virtues of building the casino and hotel—complete with an amusement park—versus those of making "a retirement village for millionaires" with "trees imported from England." They conclude, "We'll uproot a lot of these native shrubs and wild bushes and plant a beautiful English garden" (202–3).

Heart of Redness's conceptual grounding for resistance to such disastrous "development" processes is related to a form of imagining place popular in ecocriticism, bioregionalism, but it also transforms the concept by making it amenable to a "cosmopolitan" vision. As a result, Mda's novel is useful in the pursuit of two larger, emerging critical projects. The first is the effort to foreground and revise place—and especially bioregionalism—at the intersection of postcolonialism and ecocriticism. The second is to explore how African literature and environmental criticism might accommodate each other. In an early attempt to explore the relationship between African literature and ecocriticism, William Slaymaker asserted "that global ecocritical responses to what is happening to the earth have had an almost imperceptible African echo" (138) and called for both African writers and critics to embrace what he saw as a "global ecocritical movement" (140). Although he claimed that ecocriticism is global, the criteria he used to determine if a piece of writing is properly environmental came from a primarily Anglo-American ecocritical framework associated with the application of the sciences to literature and with deep ecology. Subsequent work has questioned this approach to the relationship between the two fields, and/or has examined how African texts and contexts might revise ecocritical concepts.[1] Yet, despite the recent explosion of critical work on the relationship between postcolonialism and ecocriticism,[2] there remain relatively few readings of African literary texts generated by ecocritical debates and concerns, and even fewer exploring how African literary studies might contribute to the project of revising ecocritical approaches. In its exploration of the relationship between bioregionalism and *The Heart of Redness*, this chapter aims to contribute to this small but important body of work.

As defined by one of the foremost environmental philosophers of place, Mitchell Thomashow, bioregionalism entails "a commitment to understand local ecology and human relationships" ("Toward" 125), as well as a sense of belonging based on such understanding. The bioregion itself is an ecopolitical unit integrating ecological and cultural relationships and determined by such factors as geography, ecosystem, indigenous culture, local knowledge, and environmental history. If capitalism in its various phases has made space out of place, stripping away prior signification (deterritorializing) and reshaping in order to facilitate control and exploitation, then the process of imagining or reimagining a "place" entailed by bioregionalism can be one means of countering threats of exploitation, environmental degradation, and disempowerment. This form of imaginative engagement encourages understanding of and commitment to one's place and community, as well as the places and communities of others, and it challenges the meanings imposed in the process of deterritorialization—for example, by countering commodification. In many ways, Mda's novel shares the conception and ethics of place offered by bioregionalism. For example, it encourages careful attention both to ecology and to human relationships as a means for care and stewardship of one's place, especially in respect to identifying and combating external threats.

Yet, needless to say, there are some potential pitfalls to bioregionalism. Perhaps the primary danger is what Rob Nixon, in his seminal article "Environmentalism and Postcolonialism," refers to as ecoparochialism, the threat that the focus inward toward a bioregion will result in occlusion of the ways that any region is established by relationships with other places and has permeable boundaries: "All too frequently, we are left with an environmental vision that remains inside a spiritualized and naturalized national frame" (236). As Nixon implies, bioregionalists can be overly confident in their ability to achieve representational closure. One example involves the very definition of the bioregion itself, which, as Lawrence Buell has pointed out, often elides the "malleable or problematic" nature of a bioregion's borders (*Future* 84). The potential lack of productive skepticism in bioregionalism can extend to its conception of environmental protection. Doug Aberley claims that the decentralization entailed by the bioregion enables "the achievement of cultural and ecological sustainability" (37). However, the principle of sustainability—"of more prudent, self-sufficient use of natural resources"—is no guarantee, since it "requires guesswork about what future generations will be like" and "runs contrary to the known fact that nature itself does not remain stable" (Buell *Future* 84). Finally, the notion of the "bioregion," like any bounded notion of place, can all too easily lend itself to xenophobia with its attendant nativism. For those concerned with processes of displacement resulting from the history of imperialism, this potential xenophobia can be especially disturbing.

The approach to place offered by *The Heart of Redness* is most closely approximated by Thomashow's concept of *cosmopolitan* bioregionalism, which significantly departs from more traditional versions of bioregionalism. According to Thomashow, cosmopolitan bioregionalism would recognize how a "local landscape" cannot be understood without reference to larger systems, as well as how the belief in hard boundaries "is the cause of much human suffering" ("Toward" 129). It would embrace the notion that borders are "permeable" and identities "pluralistic" and "multiple" (129). For the cosmopolitan bioregionalist, the bioregion is produced as much by "the instability and dislocation of ecological and cultural diasporas" as by indigenous nature and culture: "A bioregion is the stopping place for the migration of assorted flora and fauna, each of which makes its indelible imprint on the ecology and culture of the neighborhoods where they temporarily reside" (129). Ultimately, the kind of "bioregional sensibility" Thomashow seeks "requires multiple voices and interpretations," and is "necessarily open-ended and flexible" (130). Like Thomashow, Mda emphasizes the need for an approach that can account for shifting and multiple constructions of place and identity. In *The Heart of Redness*, representations of place are always unstable both because of change over time and because of a lack of unity at any one time; they need to be recognized as human constructions open to debate in order to be effective in protecting the local. Ultimately, Mda's novel can help develop a cosmopolitan bioregionalism not only by emphasizing the instability inherent in efforts to define a "local" identity but also by suggesting how such efforts will always be politically inflected.

Nixon calls for just this sort of revision of bioregionalism as part of the larger project of bringing together postcolonial writing and ecocriticism. An ecocritical ethics of place, especially as embodied in bioregionalism, could be very helpful for postcolonial critics theorizing the threats to local environments posed by imperial processes and the grounding for resistance. However, Nixon argues that mainstream American ecocriticism is all too often inflected with a focus on purity ("virgin wilderness and the preservation of 'uncorrupted' last great places" ["Environmentalism" 235]), with national (as opposed to cosmopolitan) frameworks, and with the suppression or subordination of history. American ecocriticism all too easily leads to "spatial amnesia" in which the histories of indigenous peoples and of the making of places in transnational and colonial contexts are suppressed (236). These aspects of American ecocriticism are at odds with most postcolonial writing and criticism, which is why, he claims, postcolonialists have remained suspicious. Ultimately what Nixon calls for is not simply the addition of a few postcolonial texts to an ecocritical canon, but the transformation of underlying ecocritical frameworks. A central part of this task, he argues, is to take up the "intellectual challenge" of drawing "on the strengths of bioregionalism without succumbing to ecoparochialism," a move which would "render ecocriticism more accommodating of what [he calls] a transnational ethics of place" (239). *The Heart of Redness* affords an ideal opportunity to explore both how "the strengths of bioregionalism" might be mobilized in efforts to resist imperial development *and* how the concept might be made amenable to "a transnational ethics of place."

Zakes Mda, a prolific playwright and novelist, is among the most acclaimed South African authors to emerge in the last twenty years. *The Heart of Redness*, the third of his novels, won numerous accolades, including the Hurston/Wright Legacy Award, the *Sunday Times* Fiction Prize, and the Commonwealth Writer's Prize for the Africa region. The novel switches between the story of postapartheid South Africa and an interconnected narrative depicting events preceding, during, and immediately after the Xhosa cattle killing in the 1850s. Mda's recounting of these events relies heavily on J. B. Peires's *The Dead Will Arise* (cited in the novel's dedication as its primary historical resource).[3] Since the eighteenth century, the amaXhosa had increasingly been dispossessed as the British expanded the size of the Cape Colony north and east. The colonial land grab was accompanied by the destruction of the amaXhosa's political and economic independence and the reshaping of their religious and cultural institutions. In addition, during the mid-1850s over half of the amaXhosa's cattle were wiped out by lung sickness caused by a pathogen introduced by imported cattle, and they endured a crop blight which ruined their maize. In the midst of this tragedy, the prophetess Nongqawuse claimed to hear the voices of the ancestors telling her that the people must kill all their cattle, destroy their grain, and refrain from agriculture to purge impurity from the land and enable the rising of the dead. The ancestors would bring with them clean animals and grain, and the English invaders would be swept away. The people became divided between believers of the prophecies and unbelievers, resulting in civil war. The results of the cattle killing were apocalyptic for the amaXhosa. Over 80,000 starved to death or were forced by starvation into the colonial labor market. The colonial governor, Sir George Grey, turned the tragedy to British advantage, taking hundreds of thousands of acres of Xhosa land for the use of white settlers.

The novel represents the cattle killing primarily through the story of a family conflict between two brothers, the amusingly named Twin and Twin-Twin. Initially, the two brothers are inseparable and fight against the British in the earlier border wars, but after Nongqawuse offers her prophecies, Twin becomes a leader among the believers while Twin-Twin joins the unbelievers. In the present, this family conflict continues. The unbelievers, headed by Twin-Twin's descendant Bhonco, claim that the believers led the people to destruction in the past by following the prophecies and are preventing "progress" in the present by rejecting the casino scheme. The believers, led by Twin's descendant Zim, argue that the unbelievers are responsible for the failure of Nongqawuse's prophecy and that they are encouraging another disaster by supporting the building of the casino. The conflict between the two groups appears to be between advocates of modernization and defenders of tradition, although the novel undoes any clear distinction between such terms.

Into this fray comes Camagu, a Xhosa man who has lived most of his life in the U.S., where he received his Ph.D. in communications and development studies and who returned to South Africa to help build a postapartheid nation. Unable to find a job, because he is not one of the "aristocrats of the revolution," he becomes disillusioned with the new dispensation. Although he has no family ties to Qolorha, when he travels to the village he becomes embroiled both in the conflict over the casino and in a love triangle involving the beautiful but cold Xoliswa Ximiya, daughter of Bhonco, and Qukezwa, the daughter of Zim. The principal of the local school, Xoliswa scorns all things "traditional" and espouses an extreme version of colonial modernity. Qukezwa works in the trading store owned by John Dalton, a man of English descent who helps lead the fight against the casino. She is one of the believers, but does not become a parody of belief. (In the novel, as in most comedy, to follow a "belief" dogmatically is to become a caricature.) Eventually, Camagu chooses Qukezwa, whom he marries, and espouses the fight against the casino. He comes up with a plan to thwart the casino through the designation of

Qolorha, the place of Nongqawuse's original prophecies, as a national heritage site and through the building of a backpacker hostel which enables sustainable development.

As this sketch suggests, *The Heart of Redness* upholds struggles to defend the "indigenous" and the "local"; yet, at the same time, it undermines rigid dichotomies between these categories and the "global" and the "modern." Anthony Vital and Rita Barnard have argued that Mda's novel offers an unresolved contradiction between romantic idealist notions of place, indigeneity, and the natural (on the one hand), and (on the other) a postmodern skepticism regarding these categories. Up to a point, these readings are inarguable. Alongside its rigorous epistemological skepticism, the novel certainly has moments when it seems to succumb to the lure of valorized, stable conceptions of "the traditional" and "the natural." Yet I would argue that *The Heart of Redness* not only persistently brings into question clearly bounded idealist categories, but also encourages critical distance from its own romantic lapses. Maintaining a skeptical posture, the novel suggests that any final representation of reality will be impossible: more narrative and dialogue will always be needed. The grounds offered for resistance and conservation constantly shift. The novel suggests that the local, the natural, and the indigenous must be seen as emerging and reemerging from specific, messy interrelationships with their supposed opposites. While *The Heart of Redness* very clearly represents the continued existence of local cultural and natural elements, it also notes how these have been transformed by "external" forces—colonialism, capitalism, the nation, and so forth. Thus, the local must be understood as a process or a set of processes.[4] Such a conception of place is closely related to cosmopolitan bioregionalism, which both encourages attempts to understand "local" places and suggests that these places can be grasped only by engaging with the messiness and resistance to categorical closure entailed by their relationships with more "global" forces.

The Heart of Redness undoes easy categorization of identity and belonging, "unsettling notions of culture as stable and unified" (Vital "Situating" 306), and demonstrating an "ambivalence about proper place and context" (Barnard *Apartheid* 161).[5] The novel achieves this effect in part through its focus on the history of the village and its environs. If the text's historical memory creates a sense of place, of a rich and unique heritage accrued through time, it also emphasizes how this place has never had a singular identity and has always challenged efforts to create clear boundaries. In the present, almost all "traditional" cultural practices and institutions have been transformed by their intersection with imperial modernity. A particularly interesting example involves changes in the landscape and the village economy resulting from the building of holiday "cottages." Upon learning of this development, Camagu is surprised, since, "The land in the rural villages is not for sale. It is given by the chief and his land-allocations committees" (68). However, he discovers that the significance of this traditional means of maintaining communal land has been changed;

"the white people" and "some well-to-do blacks" bribe the chief. In the past they used "a bottle of brandy" but now they offer "cellphones and satellite dishes" (68). If this incident suggests vestiges of traditional land tenure among the amaXhosa (which the colonists did their best to undermine following the cattle killing), it also points to their utter transformation by the pressures of economic rationality entailed by capitalism.[6]

Notions of purity are debunked in *The Heart of Redness* not only in respect to identity and culture, but also in terms of the category of nature. At the most obvious level, the novel skewers the notion of a pure nature or wilderness that is not already intertwined with the social. In his landmark essay "The Trouble with Wilderness or Getting Back to the Wrong Nature," William Cronon points out the problems with such a notion, delineating the ways that it occludes human history and even prevents a sense of ecological responsibility, since we are left with an either/or situation regarding impact—either there is no impact or such impact is negative. The novel's representations of what Alfred Crosby calls "ecological imperialism" are interesting in this regard. In the present, the bush is covered with various kinds of non-native plants which have been imported; some of these species—such as the wattle, the inkberry, and the lantana—are a serious danger to the continued existence of native species. The invasion and threatened conquest by this biota represents a kind of mixture of cultural and natural processes. Many of these plants have been intentionally imported, but their progress has not necessarily been anticipated or controlled by humans. As a result, the transformed landscape and methods of intervention cannot be understood in terms of a nature/culture dichotomy, and those who fall back on such simple categories appear misguided. We see these dynamics played out in the repeated criticisms of Qukezwa for her attempt to destroy the invasive species. Behind these criticisms is a notion of an unadulterated nature that she is wantonly attacking. When Qukezwa is brought to trial by the village elders for cutting down invasive species, even Camagu, before he understands her reasoning, thinks to himself,

> what came over Qukezwa to make her chop down trees, when she has always presented herself as their protector. Part of her objection to the planned holiday paradise is that the natural beauty of Qolorha-by-Sea will be destroyed. But here she is, standing before the graybeards of the village, being charged with the serious crime of vandalizing trees. (213)

For Camagu, all the trees are part of a singular "nature" that must be protected. During the trial, Qukezwa emphasizes that the "wilderness" has already been transformed by human history; as a result, conservation requires intervention in what appear to be "natural" processes.

Nonetheless, Qukezwa's conservation efforts raise some thorny issues regarding the novel's treatment of the categories of the indigenous and the natural. After all, she is trying to save "indigenous species" from the threat of the foreign. In addition, she seems to embody the ideal of an untutored indigenous knowledge of local ecology and of the proper relationship between humans and nature. These aspects of her character lead critics to claim that Mda perpetuates idealist notions of the indigenous and the natural. Anthony Vital, for example, sees her as embodying a kind of radical ecofeminist ideal of women's closeness to nature. He argues that in *The Heart of Redness*, Qukezwa, and more generally the female, embody "a connection with nature the male feels he has lost" as well as "traditional visionary relations with nature" which are valorized by the novel ("Situating" 310–11). Such characterizations suggest that Mda reinforces the notion of an unchanged indigenous ecosystem that existed before the impact of colonialism and advocates for a return to an indigenous, properly ecological relationship between human and nonhuman nature—a natural society and culture. I would argue, however, that the novel proposes that traditional relations with nature have been neither singular nor untroubled and that there was not and cannot be an unchanging indigenous ecosystem untransformed by human activity.

While the novel advocates for the protection of indigenous species, it also suggests that the larger contexts of which these species are parts have substantially changed in such a way that there is no access to an underlying indigenous natural "spirit" that could be salvaged. As I have pointed out, the entire "natural" environment has been utterly transformed by the history of human and nonhuman invasion; to completely destroy "foreign" species—to strive for an ecological purity—is not a realistic course of action. At one point, Qukezwa is asked, "Are you going to go out to the forest of Nogqoloza and destroy all the trees there just because they were imported from the land of the white man in the days of our father?" She responds, "The trees in Nogqoloza don't harm anybody, as long as they stay there" (216). Both Zim and Qukezwa note how the place that would seem to be the very epitome of an indigenous nature, Nongqawuse's pool, has been transformed. Zim tells his daughter, "In the days of Nongqawuse there were aloes [around the pool]. . . . Even when we were growing up, there were aloes. Also reeds. Reeds used to cover this whole place. Only forty years ago . . . when I was a young man . . . there were reeds" (46). In *The Heart of Redness* defining the "natural" identity of a place is complicated by ecosystemic changes over time, in part through the impact of "the migration of assorted flora and fauna" (Thomashow "Toward" 129). The combination of attention to ecology *and* to the challenges posed by environmental history for defining a "bioregion" affiliates the novel with a cosmopolitan bioregionalist sensibility.

In line with the novel's destabilizing of unified notions of culture and identity through historical narrative, *The Heart of Redness*'s representations of nineteenth-century amaXhosa society bring into question whether its relationship with nature was ever singular or perfectly harmonious. King Sarhili, we are told, "retreated to Manyube, a conservation area and nature reserve where people were not allowed to chop trees or hunt animals and birds. He had often told his people, 'One day these wonderful things of nature will get finished. Preserve them for future generations'" (131–32). These references to the drive for conservation among the Xhosa in the past suggest that even before the extensive spread of capitalism, the "balance" of nature had been significantly impacted by what Sarhili saw as destructive environmental practice. Furthermore, the episode points to an existing conflict regarding such practice, a conflict possibly inflected by social status. (The king wants a conservation area in part because it allows him a place "to think things over in a peaceful environment" [132].) These cultural divisions continue to be reflected in the present in the debates regarding conservation. Despite the efforts by both sides to represent themselves as cultural preservationists, the issue is which thread of "tradition" will be followed. The believers accuse Dalton, the local trader (of "English stock" but with "an UmXhosa heart" [8]), of trying to "change the ancient practices of the people" when he attempts to prevent boys from "taking the eggs of birds from their nests" and "hunting wild animals with their dogs" (147). However, he counters with the story of Sarhili: "Perhaps you need to learn more about your forefathers. . . . King Sarhili himself was a very strong conservationist" (165). Given moments such as these, it is difficult to claim that the text supports the image of the eco-indigene, in which indigenous peoples are envisioned as living in perfect harmony with nature and having an ideal ecological wisdom.[7]

Admittedly, the question of epistemologies of nature is vexed in *The Heart of Redness*. Through the characters of the colonial governor Sir George Grey and the developers, Mda articulates a colonial nature/culture binary that constructs "nature" as wild and primitive, to be subdued and made useful through European rationality. In contrast, characters like Qukezwa and her father Zim seem to point to indigenous spiritual and aesthetic ways of knowing nature that emphasize interdependence, challenge the nature/culture binary, and can serve as a foundation for indigenous principles of conservation. However, the novel does not necessarily equate these ways of knowing with a *singular* traditional, indigenous relationship with nature in the present or the past. One thread of "tradition" may lay the groundwork for a locally rooted form of ecological care, but *The Heart of Redness* suggest there are other, contradictory environmental "traditions." If the novel's focus on the history of a local community's relationships with nature aligns it with bioregionalism, the emphasis on the plural, even contradictory nature of these relationships disrupts any easy, singular conception of the bioregion's ecocultural identity. Similarly, Mda points to the existence in the West of a romantic reverential approach to nature in Camagu's recognition that "green" backpackers would have a strong appeal to certain kinds of tourists. ("There are many people out there who enjoy communing with unspoiled nature" [201].) Finally, the novel suggests that even those aspects of indigenous "tradition" that entail spiritual reverence for nature do not necessarily embody ideal ecological wisdom or practice. In a discussion of punishments for environmental transgressions, one elder notes that some tourists have been arrested (by the government) for smuggling cycads, while some village boys have been punished by village authorities "for killing the red winged starling." The other elders raise an outcry at even linking the two "crimes": "There can be no comparison here, the elders say all at once. The isomi is a holy bird. It is blessed. No one is allowed to kill it" (216). In this situation, animistic beliefs invest some species with spiritual significance while making others relatively unimportant (spiritually). Rather than being the grounds for care of biodiversity, these beliefs become a means of sanctioning biopiracy. Of course, one of the ways that *The Heart of Redness* opposes the terms of colonial discourse and the forms of exploitation it enables is precisely by challenging static, unitary categories such as "indigenous" (versus "Western") and "nature" (versus "culture").[8] Jennifer Wenzel reads this challenge in terms of Mda's treatment of time; by blurring the lines between "tradition and modernity" and "past and present," the novel undermines "the hegemonic notions of time and historical change that undergird the civilizing mission: the notion, for example, that literacy inevitably replaces orality" (*Bulletproof* 181).

The most significant problem with the reading of Qukezwa as an image of the female eco-indigene may be that it suggests *her* character is static and singular and that she represents the voice of truth in the novel. *The Heart of Redness* is far more resistant to closure than such a characterization would suggest. Qukezwa's knowledge and attitudes are not portrayed as only or even primarily the product of "tradition" or of nature; she understands not only the local ecosystem but also how tourism development schemes can work, and her desires are in part conditioned by the capitalist economy and the perception of geographic opportunity it encourages. (Near the opening of the novel, she tells her father than she has a "yearning" to go to Johannesburg because she will be able to "earn better money ... I'll be somebody in the city" [46–7].) Moreover, both Qukezwa and Camagu grow in the novel precisely to the degree to which, in their dialogues with each other, they recognize the limitations to their own fixed categories and narratives of identity. If at first Camagu is condescending with Qukezwa, believing his education and experience give him a superior understanding of the world, he nonetheless comes to respect her knowledge and her perspective on development. Qukezwa also initially draws on her own clear dichotomies in judging Camagu, seeing him as representative of a modernity that is in strict opposition to "traditional" beliefs and practices; she believes his forms of knowledge are useless for Qolorha. Over the course of the novel, however, Qukezwa comes to realize not only that his cosmopolitan "education" and experience are not necessarily at odds with traditional practices, but also that his knowledge can benefit the village as he pushes to get Nongqawuse's Valley declared a heritage site by the government in order to block the casino scheme.

Thus far, my argument has emphasized the ways that *The Heart of Redness* debunks binaries and the static categories they entail. As a distinctly *postcolonial* text, the novel joins its deconstructive moves with a focus on ways in which such categories are connected to the legacy of imperialism. For example, Sir George Grey uses the civilized/barbarous dichotomy to sell a vision of advancement, but, in trade for "the greatest gift of all: education and British civilization," the amaXhosa must relinquish their land and political control (137). If this relationship between nineteenth-century imperial rhetoric of salvation and dispossession is fairly transparent, Mda more subtly suggests a connection between the cattle-killing movement's redemptive narrative and imperialist imperatives. In Mda's narrative, the believers' faith in Nongqawuse's prophecies, which offer the promise of transcending a messy and frightening reality through *external* agency, prevent them from grappling with their conditions of existence themselves. Not surprisingly, their belief makes them "lethargic" and leads to their eventual starvation. Sir George Grey is then able to succeed "beyond his wildest dreams in turning [the Xhosa] into 'useful servants, consumers of our goods, contributors to our revenue'" (Peires 321).

In the present, the locals once again threaten to facilitate their own dispossession and loss of agency by buying into a narrative of salvation—now embedded in the discourse of economic development—based on the old colonial binaries. This danger is especially apparent in the arguments regarding the proposed plans for the casino complex. Not only do Bhonco and his band of Unbelievers accept the story of economic development for the community—in other words, that the scheme will bring jobs and further social infrastructure—but they also claim that it will offer deliverance from all that is primitive and wild: "We want to get rid of this bush which is a sign of our uncivilized state. We want developers to come and build the gambling city that will bring money to this community. That will bring modernity to our lives, and will rid us of our redness" (92). Ironically, the new development will be partly advertised by holding out the promise of the "wildness" of the wild coast, in particular for the surfers: "the waves here are more suited to the sport than the waves of other big cities in South Africa. The waves here are big and wild" (199). In this case, "development" feeds off its apparent opposite, "wildness," suggesting that these categories are the twin poles of the same construction. The creation of discrete categories makes "wildness" and "untamed nature" easily commodified and enables them to be brought more easily into a discourse of modernity.

The novel's suspicion regarding rigid, hierarchal models of identity and culture is also reflected in the debates between Camagu and Dalton regarding effective means of resistance to the casino. Though Dalton is among the leaders of the resistance, Camagu warns him that his efforts to "help" the people are bound to fail unless he is willing to relinquish authoritative (and authoritarian) representation; to truly empower them, he must become an active listener: "You know that you are 'right' and you want to impose those 'correct' ideas on the populace from above. I am suggesting that you try involving the people in decision-making rather than making decisions for them" (180). Camagu seems to be suggesting the need for Fanonian intellectuals who will develop representations of the people, their needs, and possible courses of action in dialogue with them. In "On National Culture," Fanon insists that the native intellectual "must join [the people] in that fluctuating movement which they are just giving a shape to, and which, as soon as it has started, will be the signal for everything to be called in question. Let there be no mistake about it; it is to this zone of occult instability where the people dwell that we must come" (227). If the call to join "the people" urges the intellectual to identify with a subaltern collective, the references to the "fluctuating movement" and "zone of occult instability" in which "the people" are to be found suggests that the identity of this collective is always in progress. In fact, a primary theme running throughout "On National Culture" is a warning against seeking for liberation through a static collective identity. The Fanonian aspect of Camagu's appeal becomes especially apparent when he questions Dalton's "cultural village," which produces an exoticized version of traditional culture. As Camagu notes, "I am interested in the culture of the amaXhosa as they live it today, not yesterday. The amaXhosa people are not a museum piece. Like all cultures, their culture is dynamic" (248).

Camagu's perspective on the best means to protect Qolorha is expressed not just in his discussions with Dalton, but also, more positively, in his own efforts to counter the casino scheme and to develop an alternative in a community-based form of ecotourism. The novel mostly endorses Camagu's efforts, and in this sense his Fanonism points toward the (shifting) grounding offered by *The Heart of Redness* for successful protection of local peoples, cultures, and natural environments in the face of contemporary imperial threats. When asked by the developers, "If you fight against these wonderful developments [to be brought by the casino], what do you have to offer in their place?" Camagu answers, "The promotion of the kind of tourism that will benefit the people, that will not destroy indigenous forests, that will not bring hordes of people who will pollute the rivers and drive away the birds" (201). He then proclaims, "We can work it out, people of Qolorha" (201). As this last statement indicates, Camagu's idea, which develops into the eco-friendly backpacker hostel, avoids the pitfalls of Dalton's project through its focus on collective participation; the hostel is planned, built, and owned by the village.

If there are echoes of "On National Culture" in Camagu's approach to anti-imperial forms of collective identity and agency, however, *The Heart of Redness* also significantly departs from Fanon's vision. Most obviously, Mda is not focused on the category of the nation; being both before and after the nation, Mda's local community outstrips the abstraction and teleology which that category entails. Even more important for my argument here, unlike Fanon, Mda represents the search for community in terms of a wider ecosystem. When Camagu asks Qukezwa how she knows so much "about birds and plants," she responds, "I live with them" (105). In the context of the novel, this "living" with nonhuman nature is not just a matter of living *in* a particular environment but also of seeing oneself as part of a community. The focus on ecological affiliation and on such affiliation as one basis for geopolitical identification is perhaps the most salient "bioregionalist" feature of *The Heart of Redness*.

The notion that humans are interdependently related to wider ecological communities comes into particular relief in the novel's representations of the ways that abrupt ecosystemic changes have drastic implications for human societies and cultures. Lung-sickness is a particularly good example. It was caused by microbes that came from Europe and had a dramatic impact on amaXhosa society and culture. The novel stresses that the disease cannot be reduced to social or cultural explanations, although it is tightly bound with social processes both causally and in terms of its impact. Its appearance represents something new, which the amaXhosa must try to understand in all its complexity without relying on preconceptions and definitive categories. In Mda's narrative, one problem with the cattle-killing movement is that it relied on an existing grand narrative to explain a transformation in the natural environment. Like "the people," "nature" must be listened to and actively engaged with as it emerges in the present.

As Mda's version of the cattle killing suggests, in *The Heart of Redness* a community must try to understand the wider system of ecological relationships within which it finds itself if it will determine effective courses of action for its survival. The novel makes it clear that the destruction of both resources and Qolorha's unique beauty in the wake of the casino's construction will have a dramatic impact on the community's situation; they will very quickly become completely transformed and have little control over their future. By understanding the relationships in which they find themselves, and grasping the significance of those relationships, they have a better sense of how to respond to the casino scheme. The same could be said about the issue of ecological imperialism. The community needs to understand the particular threat they face by closely examining the set of relationships in which it is embedded. At the end, through a better (if necessarily incomplete) understanding of these relationships and their significance, the community has been able to fight off both the casino scheme and the threat represented by invasive species. Driving back to Qolorha, Camagu "sees wattle trees along the road. Qukezwa taught him that these are enemy trees. All along the way he cannot see any of the indigenous trees that grow in abundance at Qolorha. Just the wattle and other imported trees. He feels fortunate that he lives in Qolorha. Those who want to preserve indigenous plants and birds have won the day there" (277). Such preservation is important, in part, because of the issue of local control over resources, one of which is, precisely, the place's uniqueness; for, of course, uniqueness is a commodity which draws people to Qolorha and its backpackers' hostel. The casino scheme, by contrast, would render Qolorha a copy, something that could be on any coast; the developers, savvy in the production of such projects, would be the ones in control.

As I have been suggesting throughout, *The Heart of Redness* shares much with a bioregional perspective. It focuses on the value of reinhabitation, the "commitment to understand local ecology and human relationships" (Thomashow "Toward" 125), and, in particular, on the ways that understanding and appreciating the uniqueness of a particular place, defined culturally and ecologically, can contribute to resistance against colonial modernity. The novel may emphasize geographical and categorical intermixing, but it does not suggest that differences among places have no meaning. In fact, in *The Heart of Redness* effective action is dependent on recognizing and bringing together the knowledge and perspectives offered by such differences. As Camagu lives in Qolorha and engages with Qukezwa, the local comes to represent not only the gaps in his education, but also something to be known—no matter how incomplete that knowledge will of necessity be. At the same time, as Camagu becomes more and more involved in the resistance movement against the gambling complex development scheme, his knowledge from Johannesburg and the United States becomes crucial in the success of the movement. The high degree of interpenetration between categories (urban and the rural, local and global, regional and national) give the differences in these categories more not less meaning.

Nonetheless, these differences are not to be understood as ahistorical or clearly bounded. Opposing the casino scheme and determining the best alternative—identifying what and who needs to be opposed, as well as why—requires thinking through the interplay of similarity and difference in shifting terms based on context and scale. It is important, for example, for Camagu to keep in mind both how Qolorha is linked with national majorities in terms of dispossession by elites *and* the differences that result from Qolorha being a marginal, rural place in respect to the urban centers of South Africa. Similarly, the novel suggests how Dalton is both different from some of his liberal white friends who have little sense of identification with places like Qolorha (or even South Africa as whole), and, at the same time, how his interests are not necessarily identical with the interests of the majority of the villagers.

It should be noted that Camagu's solutions are themselves neither ideologically pure nor necessarily adequate. He maintains that he opposes the exoticization and commodification of Xhosa culture embraced by Dalton's cultural village, but his own cooperative society produces "traditional isiXhosa costumes and accessories . . . to be marketed in Johannesburg" (161). In addition, the backpackers' hostel is sold through the claim that Qolorha can offer "unspoiled nature," and, as result, draws on a commodified notion of wilderness challenged by the novel as a whole. Most important, at the close of the novel, Camagu notes, "Sooner or later the powers that be may decide, in the name of the people, that it is good for the people to have a gambling complex at Qolorha-by-Sea. And the gambling complex shall come into being" (277). This final comment suggests that there are limitations to Camagu's strategies for resistance and that new ones will need to be produced if Qolorha is to resist the protean operation of imperial capital.

If Camagu's solution remains limited, however, the novel does not suggest that it should be rejected. After all, it has been successful in terms of preservation of local control and environment. ("Those who want to preserve indigenous plants and birds have won the day" [277] in Qolorha, Camagu thinks to himself near the end.) At the same time, its provisional status points to the need for revision. There is no once and for all. In this sense, the novel not only makes no claims to the authority of its own representations and solutions, but even encourages us to seek out its contradictions. Ironically, in so doing, we end up endorsing the one truth it does insist on: the impossibility of a "destination beyond which all knowledge ends" (97).

As the foregoing analysis implies, if one is to align *The Heart of Redness* with bioregionalism, that term must be qualified with "cosmopolitan." It is worth recalling that a *cosmopolitan* bioregionalist sensibility is "open-ended," perceiving boundaries as "permeable" and identities as "pluralistic" (Thomashow "Toward" 129–30). At the same time, the term "bioregional" denotes a difference from a cosmopolitan approach to "place" more generally.[9] The latter will not *necessarily* take account of the importance of ecology or the significance of ecological relationships for humans. To discuss 'place' in *The Heart of Redness* necessitates that one appreciates the importance of how Qolorha has been shaped by particular relationships between nature and culture, as well as by relationships between the local and global.[10]

In its dialogic approach to conceptions of place and ecology, *The Heart of Redness* encourages efforts to decenter ecocriticism. As Nixon argues, we need

> to refuse a vision of environmentalism as invented at the center and exported to (or imposed on) the periphery. Such center-periphery thinking constitutes both a source of postcolonialists' pervasive indifference to environmentalism and conversely, a source of the debilitating strain of superpower parochialism that lingers among many American ecocritics and writers. ("Environmentalism" 247)

The process of decentering will involve not only shifts in the concerns and formulations of ecocriticism but also a shift in postcolonial criticism and writing, one that brings ecology to the fore. In a sense, this analysis of *The Heart of Redness* might represent one example of such a shift; while paying close attention to the treatment of environmental concerns in the novel, it also emphasizes how different geopolitical positions relate to competing conceptions of ecology, place, and their significance. Of course, the very use of the concept of cosmopolitan bioregionalism points to the "impurity" of *my* analysis, which uses a conceptual framework from "outside" to help "make sense" of an "African" novel. It might be argued that the resistance to fixed categories (e.g., "inside," "outside") that is implied in "cosmopolitan bioregionalism" allows the concept to travel well, without necessarily representing the kind of imposition decried by Nixon. But perhaps such an argument could itself suggest a sort of smug satisfaction with the conclusions drawn here—a satisfaction I obviously want to resist. The questions I and others have raised point to the need for continued investigation, the need not to believe that we have reached "the destination beyond which all knowledge ends."

NOTES

1. See Caminero-Santangelo; Lundblad; Nixon "Environmentalism"; and Vital "Toward."

2. See Cilano and DeLoughrey; Huggan "'Greening'"; Huggan and Tiffin; Nixon "Environmentalism"; O'Brien "Articulating"; Tiffin; and Vital and Erney "Introduction."

3. A full analysis of the complicated intertextual relationship between *The Heart of Redness* and *The Dead Will Arise* is beyond the scope of this chapter. Yet, it does seem important to address, however briefly, the recent charge of "plagiarism" against Mda by Andrew Offenburger. Based on a fairly exhaustive catalogue of Mda's borrowings from Peires, Offenburger claims that the novel is "a derivative work masquerading plagiarism as intertextuality" (164) and accuses literary critics of abetting the crime. However, his argument considers only the part of the novel placed in the past and, as a result, does not address the relationship between the historical material and the novel's narrative of the present. Offenburger also ignores the fictional aspects of Mda's historical narrative (the story of the brothers Twin and Twin-Twin), as well as the oral sources on which Mda draws. Finally, Offenburger fails to define key terms such as "plagiarism" and "intertextuality" and to address their rich theoretical history. (For Mda's rebuttal to Offenburger, see "A Response.") In contrast, Jennifer Wenzel develops an insightful reading of Mda's appropriations of *The Dead Will Arise*. While acknowledging the extent of these appropriations and some of their troubling implications, she ultimately argues that "what makes *The Heart of Redness* more than a novelization of Peires's history is its engagement with questions of time" (*Bulletproof* 179).

4. In this sense, *The Heart of Redness* echoes Lawrence Buell's assertion that "place is not just a noun but also a verb, a verb of action" (*Writing* 67).

5. See also Jacobs; Koyana; and Woodward.

6. For the history of colonial attempts to do away with collective land tenure following the cattle killing, and specifically the power of the chiefs to allocate land, see Peires 290–96.

7. Recent scholarship bringing this stereotype into question includes Krech and Ross.

8. For an insightful reading of ways that Mda treats the nature/culture binary, see Klopper. Using "anthropological research on the role of diviner-prophet in Xhosa society," Klopper argues that *The Heart of Redness* interrogates the relationship between nature and culture through the notion of the prophetic.

9. See, for example, Doreen Massey's notion of a "progressive concept of place," which sees "the uniqueness of place" as stemming precisely from being "a particular, unique, point" at the intersection of "wider and local social relations," which themselves "take a further element of specificity" from history (322–33).

10. In *Sense of Place and Sense of Planet*, Ursula Heise asserts the need for what she terms "eco-cosmopolitanism," which entails a shift from the primary focus on place in many forms of American environmentalism and ecocriticism to ways of representing environmental crisis in global terms. While not entirely dismissing the usefulness of the category of place, she seeks forms of environmental imagination and advocacy based "no longer primarily on ties to local places but on ties to territories and systems that are understood to encompass the planet as a whole" (10). In *Bringing the Biosphere Home*, Thomashow also engages in the project to develop means of grasping global environmental threat. However, he claims that a global environmental sensibility must stem from a sense of place; Heise rejects this position: "The challenge for environmentalist thinking . . . is to shift the core of its cultural imagination from a sense of place to a less territorial and more systematic sense of planet" (56). Even though *The Heart of Redness* emphasizes the ways that the local must be understood in terms of specific larger national and global relationships, it too does not quite line up with Heise's notion of eco-cosmopolitanism since, as my reading suggests, the category of place is still privileged.

Works Cited

Achebe, Chinua. *Things Falls Apart*. New York: Anchor, 1994.
Adamson, Joni, Mei Mei Evans, and Rachel Stein, eds. *The Environmental Justice Reader: Politics, Poetics, and Pedagogy*. Tucson: University of Arizona Press, 2002.
Adorno, Theodor and Max Horkheimer. *Dialectic of Enlightenment*. Trans. John Cumming. New York: Continuum, 1976.
Agarwal, Anil, R. Chopra, and K. Sharma, eds. *The First Citizen's Report on the Environment in India*. New Delhi: Centre for Science and Environment, 1982.
Agnoletti, Mauro. "Introduction." *Forest History: International Studies on Socio-Economic and Forest Ecosystem Change* (Report No. 2 of the IUFRO Task Force on Environmental Change). Eds. Mauro Agnoletti and Steven Anderson. Wallingford, Oxfordshire: CABI, 2000. 1–20.
Aiu, Pua'ala'okalani D. "This Land Is Our Land: The Social Construction of Kahoolawe Island." PhD diss. University of Massachusetts, Amherst. May 1997.
Alaimo, Stacy. *Undomesticated Ground: Recasting Nature as Feminist Space*. Ithaca, NY: Cornell University Press, 2000.
Alata, Syed Hussein. *The Myth of the Lazy Native*. New York: Routledge, 1977.
Alexis, Jacques Stephen. *Les arbres musiciens*. Paris: Gallimard, 1957.
Allen, Chadwick. *Blood Narrative: Indigenous Identity in American Indian and Maori Literary and Activist Texts*. Durham: Duke University Press, 2002.
Althusser, Louis. "Ideology and Ideological State Apparatuses." *The Norton Anthology of Theory and Criticism*, ed. Vincent B. Leitch et al. New York, London: Norton, 2001. 1483–1509.
Altman, Dennis. *Global Sex*. Chicago and London: University of Chicago Press, 2001.

Amarasinghe, Sarath W. "Sri Lanka: The Commercial Sexual Exploitation of Children: A Rapid Assessment." *International Labour Organization*. 2002. http://www.ilo.org/public/english////standards/ipec/simpoc/srilanka/ra/cse.pdf.

Amodio, Emanuele. "The War of the Plants: Botanical Exchange and Agricultural Conquest of the New World during Colonial Times." *Forest History: International Studies on Socio-Economic and Forest Ecosystem Change* (Report No. 2 of the IUFRO Task Force on Environmental Change). Eds. Mauro Agnoletti and Steven Anderson, 49–64. Wallingford, Oxfordshire: CABI, 2000.

Andrews, Malcolm. *The Search for the Picturesque: Landscape Aesthetics and Tourism in Britain, 1760–1800*. Stanford: Stanford University Press, 1990.

Anzaldúa, Gloria. *Borderlands/La Frontera: The New Mestiza*. San Francisco: Aunt Lute, 1987.

Armstrong, Susan J., and Richard G. Botzler, eds. *The Animal Ethics Reader*. London: Routledge, 2003.

Arnold, David. *Famine: Social Crisis and Historical Change*. Oxford: Oxford University Press, 1988.

———. *The Problem of Nature: Environment, Culture, European Expansion*. Oxford: Blackwell, 1996.

Arnold, David and Ramachandra Guha. "Introduction: Themes and Issues in the Environmental History of South Asia." *Nature, Culture, Imperialism: Essays on the environmental history of South Asia*. Delhi: Oxford University Press, 1995. 1–20.

Arrate, José Martín Félix de. *Llave del Nuevo Mundo: Antemural de las Indias Occidentales. La Habana descrita* [1761]. http://www.cervantesvirtual.com/servlet/SirveObras/01362845434592728987891/index.htm.

Athique, Tamara Mabbott. "Textual Migrations: South Asian–Australian Fiction." Diss. University of Wollongong, 2006.

Attridge, Derek. "Against Allegory: Waiting for the Barbarians, Life and Times of Michael K, and the Question of Literary Reading." *J. M. Coetzee and the Idea of the Public Intellectual*. Ed. Jane Poyner. Athens: Ohio University Press, 2006. 63–82.

———. "Ethical Modernism: Servants as Others in J. M. Coetzee's Early Fiction." *Poetics Today* 25.4 (2004): 653–71.

Auerbach, Erich. *Scenes from the Drama of European Literature*. New York: Meridian Books, 1959.

Bacchilega, Christina. *Legendary Hawai'i and the Politics of Place: Tradition, Translation, and Tourism*. Philadelphia: University of Pennsylvania Press, 2007.

Baer, William. "An Interview with Derek Walcott." *Conversations with Derek Walcott*. Ed. William Baer. Jackson: University Press of Mississippi, 1996. 194–206.

Baker, Geoffrey. "The Limits of Sympathy: J. M. Coetzee's Evolving Ethics of Engagement." *ARIEL: A Review of International English Literature* 36.1–2 (January 2005): 27–49.

Balch, Emily Green. *Occupied Haiti*. New York: Writers Publishing, 1927.

Baldwin, James. "Stranger in the Village." *Notes of a Native Son*. 1955. Boston: Beacon Press, 1984. 159–75.

Barasch, Moshe. "Apocalyptic Space." *Apocalyptic Time*. Ed. Albert I. Baumgarten. Herndon, VA: Brill, 2000. 305–26.

Barclay, Robert. *Melal: A Novel of the Pacific*. 2002. Honolulu: University of Hawai'i Press, 2002.

Barnard, Rita. "J. M. Coetzee's *Disgrace* and the South African Pastoral." *Contemporary Literature* 44.2 (2003): 199–224.

———. *Apartheid and Beyond: South African Writers and the Politics of Place*. Oxford: Oxford University Press, 2007.
Barros, Jacques. *Haïti de 1804 à Nos Jours*. Paris: L'Harmattan, 1984. 225–51.
Bate, Jonathan. *John Clare: A Biography*. New York: Farrar, Straus and Giroux, 2003.
Bauman, Zygmunt. "Living (Occasionally Dying) Together in an Urban World." *Cities, War, and Terrorism: Towards an Urban Geopolitics*. Ed. Stephen Graham. Malden: Blackwell, 2004. 110–19.
———. *Wasted Lives: Modernity and Its Outcasts*. London: Polity, 2004.
Behn, Aphra. *Oroonoko*. London: Penguin Classics, 2003.
Beinart, William. *The Rise of Conservation in South Africa: Settlers, Livestock, and the Environment 1770–1950*. New York: Oxford University Press, 2008.
Beinart, William and Peter Coates. *Environment and History. The Taming of Nature in the USA and South Africa*. London: Routledge, 1995.
Bellegarde-Smith, Patrick. *Haiti: The Breached Citadel*. Boulder, San Francisco, and London: Westview Press, 1990. 9–22.
Benjamin, Walter. "Paralipomena to 'On the Concept of History.'" *Walter Benjamin: Selected Writings*. Vol. 4. Trans. Edmund Jephcott et al. Eds. Howard Eiland and Michael W. Jennings. Cambridge: Belknap, 2003. 401–11.
Benson, LeGrace. "A Long Bilingual Conversation Concerning Paradise Lost: Landscapes in Haitian Art." *Caribbean Literature and the Environment: Between Nature and Culture*. Eds. Elizabeth DeLoughrey, Renée Gosson, and George Handley. Charlottesville: University of Virginia Press, 2005.
———. Mangones, Albert; Marat, Francine; Monosiet, Pierre; Rodman, Selden; Turnier, Luce; Voegeli, The Rt. Rev. Alfred, Personal communications, 1982–1986.
Benton, Ted. *Natural Relations: Ecology, Animal Rights, and Social Justice*. London: Verso, 1993.
Beresford, Lucy. "Village of the Damned." Review of *Animal's People* by Indra Sinha. *New Statesman* 26 (February 2007). http://www.newstatesman.com/books/2007/02.
Berkes, Fikret. *Sacred Ecology: Traditional Ecological Knowledge and Resource Management*. 2nd edition. New York: Taylor & Francis, 2008.
Bhabha, Homi. *The Location of Culture*. New York: Routledge, 1994.
Binde, Per. "Nature in the Roman Catholic Tradition." *Anthropological Quarterly* 74.1 (2001): 21. http://www.jstor.org/stable3318300.
Blixen, Karen. *Out of Africa* (1937). New York: Penguin, 1999.
Bobadilla. Emilio. *A fuego lento*. Barcelona: Impresora de Henrich, 1903.
Bookchin, Murray. *The Ecology of Freedom: The Emergence and Dissolution of Hierarchy*. Cheshire Books, 1982.
———. *Our Synthetic Environment* New York: Knopf, 1962. Online http://dwardmac.pitzer.edu/anarchist_archives/bookchin/syntheticenviron/osetoc.html July 25, 2010.
Bosch, Juan. *Cuentos escritos en el exilio*. Santo Domingo: Editorial Librerías Dominicanas, 1962.
Botkin, Daniel. *Discordant Harmonies: A New Ecology for the Twenty-First Century*. London and New York: Oxford University Press, 1990.
Bowen-Jones, Howard. Ed. *Human Ecology in the Commonwealth*. London: Charles Knight, 1972.
Boyd, Richard. "Metaphor and Theory Change: What is 'Metaphor' a Metaphor for?" *Metaphor and Thought*. Ed. Andrew Ortony. Cambridge: Cambridge UP, 1979. 356–408.

Boyer, Paul. *By The Bomb's Early Light: American Thought and Culture at the Dawn of the Atomic Age*. Chapel Hill: U of North Carolina P, 1994.
Bradford, Helen. "Women, Gender and Colonialism: Rethinking the History of the British Cape Colony and Its Frontier Zones, c. 1806–70." *The Journal of African History* 37:3 (1996): 351–70.
Braudel, Fernand. "History and the Social Sciences: The *Longue Durée*." *On History*. Trans. Sarah Matthews. The University of Chicago Press, 1982.
Braziel, Jana Evans. "Caribbean Genesis: Language, Gardens, Worlds (Jamaica Kincaid, Derek Walcott, Édouard Glissant)." *Caribbean Literature and the Environment: Between Nature and Culture*. Eds. Elizabeth DeLoughrey, Renée Gosson, and George Handley. Charlottesville: University of Virginia Press, 2005.
Bresson, Louis. *Tourisme—l'anti-crise: la voie royale pour l'économie de l'après nucléaire*. Papeete, Tahiti, Polynésie française: Pacific Promotion Tahiti, 1993.
Breton, André. "Discours de M. André Breton à 'Savoy." *Conjonction* 193 (1992): 61–65.
———. *Surrealism and Painting*. Trans. Simon Watson Taylor. Boston: MFA Publications, 2002. 308–12.
Brockaway, Lucille. *Science and Colonial Expansion: The Role of the British Royal Botanical Gardens*. New York: Academic Press, 1979.
Brown, Robert, and Cheryl Johnson. "Thinking Poetry: An Interview with Derek Walcott." *Conversations with Derek Walcott*. Ed. William Baer. Jackson: University Press of Mississippi, 1996. 175–88.
Browne, Janet. "A Science of Empire: British Biogeography before Darwin." *Revue d'histoire des sciences* 44 (1992): 451–75.
———. *The Secular Ark*. New Haven: Yale University Press, 1983.
Bryld, Mette, and Nina Lykke. *Cosmodolphins: Feminist Cultural Studies of Technology, Animals and the Sacred*. London and New York: Zed Books, 2000.
Buell, Frederick. *From Apocalypse to Way of Life: Environmental Crisis in the American Century*. London and New York: Routledge, 2003.
Buell, Lawrence. *The Environmental Imagination: Thoreau, Nature Writing, and the Formation of American Culture*. Cambridge: Belknap Press of Harvard University Press, 1995.
———. *The Future of Environmental Criticism: Environmental Crisis and Literary Imagination*. Malden, MA: Blackwell, 2005.
———. *Writing for an Endangered World: Literature, Culture, and Environment in the U.S. and Beyond*. Cambridge: Belknap, 2001.
Bullard, Robert D. *Dumping in Dixie: Race, Class, and Environmental Quality*. Boulder: Westview Press, 1990.
Bunn, David. "Relocations: Landscape Theory, South African Landscape Practice, and the Transmission of Political Value." *Pretexts* 4 (1993): 44–67.
Buscaglia-Salgado, José F. "The Misfortunes of Alonso Ramírez (1690) and the Duplicitous Complicity between the Narrator, the Writer, and the Censor." *Dissidences: Hispanic Journal of Theory and Criticism*. http://www.dissidences.org/SiguenzaMisfortunes.html. Accessed August 9, 2008.
Cabezas, Amalia L. "Women's Work Is Never Done: Sex Tourism in Sosúa, the Dominican Republic." *Sun, Sex, and Gold: Tourism and Sex Work in the Caribbean*. Ed. Kamala Kempadoo. Lanham and Oxford: Rowman & Littlefield, 1999. 93–123.
Calarco, Matthew. *Zoographies: The Question of the Animal from Heidegger to Derrida*. New York: Columbia University Press, 2008.

Camayd-Freixas, Erik. "Introduction: The Returning Gaze." *Primitivism and Identity in Latin America: Essays on Art, Literature, and Culture*. Eds. Erik Camayd-Freixas and José Eduardo González. Tucson: University of Arizona Press, 2000. vii–xix.

Caminero-Santangelo, Byron. "Different Shades of Green: Ecocriticism and African Literature." *African Literature: An Anthology of Criticism and Theory*. Oxford: Blackwell, 2007. 698–706.

Campbell, Chris, and Erin Somerville, eds. *What Is the Earthly Paradise? Ecocritical Responses to the Caribbean*. Cambridge: Cambridge Scholars, 2007.

Cañizares-Esguerra, Jorge. *Nature, Empire, and Nation: Explorations of the History of Science in the Iberian New World*. Palo Alto: Stanford University Press, 2006.

Caplan, Lionel. "'Bravest of the Brave': Representations of 'The Gurkha' in British Military Writings." *Modern Asian Studies* 25.3 (1991): 571–97.

Carson, Rachel. *Silent Spring*. New York: Houghton Mifflin, 1962

———. *The Sea Around Us*. New York: Oxford University Press, 1951.

Carew, Jan. *Black Midas*. London: Secker & Warburg, 1958.

Carmichael, Mrs. *Domestic Manners and Social Condition of the White, Coloured and Negro Population of the West Indies*. 2 vols. London: Whittaker, Treacher, 1833.

Carpentier, Alejo. "The Baroque and the Marvelous Real." *Magical Realism: Theory, History, Community*. Eds. Lois Parkinson Zamora and Wendy B. Faris. Durham: Duke University Press, 1995. 89–108.

———. "El Gran Libro de la Selva." *El Nacional*. May 14, 1952. [Caracas].

———. *The Lost Steps*. Trans. Harriet de Onís. New York: Noonday Press, 1989.

———. "Misterios de la Naturaleza Venezolana." *El Nacional*. July 21, 1952. [Caracas].

———. "On the Marvelous Real in America." *Magical Realism: Theory, History, Community*. Eds. Lois Parkinson Zamora and Wendy B. Faris. Durham: Duke University Press, 1995. 75–88.

———. *Los pasos perdidos*. Madrid: Catedra Letras Hispánicas, 1985.

———. "Presencia de la naturaleza." *El Nacional*. Aug. 23, 1952. [Caracas].

———. "Presencia de la naturaleza." *El Nacional*. Oct. 2, 1952. [Caracas].

———. *El reino de este mundo*. New York: Rayo, 2009.

———. "El turista y el viajero." *El Nacional*. Oct. 21, 1952. [Caracas].

———. *Visión de América: fragmentos de una crónica de viajes*. Buenos Aires: Losada, 1999.

Carrigan, Anthony. *Postcolonial Tourism: Literature, Culture, and Environment*. London and New York: Routledge, 2011.

Carruthers, Jane. *The Kruger National Park: A Social and Political History*. Pietermaritzburg, South Africa: University of Natal Press, 1995.

Carter, Martin. *Selected Poems*. Ed. David Dabydeen. London: Peepal Tree Press, 1999.

Casid, Jill H. *Sowing Empire: Landscape and Colonization*. Minneapolis: University of Minnesota Press, 2005.

Casteel, Sarah Phillips. *Second Arrivals: Landscape and Belonging in Contemporary Writing of the Americas*. Charlottesville: University of Virginia Press, 2007.

Caufield, Catherine. *Multiple Exposures: Chronicles of the Radiation Age*. New York: Harper, 1990.

Cavalieri, Paola. "For an Expanded Theory of Human Rights." *The Animal Ethics Reader*. 2nd ed. Eds. Armstrong and Botzler. London and New York: Routledge, 2008. 30–32.

Cavell, Stanley, et al. *Philosophy and Animal Life*. New York: Columbia University Press, 2008.
Cazdyn, Eric. "Disaster, Crisis, Revolution." *South Atlantic Quarterly* 106.4 (2007): 647–62.
Cetacean Nation Information and Energy Center. March 14, 2009. http://www.cetacean-nation.com.
Chakrabarty, Dipesh. "The Climate of History: Four Theses." *Critical Inquiry* 35 (Winter 2009): 197–222.
———. *Habitations of Modernity: Essays in the Wake of Subaltern Studies*. Chicago: Chicago University Press, 2000.
———. *Provincializing Europe: Postcolonial Thought and Historical Difference*. Princeton: Princeton University Press, 2001.
Chamoiseau, Patrick. *Biblique des derniers gestes*. Paris: Gallimard, 2002.
Chanady, Amaryll. "The Territorialization of the Imaginary in Latin America: Self-Affirmation and Resistance to Metropolitan Paradigms." *Magical Realism: Theory, History, Community*. Eds. Lois Parkinson Zamora and Wendy B. Faris. Durham: Duke University Press, 1995. 125–44.
Chauvet, Marie. *Amour, Colère et Folie*. Paris: Gallimard, 1968.
Chaze, Michou. *Vai: La rivière au ciel sans nuages*. Papeete: Cobalt/Tupuna, 1990.
Chernus, Ira. *Dr. Strangegod: On the Symbolic Meaning of Nuclear Weapons*. Columbia: University of South Carolina Press, 1986.
Chouhan, T. R. *Bhopal: The Inside Story*. New York: 1994.
Christophe, Henri and Thomas Clarkson. *A Correspondence*. Berkeley: University of California Press, 1952.
Cilano, Cara, and Elizabeth DeLoughrey. "Against Authenticity: Global Knowledges and Postcolonial Ecocriticism." *Interdisciplinary Studies in Literature and Environment (ISLE)* 14.1 (Summer 2007): 71–87.
Clare, John. "The Fallen Elm." *"I Am": The Selected Poetry of John Clare*. Ed. Jonathan Bate. New York: Farrar, Straus and Giroux, 2003. 141–43.
———. *"I Am": The Selected Poetry of John Clare*. Ed. Jonathan Bate. New York: Farrar, Straus and Giroux, 2003.
———. "The Lament of Swordy Well." *"I Am": The Selected Poetry of John Clare*. Ed. Jonathan Bate. New York: Farrar, Straus and Giroux, 2003. 211–19.
———. "The Progress of Rhyme." *"I Am": The Selected Poetry of John Clare*. Ed. Jonathan Bate. New York: Farrar, Straus and Giroux, 2003. 120–31.
———. "Swordy Well." *"I Am": The Selected Poetry of John Clare*. Ed. Jonathan Bate. New York: Farrar, Straus and Giroux, 2003. 135.
Clarence-Smith, W. G. *Cocoa and Chocolate, 1765–1914*. London and New York: Routledge, 2000.
Clarkson, Thomas. *Papers*. Vol. 6, Haiti and Jamaica Correspondence (King Henry Christophe/Clarkson letters for 1816–1820), British Library, London, England.
Cliff, Michelle. *Abeng*. Trumansburg, NY: Crossing Press, 1974.
Clifford, James. "On Collecting Art and Culture." *Art and Its Significance: An Anthology of Aesthetic Theory*. Ed. Stephen David Ross. Albany: State University of New York Press, 1994. 621–42.
———. *Routes: Travel and Translation in the Late Twentieth Century*. Cambridge and London: Harvard University Press, 1997.
Clitandre, Pierre. *La Cathédrale du mois d'août*. Port-au-Prince: Éditions Fardin, 1979.
Code, Lorraine. *Ecological Thinking: The Politics of Epistemic Location*. London: Oxford University Press, 2006.

Coetzee, J. M. *Age of Iron*. London: Penguin Books, 1990.
———. *Diary of a Bad Year*. New York: Viking, 2008.
———. *Disgrace*. New York: Viking, 1999.
———. *Elizabeth Costello*. New York: Viking, 2003.
———. *In the Heart of the Country*. London: Penguin Books, 1982.
———. *Life and Times of Michael K*. London: Penguin Books, 1983. Reprint, 1985.
———. *The Lives of Animals*. The University Center for Human Values Series. Ed. Amy Gutmann. Princeton, NJ: Princeton University Press, 1999.
———. *Slow Man*. New York: Viking, 2005.
———. *Waiting for the Barbarians*. London: Penguin Books, 1980.
———. *White Writing: On the Culture of Letters in South Africa* (1988). New Haven: Yale University Press, 1990.
Cohen, Michael P. "Blues in the Green: Ecocriticism under Critique." *Environmental History* 9 (2004): 9–36.
Coicou, Massillon. "Impressions, 92." *Poésies Nationales*. Paris: Dujarric, 1903.
Columbus, Christopher. "The Spanish Letter of Columbus to Luis de Sant'Angel." London: B. Quaritch, 1891.
Condé, Maryse. *Traversée de la mangrove*. Paris: Mercure de France, 1992.
Conley, Verena A. *Ecopolitics: The Environment in Poststructuralist Thought*. New York and London: Routledge, 1996.
Coronil, Fernando. "Towards a Critique of Globalcentrism: Speculations on Capitalism's Nature." *Public Culture* 12.2 (2000): 351–74.
Corretjer, Juan Antonio. "Pared de la soledad." http://www.ciudadseva.com/textos/poesia/esp/corret/pared.htm. Accessed October 10, 2008.
———. "Yerba bruja." http://www.ciudadseva.com/textos/poesia/esp/corret/yerba.htm. Accessed October 10, 2008.
Cosgrove, Denis. *Apollo's Eye: A Cartographic Genealogy of the Earth in the Western Imagination*. Baltimore: Johns Hopkins University Press, 2001.
Craige, Betty Jean. *Eugene Odum: Ecosystem Ecologist and Environmentalist*. Athens: University of Georgia Press, 2002.
Crick, Malcolm. *Resplendent Sites, Discordant Voices: Sri Lankans and International Tourism*. Chur and Reading: Harwood Academic, 1994.
Cronon, William. "The Trouble with Wilderness or Getting Back to the Wrong Nature." *Uncommon Ground: Rethinking the Human Place in Nature*. New York: Norton, 1995. 69–90.
Crosby, Alfred W. *The Columbian Exchange: Biological and Cultural Consequences of 1492*. Westport, CT: Praeger, 2003.
———. *Ecological Imperialism: The Biological Expansion of Europe 900–1900*, 2nd ed. Cambridge: Cambridge University Press, 2004.
Curtin, Deane W. *Chinnagounder's Challenge: The Question of Ecological Citizenship*. Bloomington: Indiana, 1999.
———. *Environmental Ethics for a Postcolonial World*. Lanham, Maryland: Rowman & Littlefield, 2005.
Dangarembga, Tsitsi. *Nervous Conditions* London: The Women's Press, 1988.
Danta, Chris. "'Like a Dog . . . Like a Lamb': Becoming Sacrificial Animal in Kafka and Coetzee." *New Literary History* 38 (2007): 721–37.
Darwin, Charles. *On the Origin of Species*. 5th ed. London: John Murray, 1869.
Das, Saswat S. "Home and Homelessness in *The Hungry Tide*: A Discourse Unmade." *Indian Literature* 235 (2006): 179–85.
"Deathly Calm Over City of Tragedy." *Hindu*. Late ed. December 5, 1984: 1.

de Chardin, Teilhard. *The Divine Milieu*. New York: Perennial, 2001.
De Man, Paul. "The Epistemology of Metaphor." *On Metaphor*. Ed. Sheldon Sacks. Chicago: University of Chicago Press, 1979. 11–28.
de Vries, Pieter, and Hans Saur. *Moruroa and Us: Polynesians' Experiences during Thirty Years of Nuclear Testing in the French Pacific*. Lyon: Centre de Documentation et de Recherche sur la Paix et les Conflits, 1997.
de Wimpffen, Baron Alexandre-Stanislaus. *Haiti au Xve siècle: Richesse et esclavage dans une colonie française* (1797). Paris: Edition Karthala, 1993. 165.
DeGrazia, David. *Human Identity and Bioethics*. Cambridge: Cambridge University Press, 2005.
De Lisser, Herbert George. *The White Witch of Rosehall*. London. E. Benn, 1929.
DeLoughrey, Elizabeth. "Globalizing the Routes of Breadfruit and Other Bounties." *Journal of Colonialism and Colonial History*. 8:3 (Winter 2008): http://muse.jhu.edu/journals/journal_of_colonialism_and_colonial_history/v008/8.3deloughrey.html

———."Radiation Ecologies and the Wars of Light." *Modern Fiction Studies* 55.3 (2009). 468–98.

———. *Routes and Roots: Navigating Caribbean and Pacific Island Literatures*. Honolulu: University of Hawai'i Press, 2007.

———. "Solar Metaphors: 'No Ordinary Sun.'" *Ka Mate Ka Ora: A New Zealand Journal of Poetry and Poetics* 6 (Sept. 2008) <http://www.nzepc.auckland.ac.nz/kmko/index06.asp>.

DeLoughrey, Elizabeth, Renée Gosson, and George B. Handley. "Introduction." *Caribbean Literature and the Environment: Between Nature and Culture*. Charlottesville: University of Virginia Press, 2005. 1–30.

———, eds. *Caribbean Literature and the Environment: Between Nature and Culture*. Charlottesville: University Press of Virginia, 2005.

Dening, Greg. *Islands and Beaches: Discourse on a Silent Land, Marquesas 1774–1880*. Honolulu: University Press of Hawai'i, 1980.
Dennett, D. C. "Conditions of Personhood." *The Identities of Persons*. Ed. A. O. Rorty. Berkeley: University of California Press, 1976.
Derrida, Jacques. *The Animal That Therefore I Am*. Ed. Marie-Louise Mallet. Trans. David Wills. New York: Fordham University Press, 2008.

———. "White Mythology: Metaphor in the Text of Philosophy." Trans. F.C.T. Moore. *New Literary History* 6.1 (1974): 5–74.

Desai, Kiran. *The Inheritance of Loss*. New York: Atlantic Monthly Press, 2006.
Desmangles, Leslie. *The Faces of the Gods: Vodou and Roman Catholicism in Haiti*. Chapel Hill and London: University of North Carolina Press, 1992.
Devi, Mahasweta. "Dhowli." *Of Women, Outcastes, Peasants, and Rebels: A Selection of Bengali Short Stories*. Ed. and trans. Kalpana Bardhan. Berkeley: University of California Press, 1990. 185–205.

———. "Douloti the Bountiful." *Imaginary Maps*. New York, London: Routledge, 1994.

———. "Draupadi." Trans. Gayatri Chakravorty Spivak. *Bashai Tudu*. Ed. Samik Bandyopadhyay. Calcutta: Thema, 1990. 149–62.

———. "The Hunt." *Imaginary Maps*. Routledge, 1994. 1–17.

———. *Imaginary Maps: Three Stories by Mahasweta Devi*. Trans. Gayatri Chakravorty Spivak. New York: Routledge, 1995.

———. "Pterodactyl, Puran Sahay, and Pirtha." *Imaginary Maps*. Routledge, 1994. 95–196.

———. "Salt." Trans. Tapan Mitra. *Protest: An Anthology of Bengali Short Stories of the 70's.* Ed. Partha Chatterjee. Calcutta: Srijani, 1981. 21–38.

———. "Shishu" ("Children"). 1978. Trans. Pinaki Bhattacharya. *Women Writing in India: 600 B.C. to the Present.* Vol. II: The Twentieth Century. Eds. Susie Tharu and K. Lalita. Delhi: Oxford University Press, 1995. 236–51.

———. "Strange Children." *Of Women, Outcasts, Peasants, and Rebels.* Ed. Kalpana Bardhan. Berkeley: University of California Press, 1990, pp. 229–41.

Diamond, Cora. "The Difficulty of Reality and the Difficulty of Philosophy." *Partial Answers: Journal of Literature and the History of Ideas.* 1.2 (2003): 1–26.

Dodman, David, and Jane Dodman. "'Nuff Respec'? Widening and Deepening Participation in Academic and Policy Research in Jamaica." *Environmental Planning in the Caribbean.* Eds. Jonathan Pugh and Janet Henshall Momsen. Aldershot: Ashgate, 2006. 93–109.

Doniger, Wendy. "Reflections." *The Lives of Animals*, by J. M. Coetzee. Princeton: Princeton University, 1999. 93–106.

Dowie, Mark. *Refugees from Conservation: Global Conservation's Hundred Year Misunderstanding with Native People.* Boston: MIT Press, 2009.

Drayton, Richard. *Nature's Government: Science, Imperial Britain and the "Improvement of the World."* New Haven: Yale University Press, 2000.

Durrant, Sam. "J. M. Coetzee, Elizabeth Costello, and the Limits of the Sympathetic Imagination." *J. M. Coetzee and the Idea of the Public Intellectual*, by Jane Poyner. Athens: Ohio University Press, 2006. 118–34.

Duval-Carrié, Edouard. *Vodou Panthéon* (installation in Figgie Museum, Davenport, Iowa, 2005).

Eri, Vincent. *The Crocodile: A Novel of Papua New Guinea.* Ringwood, Vic: Penguin Books Australia, 1970.

Escobar, Arturo. "Constructing Nature: Elements for a Poststructuralist Political Ecology" In *Liberation Ecologies: Environment, Development, Social Movements.* Richard Peet and Michael Watts, eds. London: Routledge. 46–68.

———."Difference and Conflict in the Struggle Over Natural Resources: A Political Ecology Framework." *Development* 49 (2006): 6–13.

Esposito, Lauren. "Integrative Conservation." *SAIS Review* 22:2 (2002): 53–75.

Everest, Larry. *Behind the Poison Cloud: Union Carbide's Bhopal Massacre.* Chicago: Banner, 1986.

Eze, Emmanuel Chukwudi, ed. *Race and the Enlightenment: A Reader.* Cambridge, MA: Blackwell, 1997.

Fabian, Johannes. *Time and the Other: How Anthropology Makes Its Object.* New York: Columbia University Press, 1983.

Fanon, Frantz. *Black Skin, White Masks.* Trans. Charles Lam Markmann. 1967; London: Pluto, 1991.

———. *Peau Noir, Masques Blancs.* Paris: Gallimard, 1952.

———. *The Wretched of the Earth.* Trans Richard Philcox. New York: Grove Press, 2004.

Faris, Wendy. "Marking Space, Charting Time: Text and Territory in Faulkner's 'The Bear' and Carpentier's *Los Pasos Perdidos.*" *Do the Americas Have a Common Literature?* Ed. Gustavo Pérez-Firmat. Durham: Duke University Press, 1990. 243–65.

Fatton, Robert. *The Roots of Haitian Despotism.* Boulder, London: Lynne Rienner, 2007. 159–92.

Ferguson, Jesse Patrick. "Violent Dis-Placements: Natural and Human Violence in Kiran Desai's *The Inheritance of Loss.*" *The Journal of Commonwealth Literature* 44.2 (2009): 35–39.

Firth, Stewart. *Nuclear Playground*. Honolulu: University of Hawai'i Press, 1987.
Firth, Stewart and Karin Von Strokirch. "A Nuclear Pacific." *The Cambridge History of the Pacific Islanders*. Ed. Donald Denoon et al. Cambridge: Cambridge UP, 1997. 324–58.
Fleury-Battier, Alcibiade. *Sous les Bambous: Poésies*. Paris: Imprimerie Typographique Kugelmann, 1881.
Foning, A. R. *Lepcha, My Vanishing Tribe*. New Delhi: Sterling, 1987.
"Forensics: Age Written in Teeth by Nuclear Tests." *Nature* 437 (2005): 333–34.
Foster, John Bellamy. *Ecology against Capitalism*. Monthly Review Press, 2002.
Foucault, Michel. *The Order of Things: An Archaeology of the Human Sciences*. New York: Vintage Books, 1994.
Franssen, Paul. "Fleeing from the Burning City: Michael K, Vagrancy and Empire." *English Studies* 5 (2003): 453–63.
Freedgood, Elaine. *Victorian Writing about Risk*. Cambridge: Cambridge University Press, 2000.
French, Jennifer L. *Nature, Neo-Colonialism and the Latin American Regional Writers*. Hanover: University Press of New England, 2005.
Frisbie, Florence Johnny. *Miss Ulysses from Puka-Puka*. New York: MacMillan Co, 1948.
Fromm, Erich. *The Art of Loving*. New York: Harper & Row, 1956.
Funes Monzote, Reinaldo. *From Rainforest to Cane Field in Cuba: An Environmental History since 1492*. Trans. Alex Martin. Chapel Hill: University of North Carolina Press, 2008.
Gaard, Greta. "Tools for a Cross-Cultural Feminist Ethics: Exploring Ethical Contexts and Contents in the Makah Whale Hunt." *Hypatia* 16.1 (2001): 1–26.
Gadgil, Madhav, and Ramachandra Guha. *This Fissured Land: An Ecological History of India*. Delhi: Oxford University Press, 1993.
Ganguly, Rajat. "Poverty, Malgovernance and Ethnopolitical Mobilization: Gorkha Nationalism and the Gorkhaland Agitation in India." *Nationalism and Ethnic Politics* 11.4 (2005): 467–502.
Garber, Marjorie. "Reflections." *The Lives of Animals*, by J. M. Coetzee. Princeton: Princeton University Press, 1999. 73–84.
Garrard, Greg. *Ecocriticism*. London and New York: Routledge, 2004.
"Gas Kills Over 400 in Bhopal." *Hindustan Times* Late ed. December 4, 1984: 1.
Gautier Benítez, José. "A Puerto Rico." *Poesías*, 27. San Juan: Instituto de Cultura Puertorriqueña, 1960.
George, James. *Ocean Roads*. Wellington, NZ: Huia Press, 2006.
Gilligan, Carol. *In A Different Voice: Psychological Theory and Women's Development*. Cambridge: Harvard UP, 1982.
Ghose, Indira. *Women Travellers in Colonial India: The Power of the Female Gaze*. New Delhi: Oxford University Press, 1998.
Ghosh, Amitav. "The Author Talks." *The Hungry Tide*. Audiobook on CD. Recorded Books, 2005.
———. *The Hungry Tide*. London: HarperCollins, 2004.
Glissant, Édouard. *Caribbean Discourse: Selected Essays*. Trans. J. Michael Dash. Charlottesville: University Press of Virginia, 1989.
———. *Le discours antillais*. Paris: Seuil, 1981.
———. *La Lézarde*. Paris: Editions du Seuil, 1958.
———. *Poetics of Relation*. Trans. Betsy Wing. Ann Arbor: University of Michigan Press, 1997.

Glotfelty, Cheryll. "Introduction." *The Ecocriticism Reader: Landmarks in Literary Ecology*. Eds. Cheryll Glotfelty and Harold Fromm. Athens: University of Georgia Press. 1996.

Glotfelty, Cheryll, and Harold Fromm, eds. *The Ecocriticism Reader: Landmarks in Literary Ecology*. Athens: University of Georgia Press, 1996.

Godreau, Isar P. "Changing Space, Making Race: Distance, Nostalgia, and the Folklorization of Blackness in Puerto Rico." *Identities* 9 (2002): 282–304.

Golley, Frank Benjamin. *A History of the Ecosystem Concept in Ecology*. New Haven: Yale University Press, 1993.

Gombrich, Sir Ernst. *The Preference for the Primitive: Episodes in the History of Western Taste and Art*. London and New York: Phaidon Press, 2002.

Gomez, Juan Carlos. "Are Apes Persons? The Case for Primate Intersubjectivity." *The Animal Ethics Reader*. 2nd ed. Eds. Armstrong and Botzler. Routledge: 2008. 138–143.

Gómez de Avellaneda, Gertrudis. *Sab and Autobiography*. Trans. Nina Scott. Austin: University of Texas Press, 1993.

Gopalakrishnan, K. "Unskilled Worker Had Cleaned Tank." *Hindustan Times*. Late ed. December 5, 1984: 1.

Gordimer, Nadine. "Good Climate, Friendly Inhabitants." *Six Feet of the Country*. London: Penguin, 1986.

Gottlieb, Roger, ed. *This Sacred Earth: Religion, Nature and the Environment*. New York: Routledge, 2003.

———. "The Ingot and the Stick, The Ingot and the Gun: Mozambique-South Africa." George Carey, ed. *Frontiers*. London: BBC Books, 1990. 50–77.

———. "The Ultimate Safari." *Telling Tales*. Ed. Nadine Gordimer. New York: Farrar Straus and Giroux, 2004. 269–82.

Grace, Patricia. *Potiki*. Auckland, Penguin, 1986

Greenblatt, Stephen. *Marvelous Possessions: The Wonder of the New World*. Chicago: University of Chicago Press, 1991.

Grove, Richard H. "The Culture of Islands and the History of Environmental Concerns." Harvard Seminar on Environmental Values, April 18, 2000. http://ecoethics.net/hsev/200004txt.htm. Accessed March 10, 2008.

———. *Green Imperialism: Colonial Expansion, Tropical Island Edens and the Origins of Environmentalism, 1600–1860*. Cambridge: Cambridge University Press, 1995.

Guha, Ramachandra. *Environmentalism: A Global History*. New York: Longman, 2000.

———. "The Paradox of Global Environmentalism." *Current History* 99 (Nov. 2000): 367–70.

———. "Radical American Environmentalism: A Third World Critique." *Ethical Perspectives on Environmental Issues in India* 11 (1989): 71–83.

Guha, Ramachandra, and J. Martinez-Alier. *Varieties of Environmentalism: Essays North and South*. Delhi and New York: Oxford University Press, 1998.

Gunasekera, Rabindranath B., and Janet Henshall Momsen. "Amidst the Misty Mountains: The Role of Tea Tourism in Sri Lanka's Turbulent Tourist Industry." *Tea and Tourism: Tourists, Traditions and Transformations*. Ed. Lee Jolliffe. Clevedon: Channel View, 2007. 84–97.

Gutmann, Amy. "Introduction." *The Lives of Animals* by J. M. Coetzee. Princeton: Princeton University, 1999. 3–14.

Guy, Jeff. "A Landmark, Not a Breakthrough." *Suid-Afrikaanse Historiese Joernaal* 25 (1991): 227–231.

Hacking, Ian. "Our Fellow Animals." Review of *The Lives of Animals* by J. M. Coetzee and *Ethics into Action: Henry Spira and the Animal Rights Movement* by Peter Singer. *New York Review of Books*. June 29, 2000.

Haeckel, Ernst Heinrich Philipp August. *The History of Creation; or, The Development of the Earth and Its Inhabitants by the Action of Natural Causes. A Popular Exposition of the Doctrine of Evolution in General, and that of Darwin, Goethe, and Lamarck in Particular*. Trans. E. Ray Lankester. New York: D. Appleton, 1876.

Hagen, Joel Bartholemew. *An Entangled Bank: The Origins of Ecosystem Ecology*. Piscataway, NJ: Rutgers UP, 1992.

Half Life: A Parable of the Nuclear Age. Dir. Dennis O'Rourke. CameraWork, 1986.

Hall, Ambury, ed. *Below the Surface: Words and Images in Protest at French Nuclear Testing on Moruroa*. Auckland: Vintage NZ, 1995.

Halualani, Rona Tamiko. *In the Name of Hawaiians: Native Identities and Cultural Politics*. Minneapolis: University of Minnesota Press, 2002.

Handley, George. B. "The Argument of the Outboard Motor: An Interview with Derek Walcott." *Caribbean Literature and the Environment: Between Nature and Culture*. Eds. Elizabeth DeLoughrey, Renée Gosson, and George Handley. Charlottesville: University of Virginia Press, 2005. 127–39.

———. "Derek Walcott's Poetics of the Environment in *The Bounty*." *Callaloo* 28.1 (Winter 2005): 201–15.

———. *New World Poetics: Nature and the Adamic Imagination of Whitman, Neruda, and Walcott*. Athens: University of Georgia Press. 2007.

———. "A Postcolonial Sense of Place in the Work of Derek Walcott." *ISLE (Interdisciplinary Study of Literature and the Environment)* 6.3 (Summer 2000): 1–22.

Handy, E. S. Craighill, and Elizabeth Green Handy, with Mary Kawena Pukui. *Native Planters in Old Hawaii: Their Life, Lore, and Environment*. Honolulu: Bishop Museum Press, 1972.

Hansen, Peter. "Albert Smith, the Alpine Club and the Invention of Mountaineering in Mid-Victorian England." *The Journal of British Studies* 34.3 Victorian Subjects (1995): 300–324.

Haraway, Donna J. "Otherworldly Conversations; Terrain Topics; Local Terms." *Science as Culture* 3.1 (1992): 64–98.

———. *Primate Visions: Gender, Race and Nature in the World of Modern Science*. London: Routledge, 1989.

———."The Promises of Monsters: A Regenerative Politics for Inappropriate/d Others" in: Lawrence Grossberg, Cary Nelson, Paula A. Treichler, eds., *Cultural Studies*. New York; Routledge, 1992, pp. 295–337.

———. *Simians, Cyborgs, and Women: The Reinvention of Nature*. New York: Routledge, 1991.

———. "Teddy Bear Patriarchy: Taxidermy in the Garden of Eden, New York City, 1908–1936." *Social Text* 11 (1984): 20–64.

———. *When Species Meet*. Minneapolis: University of Minnesota Press, 2008.

Harkin, Michael E. "Staged Encounters: Indians and Tourism." *Ethnohistory* 50.3 (2003): 573–83.

Harris, Wilson. *Explorations: A Selection of Talks and Articles 1966–1981*. Ed. and Intr. Hena Maes-Jelinek. Mundelstrup: Dangaroo Press, 1981.

———."The Fabric of the Imagination." *Third World Quarterly* 12.1 (January 1990): 175–186.

———. *The Whole Armour*. London: Faber, 1962.

Harrison, Mark. "Climates and Constitutions: Health, Race, Environment and British Imperialism in India 1600–1850." *Journal of Historical Geography* 27.3 (2001): 455–57.
Harrison, Robert Pogue. *Forests: The Shadow of Civilization*. Chicago: University of Chicago Press, 1992.
Harvey, David. *Justice, Nature and the Geography of Difference*. London: Blackwell, 1996.
———. *The New Imperialism*. Oxford: Oxford University Press, 2003.
Hatzenberger, Françoise. "The Historic Evolution of the Haitian Forest." *Forest History: International Studies on Socio-Economic and Forest Ecosystem Change* (Report No. 2 of the IUFRO Task Force on Environmental Change). Eds. Mauro Agnoletti and Steven Anderson, 65–78. Wallingford, Oxfordshire: CABI, 2000.
Hau'ofa, Epeli. "The Ocean in Us." *Voyaging through the Contemporary Pacific*, eds. David Hanlon and Geoffrey M. White. Lanham, MA: Rowman and Littlefield, 2000. 113–31.
———. "Our Sea of Islands." *Asia/Pacific as Space of Cultural Production*, eds. Arif Dirlik and Rob Wilson. Durham and London: Duke University Press, 1995. 86–101.
Head, Dominic. "A Belief in Frogs: J. M. Coetzee's Enduring Faith in Fiction." *J. M. Coetzee and the Idea of the Public Intellectual*, by Jane Poyner. Athens: Ohio University Press, 2006. 100–117.
———. "The (Im)Possibility of Ecocriticism" *Writing the environment: ecocriticism and literature*. Edited by Richard Kerridge and Neil Sammells. London; New York: Zed Books, 1998. 27–39.
Heim, Otto. "Breath as metaphor of sovereignty and connectedness in Pacific Island poetry." *New Literatures Review* 47, forthcoming.
Heinl, Robert Debs. *Written in Blood: The Story of the Haitian People, 1492–1971*. Boston: Houghton Mifflin, 1978.
Heise, Ursula. "The Hitchhiker's Guide to Ecocriticism." *PMLA* 121.2 (2006): 503–16.
Held, Virginia. *The Ethics of Care: Personal, Political, Global*. Oxford University Press, 2006.
———. *Sense of Place and Sense of Planet*. Oxford: Oxford UP, 2008.
Herron, Tom. "The Dog Man: Becoming Animal in Coetzee's *Disgrace*." *Twentieth-Century Literature* 51.4 (2005): 467–90.
Hill, Christopher V. *South Asia: An Environmental History*. Santa Barbara, CA: ABC-CLIO, INC, 2008
Hodge, Merle. *Crick, Crack Monkey*. London: Heinemann, 1981.
Hofmeyr, Isabel. "Nterata"/"The Wire": Fences, Boundaries, Orality, Literacy." *International Annual of Oral History, 1990: Subjectivity and Multiculturalism in Oral History*. Ed. Ronald J. Grele. New York: Greenwood Press, 1990. 69–91.
Hogan, Linda. *People of the Whale*. New York: W. W. Norton, 2008.
———. "Silencing Tribal Grandmothers—Traditions, Old Values at Heart of Makah's Clash over Whaling." *Seattle Times*. Accessed February 28, 2009. http://community.seattletimes.nwsource.com/archive/?date=19961215&slug=2365045
Hogan, Linda and Brenda Peterson, eds. *The Sweet Breathing of Plants: Women Writing on the Green World*. New York: North Point Press, 2001.
Hollywood's Top Secret Film Studio. Dir. Peter Kuran. VCE, 1999.

Honey, Martha. *Ecotourism and Sustainable Development: Who Owns Paradise?* Washington, DC: Island Press, 1999.
Hooker, Joseph Dalton. *Himalayan Journals I: Scientific Travellers, 1789–1874*. London: Routledge, 2004.
hooks, bell. *All about Love: New Visions*. New York: Harper Perennial, 2000.
Huggan, Graham. "'Greening' Postcolonialism: Ecocritical Perspectives." *Modern Fiction Studies* 50.3 (2004): 701–33.
———. *The Postcolonial Exotic: Marketing the Margins*. London and New York: Routledge, 2001.
Huggan, Graham and Helen Tiffin. "Green Postcolonialism." *Interventions* 9.1 (2007): 1–11.
———. *Postcolonial Ecocriticism: Literature, Animals, Environment*. New York: Routledge, 2010.
Hulme, Peter. "Beyond the Straits: Postcolonial Allegories of the Globe." *Postcolonial Studies and Beyond*. Eds. Ania Loomba et al. Durham and London: Duke University Press, 2005. 41–61.
Hurbon, Laennec. "L'arbe dans le pantheon vaudou." *Haïti, Terre Délabrée; Ecologie et Dictature, Dossier 2*. Eds. Rony Smarth and Edwidge Balutansky. Port-au-Prince: l'Impremier II for Centre de Researches Sociales et de Diffusion Populaire, 1991. 69–75.
———. *Le Barbare Imaginaire*. Port-au-Prince: Édition Henri Deschamps, 1987. 228–42.
Ihimaera, Witi. "The Whale." *Pounamu Pounamu*. Auckland: Reed, 2003. 152–62.
———. *The Whale Rider*. Orlando: Harcourt, 1987.
Jackson, Wes. "Fertility and the Age of Soils." *The Land Institute*. December 1, 2000. http://www.landinstitute.org/vnews/display.v/ART/2000/12/01/3aa90b0d9. Accessed October 2, 2008.
Jacobs, J.U. "Zakes Mda's *The Heart of Redness*: The Novel as Umngqokolo." *Kunapipi: Journal of Post-Colonial Writing*. 24:1–2 (2002): 224–36.
Jacobs, Nancy J. *Environment, Power, and Injustice. A South African History*. Cambridge: Cambridge University Press, 2003.
Jones, Katie. "Land and Sea: The Castaway and the Gulf." *The Art of Derek Walcott*. Ed. Stewart Brown. Bridgend: Seren Books, 1991. 37–50.
Jordan, June. "Report from the Bahamas." 1989 *A Stranger in the Village: Two Centuries of African-American Travel Writing*. Eds. Farah J. Griffin and Cheryl J. Fish. Boston: Beacon Press, 1998. 319–29.
Jungk, Robert. *Brighter than a Thousand Suns: A Personal History of the Atomic Scientists*. New York: Harcourt, 1958.
Kafka, Franz. "A Report to an Academy." *Metamorphosis and Other Stories*. London: Penguin Books, 1992. 187–95. Originally published in *A Country Doctor: Little Tales*, Munich and Leipzig: Kurt Wolff, 1919.
Kalof, Linda, and Amy Fitzgerald, eds. *The Animals Reader*. Oxford: Berg, 2007.
Kanahele, George Sanford. *Kū Kanaka, Stand Tall: A Search for Hawaiian Values*. Honolulu: University of Hawai'i Press, 1992.
Kanahele, Pualani. "He Ko'ihonua no Kanaloa, he Moku." *Kaho'olawe: Na Leo o Kanaloa*. Eds. Walter Levin and Roland B. Reeve. Honolulu: Ai Pohaku Press, 1995.
Kapferer, Bruce. "Ethnic Nationalism and the Discourses of Violence in Sri Lanka." *Communal/Plural: Journal of Transnational and Cross-Cultural Studies* 9.1 (2001): 33–67.
Kaplan, Rachel, and Stephen Kaplan. *The Experience of Nature: A Psychological Perspective*. New York: Cambridge University, 1989.
Kapstein, Helen. "A Culture of Tourism: Branding the Nation in a Global Market." *Safundi: The Journal of South African and American Studies* 8.1 (2007): 109–15.

Kashi, Ed and Michael Watts. *The Curse of the Black Gold 50 Years of Oil in the Niger Delta*. Powerhouse, 2008.
Kaur, Rajender. "'Home Is Where the Oracella [sic] Are': Toward a New Paradigm of Transcultural Ecocritical Engagement in Amitav Ghosh's *The Hungry Tide*." *ISLE* 14.1 (Winter 2007): 125–41.
Keller, Evelyn Fox. *A Feeling for the Organism: The Life and Work of Barbara McClintock*. New York: Henry Holt, 1983.
Kennedy, Dane. *The Magic Mountains: Hill Stations and the British Raj*. Berkeley: University of California Press, 1996.
Kerridge, Richard. "Introduction." *Writing the Environment: Ecocriticism and Literature*. Eds. Richard Kerridge and Neil Sammells. London: Zed, 1998. 1–10.
Kerridge, Richard, and Neil Sammells, eds. *Writing the Environment: Ecocriticism and Literature*. London: Zed, 1998.
Khan, Ismith. *The Jumbie Bird*. Harlow, England: Longman, 1985.
Kimbrell, Andrew. *Fatal Harvest: The Tragedy of Industrial Agriculture*. Washington, DC and London: Island Press, 2002.
Kimmerle, Heinz. "The Concept of the Person in African Thought." *Ontology of Consciousness: Percipient Action*. Ed. Helmut Wautischer. Cambridge, MA, and London: MIT Press, 2008. 507–24.
Kincaid, Jamaica. *Among Flowers: A Walk in the Himalayas*. Washington, DC: National Geographic, 2005.
———. *A Small Place*. New York: Plume, 1988.
———, ed. *My Favorite Plant*. New York: Farrar, Straus and Giroux, 1998.
———. *My Garden (Book)*: New York: Farrar, Straus and Giroux, 1999.
Klein, Naomi. "The Rise of Disaster Capitalism." *Nation*. May 2, 2005. http://www.thenation.com/doc/20050502/klein.
———. *The Shock Doctrine: The Rise of Disaster Capitalism*. London: Allen Lane, 2007.
Klopper, Dirk. "Between Nature and Culture: The Place of Prophecy in Zakes Mda's *The Heart of Redness*." *Current Writing: Text and Reception in Southern Africa* 20.2 (2008):
Kolodny, Annette. *The Lay of the Land: Metaphor as Experience and History in American Life and Letters*. Chapel Hill: University of North Carolina Press, 1975.
Kothari, Rajni. "Foreword." *Staying Alive* by Vandana Shiva. London: Zed Books. ix–xiii.
Koyana, S. "Qolorha and the Dialogism of Place in Zakes Mda's *The Heart of Redness*." *Current Writing* 15:1 (2003): 51–62.
Krech, Shepard, III. *The Ecological Indian: Myth and History*. New York: W. W. Norton, 1999.
Kreps, Gary A. "Disaster as Systemic Event and Social Catalyst." *What Is a Disaster?: Perspectives on the Question*. Ed. Enrico L. Quarantelli. London and New York: Routledge, 1998. 31–55.
Kroeber, Karl. "Why It's a Good Thing Gerald Vizenor Is Not an Indian." *Survivance: Narratives of Native Presence*. Ed. Gerald Vizenor. Lincoln and London: University of Nebraska Press, 2008. 25–38.
Kroese, Ron. "Industrial Agriculture's War against Nature." *Fatal Harvest: The Tragedy of Industrial Agriculture*. Ed. Andrew Kimbrell, 20–28. Washington, DC, and London: Island Press, 2002.
Kuhn, Thomas. "Metaphor in Science." *Metaphor and Thought*. Ed. Andrew Ortony. Cambridge: Cambridge University Press, 1979. 409–419.
Kumar, Amitava. *Bombay-London-New York*. New York: Routledge, 2002.

———. "Sirens Called Them to Death." *Hindustan Times*. December 5, 1984: 1.
Kuo, Frances E., and Andrea Faber Taylor. "A Potential Natural Treatment for Attention-Deficit/Hyperactivity Disorder: Evidence from a National Study." *American Journal of Public Health* 94.9 (2008): 1580–87.
Kurlansky, Mark. *A Continent of Islands: Searching for the Caribbean Destiny*. Cambridge, MA: Da Capo Press, 1993.
Labat, Jean Baptiste. *The Memoirs of Père Labat, 1693–1705*. 1931. Trans. John Eaden. London: F. Cass, 1970.
Labuschagne, R. J. *60 Years, Kruger Park*. Pretoria: National Parks Board of Trustees, 1958.
Laguerre, Enrique. *La Llamarada*. Río Piedras: Editorial Cultural, 1979.
Lanchester, John. "A Will of His Own." *New York Review of Books*, November 17, 2005.
Lapierre, Dominic, and Javier Moro. *Five Past Midnight in Bhopal*. London: Scribner, 2002.
Laraque, Paul. "André Breton en Haïti." *Conjonction* 193 (1992): 24–32.
Las Casas, Bartolomé de. *Brevísima relación de la destrucción de las Indias*. Barcelona: Linkgua Ediciones, 2006.
Laurence, William. *Dawn over Zero: The Story of the Atomic Bomb*. NY: Alfred A. Knopf, 1946.
———. "Is Atomic Energy the Key to Our Dreams?"*Saturday Evening Post*. April 13, 1946. 9–10, 36–41.
Lazarus, Neil. *Nationalism and Cultural Practice in the Postcolonial World*. Cambridge: Cambridge University Press, 1999.
Leach, Melissa, and Mearns Robin, eds. *The Lie of the Land: Challenging Received Wisdom on the African Environment*. Oxford: James Currey, 1996.
Leech, Clifford. *Tragedy*. London and New York: Routledge, 1989.
Leopold, Aldo. *A Sand County Almanac and Sketches Here and There*. London and New York: Oxford University Press, 1949.
Lerebours, Michel-Philippe. *Haïti et ses Peintres de 1804 à 1980*. Port-au-Prince: L'Imprimeur II, 1989. 233–35 & 309–44.
Lezama Lima, José. *La expresión americana*. La Habana: Editorial Letras Cubanas, 1993.
Light, Michael. *100 Suns*. New York: Alfred A. Knopf, 2003.
Lilienthal, David E. "Atomic Energy is your Business" *Bulletin of Atomic Scientists* 3. 11 (November 1947), 335–36.
Livingstone, David N. "Tropical Hermeneutics: Fragments for a Historical Narrative." *Singapore Journal of Tropical Geography* 21.1 (2000): 92–98.
Lodge, David. "Disturbing the Peace." Review of *Elizabeth Costello* by J. M. Coetzee. *New York Review of Books*. November 20, 2003.
Lohmann, Larry. "Green Orientalism." *Ecologist* 23.6 (1993): 202.
Lokugé, Chandani. *Turtle Nest*. New Delhi: Penguin, 2003.
Lutts, Ralph H. "Chemical Fallout: *Silent Spring*, Radioactive Fallout, and the Environmental Movement." *And No Birds Sing: Rhetorical Analyses of Rachel Carson's* Silent Spring. Ed. Craig Wadell. Carbondale: Southern Illinois UP, 2000. 17–42.
Lyons, Paul. *American Pacificism: Oceania in the US Imagination*. New York: Routledge, 2006.
Maathai, Wangari. *The Challenge for Africa*. New York: Pantheon Books, 2009.
Madiou, Thomas. *Histoire d'Haïti, Tome IV (1847–1848)*. Port-au-Prince: Editions Henri Deschamps, 1989. 510–43.

Magome, Hector, and Murombedzi, James. "Sharing South African National Parks: Community Land and Conservation in a Democratic South Africa." *Decolonizing Nature: Strategies for Conservation in a Post-Colonial Era*. Eds. William M. Adams and Martin Mulligan. London: Earthscan, 2003. 108–34.

Malkki, Liisa. *Purity and Exile: Violence, Memory, and National Cosmology among Hutu Refugees in Tanzania*. Chicago: University of Chicago Press, 1995.

Mallick, Ross. "Refugee Resettlement in Forest Reserves: West Bengal Policy Reversal and the Marichjhapi Massacre." *Journal of Asian Studies* 58.1 (1999): 104–25.

Mander, Jerry. "Machine Logic: Industrializing Nature and Agriculture." *Fatal Harvest: The Tragedy of Industrial Agriculture*. Ed. Andrew Kimbrell, 16–19. Washington, DC, and London: Island Press, 2002.

Marcone, Jorge. "Jungle Fever: Primitivism in Environmentalism: Rómulo Gallego's Canaima and the Romance of the Jungle." *Primitivism and Identity in Latin America: Essays on Art, Literature, and Culture*. Eds. Erik Camayd-Freixas and José Eduardo González. Tucson: University of Arizona Press, 2000. 157–72.

Marshak, Robert and Eldred C. Nelson, and Leonard I. Schiff. *Our Atomic World*. Los Alamos Atomic Bomb Laboratory. Albuquerque: University of New Mexico Press, 1946.

Martinez-Alier, Joan. *The Environmentalism of the Poor*. Cheltenham, UK, and Northampton, MA: Edward Elgar, 2002.

Marzec, Robert. *An Ecological and Postcolonial Study of Literature: From Daniel Defoe to Salman Rushdie*. New York: Palgrave, 2007.

———. "Enclosures, Colonization and the Robinson Crusoe Syndrome." *Boundary 2* 29.2. (2002): 129–56.

Masco, Joseph. *The Nuclear Borderlands: The Manhattan Project in Post-Cold War New Mexico*. Princeton: Princeton UP, 2006.

Maslin, Janet. "The Mockery Can Still Sting with a Target in the Mirror." Review of *Elizabeth Costello* by J. M. Coetzee. *New York Times*. October 21, 2003.

Massey, Doreen. "A Global Sense of Place." in *Reading Human Geography*. Eds. Trevor Barnes and Derek Gregory. London: Arnold, 1997. 315–23.

Mateo Palmer, Margarita. "El mito americano en Los pasos perdidos." *Alejo Carpentier: acá y allá*. Ed. Luisa Campuzano. Pittsburgh: University of Pittsburgh, 2007. 145–64.

Mathers, Kathryn, and Loren B. Landau. "Tourists or 'Makwerekwere': Good versus Bad Visitors and the Possibilities of Ethical Tourism in South Africa." *Forced Migration Working Paper Series #27*, Forced Migration Studies Programme, University of Witwatersrand. Paper presented to the International Sociological Association Congress Durban, South Africa, July 2006. 1–16.

Mazel, David. "American Literary Environmentalism as Domestic Orientalism." *The Ecocriticism Reader: Landmarks in Literary Ecology*. Eds. Cheryll Glotfelty and Harold Fromm. Athens: University of Georgia Press, 1996. 137–46.

Mazuchelli, Elizabeth Sarah. *The Indian Alps and How We Crossed Them: Being a Narrative of Two Years Residence in the Eastern Himalaya and Two Months' Tour into the Interior. By a Lady Pioneer, Illustrated by Herself*. Boston: Adamant Media Corporation, 2002.

McClintock, Anne. *Imperial Leather: Race, Gender and Sexuality in the Colonial Contest*. New York: Routledge, 1995.

McGregor, Davianna Pomaika'i. *Na Kua'aina: Living Hawaiian Culture*. Honolulu: University of Hawai'i Press, 2007.

McKibben, Bill. *The End of Nature*. New York: Random House, 1989.
Mda, Zakes. *The Whale Caller*. New York: Picador, 2005.
———. *Heart of Redness*. New York: Picador, 2000.
———. "A Response to 'Duplicity and Plagarism in Zakes Mda's *The Heart of Redness* by Andrew Offenburger.'" *Research in African Literatures* 39:3 (2008): 200–203.
Meeker, Joseph W. *The Comedy of Survival: In Search of an Environmental Ethic*. 2nd ed. Los Angeles: Guild of Tutors Press, 1980.
———. *The Comedy of Survival: Literary Ecology and a Play Ethic*. 3rd ed. Tucson: University of Arizona Press, 1997.
Melville, Elinor G. K. *A Plague of Sheep: Environmental Consequences of the Conquest of Mexico*. Cambridge: Cambridge University Press, 1994.
Melville, Herman. *Moby Dick*. Ed. Harrison Hayford and Hershel Parker. New York: W. W. Norton, 1967.
Mercer, Kobena. "Welcome to the Jungle." *Identity*. Ed. J. Rutherford. London: Lawrence and Wishart, 1990.
Merchant, Carolyn. *The Death of Nature: Women, Ecology, and the Scientific Revolution*. San Francisco: Harper and Row, 1980.
———. *Earthcare: Women and the Environment*. Routledge, 1995.
———. *Ecology: Key Concepts in Critical Theory* 2nd edition. Amherst, NY: Prometheus (Humanity) Books, 2008.
———. *Reinventing Eden: The Fate of Nature in Western Culture*. New York: Routledge, 2003.
Meyer, Manulani Aluli. "Hawaiian Epistemology and the Triangulation of Meaning." *Handbook of Critical and Indigenous Methodologies*. Eds. Norman K. Denzin, Yvonna S. Lincoln, and Linda Tuhiwai Smith. London and Los Angeles: Sage, 2008. 217–32.
Mies, Maria, and Vandana Shiva. *Ecofeminism*. London & New Jersey: Zed Books, 1993.
Miller, David Philip, and Peter Hanns Reill, eds. *Visions of Empire: Voyages, Botany, and Representations of Nature*. New York: Cambridge University Press, 1996.
Miller, Shawn. *An Environmental History of Latin America*. Cambridge: Cambridge University Press, 2007.
Milne, Anne. "Ecocritism." *The Johns Hopkins Guide to Literary Theory and Criticism*. 2nd ed. 2005. Online. http://litguide.press.jhu.edu/cgi-bin/view.cgi?eid=84.
Milton, John. *Paradise Lost*. Ed. Gordon Teskey. New York: Norton, 2005.
Mir, Pedro. *Hay un país en el mundo*. Mexico: Librería G. Monge, 1949.
Misra, R.P. *Environmental Ethics: A Dialogue of Cultures*. Delhi: Sustainable Development Foundation, 1992.
Mitter, Partha. *Much Maligned Monsters: A History of European Reactions to Indian Art*. Chicago: University of Chicago Press, 1992.
Montenegro, David. "An Interview with Derek Walcott." *Conversations with Derek Walcott*. Ed. William Baer. Jackson: University Press of Mississippi, 1996. 135–50.
Montero, Mayra. *In the Palm of Darkness*. Translated by Edith Grossman. New York: HarperCollins, 1997.
Moore, Donald S., Anand Pandian, and Jake Kosek. "Introduction: The Cultural Politics of Race and Nature." *Race, Nature, and the Politics of Difference*. Durham, NC: Duke University Press, 2003.
Morales, Rodney, ed. *Ho'i Ho'i Hou: A Tribute to George Helm and Kimo Mitchell*. Honolulu: Bamboo Ridge Press, 1984.

Moréau de Saint-Méry, Médéric Louis Elie. *A Topographical, Political Description of St. Domingo: Its Climate, Population, Character, Manners of the Inhabitants, and Government*. Boston: J. Bumsteadm, 1808.

Mortimer-Sandilands, Catriona. "Queering Ecocultural Studies." *Cultural Studies* 22.3-4 (2008): 455-76.

Morton, Timothy. *Ecology without Nature: Rethinking Environmental Aesthetics*. Cambridge, MA: Harvard University Press, 2007.

Mufti, Aamir R. *Enlightenment in the Colony: The Jewish Question and the Crisis of Postcolonial Culture*. Princeton: Princeton University Press, 2007.

Mukherjee, Pablo. *Postcolonial Environments: Nature, Culture and the Contemporary Indian Novel in English*. New York: Palgrave, 2010.

———. "Surfing the Second Wave: Amitav Ghosh's Tide Country." *New Formations* 59 (2007): 144-75.

Murombedzi, James, "Devolving the Expropriation of Nature: The 'Devolution' of Wildlife Management in Southern Africa." *Decolonizing Nature: Strategies for Conservation in a Post-Colonial Era*. Eds. William M. Adams and Martin Mulligan. London: Earthscan, 2003. 135-51.

Murphy, Patrick D. *Literature, Nature, and Other: Ecofeminist Critiques*. Albany: State University of New York Press, 1995.

———, ed. *Literature of Nature: An International Sourcebook*. Chicago and London: Fitzroy Dearborn Publishers, 1998.

Mwangi, "Nobel Prize: A Shot in the Arm to African Ecocriticism" *The Nation* (Nairobi) 24 October 2004. http://www.asle.org/site/resources/ecocritical-library/intro/nobel/ Accessed July 25, 2010.

Nadal-Gardère, Marie-José, and Gérald Bloncourt. *La Peinture Haïtienne/Haitian Arts*. Évreux: Nathan, 1986. 94.

Naess, Arne. "The Third World, Wilderness, and Deep Ecology." *Deep Ecology in the Twenty-First Century*. Ed. George Sessions. Boston: Shambhala, 1995. 397-407.

Nandy, Ashis. "History's Forgotten Doubles." *History & Theory* 34.2 (1995): 44-66.

Nash, Richard, and Ron Broglio. "Introduction to Animal Issue." *Configurations* 14.1 (2008): 1-7.

Ndebele, Njabulo S. *Fine Lines from the Box. Further Thoughts about Our Country*. Houghton, South Africa: Umuzi, 2007.

———. "Game Lodges and Leisure Colonialists." *Blank: Interrogating Architecture after Apartheid*. Eds. Hilton Judin and Ivan Vladislavic. Cape Town: David Phillips, 1998. 10-14.

———. "Rediscovery of the Ordinary." *Essays on South African Literature and Culture*. Johannesburg: COSAW, 1991.

Neruda, Pablo. *Canto General*. Trans. Jack Schmitt. Berkeley: University of California Press, 2000.

———. *Obras completas*. Vols. I-V. Ed. Hernan Loyola with advice from Saúl Yurkievic. Barcelona: Galaxia Gutenberg.

New American Bible. Camden, NJ: Thomas Nelson, 1970. 3.

Nixon, Rob. "Environmentalism and Postcolonialism." *Postcolonial Studies and Beyond*. Ed. Ania Loomba et al. Durham: Duke University Press, 2005. 233-51.

———. "Slow Violence." Paper presented at the MLA Convention, Chicago, December 2007.

———. "Slow Violence, Gender, and the Environmentalism of the Poor." *Journal of Commonwealth and Postcolonial Studies* 13.2/14.1 (Fall 2006-Spring 2007): 3-12.

Northcott, Michael S. *The Environment and Christian Ethics*. Cambridge: Cambridge University Press, 1996.

———. *A Moral Climate: The Ethics of Climate Change*. New York: Orbis, 2009.

Nunez, Elizabeth. *Prospero's Daughter*. New York: Ballantine Books, 2006.

Nussbaum, Martha C. *Frontiers of Justice: Disability, Nationality, Species Membership*. Cambridge, MA: Harvard University Press, 2004.

———. "The Moral Status of Animals." *Chronicle of Higher Education* 52:22 (February 3, 2006): 1–6. page B6: http://chronicle.com/article/The-Moral-Status-of-Animals/25792/

———. "The Moral Status of Animals." *The Animals Reader: The Essential Classic and Contemporary Writings*. Eds. Linda Kalof and Amy Fitzgerald. Virginia: Berg, 2007. 30–36.

O'Brien, Susie. "Articulating a World of Difference: Ecocriticism, Postcolonialism and Globalization." *Canadian Literature*. 170/171 (Winter 2001): 140–58.

———. "The Garden and the World: Jamaica Kincaid and the Cultural Borders of Ecocriticism." *Mosaic: A Journal for the Interdisciplinary Study of Literature* 35.2 (2002): 167.

O'Connell Davidson, Julia. *Children in the Global Sex Trade*. Cambridge: Polity, 2005.

O'Connor, James. *Natural Causes: Essays in Ecological Marxism*. Guilford Press, 1997.

Odum, Eugene P. "Ecology and the Atomic Age." *ASB Bulletin* 4.2 (1957): 27–29.

Offenburger, Andrew. "Duplicity and Plagiarism in Zakes Mda's *The Heart of Redness*." 39:3 (2008): 164–99.

Operation Greenhouse. Nar. Carey Wilson. Prod. Atomic Energy Commission and Joint Task Force 3. Lookout Mountain Laboratory, 1951.

Ormerod, Beverley. *An Introduction to the French Caribbean Novel*. London: Heinemann, 1985.

Pal, Indra. "Chipko Movement Is 300 Years Old," in Misra, R.P. *Environmental Ethics*. 62–63.

Parini, Jay. "The Greening of the Humanities." *New York Times Magazine*. October 19, 1995. 52–53.

Peet, Richard, and Michael Watts, eds. *Liberation Ecologies: Environment, Development, Social Movements*. London and New York: Routledge, 2004.

Peires, J. *The Dead Will Arise: Nongqawuse and the Great Xhosa Cattle Killing Movement of 1856-7*. Bloomington: Indiana UP, 1989

Persaud, Lakshmi. *For the Love of My Name*. Leeds, England: Peepal Tree Press, 2000.

Peterson, Brenda. "Apprenticeship to Animal Play." *Intimate Nature: The Bond between Women and Animals*. Eds. Linda Hogan, Deena Metzger, and Brenda Peterson. New York: Ballantine, 1998. 428–37.

———. "Who Will Speak for the Whales? Elders Call for a Spiritual Dialogue on Makah Tribe's Whaling Proposal." *Seattle Times*. December 22, 1996. http://seattletimes.nwsource.com. Accessed February 28, 2009.

Peterson, Brenda, and Linda Hogan. *Sightings: The Gray Whales' Mysterious Journey*. Washington, DC: National Geographic Society, 2002.

Phillips, Dana. *The Truth of Ecology: Nature, Culture, and Literature in America*. Oxford: Oxford University Press, 2003.

Phillips, Joan L. "Tourist-Oriented Prostitution in Barbados: The Case of the Beach Boy and the White Female Tourist." *Sun, Sex, and Gold: Tourism and Sex Work in the Caribbean*. Ed. Kamala Kempadoo. Lanham and Oxford: Rowman & Littlefield, 1999. 183–200.

Plant, Judith. *Healing the Wounds: The Promise of Ecofeminism*. London: Green Print, 1989.

Plummer, Brenda Gayle. *Haiti and the United States: The Psychological Moment.* Athens: University of Georgia Press, 1992. 110–14.
Plumwood, Val. *Environmental Culture: The Ecological Crisis of Reason.* London and New York: Routledge, 2002.
———. *Feminism and the Mastery of Nature.* London and New York: Routledge. 1993.
Pompilus, Pradel. "Le Paysan dans le Littérature Haitienne." *Littérature et Société en Haïti.* Ed. Claude Souffrant. Port-au-Prince: Editions Henri Deschamps, 1991. 19–25.
Poyner, Jane. *J. M. Coetzee and the Idea of the Public Intellectual.* Athens: Ohio University Press, 2006.
Pratt, Mary Louise. *Imperial Eyes: Travel Writing and Transculturation.* 2nd ed. New York: Routledge, 1992; 2008.
Prentice, Chris. "Riding the Whale? Postcolonialism and Globalization in *Whale Rider.*" *Global Fissures: Postcolonial Fusions.* Eds. Clara A. B. Joseph and Janet Wilson. Amsterdam and New York: Rodopi, 2006. 247–68.
Prest, John. *The Garden of Eden: The Botanic Garden and the Re-Creation of Paradise.* New Haven: Yale University Press, 1981.
Price-Mars, Jean. *Ainsi Parla L'Oncle.* Port-au-Prince: Bibliothèque Haïtienne, 1928. Ottawa: Lemeac, 1973.
———. *So Spoke the Uncle.* Trans. Magdaline W. Shannon. Washington, DC: Three Continents Press, 1983.
Prigogine, Ilya, and Isabelle Stengers. *Order Out of Chaos: Man's New Dialogue with Nature.* Toronto, New York: Bantam Books, 1984.
Protect Kaho'olawe 'Ohana. *Aloha 'Āina.* Kaunakakai, Hawai'i: Newsletter Published by Protect Kaho'olawe Fund (1988–89): 2.
Pyne, Stephen J. *How the Canyon Became Grand.* New York: Viking, 1998.
Quarantelli, Enrico L. "Epilogue Where We Have Been and Where We Might Go: Putting the Elephant Together, Blowing Soap Bubbles, and Having Singular Insights." *What Is a Disaster: Perspectives on the Question.* Ed. Enrico L. Quarantelli. London and New York: Routledge, 1998. 234–73.
Quayson, Ato. *Calibrations: Reading for the Social.* Minneapolis: University of Minnesota Press, 2003.
Radio Bikini. Dir. Robert Stone. New Video Group, 1987.
Rajan, Ravi. *Modernizing Nature: Forestry and Imperial Eco-Development, 1800–1950.* Oxford University Press, 2006.
Raleigh, Walter. *The Discovery of Guiana.* New York: Cassell, 1886.
Renda, Mary A. *Taking Haiti, Military Occupation and the Culture of U.S. Imperialism.* Chapel Hill and London: University of North Carolina Press, 2001.
Rhodes, Richard. *The Making of the Atomic Bomb.* New York: Simon, 1990.
Rhys, Jean. *Wide Sargasso Sea.* New York: W. W. Norton, 1966.
Rice, Alison. "Post-Tsunami Reconstruction and Tourism: A Second Disaster?" *Tourism Concern.* 2005. http://www.tourismconcern.org.uk/pdfs/Final%20report.pdf.
Richards-Pillot, Eunice. *Les Terres noyées.* Matoury: Ibis Rouge, 2006.
Ricoeur, Paul. *The Rule of Metaphor: Multi-Disciplinary Studies in the Creation of Meaning in Language.* Trans. Robert Czerny et al. London: Routledge, 1978.
Ring, Jim. *How the English Made the Alps.* London: John Murray, 2001.
Roberts, Ronald Suresh. *No Cold Kitchen: A Biography of Nadine Gordimer.* Johannesburg: STE, 2005.

Rollason, Christopher. "'In Our Translated World': Transcultural Communication in Amitav Ghosh's *The Hungry Tide*." *Atlantic Literary Review* 6.1–2 (2005): 1–14.

Rose, T. S. R. "English Artists in the Val D'Aosta." *Journal of the Warburg and Courtauld Institutes* 19.3/4 (1956): 283–93.

Rosenthal, Peggy. "The Nuclear Mushroom Cloud as Cultural Image." *American Literary History* 3 (1991): 63–92.

Ross, Andrew. *The Chicago Gangster Theory of Life: Nature's Debt to Society*. London: Verso, 1994.

Roumain, Jacques. *Gouverneurs de la Rosée*. Paris: Messidor, 1946.

Ruiz Marrero, Carmelo. "The Poetry that Saved a Forest." *World Rainforest Movement Bulletin* 66 (January 2003). http://www.wrm.org.uy/bulletin/66/CA.html. Accessed October 9, 2008.

Ruskin, John. "Of the Pathetic Fallacy." *Modern Painters*. Vol. 3. Sunnyside: George Allen, 1888. 157–72.

Ryan, Chris, and C. Michael Hall. *Sex Tourism: Marginal People and Liminalities*. London and New York: Routledge, 2001.

Rytkheu, Yuri. "When the Whales Leave." *Soviet Literature* 1977. 12: 3–73.

Sachs, Wolfgang. "Environment." *The Development Dictionary*. London: Zed Books, 1992. 26–37.

Said, Edward W. *Culture and Imperialism*. New York: Vintage, 1994.

———. "Traveling Theory." *The World, the Text and the Critic*. Cambridge: Harvard University Press, 1983. 241–42.

———. *The World, the Text, and the Critic*. Cambridge: Harvard University Press, 1983.

———. "Yeats and Decolonization." *Nationalism, Colonialism, and Literature*. Ed. Terry Eagleton et al. Minneapolis: University of Minnesota Press, 1990. 69–95.

Salgado, Minoli. *Writing Sri Lanka: Literature, Resistance and the Politics of Place*. London and New York: Routledge, 2007.

Saro-Wiwa, Ken. *Genocide in Nigeria*. Reissue. Saros International, 2000.

Saura, Bruno. *Entre terre et culture. La mise en terre du placenta en Polynésie française*. Papeete: Haere Po, 2005.

Sawyer, Suzana, and Arun Agrawal. "Environmental Orientalism." *Cultural Critique*. 45 (Spring 2000): 71–108.

Scafi, Alessandro. *Mapping Paradise: A History of Heaven on Earth*. Chicago and London: University of Chicago Press and British Library, 2006.

Schmidt, Hans. *The United States Occupation of Haiti 1915–1934*. New Brunswick: Rutgers University Press, 1995.

Scholtmeijer, Marian Louise. *Animal Victims in Modern Fiction: From Sanctity to Sacrifice*. Toronto and London: University of Toronto Press, 1993.

Seabrook, Jeremy. *Travels in the Skin Trade: Tourism and the Sex Trade*. 2nd ed. London: Pluto, 2001.

Searle, John R. "Metaphor." *Metaphor and Thought*, 2nd ed. Ed. Andrew Ortony. Cambridge: Cambridge University Press, 1993. 83–111.

Sen, Amartya. "Population: Delusion and Reality." September 22, 1994 http://www.uwmc.uwc.edu/geography/malthus/sen_NYR.htm.

Senior, Olive. *Gardening in the Tropics*. Toronto: McClelland and Stewart, 1994.

Serres, Michel. *The Natural Contract*. Trans. Elizabeth MacArthur and William Paulson. Ann Arbor: University of Michigan Press, 1995.

Shakespeare, William. *King Lear*. Harmondsworth: Penguin, 1972.

Shanmugaratnam, Nadarajah. "Challenges of Post-Disaster Development of Coastal Areas in Sri Lanka." *South Asia Citizens Web*. 2005. http://www.sacw.net/peace/ChallengesPostdisasterShanNovember2005.pdf.

Sharrad, Paul. "Estranging an Icon: Eucalyptus and India." *Interventions: International Journal of Postcolonial Studies* 9.1 (2007): 31–48.

Shepard, Paul. "The Pet World." *The Animal Ethics Reader*. 2nd ed. Eds. Susan Armstrong and Richard Botzler. New York and London: Routledge, 2008. 510–12.

Shinebourne, Jan Lowe. *The Last English Plantation*. Leeds, England: Peepal Tree Press, 2002.

Shiva, Vandana. *Biopiracy: The Plunder of Nature and Knowledge*. Boston: South End Press, 1999.

———. *Ecology and the Politics of Survival: Conflicts over Natural Resources in India*. New Delhi: Sage, 1991.

———. *Staying Alive: Women, Ecology and Development*. London: Zed Books, 1988.

———. *Tomorrow's Biodiversity*. London: Thames and Hudson, 2000.

———. *The Violence of the Green Revolution: Agriculture, Ecology, and Politics in the South*. London: Zed Books, 1991.

Shulevitz, Judith. "Author Tour: Elizabeth Costello." *New York Times*. October 26, 2003.

Sigüenza y Sonora, Carlos de. Excerpt from *Misfortunes of Alonso Ramírez*. Trans. José Buscaglia Salgado. *Dissidences: Hispanic Journal of Theory and Criticism*. http://www.dissidences.org/SiguenzaMisfortunes.html. Accessed August 9, 2008.

Silva, Noenoe. *Aloha Betrayed: Native Hawaiian Resistance to American Colonialism*. Durham: Duke University Press, 2004.

Singer, Peter. "Animal Liberation." *Review of Animals, Men and Morals*. Eds. Stanley Godlovitch, Roslind Godlovitch, and John Harris. *New York Review of Books*. April 5, 1973.

———. "Practical Ethics." *The Animal Ethics Reader*. 2nd ed. Eds. Susan Armstrong and Richard Botzler. New York and London: Routledge, 2008. 33–44.

Singh, Samar, Karan Singh, and Najma Heptulla. *The World Charter for Nature*. New Delhi: Full Circle, 2003.

Sinha, Indra. *Animal's People*. London: Pocket Books, 2008.

Slaymaker, William. "Echoing the Other(s): The Call of Global Green and Black African Responses." *PMLA* 116 (2001): 129–144.

Smarth, Rony, and Edwidge Balutansky. *Haïti, Terre Délabrée; Ecologie et Dictature, Dossier 2*. Port-au-Prince: l'Impremier II for Centre de Researches Sociales et de Diffusion Populaire, 1991. 17, 54–55.

Smith, Bernard. *European Vision and the South Pacific*. New Haven: Yale University Press, 1985.

Smith, H. Alley. "Where's That Crazy Weather Coming From?" *Saturday Evening Post* 226.5 (August 1, 1953): 30, 89–90.

Smith, Jeff. *Unthinking the Unthinkable: Nuclear Weapons and Western Culture*. Bloomington: Indiana University Press, 1989.

Smith, Linda Tuhiwai. *Decolonizing Methodologies*. London and New York: Zed Books; Dunedin: University of Otago Press; New York: St. Martin's Press, 1999.

Smith, Neil. "Disastrous Accumulation." *South Atlantic Quarterly* 106.4 (2007): 769–87.

Smuts, Barbara. "Reflections." *The Lives of Animals*, by J. M. Coetzee and Amu Gutmann. Princeton: Princeton University Press, 1999. 107–20.

Sofield, Trevor H. B. *Empowerment for Sustainable Tourism Development*. Amsterdam and London: Pergamon, 2003.

Sönmez, Sevil F. "Sustaining Tourism in Islands under Sociopolitical Adversity." *Island Tourism and Sustainable Development: Caribbean, Pacific, and Mediterranean Experiences*. Eds. Yorghos Apostolopoulos and Dennis John Gayle. Westport and London: Praeger, 2002. 161–80.

———. "Tourism, Terrorism, and Political Instability." *Annals of Tourism Research* 25.2 (1998): 416–56.

Souffrant, Claude. *Littérature et Société en Haïti*. Port-au-Prince: Editions Henri Deschamps, 1991.

Spitz, Chantal. *L'île des rêves écrasés*. Papeete: Au vent des îles, 2003.

———. *Island of Shattered Dreams*. Trans. Jean Anderson. Wellington, NZ: Huia, 2007.

Spivak, Gayatri Chakravorty. *A Critique of Postcolonial Reason: Towards a History of the Vanishing Present*. Cambridge, MA: Harvard University Press, 1999.

———. *Death of a Discipline*. New York: Columbia UP, 2003.

———. "Ethics and Politics in Tagore, Coetzee, and Certain Scenes of Teaching." *Diacritics* 32.3–4 (2002): 17–31.

———. "Woman in Difference." *Outside in the Teaching Machine*. New York and London: Routledge, 1993. 77–96.

"Sri Lanka [LTTE]." *The International Institute for Strategic Studies Armed Conflict Database*. http://acd.iiss.org/armedconflict/MainPages/dsp_ConflictSummary.asp?ConflictID=174.

Steady, Filomina Chioma. *Environmental Justice in the New Millennium: Global Perspectives on Race, Ethnicity, and Human Rights*. New York: Palgrave Macmillan, 2009.

Stearn, William T. "The Influence of Leyden on Botany in the Seventeenth and Eighteenth Centuries." *British Journal for the History of Science* 1.2 (1962): 137–58.

Stepan, Nancy. *Picturing Tropical Nature*. Ithaca, NY: Cornell University Press, 2001.

Stephenson, Michael and John Weal. *Nuclear Dictionary*. London: Longman, 1985.

Stevenson-Hamilton, James. *South African Eden*. London: Cassell, 1937.

Strachan, Ian Gregory. *Paradise and Plantation: Tourism and Culture in the Anglophone Caribbean*. Charlotte: University of Virginia Press, 2002.

Sturgeon, Noel. *Ecofeminist Natures: Race, Gender, Feminist Theory and Political Action*. New York: Routledge, 1997.

Sublette, Carey. *The Nuclear Weapons Archive: A Guide to Nuclear Weapons*. <http://nuclearweaponarchive.org>.

Sullivan, Robert. *A Whale Hunt*. New York: Scribner, 2000.

Swami, Vandana. "Environmental History and British Colonialism in India: A Prime Political Agenda." *CR: The New Centennial Review* 3.3 (2003): 113–20.

Tansley, Alfred George. "The Use and Abuse of Vegetational Concepts and Terms." In *The Philosophy of Ecology*. Eds. David R. Keller and Frank B. Golley. U of Georgia P, 2000, 55–70.

Taylor, Frank Fonda. *To Hell with Paradise*. Pittsburgh: University of Pittsburgh Press, 1993.

Taylor, Peter J., and Frederick H. Buttel. "How Do We Know We Have Global Environmental Problems?" *GeoForum* 23: (1992) 405–416.

Taylor, Theodore. *The Cay*. New York: Avon, 1969.

Teaiwa, Teresia. "bikinis and other s/pacific n/oceans." *The Contemporary Pacific* 6 (1994). 87–109.

———. "Militarism, Tourism and the Native: Articulations in Oceania." PhD diss., University of California, Santa Cruz, 2001.

———. "Microwomen: U.S. Colonialism and Micronesian Women Activists," *Pacific History: Papers from the 8th Pacific History Association Conference*. Ed. D. Rubinstein, University of Guam, 1992. 125–42.

———. "Reading Paul Gauguin's *Noa Noa* with Epeli Hau'ofa's *Kisses in the Nederends*: Militourism, Feminism, and the 'Polynesian' Body." *Inside Out: Literature, Cultural Politics and Identity in the New Pacific*. Ed. Vilsoni Hereniko and Rob Wilson. Lanham, MD: Rowman and Littlefield, 2001. 249–69.

Terada, Rei. *Derek Walcott's Poetry: American Mimicry*. Boston: Northeastern University Press, 1992.

Thieme, John. *Derek Walcott*. Manchester: Manchester University Press, 1999.

———. *Bringing the Biosphere Home*. Cambridge, MA: MIT, 2002.

Thoby-Marcelin, Philippe and Pierre Marcelin. *The Beast of the Haitian Hills*. New York: Time-Life Books, 1964. xv–xxi.

Thomas, Ned. "Interview." *Conversations with Derek Walcott*. Ed. William Baer. Jackson: University Press of Mississippi, 1996. 64–69.

Thomashaw, Mitchell. "Toward a Cosmopolitan Bioregionalism." *Bioregionalism*. Ed. Michael Vincent McGinnis. London: Routeldge, 1999. 121–31

———. *Bringing the Biosphere Home*. Cambridge, MA: MIT, 2002.

———. "Croix-des-Missions, Port-au-Prince; February 1928." Trans. Kevin Meehan and Marie Léticée. *Callaloo* 23.4 (2000): 1386–87.

Threadgold, Terry. *Feminist Poetics: Poiesis, Performance, Histories*. London: Routledge. 1997.

"350 Killed as Poisonous Gas Leaks from Bhopal Plant." *Hindu*. Late ed. December 4, 1984. 1.

Thrift, Nigel, and Sarah Whatmore, eds. *Cultural Geography: Critical Concepts in the Social Sciences*, 2 vols. London and New York: Routledge, 2004.

Tiffin, Helen. "Introduction." *Five Emus to the King of Siam: Environment and Empire*. Amsterdam. New York: Rodopi, 2007.

Tillich, Paul. *The Shaking of the Foundations*. New York: Charles Scribner's Sons, 1948.

Tobin, Beth Fowkes. *Colonizing Nature: The Tropics in British Arts and Letters, 1760–1820*. Philadelphia: University of Pennsylvania Press, 2005.

Tomsky, Terri. "Amitav Ghosh's Anxious Witnessing and the Ethics of Action in *The Hungry Tide*." *Journal of Commonwealth Literature* 44.1 (2009): 53–65.

Torres Vargas, Diego de. "Descripción de la Isla y Ciudad de Puerto Rico." *Crónicas de Puerto Rico: Desde la Conquista hasta nuestros días*. 7th ed. Ed. Eugenio Fernández Méndez. San Juan: El Cemí, 1997. 52–196.

Trask, Haunani-Kay. *From a Native Daughter: Colonialism and Sovereignty in Hawai'i*. Honolulu: University of Hawai'i Press, 1999.

Tropp, Jacob A. *Natures of Colonial Change: Environmental Relations in the Making of the Transkei*. Athens: Ohio University Press, 2006.

Tsing, Anna Lowenhaupt. *Friction: An Ethnography of Global Connection*. Princeton: Princeton University Press, 2005.

———. "Transitions as Translations." *Transitions, Environments, Translations: Feminisms in International Politics*. Eds. Joan Scott, Cora Kaplan, and Debra Keates. New York: Routledge, 1997. 253–72.

Tsuji, Teruyuki. "Villaging the Nation: The Politics of Making Ourselves in Postcolonial Trinidad." *Sargasso* 31.4 (2008): 1148–74.

Tuwhare, Hone. *No Ordinary Sun*. Auckland: Blackwood and Janet Paul, 1964.

Unterhalter, Elaine. *Forced Removal: The Division, Segregation and Control of the People of South Africa*. London: Idaf, 1987.
USAID Country Studies. http://www.usaid.gov/pubs/cp97/countries/ht.htm.
Vern, Jules. *The Mighty Orinoco*. Trans. Stanford Luce. Middletown, CT: Wesleyan University Press, 2005.
Viljoen, Hein. "Journeys from the Liminal to the Sacred in the Interior of South Africa." *Beyond the Threshold: Explorations of Liminality in Literature*. New York: Peter Lang, 2007. 193–208.
Virilio, Paul. *The Vision Machine*. Bloomington: Indiana UP, 1994.
———. *War and Cinema: The Logistics of Perception*. London: Verso, 1989.
Visual Concept Entertainment. <www.vce.com>.
Vital, Anthony. "Situating Ecology in Recent South African Fiction: J. M. Coetzee's *The Lives of Animals* and Zakes Mda's *The Heart of Redness*." *Journal of Southern African Studies* 31.2 (2005): 297–313.
———. "Toward an African Ecocriticism: Postcolonialism, Ecology and Life and Times of Michael K." *Research in African Literatures* 39.1 (Winter 2008): 87–106.
———. "Toward an African Ecocriticism: Postcolonialism, Ecology and Life and Times of Michael K." Postcolonial-ecology.net. August 29, 2008. http://www.postcolonial-ecology.net/TowardanAfricanEcocriticism.pdf. Accessed February 14, 2009.
Vital, Anthony, and Hans-Georg Erney. "Introduction: Postcolonial Studies and Ecocriticism." *Journal of Commonwealth and Postcolonial Studies* 13.2/14.1 (Fall 2006–Spring 2007): 3–12.
———, eds. *Journal of Commonwealth and Postcolonial Studies (Special Issue: Postcolonial Studies and Ecocriticism)* 13.2/14.1 (Fall 2006–Spring 2007).
Vizenor, Gerald. "Aesthetics of Survivance: Literary Theory and Practice." *Survivance: Narratives of Native Presence*. Ed. Gerald Vizenor. Lincoln and London: University of Nebraska Press, 2008. 1–23.
———. *Manifest Manners: Post-Indian Warriors of Survivance*. Middleton, CT: Wesleyan University Press, 1993.
von Braun, Joachim and Ruth Meinzen-Dick. "'Land Grabbing' by Foreign Investors in Developing Countries: Risks and Opportunities." *IFPRI Policy Brief* 13 (April 2009): 1–3.
Walcott, Derek. "The Antilles: Fragments of Epic Memory." *What the Twilight Says*. New York: Farrar, Straus and Giroux, 1998. 65–84.
———. *The Arkansas Testament*. New York: Farrar, Straus and Giroux, 1987.
———. "The Banyan Tree, Old Year's Night." *Collected Poems 1948–1984*. New York: Farrar, Straus and Giroux, 1984. 48–49.
———. "The Bounty." *Selected Poems*. Ed. Edward Baugh. New York: Farrar, Straus and Giroux, 1997. 3–16.
———. "The Castaway." *Collected Poems 1948–1984*. New York: Farrar, Straus and Giroux, 1984, 57–58.
———. *The Castaway and Other Poems*. London: Cape, 1965.
———. *Collected Poems 1948–1984*. New York: Farrar, Straus and Giroux, 1984.
———. "The Fortunate Traveller." *Collected Poems: 1948–1984*. New York: Farrar, Straus and Giroux, 1984. 456–63.
———. "From This Far." *Collected Poems 1948–1984*. New York: Farrar, Straus and Giroux, 1984. 315.
———. *In a Green Night*. London: Jonathan Cape, 1962.
———. *The Gulf and Other Poems*. New York: Farrar, Straus and Giroux, 1970.

———. "Isla Incognita." *Caribbean Literature and the Environment*. Eds. Elizabeth DeLoughrey, Renée Gosson, and George B. Handley. Charlottesville: University of Virginia Press, 2005. 51–57.

———. *Midsummer*. New York: Farrar, Straus and Giroux, 1984.

———. "The Muse of History." *The Routledge Reader in Caribbean Literature*. Eds. Alison Donnell and Sarah Lawson Welsh. London: Routledge, 1996. 354–58.

———. "Nights in the Gardens of Port of Spain." *Collected Poems 1948–1984*. New York: Farrar, Straus and Giroux, 1984. 67.

———. *Omeros*. New York: Farrar, Straus and Giroux, 1990.

———. "Orient and Immortal Wheat." *Collected Poems 1948–1984*. New York: Farrar, Straus and Giroux, 1984. 36–37.

———. *The Prodigal*. New York: Farrar, Straus and Giroux, 2004.

———. "Sainte Lucie." *Collected Poems 1948–1984*. New York: Farrar, Straus and Giroux, 1984. 309–23.

———. "Sea Canes." *Collected Poems 1948–1984*. New York: Farrar, Straus and Giroux, 1984. 331–32.

———. *Sea Grapes*. London: Jonathan Cape, 1976.

———. *Selected Poems*. Ed. Edward Baugh. New York: Farrar, Straus and Giroux, 1997.

———. *The Star-Apple Kingdom*. New York: Farrar, Straus and Giroux, 1980.

———. *Tiepolo's Hound*. New York, Farrar, Straus and Giroux, 2000.

———. "To Return to the Trees." *Collected Poems 1948–1984*. New York: Farrar, Straus and Giroux, 1984. 339–41.

Warren, Karen J. (ed.) *Ecological Feminist Philosophies*. Bloomington: Indiana University Press, 1996.

Weart, Spencer R. *Nuclear Fear: A History of Images*. Cambridge, MA: Harvard University Press, 1988.

Weik, Alexa. "The Home, the Tide, and the World: Eco-cosmopolitan Encounters in Amitav Ghosh's *The Hungry Tide*." *Journal of Commonwealth and Postcolonial Studies* 13.2–14.1 (2006–2007): 120–41.

Weisgall, Jonathan M. *Operation Crossroads: The Atomic Tests at Bikini Atoll*. Annapolis: Naval Institute Press, 1994.

Wells, Nancy. "At Home with Nature: Effects of 'Greenness' on Children's Cognitive Functioning." *Environment and Behavior* 32.6 (2000): 775–95.

Welsome, Eileen. *The Plutonium Files: America's Secret Medical Experiments in the Cold War*. New York: Dial, 1999.

Wendt, Albert. *Black Rainbow*. Auckland: Penguin Books, 1992.

———. Ed. *Nuanua: Pacific Writing in English Since 1980*. Honolulu: University of Hawai'i Press, 1995.

Wenzel, Jennifer. *Bulletproof: Afterlives of Anticolonial Prophecy in South Africa and Beyond*. Chicago: Chicago University Press, 2009.

———. "Epic Struggles over India's Forests in Mahasweta Devi's Short Fiction." *Alif: Journal of Comparative Poetics* 18 (1998), Special Issue on Post-Colonial Discourse in South Asia: 127–58.

———. "The Pastoral Promise and the Political Imperative: The Plaasroman Tradition in an era of Land Reform." *Modern Fiction Studies* 46.1 (Spring 2000): 90–113.

West, Elliott. "Wallace Stegner's West: Wilderness and History." *Wallace Stegner and the Continental Vision*. Ed. Curt Meine. Washington, DC: Island Press, 1997. 85–96.

Whale Rider. Dir. Niki Caro. DVD. Newmarket Films, 2003.

Whaledreamers. Dir. Kim Kindersley. DVD. Monterey Video, 2007.

Whatmore, Sarah. "Hybrid Geographies: Rethinking the 'Human' in Human Geography." *The Animals Reader: The Essential Classic and Contemporary Writings*. Eds. Linda Kalof and Amy Fitzgerald. Virginia: Berg, 2007. 338–49.

White, Lynn Jr. "Christian Myth and Christian History." *Journal of the History of Ideas* 3.2 (1942): 145–58.

Whitehouse, David. *The Sun: A Biography*. London: John Wiley & Sons, 2006.

Williams, Michael. *Deforesting the Earth: From Prehistory to Global Crisis (An Abridgment)*. Chicago: University of Chicago Press, 2006.

Williams, Raymond. *The Country and the City*. Oxford: Oxford University Press, 1975.

———. *The Country and the City*. London: Chatto & Windus, 1973.

———. *Keywords: A Vocabulary of Culture and Society*. New York: Oxford University Press, 1985.

Wilson, Jason. "Alejo Carpentier's Re-invention of América Latina as Real and Marvellous." *A Companion to Magical Realism*. Eds. Stephen M. Hart and Wen-Chin Ouyang. Woodbridge, England: Tamesis, 2005. 67–78.

Woodward, Wendy. "Laughing Back at the Kingfisher: Zakes Mda's *The Heart of Redness* and Postcolonial Humor." in *Cheeky Fictions: Laughter and the Postcolonial*. Eds. Susanne Reichl and Mark Stein. Amsterdam: Rodopi, 2005. 287–99.

Worster, Donald. *Nature's Economy: A History of Ecological Ideas*. 2nd ed. Cambridge: Cambridge University Press, 1994.

———. *Rivers of Empire: Water, Aridity, and the Growth of the American West*. New York: Oxford University Press, 1985.

———. *Wealth of Nature: Environmental History and the Ecological Imagination*. New York: Oxford UP, 1993.

Wright, Laura. *Wilderness into Civilized Shapes: Reading the Postcolonial Environment*. Athens: University of Georgia Press, 2010.

Wyndham, Susan. "Region's Tales Should Be Brought to Book." *Sydney Morning Herald* 2005. http://www.asialink.unimelb.edu.au/__data/assets/pdf_file/0008/4202/Regions_Tales.pdf.

Wynter, Sylvia. "Novel and History, Plot and Plantation." *Savacou* 5 (1971): 95–102.

Wytenbroek, J. R. "Cetacean Consciousness in Katz's *Whalesinger* and L'Engle's *A Ring of Endless Light*." *Mythlore: A Journal of J. R. R. Tolkien, C. S. Lewis, Charles Williams, and the Genres of Myth and Fantasy Studies* 21.33 no. 2 (Winter 1996): 435–38.

Yoneyama, Lisa. *Hiroshima Traces: Time, Space and the Dialectics of Memory*. Berkeley: U of California P, 1999.

Young, Robert J. C. "'Dangerous and Wrong': Shell, Intervention and the Politics of Transnational Companies." *Interventions* 1.3 (1999): 439–64.

———. *Postcolonialism: A Very Short Introduction*. Oxford and New York: Oxford University Press, 2003.

———. Parkinson. *The Inordinate Eye: New World Baroque and Latin American Fiction*. Chicago: University of Chicago Press, 2006.

———. "Magical Ruins/Magical Realism: Alejo Carpentier, François de Nomé, and the New World Baroque." *Poetics of the Americas: Race, Founding, and Textuality*. Eds. Bainard Cowan and Jefferson Humphries. Baton Rouge: Louisiana State University, 1997. 63–103.

Zimmerman, Michael E. *Contesting Earth's Future: Radical Ecology and Postmodernity*. Berkeley: University of California Press, 1994.

Index

Aberley, Doug, 293
Activism, 136, 254, 256, 262
Adorno, Theodor, 16, 26, 239, 242, 250
Aesthetics, 27–28, 30, 32, 34, 44, 47, 48, 50, 59, 82, 84, 121, 123, 132, 204, 240, 250, 274, 281
  of belonging, 30
  of colonialism, 48, 59
  and ethics, 204
  of the Earth, 27, 28, 34
  of landscape, 47, 84, 178n.11
  of the picturesque, 44, 50
  postcolonial, 274, 281
  of rupture, 34, 121, 132
  of survivance, 184
  of violence, 240, 250
Africa, 6, 12–13, 26, 32, 34, 81, 160–163, 172, 177–179, 292
  Haitian *Lan Giné*, 63, 64, 65, 67, 69, 70, 71, 72, 74, 75
African Wilderness, 160, 161, 163, 167–168, 176
Agnolleti, Mauro, 102,
Agriculture, 13, 50, 53, 58, 63–65, 69–70, 73, 82, 85, 100–101, 107, 110–111, 136, 139, 140, 149, 162, 170, 176, 218, 295
  See also Plantation
Alexis, Jacques–Stephen, 109
Alterity, 4, 7–9, 16, 20, 25, 28, 35n.7
Althusser, Louis, 140
Altman, Dennis, 280–281
Amarasinghe, Sarath, 285
American Ecocriticism, 8–10, 14–23, 140, 150, 153, 241, 281–282, 292, 294, 305
American consumption, 25–26
American Empire, 75, 238, 241, 242, 245, 260
American media, 218, 223
American Studies, 20
Amodio, Emanuele, 99, 104
Anderson, Warren, 218
Andeyo (Haiti) 62, 63, 64, 65, 67, 69, 70, 71
Andrews, Malcolm, 60n.4
Animal, 11, 13, 21, 32–34, 182–190, 192, 194–197, 216–217, 220–230, 274, 277–278, 279, 283–284, 288
  animal rights, 201, 204, 207, 211, 213
  animal studies, 32, 200–201

Animal (*continued*)
  animality, 209–210
  See also Nonhuman
Animism, 104, 118
Anthropocene, 26
Anthropocentrism, 25, 118, 119, 120, 137, 186, 195, 196, 205–206, 209, 230, 255, 266, 278, 283
Anti-colonialism, 4, 13, 167, 254, 257, 268
Anzaldua, Gloria, 174
Aotearoa. *See* New Zealand
Apartheid, 165, 169, 171, 176, 205, 214n.17, 221, 230, 295
Apocalypse, 151, 154–155n.26, 250–251, 281, 282, 286, 287
Arrate y Acosta, José Martin Félix de, 106–107, 111, 114
Ashraf, Lalla, 220
Astrology, 183
Asturias, Miguel Angel, 117
Atavism, 176
Atomic Age, 236, 238–239, 243, 246–247
Atomic Energy Commission (AEC), 33, 236–238, 240, 243, 245–246
Attridge, Derek, 205, 214n.16
Auden, W.H., 84
Auerbach, Erich, 79n.2
Australia, 279, 285
Australian Flora and Fauna Act, 36n.17

Bacchilega, Christina, 263–264
Baldwin, James, 167
Bantustans, 160, 166, 172
Barbados, 94, 106, 115n.2, 279
Barnard, Rita, 205, 214n.17, 296
Bate, Jonathan, 85, 95n.14
Bauman, Zygmunt, 38n.42, 149
Behn, Aphra, 103, 114–115
Bellegard-Smith, Patrick, 63
Benjamin, Walter, 150
Bentham, Jeremy, 222
Beresford, Lucy, 227
Bhabha, Homi, 23, 46
Bhopal (Gas Tragedy), 33, 216–220, 224, 227, 229
Bigaud, Wilson, 67–68, 70, 71, 73, 74–75, 76, 78
Bikini Atoll, 240, 243, 244
Binde, Per, 72

Biocentrism, 21, 32, 120, 129, 130, 134n.11
Biodiversity, 102, 122, 128, 159–160, 176–177, 181n.36, 300
Biopiracy, 11, 16, 21, 300
Bioregionalism, 292–294, 298–299, 303–305
Bobadilla, Emilio, 115n.4
Bollywood, 57
Bong Busti, 55
Bookchin, Murray, 15, 37n.33
Border, 169, 172, 173–175
  Borderland, 174
  Border zone, 169, 173, 179
Botanical garden. *See* Garden
Boyer, Paul, 236, 240, 244, 246
Braudel, Fernand, 250
Braziel, Jana Evans, 83
Breton, André, 65–66, 70, 71
British imperialism, 6, 11, 13, 30, 43–49, 51, 53, 55–56, 59, 64, 81, 82, 90, 101, 103, 107, 120, 138, 171, 245, 294, 295, 301
Brodsky, Joseph, 95n.13
Brown, Robert and Johnson, Cheryl, 82
Browne, Janet, 11
Bryld, Mette, 32, 183–184
Buell, Frederick, 154n.26, 281–282
Buell, Lawrence, 8, 14, 36n.24, 80, 94n.1, 136, 152n.5, 153n.13, 182–183, 199, 250, 276, 293
Burke, Edmund, 46
Buscaglia Salgado, José, 105
Buttel, Frederick, 38n.41

Cabezas, Amalia, 279
Camayd-Freixas, Erik, 118
Capitalism, 11, 16, 22–23, 29, 148, 202, 209, 211, 215n.22, 223, 226, 228, 258, 267, 273–274, 287
Caplan, Lionel, 55–56
Carew, Jan, 115n.4
Caribbean, 5, 7–8, 27, 30–31, 34, 45, 62–79, 81–96, 99–116, 166, 167, 178n.14
Caribs, 106, 114
Carmichael, Mrs., 95n.8
Carpentier, Alejo, 32, 117–135
Carruthers, Jane, 171

Carson, Rachel, 15, 31, 110, 183, 238, 245
Carter, Martin, 5–7
Casid, Jill, 81, 94n.3
Casteel, Sarah, 133n.3
Catastrophe, 271, 281–282
  See also Apocalypse
Catharsis, 283, 286
Catholics, 63, 66, 68, 73, 103, 104, 123
Cavalieri, Paola, 222
Cazdyn, Eric, 149–150
Centre d'Art, (Haiti), 63, 65, 67, 70–71, 75
Centre d'Expérimentation du Pacifique (CEP), 260, 267
Césaire, Aimé, 64
Cetacean(s), 182–187, 190, 195–6
  See also Whale
Chakrabarty, Dipesh, 29–30
Chamoiseau, Patrick, 116n.6
Chanady, Amaryll, 124, 132
Chaos theory, 119, 129
Chauvet, Marie, 108–109
Chaze, Michou, 34
Chaze, Rai (Michou Chaze), 266–267, 269
Chouhan, T.R., 220
Christ, Jesus, 65, 66, 73, 79n.2, 88
Christianity, 6, 7, 31, 63, 65–67, 70–73, 75
  See also Catholics
Christophe, Henri, 68–69
Cilano, Cara, 38n.48, 39n.52, 39n.61, 201–202, 214n.8, 276
Clare, John, 30, 84–87, 89, 93
Clarence-Smith, W.G, 106
Clarkson, Thomas, 68–69
Clifford, James, 118–119, 257
Climate change, 4, 13, 25–27, 29, 39n.58, 106, 109, 147, 151–152, 155n.26, 236, 251, 276
Clitandre, Pierre, 109
Code, Lorraine, 35n.3
Coetzee, J.M., 33, 200–215
  Age of Iron, 206
  Diary of a Bad Year, 205
  Disgrace, 201, 204–205, 213n.7, 214n.17
  Elizabeth Costello, 201–206, 214n.18
  In the Heart of the Country, 205–206
  Life and Times of Michael K, 206
  The Lives of Animals, 200–215
  Slow Man, 203, 205–206
  Waiting for the Barbarians, 206
Coicou, Masilon, 108
Coleridge, Samuel Taylor, 93
Colonialism, 44, 87, 88, 187, 195, 223, 257, 274, 276
  See also British Imperialism,
  See also American Empire
Columbian Exchange, 13
Columbus, Christopher, 99, 114, 115
Commons, the, 139, 146
Companion species, 183, 185–186, 193, 195, 200, 204, 213
  See also Haraway, Donna
Condé, Maryse, 112
Conservation, 8, 12, 17–18, 20–22, 32, 194
Corretjer, Juan Antonio, 15, 31, 110
Cosmology, 255, 261
Cosmopolitanism, 292–294, 296, 298, 305–306
Cranach, Lucas, 67–68, 71
Creole, 63, 65, 67, 72, 82, 86, 91, 103, 105, 106, 108, 109, 111, 112, 114, 117, 120
Crick, Malcolm, 275
Crisis (environmental), 10, 24, 25, 31–32, 136–137, 138, 139, 141, 147, 149–151, 235, 241, 273–276, 282, 283, 285, 287
  See also Catastrophe
Cronon, William, 35n.13, 178n.11, 297
Crosby, Alfred, 13, 297
Crusoe, Robinson, 90, 93
Cuba, 106–108
Curtin, Deane, 22, 38n.48, 36n.25, 37n.31, 38n.48, 137

Dahomey, 66
Dalí, Salvador, 123
Dangarembga, Tsitsi, 24
Dannett, Daniel, 226
Dante, 88
Darjeeling, 43–46, 48, 50–51, 53–57, 59n.3, 60
Darwin, Charles, 280, 289n.7
de Chardin, Teilhard, 73

De Man, Paul, 92
de Vries, Pieter, 267
de Wimpffen, Baron Alexandre-Stanislaus, 68
Decolonization, 4–6, 8, 15, 110, 120, 154, 176, 202, 205, 213, 254
Deep ecology, 15, 21–23, 38n.47, 118, 258–259, 292
Deep time, 24–25, 29
Defoe, Daniel, 85
Deforestation, 4, 16, 50, 60n.7, 100–103, 106, 107–108, 110–112, 113, 116n.6, 138, 141, 147
  effects of, 102–103, 106, 108, 116
  in Barbados, 115n.2
  in Cuba, 107
  in Haiti, 110
  problem of, 106, 111
  threat of, 100, 113
DeLoughrey, Elizabeth, 3, 33, 38n.40, 38n.48, 39n.52, 39n.61, 64, 81, 96n.13, 100, 201–202, 214n.8
Demeter, 88
Dening, Greg, 288
Derrida, Jacques, 237, 251, 260
Desai, Kiran, 30, 43–44, 46–53, 56–59
Desmangles, Leslie, 63
Development, 273–274, 276, 279, 281, 285, 286–288, 289n.1
Devi, Mahasweta, 31, 136–138, 143–145, 147, 152n.1, 153n.6
  "Dhowli," 137–154
  "Douloti the Bountiful," 143–144, 154n.15
  "Draupadi," 138, 144–145, 154n.15
  "The Hunt," 137, 143, 154n.19
  "Pterodactyl," 136–137
Diamond, Cora, 185
Diller, Elizabeth, and Ricardo Scofidio, 275
Disaster, 149, 217, 219, 273–288
  See also Apocalypse
Dolphin(s), 182–185, 193, 195–196
  See also Cetacean(s)
Dominica, 106, 112
Dominican Republic, 108
Doyle, Sir Alfred Conan, 125, 134n.13
Drayton, Richard, 82, 94n.7
Duval-Carrié, Edouard, 72

Earth, 188–189, 195, 217, 226–227
Ecocriticism, 8–10, 14–19, 20–25, 32, 36n.24, 39n.52, 44, 80–81, 84–85, 119, 124, 136–137, 140, 150, 153, 192, 195, 201–202, 204, 209, 211, 213, 237, 251, 276, 282, 292, 294, 305
  See also American Ecocriticism,
  See also Postcolonial Ecocriticism
Ecofeminism, 9, 14, 16, 22–24, 26, 27, 32, 35n.7, 36n.19, 36n.24, 37n.27, 37n.31, 38n.47, 38n.48, 39n.59, 146, 203–204, 208–209, 214n.10, 258, 284, 298, 300
Ecological Imperialism, 291, 294, 297, 303
Ecological Indian, 187, 195, 198n.11
Ecological thinking, 204, 256, 259, 270
Ecological thought, Franciscan, 73
Ecology, 44, 48, 52, 58–59, 60n.6, 137–138, 141, 153n.8, 182, 187, 189, 195–196, 198, 235–239, 243, 246, 257, 259, 273–274, 276–278, 280–283, 285–288
  See also Deep Ecology,
  See also Ecocriticism,
  See also Ecosystem
Economic development, 17, 18, 26, 31, 34, 110, 111, 113, 146, 275
Ecopoetics, 80, 81
Ecosystem, 62, 64, 71, 74, 78, 176, 182–183, 185, 187, 192–196, 282, 283
  See also Ecology
Eden, 12, 30, 43, 44, 63, 72, 88, 167, 178–180
  expulsion from, 71–72, 77
  the tropics as, 121, 126, 127–128
  See also Paradise
El Dorado, 125, 134n.13
Elbert, Samuel, 254
Enclosure, 84–85, 86, 89, 160, 162
Enewetak Atoll, 238, 240
Enlightenment, 10, 12, 16, 24–26, 57, 163, 167, 239, 242
Environment, 4, 7, 9–10, 12–26, 28–31, 33–34, 38n.46, 183, 185–187, 188, 190, 192, 194–195, 196, 216–217, 219, 221, 223, 226, 228, 230–231, 268, 273–277, 279–288
  See also Ecology,
  See also Ecosystem

Environmental Ethics. *See* Ethics
Environmental Justice, 9, 14, 23, 36n.24, 39n.53, 137, 274
Environmental Protection Agency, 219
Environmental racism, 259
Environmentalism of the Poor, 8, 28
Environmentalism, 8, 12, 15, 20–21, 23, 27–28, 182–183, 185, 191–192, 195–196, 204, 213
Epistemology, 136, 153n.8, 256, 257, 260, 261, 268, 284
Esposito, Lauren, 113
Ethics, 15, 23, 25–27, 33–34, 208, 213, 231, 216, 274, 283, 284, 287
   animal, 11, 13, 21, 32–34, 201, 204, 207, 211, 213
   environmental, 4, 7, 9–10, 12–26, 28–31, 33–34, 38n.46, 185, 238–239
   global, 4, 8–10, 12–13, 17–22, 25–34, 35n.5
   of belonging, 30
   of care, 27, 39n.59
   of place, 23, 34
Eurocentrism, 282
Europe, 63, 67, 73, 168, 170, 175–76
Everest, 47, 50
Ezili, 66–67

Fallout. *See* radioactivity
Fanon, Frantz, 3–4, 35n.1, 260, 302, 317
Faulkner, William, 132
Feedlots, 201, 207–209, 211–213
Fetta, S., 265
Fleury-Battier, Alcibiade, 108
Foning, A.R., 48, 51–54, 61n.9
Forests, 12, 31, 187, 193, 226–228
   books about, 115n.4
   destroying of, 100–106, 112–114
   fate of, 100
   in India, 137–141, 147, 154n.21, 148, 150, 153n.6, 154n.19;
   protection of, 107
   as refuge, 138–140, 144;
   role of, 99, 109, 136–138
   symbolism of, 101, 113, 115
   See also deforestation
Foucault, Michel, 11
France, 260–261, 266
French Polynesia, 255, 267
   See also Tahiti

Fromm, Erich, 262
Frontier, 169, 171–172, 175, 180
Fuentes, Carlos, 119
Funes Monzote, Reinaldo, 99

Gadgil, Madhav, 140, 153n.8, 154n.21
Gallegos, Rómulo, 117
Game lodge, (African), 161, 163–165, 167–169, 177–178
Game reserves, (African), 159–160, 166–167, 170–171, 176, 178, 180
Gandhi, Mahatma, 15, 17
Ganguly, Rajat., 55, 60n.7
García Márquez, Gabriel, 119–120
Garden, 43–44, 47, 49–51, 53, 55, 58–59, 63, 75, 83
   See also Eden
Garrard, Greg, 15, 84, 95, 137–138, 139
Gaud, William, 36n.21
Gautier Benítez, José, 109
Gazankulu, 171–172, 174
Genealogy, 186, 264, 269
Genette, Girard, 245
Genocide, 10, 31, 146–147, 150
George, James, 243
Geothermal plants, 265
Ghosh, Amitav, 21, 32, 35n.2, 182, 185, 192–195, 199
Glissant, Édouard, 6–8, 23, 27–29, 34, 83, 121, 132
Global Warming. *See* Climate Change
Global Climate Justice, 25
Global Humanitarian Forum, 26
Global South, 4, 8–9, 19, 22, 26, 30, 33
Global, 4, 8–10, 12–13, 17–22, 25–34, 35n.5
   See also Earth,
   See also Planetarity
Globalization, 3–4, 9–10, 17, 23, 28–29, 33–34, 193, 231, 236–237, 241, 243, 274–276, 281, 286
Glotfelty, Cheryll, 14, 36n.36, 80
Ghose, Indira., 44–45
Goethe, Johann Wolfgang von, 126
Gómez de Avellaneda, Gertrudis, 114
Gopalakrishnan, K., 218
Gordimer, Nadine, 32, 169
Gorkha National Liberation Front, 30, 50–59
Gosson, Renée, 27, 35n.8, 64, 81, 100
Grace, Patricia, 23

Grassroots organizations, 254
  See also Activism
Green postcolonialism
  See also postcolonial ecocriticism
Green Revolution, 13, 36n.21, 149
Greenblatt, Stephen, 120
Groode, Mary, 265
Grove, Richard, 11–12, 104, 238
Guha, Ramachandra, 21–23, 38n.49, 39n.52, 140, 153n.8, 154n.21, 194
Gurkha (Gorkha/Ghorka), 51, 56
Guttal, Shalmali, 274
Guyana, 114

Haeckel, Ernst Heinrich Philipp August, 60n.6
Hagen, Joel Bartholomew, 238
Haiti, 62–79, 102, 108–109, 113
Hamel, the Obeah Man (1827), 115n.3
Handley, George, 64, 81, 83, 84, 94n.5, 100
Haraway, Donna., 8, 14, 19, 35n.7, 50, 183, 185
Harewood, Baron, 94n.3
Harris, Wilson, 4, 5, 6
Harrison, Mark., 59n.2
Harrison, Robert Pogue, 140, 135n.16
Hatzenberger, Françoise, 102
Hau'ofa, Epeli, 198n.10, 255, 256, 261, 267, 268
Hawai'i, 254–272
Hawaiian language ('ōlelo hawai'i), 260–261
Hawaiian Sovereignty, (Aloha 'āina), 254–255, 260–261, 268–269
Heise, Ursula, 14, 37n.28
Helm, George, 268
Hermanus (South Africa), 190, 192
Hernández, Franciso, 104
Himalayas, 15, 30, 44, 46–48, 50–51, 57, 59, 60n.6
Hiroshima, 236, 243–244, 246
HMS *Bounty*, 88
Hodge, Merle, 24
Hodgson, Brian, 56
Hogan, Linda, 32, 182, 184–190, 198
Hooker, Joseph, 51–52, 56
hooks, bell, 262
Horace, 93
Horkheimer, Max, 16, 26, 239, 242, 250

Horticulture, 54
Hotere, Ralph, 242
Huggan, Graham, 9, 17, 22, 25, 39n.52, 100, 184, 195, 197, 204–205, 209, 212, 214n.12, 258, 260
Huggan, Graham, and Helen Tiffin, 9, 17, 258, 274, 279
Hulme, Peter, 279
Human, 4, 5, 6, 13, 16, 17–18, 21, 23–26, 29, 33, 47, 50, 54, 59, 70, 71, 75, 83, 85, 88, 90, 105, 119, 121, 126, 128–133, 145–146, 148, 185, 186, 192, 195, 203, 207, 209, 213, 217, 221–231, 242, 244, 259, 261, 265, 267
Human Rights, 18, 33, 115, 201, 216–217, 221–224, 228, 230
Humanism, 29, 120, 202, 208, 214n.18, 282
Hybridity, 23, 30, 31, 45–46, 50, 53, 118, 168
Hyppolite, Hector, 65–67, 70–75, 76, 77–78

Ihimaera, Witi, 32 182, 184–187, 190, 197, 237, 241
India, 13, 17, 21, 30, 31, 33, 44–46, 51, 53–54, 57–58, 184–185, 187–188, 193–195
Indigeneity, 100–101, 281, 296–298, 300
Indigènism, 64–65, 77, 117, 122
Indigenous, 81, 136, 140, 184, 186–187, 193, 196, 257, 260
  indigenous epistemologies, 11, 193, 251, 256, 260
  indigenous response to nuclearization, 237, 241–251
Indo-saracenic, 49
Inter-American Commission of Human Rights, 115
International Monetary Fund, 16, 18, 275
Island, 238, 239, 240, 244, 250, 261, 274, 275, 277, 282–283, 284, 287–288

Jackson, Wes, 109
Jamaica, 46, 94n.4
Japan, 236, 243–244, 246, 260
Jordan, June, 166, 178
Jungk, Robert, 245–246
Jungle, 118, 123, 126, 127, 130–132

Index

Kafka, Franz, 206, 209, 212, 214n.18
Kahoʻolawe (Hawaiian Islands), 255, 268
Kalimpong, 43–44, 46, 48–50, 53–57, 59
Kanahele, Pualani, 263
Kanaka Maoli (Native Hawaiians), 255, 260–261, 265
Kanawha valley, 219
Kanchenjunga, 46, 51, 52, 58, 59
Keller, Evelyn Fox, 73
Kennedy, Dane., 46–47, 49–50, 60n.5
Kerridge, Richard, 136, 276
Kew Gardens, 11, 95n.7
Khan, Ismith, 113–114
Khoikhoi, 190
Kimmerle, Heinz, 69
Kincaid, Jamaica, 10–11, 83, 91, 95, 166, 178
Klein, Naomi, 274–275, 286, 287
Kleinhans, J.P., 160–161
Kolodny, Annette, 14
Koshe, P.R., 220
Kothari, Rajni, 147
Krech, Shepard III, 198n.11
Kreyol (Haitian), 67, 70
Kruger National Park, 32, 169, 171, 178–181
Kumar, Amitava, 168, 218

Labat, Jean Baptiste, 112, 114
Labor, 160, 162, 166–167, 169–174, 178–180
Laguerre, Enrique, 111, 114
Lam, Wifredo, 123
Land Ethic, 24, 32
Land, 182, 184, 186–187, 190, 194, 196, 256, 262, 274, 285, 286, 287
Landscape (African), 162, 166, 176, 178–179
Landscape painting, 62, 71
Language, 5–7, 10–12, 20, 25, 29–31
Lapierre, Dominique and Moro, Javier, 219–220
Las Casas, Bartolomé de, 31, 101
Latin American modernism, 117, 122–123
Latour, Bruno, 223
Laurence, William, 246
Lazarus, Neil, 148
Leopold, Aldo, 14, 24, 39n.59

Lepcha, 47–48, 51–55
Lezama Lima, José, 119, 123, 127
Light, 237, 239–242, 247
Liliʻuokalani (Queen), 257
Linnaeus, Carolus, 10–11
Lions, 160–163, 173, 175
Lo real maravilloso [marvelous reality], 119–120, 122, 125, 126, 132
  See also Magical realism
Locke, John, 92, 93
Lokugé, Chandani, 34, 274, 276–288
Love, 257, 262
Lykke, Nina, 32, 183–184

Maʻohi (Tahitians), 260–261, 266–267
Maathai, Wangari, 18, 20
Magical realism, 119, 186, 206
  See also *Lo real maravilloso*
Magome, Hector, 176
Makah whale hunt, 184, 189
Malden Island, 240
Maldives, 26
Maori, 184, 186–187, 241–242, 245, 250–253, 258
Marcelin, Pierre, 65, 71
Marcone, Jorge, 118
Marichjhapi Massacre, 21
Marshall Islands, 256
Martinez-Alier, Joan, 8–9, 39n.52
Martinique, 106, 116
Marx, Leo, 24
Marzec, Robert, 85, 120–121
Masculinity, 142, 188, 277, 279, 280–281, 285
Mateo Palmer, Margarita, 134n.13
Mazel, David, 152
Mazuchelli, Elizabeth Sarah, 48
McClintock, Anne, 163
McGregor, Davianna Pomaikaʻi, 262–263
McKibben, William, 26
Mda, Zakes, 32, 34, 182, 185, 190–192, 196, 198–199, 291–306
Meeker, Joseph, 282–284, 289n.9
Megafauna (Charismatic), 160, 162, 164, 167, 169, 172, 175–177, 181, 183–184, 191, 194, 196, 280
  See also Whales
Mellon Institute, 219
Melville, Elinor, 102

Mercer, Kobena, 256
Merchant, Carolyn, 14, 37n.33, 183
Methyl Isocyanite (MIC), 216
Meyer, Manulani Aluli, 256, 259
Micronesia, 238
Militarism, 138, 140, 215n.23, 266
Militarization, 236–237, 239–241, 251
Militourism, 33, 240, 257, 265, 268
Miller, Shawn, 122
Milton, John, 93
Mimesis, 121–124, 126, 128, 130, 132
Mitter, Partha, 44, 46
Modernity, 23, 26, 27, 29, 31, 33, 85, 112, 118, 123, 163, 167–168, 173, 183, 185, 237–239, 242–243, 249, 295, 300
Modernization. *See* Economic development
Montenegro, David, 81
Montero, Mayra, 112, 115
Moreau de Saint-Méry, Médéric Louis Élie, 107–108, 111
Moreno Fraginals, Manuel, 99
Morichjhāpi, 193–194
Mortimer-Sandilands, Catriona, 54
Morton, Timothy, 126, 134n.11
Moruroa (Tahiti), 255–256, 260–262
Moun andeyo (Haiti) 63, 64, 65, 67, 68, 71, 77
Mozambique, 169, 171–172, 175, 179–181
Mufti, Aamir, 57
Mukherjee, Pablo, 276
Muñoz Marín, Luis, 110
Munoz, Edward, 219
Murombedzi, James, 176
Murphy, Patrick, 22, 36n.25

Naess, Arne, 15, 21
Nagasaki, 243–244
Nation, 189, 194
National defense (France), 267
National security (U.S.), 257, 267, 269
Native Hawaiian. *See* Kanaka Maoli
Nature, 4–9, 11–14, 16–20, 22–27, 31, 45–47, 51–53, 54, 56, 57, 69, 72, 81–89, 93, 100, 108, 118, 120–125, 126–131, 137–138, 144–146, 183, 184, 186–187, 190–191, 194–195, 259, 265, 276, 277, 279–282, 283–284, 286, 297–300, 303

Feminization of, 277, 279, 281, 284, 286
as indifferent to human suffering, 144–146, 149–150;
in literary representation, 150–152;
as private property, 144–148
Natureculture, 50, 59
Navy (U.S.), 260, 263
Ndebele, Njabulo, 32, 160, 163, 177
Négritude (see also *Indigènism*) 64, 117, 122
Neocolonial, 3, 17, 32, 34, 81, 126, 131, 268, 270, 274
Neoliberal, 16, 136, 146, 148, 273, 275, 287
Neruda, Pablo, 5–6
New World Baroque, 32
New York Times, The, 218
New Zealand, 32, 184, 186–187, 243, 255
Nickson, Henry, 78
Nigeria, 6, 10, 19, 23, 38n.44
Nixon, Rob, 10, 20, 23–24, 32, 34, 36n.26, 38n.45, 38n.47, 147, 297–300, 303
Noble Savage, 183–184, 263
Nonhuman, 4, 8, 21, 25, 32, 34, 185, 193, 195, 197, 259, 261, 265, 267, 274, 276
Non-Human Rights, 204–205, 207, 213, 215n.24, 227
Northcott, Michael, 26, 39n.59
Nuclear weapons, 33–34, 236–240, 243–247, 255–256, 260–262
Nuclear Free and Independent Pacific Movement, 241
Nuclearization, 33–34, 236–245, 264, 259, 266, 268
See also Radiation
Nunez, Elizabeth, 95
Nussbaum, Martha, 32, 215n.24, 222

O'ahu (Hawaiian Islands), 265
O'Brien, Susie, 28
O'Connell Davidson, Julia, 278
Ocean, 8, 18, 93, 182–183, 186–189, 193, 195, 261
Oceania (Pacific Ocean), 86, 90, 255–256, 267
Odum, Eugene, 238

Ootacamund, 46
Oppenheimer, Robert, 245
Orientalism, 18–19, 20, 55, 56, 57
Original sin, 71–72
Orinoco, 125, 126
Ormerod, Beverly, 8
Ortiz, Fernando, 107
Owens, Louis, 33, 252n.12

Pacific Island Literature, 241–251, 263–265, 266–268, 269–270
Pacific Islands, 33, 34, 237, 239–249, 255, 257
  See also Oceania
Pacific Way, The, 239–241
Pagan, 68, 73
Paikea, 186, 195
Palau, 241
Pales Matos, Luis, 117
Papeete (Tahiti), 256
Paradise, 62–64, 67–68, 70, 72, 74–76
  See also Eden
Parkinson Zamora, Lois, 119, 124, 129
Paz, Octavio, 83
Pastoral, 5, 8, 24, 46, 54, 82, 84, 86, 120, 125, 127, 130, 140, 176, 185
Pathetic fallacy, 31, 144–145, 148, 150, 153n.13
Pearl Harbor (Hawaiian Islands), 260
Peasant, 68–71, 75, 77, 104, 105, 107, 110–112, 114
Peires, J. B., 294
Pele, 265
Persaud, Lakshmi, 113
Persephone, 88
Pesticide, 148, 216, 220
Peters, Dewitt, 67
Phillips, Joan, 279
Picturesque, 24, 30, 43–52, 58–59, 129
Place, 4–6, 9, 11–14, 16, 20, 23–24, 27, 29–32, 34, 119, 224, 263, 267, 292–294, 296–297, 305
  place claims, 262
  place-based epistemologies, 257
  sacred place, 255
Planetarity, 25, 28, 243–244
  See also Earth
Plantation, 5, 13, 68, 81, 82, 94n.3, 94n.4, 95n.8
  See also Agriculture

Plants, 11, 12, 13, 30, 45–47, 49, 59, 67, 81–84, 87–93, 128, 172, 198n.13, 297, 303, 305
Plumwood, Val, 14, 35n.5, 37n.27, 38n.48, 38n.51, 183, 203–204, 208–209, 214n.10, 258, 284
Poetics of Relation, 27–30
Poiesis, 124, 129
Polynesia, 242, 254–257, 262, 267
  See also Pacific Islands
Pompilus, Pradel, 64
Population, 13, 19, 21, 31, 38n.42
Port-au-Prince (Haiti), 62, 64, 77
Postapartheid, 159–160, 162–165, 168, 175–177, 179
Postcolonial, 201, 205–206, 209, 213
Postcolonial Ecocriticism, 4, 10, 14, 20–25, 25–28, 33, 35n.13, 36n.25, 39n.52, 80–81, 137, 150–151, 154, 201–202, 204, 209, 211, 213, 214n.8, 215n.22, 279, 288
Postcolonial ecology, 4–5, 7–8, 10, 13, 16–17, 19–20, 22–23, 26–28, 30, 34, 182, 187, 189, 195–6, 256, 258–259, 268, 270
Pragnell, Alfred, 96
Pratt, Mary Louise, 10, 46, 52, 117, 120
Price-Mars, Jean, 64, 70–71
Primitivism, 117–118, 123, 132
Progress, 145, 150
Project Tiger, 21
Prostitution/sex work, 142–143, 148, 153n.9, 154n.19, 278
Protect Kaho'olawe 'Ohana (PKO), 254, 262, 265
Protestant, 68, 73
Puerto Rico, 103, 105, 108, 110
Puna, 265

Quarantelli, Enrico, 274, 289n.2
Queer Nature, 30, 50, 53, 54, 58–59

Radiation, 33, 237–238, 241, 243, 244–246, 247
  radiation ecology; 235–239
  radioactive fallout; 244–245, 236–238
  See also Nuclearization
Raleigh, Sir Walter, 31, 101, 114, 115
Reconstruction, 273–274, 287
Refugees, 164, 169, 172–175, 178–180

Regionalism, Latin American, 117, 122
Renaissance,
   European, 63, 67, 73
   Haitian, 74
   Maori, 187
Reserves, (African), 160, 166, 167, 170–171, 176, 178, 180
Rhys, Jean, 112
Rice, Alison, 274
Richards-Pillot, Eunice, 112
Rilke, Rainer Marie, 182
Ring, Jim, 75
Romanticism, 81, 108, 125, 129
Rosaldo, Renato, 183
Rosenthal, Peggy, 246
Roumain, Jacques, 71, 77, 108–109
Rule, Jane, 54
Ruskin, John, 145, 153n.13
Rwanda, 281
Ryan, Chris, and C, Michael Hall, 278

Sacred, the, 6, 15, 27–28, 31, 183, 187, 189–190, 193, 196
Said, Edward, 3–6, 13, 16, 23, 137, 151
Saint Francis, 73
Saramaka people, 114–115
Sarmiento, Domingo, 127
Saro-Wiwa, Ken, 10, 23
Saura, Bruno, 269
Scafi, Alessandro, 63
Scholtmeijer, Marian, 278, 283, 289n.6
Science, 10–11, 12, 26, 29, 34, 68, 73, 177n.2, 238–239, 246, 252n.19, 260, 292
Sea. *See* Ocean
Seabrook, Jeremy, 286
Senior, Olive, 83
Serres, Michel, 27–28
Seur, Han, 267
Shakespeare, William, 86
Shangaan, 172, 175, 180–181
Shanmugaratnam, Nadarajah, 286
Sharrad, Paul., 60n.8
Shepard, Paul, 222
Shinebourne, Jan Lowe, 116
Shiva, Vandana, 11, 15, 31, 38n.45, 136–137, 146–147, 149–150, 194, 269
Sierra Leone, 281
Sigüenza y Góngora, Carlos de, 105

Sikdar, Radhanath, 47
Silva, Noenoe, 257, 265
Singer, Peter, 206–210, 215n.21, 221–222
Sinha, Indra, 23, 33, 217, 221, 224, 226–227, 229–230
Sinhalese, 275, 281
Sino-Indian War (1962), 55
Slaymaker, William, 292
Smith, Linda Tuhiwai, 258
Social ecology, 258–259
   See also Postcolonial Ecologies
Sönmez, Sevil, 287
South Africa, 159–160, 163, 165–166, 168–173, 175–181, 185, 190, 205–206, 213n.7
Sovereignty, 20, 21, 24, 34, 57, 189, 236, 241, 264–265, 275
Spectacle, 164–165, 167, 176
Spitz, Chantal, 34, 264–265
Spivak, Gayatri Chakravorty, 7–8, 28, 149, 154n.18, 209, 243–244, 245, 251
Sri Lanka, 273–290
St. Lucia, 83, 86, 88, 90, 94n.5, 95n.12
Statesman, The, 218
Stearn, William, 68
Stepan, Nancy, 121
Stockholm Declaration, 17–18, 38n.38
Strachan, Ian Gregory, 81
Subjectivity, 255, 265
Sublime, 44, 46–48, 59, 60n.5, 166–167, 171, 180
Sullivan, Robert, 258
Sun, the, 236, 240, 245–246
Sundarbans, 185, 193
Surinam, 103, 114–115
Surrealism, 123, 124
Surrealism, 65, 66, 123, 124, 127,
Survivance, 184–187, 189, 195–196
Sustainability, 3, 8, 12, 15, 17–18, 25, 29, 141, 146, 160, 197, 254, 267, 273–74, 275–83, 285, 287–288
Swami, Vandana, 100
Switzerland, 168
Syncretism, 119

Tahiti, 242–243
Taíno, 69, 72, 101, 104, 111
Tamil, 275, 281
Tansley, Alfred George, 238
Taylor, Frank, 81, 94n.4

Index

Taylor, Peter, 38n.41
Teaiwa, Teresia, 33, 240, 257, 260, 268
Temporality, 4, 31–32, 141, 145, 151, 153n.14, 154n.26, 174, 274, 281–282, 286
Terada, Rei, 83
Terra nullius, 257, 286
Thieme, John, 83
Thoby-Marcelin, Philippe, 65, 71, 77
Thomashaw, Mitchell, 292
Thoreau, Henry David, 80
Threadgold, Terry, 94n.2
Tiffin, Helen, 9, 17, 258, 260
Tiger(s), 194
Tillich, Paul, 66, 73
Tobin, Beth Fowkes, 101
Torres Vargas, Diego de, 103–104, 110–111, 113–114
Tourism, 162, 164, 167–168, 171–173, 175, 176–177, 185, 190–191, 196, 257, 265, 268, 273–77, 279, 281, 284, 285–289, 291, 299–300, 302–304
  Sex tourism, 274–280, 284–285, 286, 289n.5
Toussaint L'Ouverture, 68
Toxicity, 216, 228
  See also Pollution
Tragedy, 276–277, 281–284, 286–287, 289n.8, 289–90n.10
Trask, Haunani Kay, 257
Travel Writing, 43–44, 47
Trinidad and Tobago, 110–111
Trinity test, 242–243, 245, 246
Tsing, Anna, 159, 166
Tsuji, Teruyuki, 111
Tsunami, 273–274, 276, 281, 285–287
Turner, J.M.W., 64
Tuwhare, Hone, 243, 245, 247–251

Union Carbide, 216–221, 223, 226, 230
United Nations, 17, 150, 236, 241
United States Occupation of Haiti, (1914–1936), 64, 69, 77, 109
United States, 65, 69, 257, 260–261, 269
  See also American Empire

Verne, Jules, 125
Viljoen, Hein, 190
Virgin Mary, 65, 66

Virilio, Paul, 239
Vital, Anthony, 44, 52–53, 59n.1, 215n.22, 296, 298
Vizenor, Gerald, 184
Vodou, 31, 63–66, 69–74, 76–77, 108, 109
  lwa, 63, 65–67, 72, 74–75
  poto mitan, 66, 75–76

Walcott, Alix, 86, 88
Walcott, Derek, 8, 30, 80–83, 85–93, 94n.5, 95n.12, 95n.13, 96n.17, 113, 115
  Collected Poems 1948–1984, 80, 89–90, 92
  In A Green Night, 89
  "Isla Incognita," 80
  "Nights in the Gardens of Port of Spain," 89
  "Orient and Immortal Wheat" 89
  Omeros, 89
  "Sainte Lucie," 80
  Sea Grapes, 89
  "Sea Canes," 89
  Selected Poems, 91, 93
  "The Antilles: Fragments of Epic Memory" 81, 91
  "The Almond Trees", 83
  The Arkansas Testament, 92
  "The Banyan Tree, Old Year's Night," 89
  "The Bounty," 83–84, 86–90, 93
  The Castaway, 83
  The Gulf, 83
  "The Hotel Normandie Pool," 92
  The Prodigal, 93
  The Star- Apple Kingdom, 89
  Tiepolo's Hound, 91
  "To Return to the Trees," 89
War, 183, 188, 211–212, 274–276, 281, 282, 287, 289n.5
  See also Militarism
Welsome, Eileen, 244
Wendt, Albert, 241
Wenzel, Jennifer, 214n.15, 300
Whale(s), 182–193, 195–196
  whale crier, 185, 190–191
  whale stranding, 187, 190
  whale watching, 190–191
  whaling, 188–189, 196

Whatmore, Sarah, 223, 226
White, George Francis, 47
White, Lynn, 68, 72
Wilderness concept, 4, 5, 15, 20–24, 31, 35n.13, 118, 119, 120, 140, 162–163, 167–168, 171, 194, 294
Williams, Eric, 110
Williams, Michael, 101
Williams, Raymond, 24, 95, 120, 127
Wilson, Jason, 123, 133n.7
Wordsworth, William, 84

World Bank, 147, 150, 275
World Wildlife Fund, 21
Worster, Donald, 7, 10, 39n.60, 236
Wyndham, Susan, 285

Yellowstone, 169
Yoruba, 66
Yugoslavia, 281

Zulu, 162–163, 172, 177

Made in the USA
Lexington, KY
10 June 2014